Maximizing SAP® ERP Financials Accounts Payable

 **PRESS**

SAP PRESS is a joint initiative of SAP and Galileo Press. The know-how offered by SAP specialists combined with the expertise of the Galileo Press publishing house offers the reader expert books in the field. SAP PRESS features first-hand information and expert advice, and provides useful skills for professional decision-making.

SAP PRESS offers a variety of books on technical and business related topics for the SAP user. For further information, please visit our website: *www.sap-press.com*.

Shivesh Sharma
Optimize Your SAP ERP Financials Implementation
2008, 696 pp.
978-1-59229-160-1

Manish Patel
Discover SAP ERP Financials
2008, 544 pp.
978-1-59229-184-7

Aylin Korkmaz
Financial Reporting with SAP
2008, 672 pp.
978-1-59229-179-3

Paul Theobald
Migrate Successfully to the New SAP GL
2007, 104 pp.
1-978-159229-166-3

Martin Ullmann

Maximizing SAP® ERP Financials Accounts Payable

Galileo Press

Bonn • Boston

ISBN 978-1-59229-198-4

© 2009 by Galileo Press Inc., Boston (MA)

1st Edition 2009

Galileo Press is named after the Italian physicist, mathematician and philosopher Galileo Galilei (1564–1642). He is known as one of the founders of modern science and an advocate of our contemporary, heliocentric worldview. His words *Eppur si muove* (And yet it moves) have become legendary. The Galileo Press logo depicts Jupiter orbited by the four Galilean moons, which were discovered by Galileo in 1610.

Editor Stephen Solomon
Copy Editor Julie McNamee
Cover Design Jill Winitzer
Photo Credit Getty Images/Joe Sohm
Layout Design Vera Brauner
Production Kelly O'Callaghan
Typesetting Publishers' Design and Production Services, Inc.
Printed and bound in Canada

Contents at a Glance

Contents

2 Accounting Document Principles 83

3 Business Transactions in Accounts Payable 93

15 Periodic Processing 423

16 Authorization Concept 433

Acknowledgements

The author would like to thank Stephen Solomon and Julie McNamee for their work in editing the manuscript for this book.

Special thanks go to Ariston Consulting for allowing the author to use its SAP system for completing this book.

Vendor Master Data is the central master data store within Accounts Payable. Vendor Master Data contains all of the relevant information for Accounting and Purchasing and is necessary for performing invoicing, payments, and purchases.

1 Vendor Master Data

In this chapter, we'll discuss Vendor Master Data and its importance to the Accounts Payable (AP) process. We'll explore configuration steps, dependencies, and vendor master enhancements.

Vendor Master Data is used in the accounting component as well as in the materials management component. All vendor master data is stored centrally and shared throughout the organization.

1.1 Organization of Vendor Master Data

Vendor master data is organized according to two criteria:

▶ Your organizational structure, such as company code or purchasing organization, which represent a legal or company division

▶ Your business purpose perspective, by vendor groups

1.1.1 Vendor Master Data and Organization Structure

Within the SAP software, you have to map your organization to the relevant SAP organizational elements. Within AP, the relevant organizational elements are the company code and the purchasing organization.

The *company code* is used to structure your organization from a financial accounting perspective. The company code represents an independent legal accounting entity for which a complete self-containing set of accounts can be drawn up. Your organization can have one or many company codes, which are assigned to one or many charts of accounts. Also, each company code can manage its own currency;

for example,, two of your company codes are located in the United States with currency USD, and another company code is in Canada with currency CAD.

Within AP, a vendor must be created for each instance of a company code related to that vendor to be able to process financial transitions, such as invoices or payments.

From a purchasing point of view, your organization is structured by purchasing organization. The purchasing organization is responsible for negotiating the terms and conditions of purchases with vendors. The purchasing organization assumes legal responsibility for all external transactions. One purchasing organization can be assigned to one or multiple company codes. However, a company code can't be assigned to multiple purchasing organizations.

As an example, Figure 1.1 shows three company codes, where company code **1001** and **2001** are assigned to the same purchasing organization, and company **1002** is assigned to a separate purchasing organization.

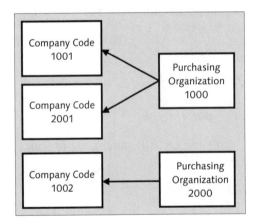

Figure 1.1 Company Codes and Purchasing Organization

So, what does the organizational structure now mean for your vendor master data? Every vendor for which you're planning to process financial transitions, such as invoices or payments, needs to be created in a company code. For purchasing-related transactions, such as requisitions or purchase orders, the vendor also must be created within your purchasing organization.

Further complicating matters, you can create a vendor in the purchasing organization only. That allows you to create a purchase order, but you can't create an invoice for the vendor.

Table 1.1 lists the different possible combinations of vendors created in company codes and purchasing organizations and examples for these combinations.

Company Code	Purchasing Organization	Examples
Created	Created	▶ Regular vendor. Purchase orders are created and invoice are received from this vendor.
Created		▶ For these vendors, no purchasing-related transactions can be created. This combination is typical for utility vendors or remittance addresses.
	Created	▶ Vendor exists only in Purchasing. No invoices can be created for this vendor. ▶ This combination is typically used for vendors with multiple ordering addresses. The ordering addresses are set up only in Purchasing to avoid invoices created by mistake.

Table 1.1 Examples of Vendors and Organizational Elements

Now that you understand the different organizational elements used within AP, let's explore the main criteria for how to group vendor master data, the vendor account group.

1.1.2 Vendor Master Account Groups

The vendor account group determines the following:

▶ The number range interval of the vendor

▶ Whether the number is assigned internally by the system or externally by the user (type of number assignment)

▶ Which fields are ready for input or must be filled when creating and changing master records (field status)

▶ Whether a vendor is a one-time vendor

Vendors within the same account group usually have the same characteristics and purposes. SAP software delivers a variety of sample vendor groups, for example, KRED (Vendor), 0003 (Alternative payee), or CPD (One-time vendor).

During an implementation, you need to decide how to group your vendors and which vendor account groups need to be created. This is usually a lengthy process that could end up delaying the implementation process. To help you with the decision process, the following list contains characteristics that justify separate account groups:

▶ Regular vendors with company code and purchasing data

▶ Vendors require special access authorization

▶ Vendors contain sensitive information

▶ Vendors are one-time vendors

▶ Vendors are only used for special purposes, that is, remittance addresses only or additional ordering addresses only

Vendor account groups that are not clearly defined is a common mistake during implementation that causes confusion for end users and results in duplicate vendors as well as vendors created in the incorrect group. Table 1.2 describes sample vendor account groups and lists their purpose.

Account Group	Description	Purpose
VEND	Regular vendor	▶ Purchase orders are created and invoices are received from this vendor.
REMT	Remittance vendor	▶ This vendor group is used for additional remittance addresses for vendors. No purchasing documents or invoices can be created
ORDR	Ordering addresses	▶ This vendor group is used for a vendor with multiple ordering addresses in purchasing. No invoices can be created.
EMPL	Employees	▶ No purchase orders can be created
PYRV	Payroll vendors	▶ Payroll vendors are used for invoices that need to be created as a result of payroll, for example, IRS, Social Security, or garnishments. Special authorizations to display the vendors and transactions apply.

Table 1.2 Sample Vendor Account Groups

As you can see, a meaningful four-character code for the vendor account groups, which matches the description and the purpose, is used. You can delete the pre-delivered SAP sample vendor groups and create your own groups. For example, the vendor account group for regular vendors is called VEND, instead of the predefined SAP account group KRED. These simple but effective guidelines will help your end-user community better understand the purposes of the different groups.

It's not recommended to group vendor master data by reporting criteria, such as service vendors, material suppliers, or 1099 vendors, because these criteria can change frequently, and then the groups will become inconsistent. A better way is to use fields within the vendors, such as the industry code.

The configuration steps of the vendor account groups are described in Section 1.5 Vendor Master Configuration Step.

The vendor master data is organized in three different data views:

▶ General data

▶ Company code data

▶ Purchasing data

The next section describes each data view in more detail.

1.2 General Data View

The *general data view* contains data of a vendor master, which are shared in all company codes as well in the different purchasing organizations of this vendor. This data are therefore company code and purchasing organization independent. The general data view contains following tabs:

▶ Address

▶ Control

▶ Payment Transactions

▶ Contact Persons

1.2.1 Address

The initial screen of the vendor master is the address screen as shown in Figure 1.2. The vendor master uses Business Address Services (BAS) for the vendor master address. BAS is also known as Central Address Management. BAS is an application-independent function for address management. When BAS was introduced by SAP in version 4.5, additional fields became available in the address screen, such as e-mail.

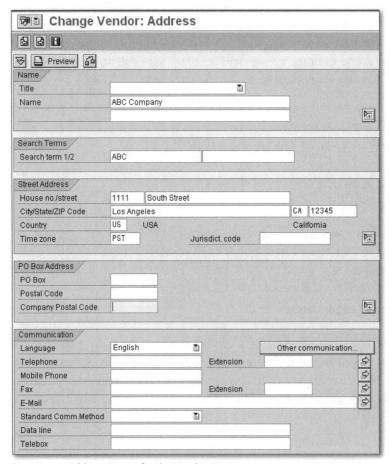

Figure 1.2 Address Screen for the Vendor Master

Title

The title is the salutation of the vendor. If the vendor is a company, choose the company title; otherwise, use the appropriate salutation. The titles can be configured in the IMG via the navigation path **IMG • SAP NetWeaver • Application Server • Basis Services • Address Management • Forms of Address and Name Components • Maintain Forms of Address.**

Names

You can store up to four names for your vendors. The names of the vendors should be consistent to avoid duplicate vendors. When deciding the use of the different names, keep in mind how many characters you have available in your vendor correspondences. For example, only NAME1 and NAME2 will fit on vendor check. In addition, only the first 35 characters may be printed in some forms. See OSS Note 145753 for more details.

Search Terms

Search terms can be used to find vendors in search-help easier. Two fields, search term 1 and search term 2, are available, and both fields are not case sensitive. If you decide to use these fields, you need to use them consistently throughout your organization. As a general rule for your organization, you could use a person's last name or the company name as the search term.

Street Address

The street address contains the address of your vendor, including house number, street, city, state (region), and postal code.

As shown in Figure 1.2, the address is displayed in the U.S. format. The SAP software delivers four address screen layouts, which can be set in the IMG via the navigation path **IMG • SAP NetWeaver • Application Server • Basis Services • Address Management • International Settings • Choose Address Screen Layout**. You can make this configuration change anytime because the data and fields don't change, just the appearance on the screen.

The SAP software also allows validating the addresses with valid addresses according to your postal office standards. To do that, you have to upload the postal codes, cities, districts, streets, and PO boxes using the procedure described in OSS Note 132948 and activate Regional Structure/City file validation in the BAS configuration.

PO Box Address

The **PO Box Address** section consists of three fields, **PO Box, Postal Code**, and **Company Postal Code**. The values in the **PO Box Address** section take priority over the values in the **Street Address** fields in correspondences. For example, a vendor has a street and house number as well as a PO box. In the check, the PO box is printed instead of the street and house number.

Communication

The communication fields are used not only for information purposes but also for defining the standard communication method to vendors, for example, through fax or e-mail. The information should therefore be updated regularly.

Comments

A 50-character comment field is also available below the **Communication** section, which is not shown in Figure 1.2.

1.2.2 Control Screen

The control screen shown in Figure 1.3 contains mainly tax information as well as reference information.

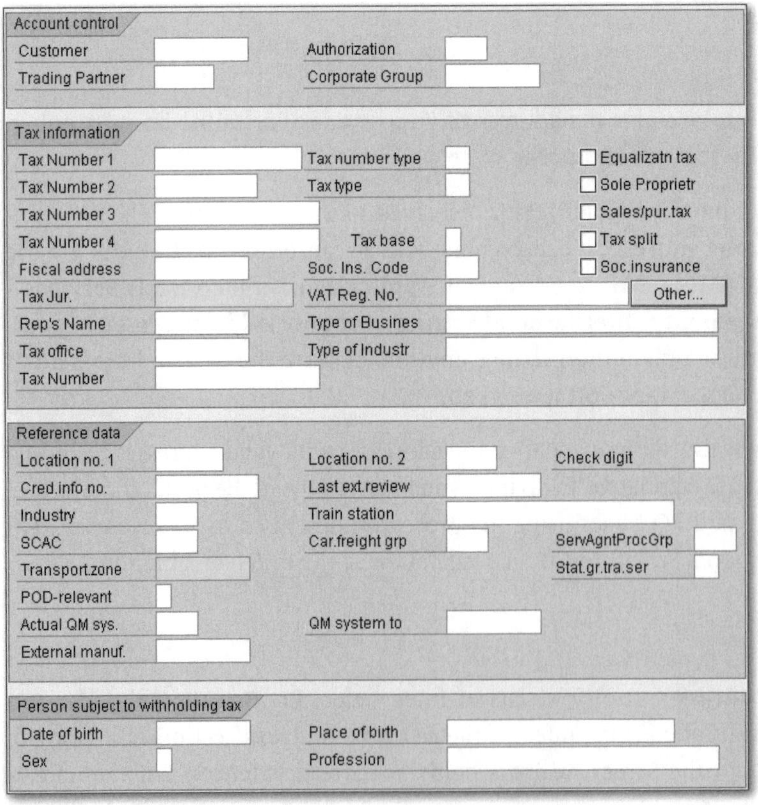

Figure 1.3 Control Screen for the Vendor Master

Customer

If a vendor is also a customer, you can use the **Customer** field to enter the customer number. After you enter the customer number, the Vendor number field in the customer master is filled automatically.

If you also require clearing between vendor and customer line items, in other words, an open AP invoice should be offset with an open AR invoice, you need to set the Clearing with vendor checkbox in the customer as well as the Clearing with customer checkbox in the vendor. Both checkboxes are located in the Payment Transaction screen in the "Company Code Data View" section later in this chapter.

Authorization

After a value in the authorization field is entered, the system checks whether the user has authorization for this value via the authorization object F_LFA1_BEK. This authorization object allows you to protect master data as well as transactional data such as invoices or payments. More detailed information about the authorization concept in AP can be found in Chapter 16, Authorization Concepts.

Trading Partner

The trading partner function is used within the consolidation functionality of SAP. It allows you to eliminate company internal business transactions. The trading partner can be configured under the navigation path **IMG • Enterprise Structure • Definition • Financial Accounting • Define Company.**

Corporate Group

The group key is a 10-character field that can't be configured. The group key can be used as a grouping characteristic of multiple vendors of the same organization to improve vendor search capabilities.

Tax Numbers 1, 2, 3, and 4

The fields **Tax Number 1**, **2**, **3**, and **4** have different meanings depending on the country of the vendor. For example in the United States, **Tax Number 1** is used for the social security number, and **Tax Number 2** for the Employer Identification Number (EIN).

The field format of **Tax Numbers 1** and **2** are validated based on the length and checking rule in your country-specific checks. The rules can be configured under the navigation path **IMG • SAP NetWeaver • General Settings • Set Countries • Set Country-Specific Checks.** For example, if the social security number should be entered in the format 999-99-9999, you should set the length of **Tax Number 1** to 11 characters and use **Checking rule 3 (Length to be kept to exactly, without gaps)** as shown in Figure 1.4.

In addition, you could use user-defined validation rules as described in Section 1.7 to validate field values and formats.

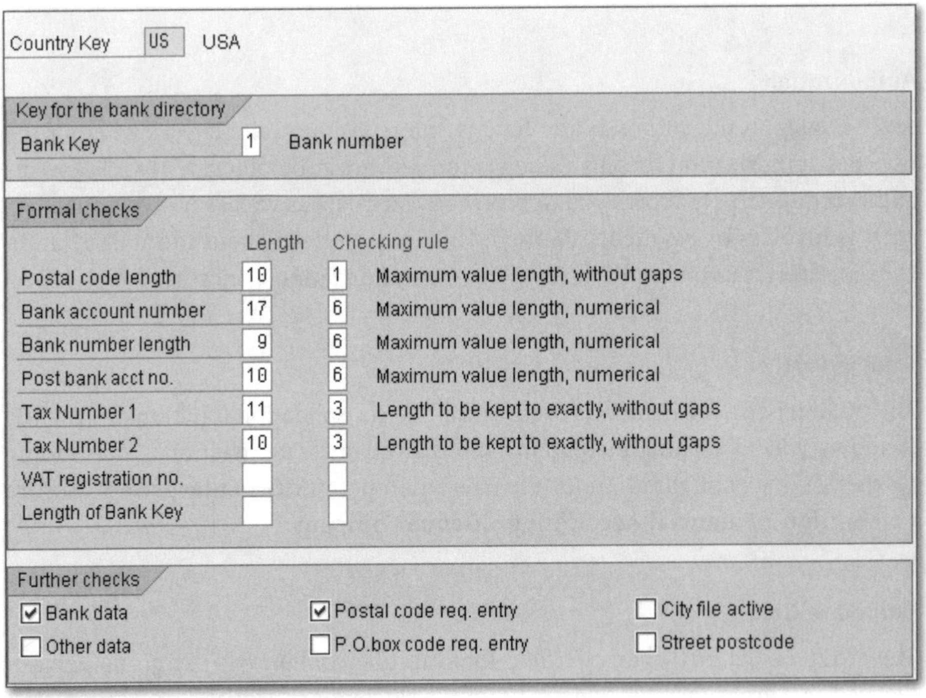

Figure 1.4 Country-Specific Checks

Fiscal Address

The **Fiscal address** field has a special function for tax reporting; for example, in the United States, it combines all transactions of multiple vendors under the same fiscal address vendor for 1099 MISC reporting.

Tax Jurisdiction

The tax jurisdiction code is used mainly in North America and is either entered in the address screen or determined based on the address information from an external tax package, such as Taxware or Vertex.

Other Tax Fields

All other fields in the tax information section are country specific.

International Location Number (ILN)

The International Location Number (ILN) is also known as Global Location Number (GLN) and is used by companies to identify legal, functional, or physical entities. The ILN number is a worldwide unique 13-digit number that is divided into 3 fields within SAP, **Location no. 1**, **Location no. 2,** and **Check digit**.

Credit Information Number/Last Review Date

The fields **Cred. info. no.** and **Last ext. review** are used for information purposes only. These fields can be used in conjunction with D&B data and are filled automatically if these services are used.

Industry Key

The industry key is a way to group similar vendors for reporting purposes, such as government vendors, banking, and trade groups. The industry key can be configured under the navigation path **IMG • Financial Accounting • Accounts Receivable and Payable • Vendor Accounts • Master Data • Preparations for Creating Vendor Master Data • Define Industries.**

Standard Carrier Alpha Code (SCAC)

The National Motor Freight Traffic Association (NMFTA) in the United States maintains the Standard Carrier Alpha Code (SCAC). The NMFTA is a nonprofit membership organization with more than 1,000 motor-carrier members, regulated by the U.S. Department of Transportation's Surface Transportation Board and various state and federal agencies.

The four-character SCAC code is used to identify a shipping carrier. The SCAC code is frequently used in EDI, on the 856 Advance Ship Notice, the 850 Purchase order, and all motor, rail, and water carrier transactions where carrier information is required.

Forwarding Agent Freight Group

The freight groups are used for calculating freight costs. The freight group can be maintained under the navigation path **IMG • Logistics Execution • Transportation • Basic Transportation Functions • Maintain Freight Code Sets and Freight Codes.**

Service-Agent Procedure Group

The service agent procedure group is assigned to a forwarding agent and is used to calculate the correct freight costs. The group is assigned to a pricing procedure for calculating freight costs. The service agent procedure group can be maintained under the navigation path **IMG • Logistics Execution • Transportation • Shipment Costs • Pricing • Pricing Control • Define and Assign Pricing Procedures.**

POD-Relevant

The **POD-relevant** field controls whether proof of delivery (POD) information needs to be sent to your vendor during the goods receipt process.

Vendor's QM system

Many government agencies require that the quality management (QM) systems used by a vendor meet certain levels of verifications, such as ISO 9002 or ISO 9003. These fields are used by the QM in procurement functionality.

External Manufacturer Code Name or Number

This 10-character field can be used to identify the vendor by a different name or number.

Person Subject to Withholding Tax

The fields in this tab contain information about individuals who are subject to withholding tax. These fields are not used within the United States.

1.2.3   Payment Transactions

The payment transaction screen shown in Figure 1.5 contains payment transaction information for a vendor that is company code independent. Some of the fields, such as **Alternative Payee** or **Permitted Payee**, can also be maintained as company code dependent as described in the "Company Code Data View" section later in this chapter.

Bank details										
Ctry	Bank Key	Bank Account	Acct holder	C..	IBAN	BnkT	Reference details	Col..	Name of bank	
					⇨			☐		
					⇨			☐		
					⇨			☐		
					⇨			☐		
					⇨			☐		

Bank Data...	Delete Bank Details

Payment transactions		Alternative payee in document	
Alternative payee		☐ Individual spec.	
DME Indicator		☐ Spec. per reference	Permitted Payee
Instruction key			
ISR Number			

Figure 1.5   Payment Transaction Screen

The **Bank details** section contains information relevant for payments to the vendor that should be made electronically, for example, through ACH payments.

Bank Country Key

The bank country key (**Ctry**) field identifies the country in which the vendor bank is located.

Bank Key

The bank key, also known as the routing number or ABA number, identifies the unique bank. The bank key is maintained with Transaction FI01 and is validated based on country-specific checks as described under the "Tax Number 1" and "Tax Number 2" sections.

Bank Account

The bank account is the bank account number of the vendor at the bank. Similar to the bank key, the bank account must follow country-specific rules.

Account Holder Name

The account holder name is the company or individual under whom the bank account is opened.

Bank Control Key

The bank control key is country-specific and identifies the type of bank account, such as checking account or savings account. This field isn't relevant for all countries.

International Bank Account Number (IBAN)

The International Bank Account Number (IBAN) is an international standard for identifying bank accounts across national borders in Europe. At present, the United States doesn't participate in the IBAN standard. Even though the IBAN number is a European standard, the length of the IBAN number varies by country.

Partner Bank Type

If a vendor has multiple bank accounts, you can use the Partner Bank Type (**BnkT**) field to further specify the bank account. This allows you to select the bank to which the payments should be transferred during invoice entry. The payment program then issues the payments to the selected partner bank. Otherwise, all payments are issued to the first bank in the table.

Reference Details/Collection Authorization

The **Reference Details** and Collection Authorization (**CollectAuth**) fields are only relevant for customers, where you perform payment collections.

Alternative Payee

If you enter a vendor in the **Alternative payee** field, all payments are issued to this vendor. This field should only be used if you always need to issue the payment to the same vendor. In Chapter 3, Business Transactions in Accounts Payable, the different alternative payee options are explained in more detail.

DME Indicator

This field is used in Germany only and controls whether foreign payments should be included in a report to the German Bundesbank.

Instruction Key

For automatic payment transactions, this field controls which statements are given to the participating banks when carrying out the payment order. This field is used in countries such as Germany, Austria, the Netherlands, Spain, Norway, Finland, and Japan, as well as for the SWIFT format, MT100.

ISR Number

ISR (inpayment slip with reference number) is a special payment procedure of the Swiss Postal Service. The field is therefore only relevant in Switzerland.

Alternative Payee in Document Allowed

When this indicator is set, you can enter the individual payee information, such as name, street, and city, in the invoice directly, similar to a one-time vendor. This can be useful, if you have to issue payments to the same vendor but have to enter additional information in the additional name fields, for example, payments to lawyers, where you have to specify the claimants on the payment as well. Chapter 3 explains the different alternative payee options in more detail.

Permitted Payee

The permitted payee function allows you to link multiple remittance vendor addresses to your vendor. These remittance vendors can then be selected during invoice entry. This option ensures a controlled way to issue payments to multiple remittance addresses.

1.2.4 Contact Persons

The contact person screen shown in Figure 1.6 lets you save additional contact information for your vendor.

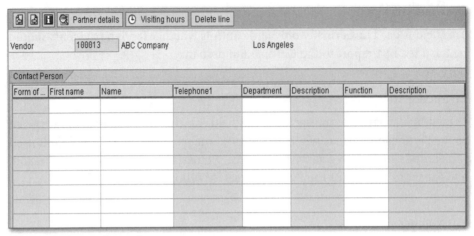

Figure 1.6   Contact Person Screen

At a minimum, you need to enter the first and the last name of the contact person. If you choose the **Partner details** functions, you can enter additional information such as communication details.

Both fields **Department** and **Function** can be configured under the navigation path **IMG · Materials Management · Purchasing · Vendor Master · Contact Persons**

1.3   Company Code Data View

The *company code data view* contains vendor master data, which is company code dependent. If a vendor exists in multiple company codes, all company code relevant data have to be entered multiple times. Usually, the accounting department is responsible for maintaining company code dependent data. The company code data view contains the following tabs:

- ▶ Accounting information
- ▶ Payment Transaction
- ▶ Correspondence
- ▶ Withholding Tax

1.3.1 Accounting Information

The first screen of the company code dependent data is the **Accounting information** screen (see Figure 1.7), which contains accounting information, as well as information relevant for tax withholding and interest calculation purposes.

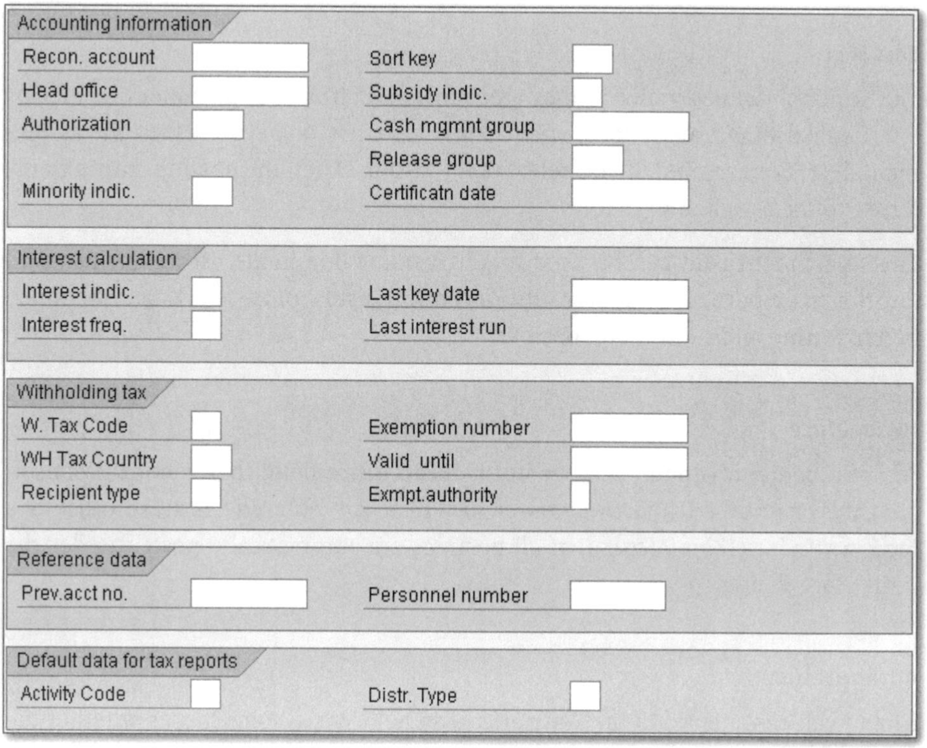

Figure 1.7 Account Information Screen

Reconciliation Account

The reconciliation account is updated parallel to the sub-ledger vendor account for all regular vendor-related postings, such as invoices or payments. For special postings, such as down payments, this account is replaced by a special GL reconciliation account.

The reconciliation account has to be created in GL with Transaction FS00, and the account type for this GL account must be set to K (vendors).

Without a value in the reconciliation account (**Recon. account**) field, no invoices can be processed against this vendor. If you want to issue payments against a vendor but avoid entering invoices against a specific vendor, such as a remittance address vendor, you need to create the company code dependent data but suppress the **Recon. account** field.

Sort Key

The sort key defines which values are transferred from the document header or line items during transactions, such as invoice entry or payments, to the assignment field. For example, if you select 001 (Posting Date), the posting date is transferred to the assignment field.

This assignment field can be used to sort vendor line items. However, the field lost this main purpose after SAP introduced ALV list layouts, which provide much better sorting and subtotaling options.

Head Office

After you enter a vendor number in the **Head office** field, that vendor is considered the head office, and the vendor in which you entered the head office is a branch vendor. The effect is that all postings are automatically posted under the head office vendor.

Authorization

After a value is entered in the **Authorization** field, the system checks whether the user has authorization for this value via the authorization object `F_LFA1_BEK`. This authorization object allows you to protect master data as well as transactional data such as invoices or payments. More detailed information about the authorization concept in AP can be found in Chapter 16.

Cash Management Group

After you've activated the Cash Management component and require that vendor transactional information is transferred to Cash Management for cash forecasting purposes, you need to fill this field with a Cash Management group. In Cash Management, all transactions are then summarized based in this planning group.

Release Group

The release approval group is only relevant for AP-specific workflows. Based on the release approval group, the workflow can be routed specifically for these vendors. The release approval groups can be configured under the navigation path **IMG • Financial Accounting • Accounts Receivable and Payable • Business Transactions • Incoming Invoices/Credit Memos • Carry Out and Check Settings for Document Parking • Define Release Approval Groups for Parking Documents.**

Minority Indicator

The minority indicator is mainly used in the United States to classify minority-owned businesses. The minority indicators can be maintained under the navigation path **IMG • Financial Accounting • Accounts Receivable and Payable • Vendor Accounts • Master Data • Preparations for Creating Vendor Master Data • Define Minority Indicators.**

Certification Date

The certification date for the **Minority indic.** field is the date when the vendor was certified as a minority business.

Interest Calculation

If you're required to pay interest to your vendor, the interest indicator **(Interest indic.)** and interest frequency **(Interest freq.)** have to be maintained. The **Last key date** and **Last interest run** fields are usually populated automatically during the interest calculation run.

Withholding Tax

Depending on whether you're using Classic or Extended Withholding Tax Reporting, either the tax withholding fields in the Account Information screen or the fields in the Withholding Tax screen have to be filled out. In Chapter 10, Withholding Tax Reporting, the different options are described in more detail.

Previous Account Number

The previous account number **(Prev.acct no.)** field is usually used after you migrate vendors from a legacy system to the SAP application. This field stores the vendor number from your legacy system.

Personnel Number

For vendors that are also employees, this field stores the unique personnel number of an employee. An enhancement is available from SAP that allows you to switch off the personnel number validation, which is described in the "Vendor Master Data Enhancement" section of this chapter.

1.3.2 Payment Transaction

The screen shown in Figure 1.8 contains company-dependent fields for invoice and payment processing. Some of the fields, such as **Alternat. payee** or **Permitted Payee**, have been described in the Payment Transaction screen of the previous "General Data View" section.

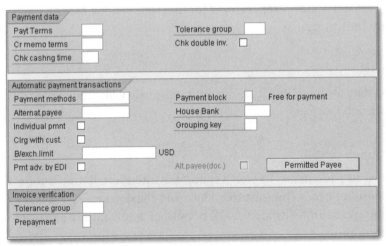

Figure 1.8 Payment Transaction Screen

Payment Terms

The payment term entered here is the most commonly used payment term for this vendor, that is, net 30 days. This payment term is defaulted into the invoice after you process an invoice in AP. If you enter a purchasing-related invoice in Logistic Invoice Verification (LIV), the payment term from the purchase order is defaulted. The payment terms can be configured under the navigation path **IMG • Financial Accounting • Accounts Receivable and Payable • Business Transactions • Incoming Invoices/Credit Memos • Maintain Terms of Payment.** The payment terms are described in more detail in Chapter 5, Outgoing Payment Processing.

Tolerance Group

You can define vendor-specific tolerance groups that are used for dealing with differences in payment and residual items that can occur during payment settlement. The tolerance group contains following tolerance details:

▸ Tolerances up to which differences in payment are posted automatically to expense or revenue accounts when clearing open items

▸ The handling of the terms of payment for residual items, if they are to be posted during clearing

The tolerance group can be configured under the navigation path **IMG • Financial Accounting • Accounts Receivable and Payable • Business Transactions • Outgoing Payments • Manual Outgoing Payments • Define Tolerances (Vendors)**.

Figure 1.9 shows a sample tolerance group that allows up to $100 and 10% payment differences if the invoice amount is higher than the payment amount, which would result in a gain. The system allows a maximum of $100 or 10%, whatever amount is smaller. On the other side, the loss will be restricted to $50 or 5%.

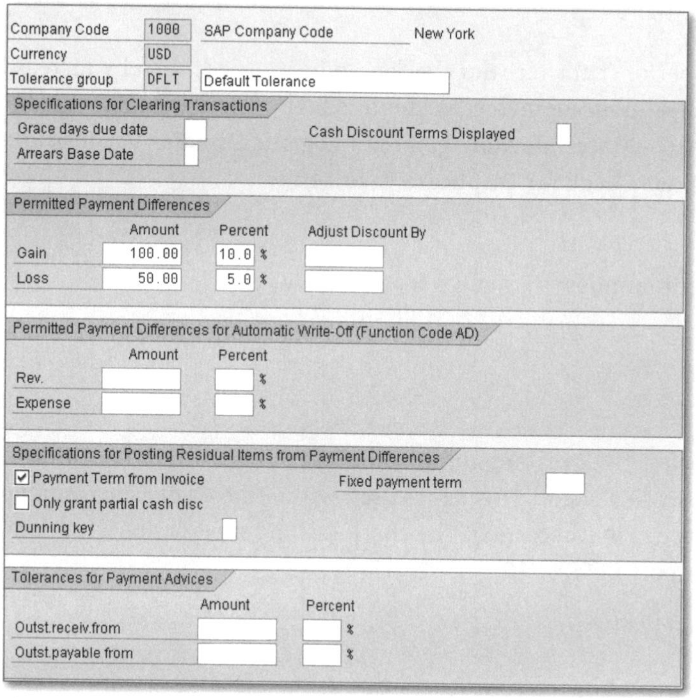

Figure 1.9 Tolerance Groups

Credit Memo Terms

A different payment term for credit memos can be entered in the credit memo terms (**Cr memo terms**) fields. If no term is entered, "*" can be entered in the payment term (**Payt Terms**) field during credit memo entry, and the invoice payment term will be defaulted.

Check Flag for Double Invoices or Credit Memos

If this flag is set, the system checks whether invoices are already entered and issues a message accordingly. The message is issued if an invoice is already entered and the following values are the same:

- Company code
- Vendor
- Currency
- Invoice amount
- Reference document number
- Invoice date

Within LIV, the number of characteristics checks can be reduced, thereby increasing the likelihood that a duplicate invoice is identified. The following fields can be switched off under **IMG • Materials Management • Logistics Invoice Verification • Incoming Invoice • Set Check for Duplicate Invoices**:

- Company code
- Reference document number
- Invoice date

Check Cashing Time

The check cashing time (check cashing time) defines the average number of days it takes the vendor to cash a check. This day is used within the Cash Management component for accurate cash forecasting. The check cashing time can be automatically updated with Report RFSRUE10.

Payment Methods

The **Payment methods** field contains the valid payment methods that can be used for this vendor during the execution of the automatic payment program (Transaction F110). If you specify a particular payment method during the invoice entry, this payment method has priority over the payment method in the vendor master data. You may also specify payment methods in the invoice that are not listed in the master record. Up to 10 different payment methods can be entered.

The payment methods can be configured under the navigation path **IMG • Financial Accounting • Accounts Receivable and Payable • Business Transactions • Outgoing Payments • Automatic Outgoing Payments • Payment Method/Bank Selection for Payment Program** and are described in more detail in Chapter 5.

Payment Block

You can enter a payment block if you want to prevent open items from being paid automatically. The payment block reasons can be configured under the navigation path **Financial Accounting • Accounts Receivable and Payable • Business Transactions • Outgoing Payments • Outgoing Payments Global Settings • Payment Block Reasons • Define Payment Block Reasons.** The payment block reasons are described in more detail in Chapter 5.

Alternative Payee

If you enter a vendor in this field, all payments within this specific company code are issued to this vendor. This field should only be used if you always require issuing the payment to the same vendor. In Chapter 3, Business Transactions, the different alternative payee options are explained in more detail.

House Bank

If the house bank is entered, all payments for this vendor are issued from the same house bank. The bank selection needs to be configured in the payment program. This configuration isn't being considered if the **House Bank** field is filled.

Individual Payment Flag

All items are paid individually rather than combined if this flag is set.

Key for Payment Grouping

Payments can be grouped together based on the payment grouping key specified in the vendor master. For example, all invoices with the same invoice reference could be paid together.

Clearing Between Customer and Vendors Flag

If clearing between vendor and customer line items is required, in other words, an open AP invoice should be offset with an open AR invoice, you need to set the Clearing with vendor checkbox in the customer as well as the Clearing with Customer checkbox in the vendor.

Bill of Exchange Limit

Bill of Exchange payments are mainly used in Europe. The limit of a bill of exchange can be entered in this field.

Payment Advices by EDI

All payment advices are sent via EDI (electronic data interchange), if this flag is set.

Permitted Payee

The permitted payee function allows you to link multiple remittance vendor addresses to your vendor. These remittance vendors can then be selected during invoice entry. This option ensures a controlled way in issuing payments to multiple remittance addresses. Chapter 3 explains the different alternative payee options in more detail.

Tolerance Group: Invoice Verification

You can define vendor-specific tolerance groups for LIV to be used during invoice processing and automatic invoice reduction. They can be configured via **IMG • Materials Management • Logistics Invoice Verification • Incoming Invoice • Configure Vendor-Specific Tolerances.** In Chapter 4, Logistic Invoice Verification, the tolerance group will be explained in more detail.

Prepayment Relevance

When this flag is set, vendor invoices can be prepaid during LIV. Chapter 4 explains the prepayment functionality in more detail.

1.3.3 Correspondence

The Correspondence screen shown in Figure 1.10 contains two sections: **Dunning data** and **Correspondence**. Because very few companies dun their vendors, only the **Correspondence** section is covered in this chapter.

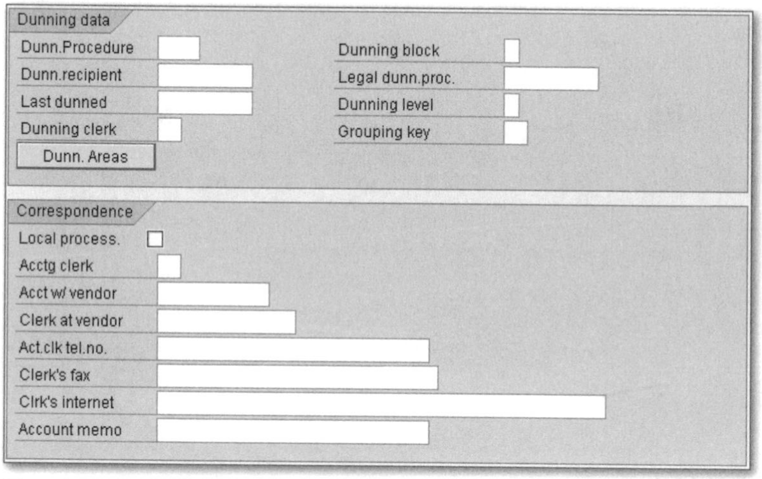

Figure 1.10   Dunning and Correspondence Screen

Accounting Clerk

Here you can enter the clerk responsible for this vendor for reporting or correspondence purposes. The accounting clerk can be configured via **Financial Accounting • Accounts Receivable and Payable • Vendor Accounts • Master Data • Preparations for Creating Vendor Master Data • Define Accounting Clerks.**

Account with Vendor

This field contains the account number of your company at your vendor.

Vendor Clerk Information

All other information on this screen contains information about the clerk's information at your vendor.

1.3.4 Withholding Tax

The **Withholding Tax** screen shown in Figure 1.11 is only visible if extended withholding tax reporting is active in your company code. Withholding tax reporting is covered in detail in Chapter 10, Tax Withholding.

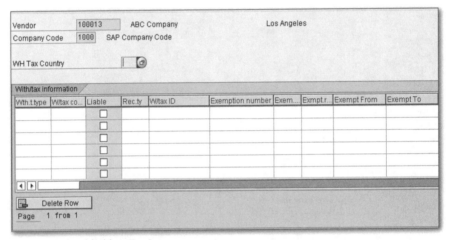

Figure 1.11 Withholding Tax Screen

1.4 Purchasing Data View

The *purchasing data view* is only relevant if purchasing-related transactions, such as purchase requisitions or purchase orders, need to be processed for a vendor. The purchasing data view consists of two screens:

▶ Purchasing Data

▶ Partner Functions

1.4.1 Purchasing Data

The **Purchasing Data** screen is divided into multiple sections for vendor conditions, control, or default data. Only the most common fields are described in detail in this section. Figure 1.12 shows the **Conditions** and **Sales data** sections of the **Purchasing Data** screen.

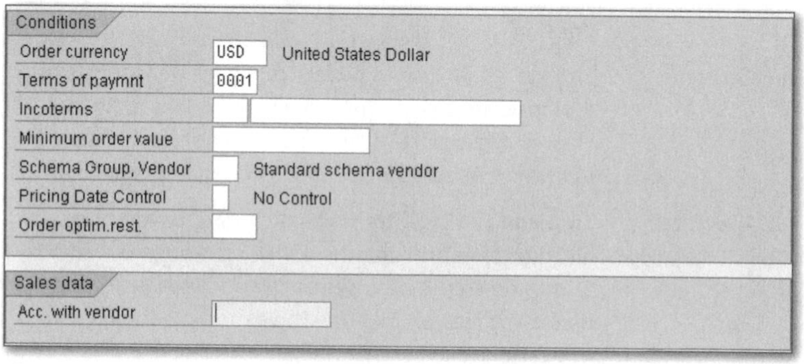

Conditions		
Order currency	USD	United States Dollar
Terms of paymnt	0001	
Incoterms		
Minimum order value		
Schema Group, Vendor		Standard schema vendor
Pricing Date Control		No Control
Order optim.rest.		

Sales data		
Acc. with vendor		

Figure 1.12 Conditions and Sales Data

Order Currency

The order currency to be used in purchase orders can be entered here. It's usually the currency of your vendor's country.

Terms of Payment

The payment term entered here is the most common payment term used in purchase orders for this vendor, that is, net 30 days. This payment term is defaulted into purchase orders upon creation of a purchase order. The payment terms can be configured via the navigation path **IMG • Financial Accounting • Accounts Receivable and Payable • Business Transactions • Incoming Invoices/Credit Memos • Maintain Terms of Payment.** The payment terms are described in more detail in Chapter 5.

Incoterms

Incoterms are internationally accepted commercial terms that define the respective roles of buyers and sellers in the arrangement of transportation and clarify when the ownership of the merchandise takes place. The Incoterm 2000 standard contains currently 13 different incoterms as displayed in Table 1.3.

Incoterm	Description	Term Details
EXW	Ex Works	Title and risk pass to buyer, including payment of all transportation and insurance cost from the seller's door.
FCA	Free Carrier	Title and risk pass to buyer, including transportation and insurance cost when the seller delivers goods cleared for export to the carrier. Seller is obligated to load the goods on the buyer's collecting vehicle.
FAS	Free Alongside Ship	Title and risk pass to buyer, including payment of all transportation and insurance cost once delivered alongside ship by the seller. Used for sea or inland waterway transportation. The export clearance obligation rests with the seller.
FOB	Free On Board	Free on board and risk pass to buyer, including payment of all transportation and insurance cost once delivered on board the ship by the seller. Used for sea or inland waterway transportation.
CFR	Cost and Freight	Title, risk, and insurance cost pass to buyer when delivered on board the ship by seller who pays the transportation cost to the destination port. Used for sea or inland waterway transportation.
CIF	Cost, Insurance and Freight	Title and risk pass to buyer when delivered on board the ship by seller who pays transportation and insurance cost to destination port. Used for sea or inland waterway transportation.
CPT	Carriage Paid To	Title, risk, and insurance cost pass to buyer when delivered to carrier by seller who pays transportation cost to destination. Used for any mode of transportation.
CIP	Carriage and Insurance Paid To	Title and risk pass to buyer when delivered to carrier by seller who pays transportation and insurance cost to destination. Used for any mode of transportation.
DAF	Delivered at Frontier	Title, risk, and responsibility for import clearance pass to buyer when delivered to named border point by seller. Used for any mode of transportation.

Table 1.3 Incoterms According to Incoterms 2000

Incoterm	Description	Term Details
DES	Delivered Ex Ship	Title, risk, responsibility for vessel discharge, and import clearance pass to buyer when seller delivers goods on board the ship to destination port. Used for sea or inland waterway transportation.
DEQ	Delivered Ex Quay (Duty Paid)	Title and risk pass to buyer when delivered on board the ship at the destination point by the seller who delivers goods on dock at destination point cleared for import. Used for sea or inland waterway transportation.
DDU	Delivered Duty Unpaid	Title, risk, and responsibility of import clearance pass to buyer when seller delivers goods to named destination point. Used for any mode of transportation. Buyer is obligated for import clearance.
DDP	Delivered Duty Paid	Title and risk pass to buyer when seller delivers goods to named destination point cleared for import. Used for any mode of transportation.

Table 1.3 Incoterms According to Incoterms 2000 (Cont.)

Vendor Schema Group

The vendor schema group defines which pricing procedure is used for this vendor. The schema can be configured via navigation path **IMG • Materials Management • Purchasing • Conditions • Define Price Determination Process • Define Schema Group.**

Price Determination Control Date

The control dates defines which date is used in the pricing procedure, that is, purchase order date or delivery date.

Account with Vendor

This field contains the account number of your company at your vendor.

Figure 1.13 shows the **Control data** and **Default data material** sections. The **Control data** fields control which functions are allowed for this vendor, whereas the **Default data material** section contains information that is copied in the purchase order.

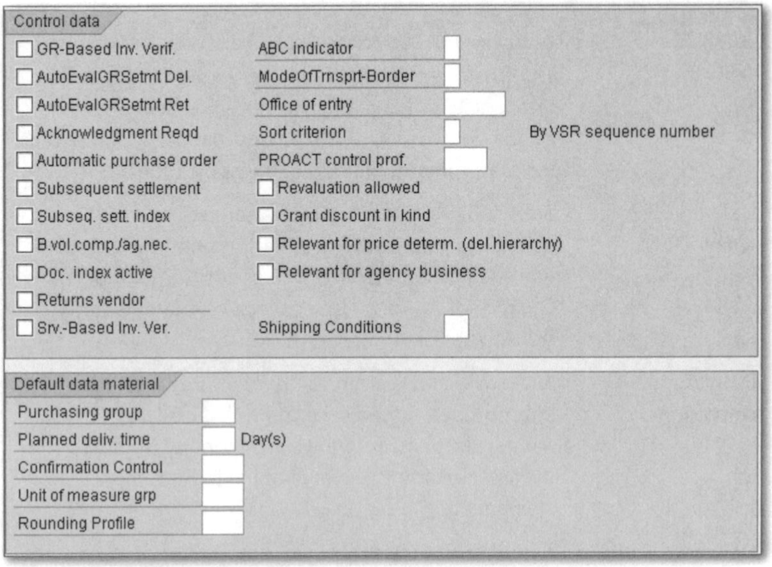

Figure 1.13   Control and Default Data Material

Goods Receipt Based Invoice Verification

This indicator **(GR-Based Inv. Verif.)** is copied into the info record or purchase order upon creation for this vendor. If Invoice Verification based on goods receipt has been defined for a purchase order item, an invoice for the order item can be entered with reference to a goods receipt document or a delivery note number entered at the time of goods receipt. In this process, a separate invoice item is created for each goods receipt. Price and formal accuracy of the invoice are checked at this item level. Note that this flag isn't a requirement to perform a three-way match. Goods Receipt Based Invoice Verification is described in detail in Chapter 4.

Automatic Evaluated Receipt Settlement Delivery/Return

These indicators define whether the Evaluated Receipt Settlement (ERS) functionality is allowed for this vendor. The ERS process is described in detail in Chapter 4 Logistic Invoice Verification.

Acknowledgement Required

This indicator determines whether the vendor requires sending an acknowledgement when the order is received.

Automatic Purchase Order

A purchase order can be automatically created from a requisition, if the requisition has been assign to the vendor in the Source of supply field. The Source of supply field can be found in the requisition line item.

Service-Based Invoice Verification

This indicator is copied into purchase order line items upon creation of a service-related purchase order. In service-based Invoice Verification, the quantities and values of services performed and ordered to date are available for checking purposes. If service-based Invoice Verification is active, the acceptance posting is carried out at the level of the services in the entry sheet, and the quantities and values of the accepted and invoiced services are shown in the purchase order history.

ABC Indicator

The **ABC indicator** classifies the vendor by the purchasing volume your company does with this vendor. "A" vendors are vendors with the highest volume. Usually the 80/20 role for purchases applies, where 80% of the volume is done with 20% of the vendors.

1.4.2 Partner Functions

The **Partner Function** screen shown in Figure 1.14 is used to define the relationship between the vendor and your company. A business partner can assume different roles with your company, such as ordering address, supplier, or invoicing party. Table 1.4 lists the different partner function roles available as well as which roles are used in Purchasing.

P...	Name	Number	Name	D...
OA	Ordering address	100013	ABC Company	☐
VN	Vendor	100013	ABC Company	☐
PI	Invoicing Party	100013	ABC Company	☐
				☐
				☐
				☐

Figure 1.14 Partner Function Screen

Partner Function	Description	Used in Purchasing?
CA	Contract Address	No
CP	Contact Person	No
ER	Employee Responsible	No
GS	Goods Supplier	Yes
OA	Ordering Address	Yes
PI	Invoicing Party	Yes
VN	Vendor	Yes

Table 1.4 Partner Function Options

After a purchase order is created, the partner roles are copied from the vendor master data to the purchase order header into the Partners tab. As a minimum, the following partner function roles must be assigned to a vendor:

▶ VN: Vendor

▶ OA: Ordering Address

▶ PI: Invoicing Party

The partner function roles have special functions.

OA: Ordering Address

If you define a different partner for the partner role OA, the purchase order is sent to the address of this partner. If multiple partners with partner role OA are defined in the vendor, you'll be asked to select the correct ordering address when you create a purchase order for this vendor.

GS: Goods Supplier

The partner role GS is used to define a different goods supplier than the vendor. In this case, purchasing declarations forms are created for the goods supplier. The address of the goods suppliers is used for returns.

PI: Invoicing Party

If you define a different partner for the partner role PI, the invoice will be posted to this partner instead of the vendor during LIV.

The partner functions are configured in multiple steps.

1. Define permissible partner roles per account group via **IMG • Materials Management • Purchasing • Partner Determination • Partner Roles • Define Permissible Partner per Account Group.** In this step, you define which partner roles are allowed for a vendor account group. As a minimum, assign VN, OA, GS, and PI to your vendor account group.

2. Define partner schemas via **IMG • Materials Management • Purchasing • Partner Determination • Partner Settings in Vendor Master Record • Define Partner Schemas.** The partner schema defines the mandatory partner roles and which roles can be changed. All mandatory partner roles are assigned automatically upon creation of a vendor.

3. Assign partner schemas to account groups via **IMG • Materials Management • Purchasing • Partner Determination • Partner Settings in Vendor Master Record • Assign Partner Schemas to Account Groups.** In this last step, the partner schemas need to be assigned to the vendor account groups.

1.5   Vendor Master Configuration Steps

The configuration of the Vendor Master Data is done in multiple steps. All configuration steps can be found in the same IMG navigation path: **IMG • Financial Accounting • Accounts Receivable and Payable • Business Transactions • Vendor Accounts • Master Data • Preparation for Creating Vendor Master Data.** The definition of the accounting clerk, industries, and minority indicators were already covered in previous sections. Enhancements for Vendor Master Data are described in a later section of this chapter.

In detail, the following steps are covered in this section:

▶ Define account groups with screen layouts.

▶ Define screen layouts per company code.

▶ Define screen layouts per activity.

▶ Change message control for vendor master data.

▶ Create number ranges for vendor accounts.

▶ Assign number ranges to vendor account groups.

▶ Define text IDs for central text.

▶ Define text IDs for accounting text.

▶ Define text IDs for purchasing organization.

The screen layouts of the Vendor Master Data are defined in steps 1 through 3. Step 1 defines the screen layouts of the vendor master group, step 2 the screen layout of the company code screens, and step 3 the screen layout of the activity. In every step, you can define a field on the screen as one of the following:

▶ Suppressed or hidden field

▶ Required field

▶ Optional field

▶ Display field

These three screen layout configuration steps work in combination with each other. The ultimate field status for a vendor master field depends on the configuration of all three steps for controlling the field status: Account Group, Company code, and Activity. The fields take on the status that has the *highest* priority. Hiding a field has the highest priority, followed by a display field, a required field, and then an optional field. Table 1.5 shows the different field status combinations and the resulting field status.

Account Group	Company Code	Activity	Resulting Field Status
Suppress	Required	Optional	Suppress
Suppress	Required	Display	Suppress
Required	Optional	Display	Display
Required	Optional	Optional	Required
Optional	Optional	Display	Display
Optional	Optional	Optional	Optional

Table 1.5 Field Status Combinations and Resulting Field Status

1.5.1 Define Account Groups with Screen Layouts

The first step is the creation of the vendor account groups. Figure 1.15 shows sample vendor account groups.

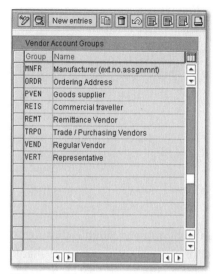

Figure 1.15 Configuration of Vendor Account Groups

The detailed field status can be maintained by either double-clicking on the vendor account group or by using the Details function. The **Field status** for all views, such as **General data**, **Company code data**, and **Purchasing data**, can be configured within the vendor account group as shown in Figure 1.16.

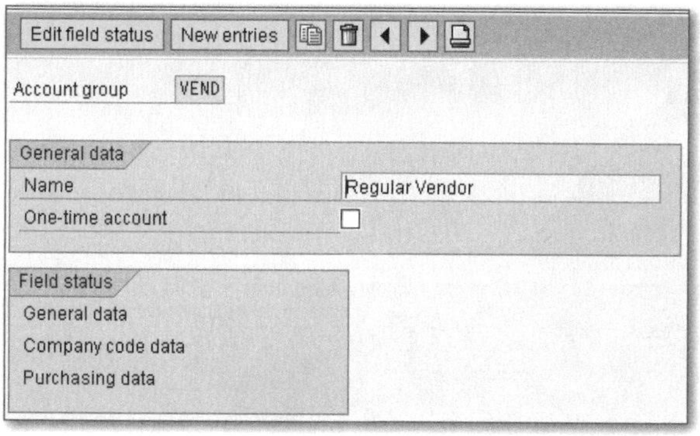

Figure 1.16 Field Status of Vendor Account Groups

By double-clicking on the individual views or selecting the **Edit field status** function, the individual tabs within each view become available for maintenance. As shown in Figure 1.17, the field status of the **Address**, **Communication**, **Control**, **Payment transactions**, and **Contact person** groups can be configured within the **General Data** view.

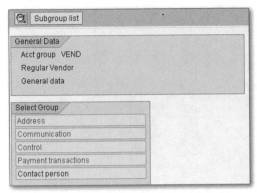

Figure 1.17 Groups Within the General Data View

Within the group, you can display the individual subgroups by double-clicking on the individual group. All individual fields or groups of fields then become available for maintenance. Figure 1.18 shows that the fields **Name 1** and **Search term** are required fields, and all other fields are optional.

In some cases, multiple individual fields are grouped into a single group of fields. For example, the International location number field group consists of three individual fields, International location number 1, International location number 2, and a Check digit field. By double-clicking on the individual group, you can see the single fields, which are included in this group.

	Suppress	Req. Entry	Opt. entry	Display
Name 1	○	●	○	○
Form of address	○	○	●	○
Search term	○	●	○	○
Name 2	○	○	●	○
Name 3, name 4	○	○	●	○
Postal code, city	○	○	●	○
Street	○	○	●	○
District	○	○	●	○
Region	○	○	●	○
PO Box	○	○	●	○

Field check — General Data — Acct group VEND — Regular Vendor — General data — Page 1 / 2 — Address

Figure 1.18 Field Status of the Address Group

1.5.2 Define Account Layout per Company Code

In this first step, the company code specific field status groups can be maintained. You can either maintain the fields status groups for each company code individually or for all company codes if "*" is entered as the company code value. The single configuration steps are the same as in the preceding "Define Account Groups with Screen Layouts" section.

1.5.3 Define Screen Layout per Activity

In this step, the field status groups per activity can be configured. The activity represents the transaction code you choose for the maintenance of the vendor master. Table 1.6 lists the activity and the corresponding transaction code.

Activity Types	Transaction Code
Create Vendor (Accounting)	FK01
Change Vendor (Accounting)	FK02
Display Vendor (Accounting)	FK03
Create Vendor (Purchasing)	MK01
Change Vendor (Purchasing)	MK02
Display Vendor (Purchasing)	MK03
Create Vendor (Centrally)	XK01
Change Vendor (Centrally)	XK02
Display Vendor (Centrally)	XK03

Table 1.6 Activity and Corresponding Transaction Code

Not all vendor master views are available for all transactions. The accounting transactions allow you to maintain the General view and Accounting view of a vendor. The purchasing transactions allow you to maintain the General view and the Purchasing view. All views, General view, Accounting view, and Purchasing view can be maintained with the central transaction.

The single configuration steps are the same as in the "Define Account Groups with Screen Layouts" section. Note that in the display, transactions fields can only be hidden or displayed. The other settings don't have any effect.

1.5.4 Define Message Control for Vendor Master Data

Message control is a feature within SAP that allows you to change the standard message type. Different specifications are possible for the online mode and for batch input sessions processed in the background. You can make the specifications globally or individually by user. If you enter a user name, the specifications only apply to this particular user. If you leave the field blank then the settings apply to all users.

Figure 1.19 shows an example where Message 144 is changed from switched-off in the standard setting to an information (I) message. The SAP application predefines which messages and which message types can be changed.

Area	F2	Master Data Maintenance: Customer, Vendor				
Message Control by User						
Msg...	Message Text		User Name	Online	Batchl	Standard
144	Vendors found with same address; check			I	I	-
217	Jurisdiction code could not be determined			W	W	S

Figure 1.19 Message Control for Vendor Master Data

1.5.5 Create Number Ranges for Vendor Accounts

In this step, you create the number ranges for vendor accounts. A two-character key identifying the number range needs to be defined and specifies the following:

▶ A number interval from which the account number for the vendor accounts is to be selected

▶ The type of number assignment (internal or external)

If a number range is defined as internal, the system automatically determines the next available number within the number range. On the other side, the vendor number has to be entered manually upon creation of the vendor, if the number range is defined externally. Only numeric values are allowed for internal number ranges. For external number ranges, numeric and alphanumeric values can be entered.

External number assignment is useful, for example, if you transfer vendor master data from other systems or for one-time vendors. In all other cases, you should use the internal number assignment.

> **Note**
>
> Number ranges are not automatically transported. Although you can manually transport them, it's strongly recommended that new number ranges be manually created in each client. Otherwise, number ranges could be overwritten by transports and cause inconsistencies.

Figure 1.20 shows multiple internal number ranges and one external number range with alphanumeric characters.

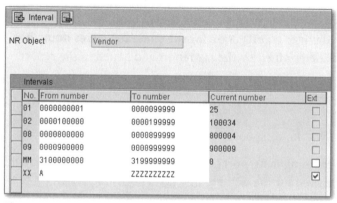

Figure 1.20 Vendor Number Ranges

1.5.6 Assign Number Ranges to Vendor Account Groups

In this step, you assign the number ranges created in the previous step to the vendor account groups. You can assign the same number range to multiple vendor account groups.

1.5.7 Define Text IDs for Central Text (Vendors)

In this step, you define text IDs for the general view of the vendor master records. Text can then be entered in the master records for each text ID. In this way, you can store additional information about the vendor in the master record, such as a memo note about purchasing activities. Standard SAP delivers two text IDs:

- 0001 Accounting note
- 0002 Purchasing memo

You can create additional text IDs. If the Relevant text flag isn't set, the text ID isn't visible.

1.5.8   Define Text IDs for Accounting Text (Vendors)

In this step, you define text IDs for the company code-dependent area of the vendor master records. For each text ID, a text can be entered when maintaining the master records. This means that you can store information on the vendor in the master record, specific to each company code.

For example, specific information on the vendor is required for the withholding tax report in Italy, such as sex, date of birth, and place of birth. You can store this data in the master record under text ID 0002 for **the company codes doing business in Italy**. The text is determined by the tax report and issued in the report.

Standard SAP delivers two text IDs:

- 0001 Accounting note
- 0002 Information on withholding tax

The text ID for the withholding tax report is delivered with the standard system. No other text ID may be used for the withholding tax report.

1.5.9   Define Text IDs for Purchasing Organization Texts

Text IDs for the purchasing organization can be maintained under the IMG path **IMG • Materials Management • Purchasing • Vendor Master • Define Text Types for Central Texts.**

The text IDs for the purchasing organization can be entered when maintaining the master records. This means that you can store information on the vendor in the master record, specific to each purchasing organization.

Standard SAP delivers two text IDs:

- 0001 Purchasing memo
- 0002 Purchase order text

1.6 Vendor Master Data Transactions

In the previous section, we discussed the different fields and configuration options. This section describes the different transaction codes available for vendor master maintenance.

1.6.1 Creating, Changing, and Displaying Vendor Master Data

Different transaction codes are available for vendor maintenance depending on the business function of an individual. Depending on the transaction code you choose, different views can be maintained. Table 1.7 lists the different views that can be created, changed, and displayed for the different transaction codes.

Transaction Code	Transaction Code Description	General View	Accounting View	Purchasing View
FK01	Create Vendor (Accounting)	YES	YES	NO
FK02	Change Vendor (Accounting)	YES	YES	NO
FK03	Display Vendor (Accounting)	YES	YES	NO
MK01	Create Vendor (Purchasing)	YES	NO	YES
MK02	Change Vendor (Purchasing)	YES	NO	YES
MK03	Display Vendor (Purchasing)	YES	NO	YES
XK01	Create Vendor (Centrally)	YES	YES	YES
XK02	Change Vendor (Centrally)	YES	YES	YES
XK03	Display Vendor (Centrally)	YES	YES	YES

Table 1.7 Transaction Codes and Vendor Master Data View

Typically, within an organization, the accounting department maintains the accounting data, and the purchasing department maintains the purchasing data. Because the General data can be maintained in accounting as well as in purchasing, the question always arises as to who is allowed to create the vendor master data in the first place. As a general rule, organizations that have a central vendor desk handle vendor creation in that department. For decentralized organizations, the responsibility is usually shared.

The accounting transaction codes can be found using the navigation path **SAP Menu • Accounting • Financial Accounting • Accounts Payable • Master Records.**

The central transaction codes can be found using the navigation path **SAP Menu • Accounting • Financial Accounting • Accounts Payable • Master Records • Maintain Centrally.**

The purchasing transaction codes can be found using the navigation path **SAP Menu • Logistics • Materials Management • Purchasing • Master Data • Vendor • Purchasing.**

Figure 1.21 shows the initial screen for creating a vendor centrally. The **Company Code**, **Purchasing Organization**, and **Account group** can be entered. If you reference an existing vendor and reference a company code or purchasing organization, the respective values are defaulted in the new vendor.

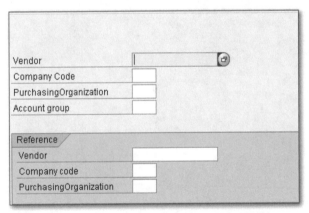

Figure 1.21 Central Vendor Creation Screen Using XK01

1.6.2   Display Vendor Account Changes

Vendor Account Changes allows you to display vendor master changes of a single vendor only. A report is listed in the report section that can be used to display changes of multiple vendors.

Depending on the transaction code you choose, general, accounting, or purchasing changes are displayed:

- ▶ FK04: Vendor Account Changes – Accounting Data
- ▶ MK05: Vendor Account Changes – Purchasing Data
- ▶ XK06: Vendor Account Changes – Central Data

1.6.3 Vendor Block/Unblock

The vendor block/unblock is used to prevent further transactions with this vendor within a company code or purchasing organization if the block indicator is set.

Depending on the transaction code you choose, posting, purchasing, or all vendor blocks can be maintained:

- ▶ FK05: Posting Blocks
- ▶ MK05: Purchasing Blocks
- ▶ XK05: Posting and Purchasing Blocks

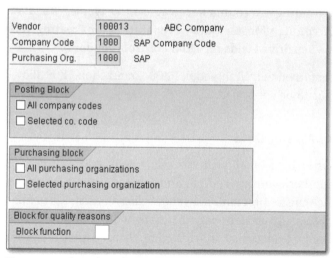

Figure 1.22 Central Vendor Block/Unblock Screen Using XK05

The postings block refers to financial transactions, such as invoices and payments. The **Posting Block** can be set for **All Company Codes** or **Selected co. code** (only the company code that was selected in the initial screen of the blocking transaction) as shown in Figure 1.22.

The **Purchasing block** refers to procurement-related transactions, such as purchase requisitions and purchase orders. No purchasing-related transactions can be executed after the block flag is set. The **Procurement block** can be set for **All purchasing organizations** or **Selected purchasing organization** (only the purchasing organization selected in the initial screen of the blocking transaction).

The **Block for quality reasons** function applies only if QM for Procurement is active. The block function defines which functions are blocked for this vendor.

1.6.4 Confirmation of Changes

This function is also known as dual control of sensitive fields. If you define a field in the vendor master record as *sensitive*, the corresponding vendor account is blocked for the payment run if the entry is changed in one of the vendor change transactions. The block is removed when a second person with authorization checks the change and confirms or rejects it. In other words, the individual who made the change can't confirm his own changes.

The fields, which are subject to dual control, are configured under IMG navigation path **IMG • Financial Accounting • Accounts Receivable and Payable • Business Transactions • Vendor Accounts • Master Data • Preparation for Creating Vendor Master Data • Define Sensitive Fields for Dual Control (Vendors)**.

A single vendor can be confirmed with Transaction FK08. Transaction FK09 allows the list of multiple vendors to be confirmed.

1.6.5 Transfer Vendor Master Data

The Transfer Vendor Master Data functionality is available to create or change vendor master data in another company code in a mass run. Figure 1.23 shows the selection screen of the transfer program. If a vendor doesn't exist, the vendor is created. If the vendor is already created, only the changes are transferred. Due to performance reasons, only vendors that are created or changed after the **From change date** are transferred.

Two transfer options are available. Either the vendor data are copied directly (direct data transfer), or the data are written to a sequential file first. With the second option, the vendor data have to be imported in a subsequent step with Transaction FK16.

Activity	Function	Transaction
H	SPACE	Create
V	SPACE	Change
V	S	Block
V	L	Delete
A	SPACE	Display

Table 1.8 Parameters for BTE 00001460

Listing 1.3 shows an example code with the preceding activity and function values.

```
FUNCTION Z_INTERFACE_00001460.
*"----------------------------------------------------------------
*"*"Local Interface:
*"  IMPORTING
*"     VALUE(I_AKTYP) LIKE  T020-AKTYP
*"     VALUE(I_FUNCL) LIKE  T020-FUNCL
*"     VALUE(I_LFA1) LIKE  LFA1 STRUCTURE  LFA1
*"     VALUE(I_LFB1) LIKE  LFB1 STRUCTURE  LFB1
*"----------------------------------------------------------------

  CASE I_AKTYP.
    WHEN 'H'.            "Create
    WHEN 'V'.
      CASE I_FUNCL.
        WHEN SPACE.      "Change
        WHEN 'S'.        "Block
        WHEN 'L'.        "Delete
      ENDCASE.
    WHEN 'A'.            "Display
  ENDCASE.

ENDFUNCTION.
```

Listing 1.3 Example for BTE 00001460

1.7.3 Vendor Master Data — User Defined Screen

If your organization requires additional master data fields, SAP allows you to add up to 32 additional tabs or screens to your vendor master. In the following example, a new screen was added to capture contractor license and expiration date information. In addition, this screen should only be visible for Transactions XK01, XK02, and XK03.

Multiple steps must be performed for this user-defined screen. It's a combination of configuration and programming. The following steps show only the minimum required configuration and programming.

Step 1: Create Screen Groups and Tab Pages

The first configuration step defines the screen group and the different tabs for the user-defined screen. This can be maintained under the IMG path **IMG • Financial Accounting • Accounts Receivable and Payable • Vendor Accounts • Master Data • Preparation for Creating Vendor Master Data • Adoption of Customer's Own Master Data Fields • Prepare Modification-Free Enhancement in Vendor Master Record.**

In this example, the screen group **Z1 Additional License data** is created as shown in Figure 1.24.

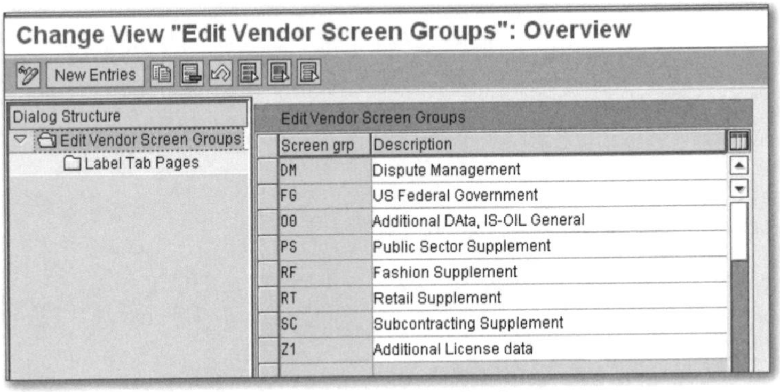

Figure 1.24 Create Screen Group for User-Defined Screen

Within each screen group, the different tabs need to be defined. To define the tabs, select the screen group and navigate to **Label Tab Pages**.

As shown in Figure 1.25, one tab page is defined with the following details:

- **Number: 10**
- **Description: License Data**
- **Icon: ICON_LINK**

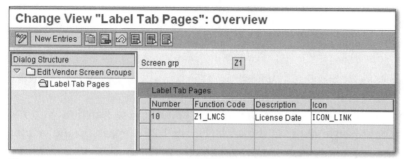

Figure 1.25 Tab Pages for a User-Defined Screen

Step 2: Create BAdI for Master Data Enhancement

In the second step, a BAdI needs to created, which includes the logic for the screen processing. This can be maintained under the IMG path **IMG • Financial Accounting • Accounts Receivable and Payable • Vendor Accounts • Master Data • Preparation for Creating Vendor Master Data • Adoption of Customer's Own Master Data Fields • Business-Add-In: Processing of Customer Master Data Enhancements.** This BAdI includes a variety of methods that allow you to execute many functions, such as the following:

▶ Validate data: Method `CHECK_ALL_DATA`

▶ Multiple methods for default values

▶ Initialize data

▶ However, only method `CHECK_ADD_ON_ACTIVE` is required. This method defines under which conditions the user-defined screens are active. In our example, we wanted to have the screen only active with Transactions XK01, XK02, and XK03. Listing 1.4 shows an example code for Method `CHECK_ADD_ON_ACTIVE`. This method was created under implementation `Z_LICENSE_ADD_DATA`.

```
method IF_EX_VENDOR_ADD_DATA~CHECK_ADD_ON_ACTIVE.
*-----------------------------------------------------
* The License Data screen (Screen Group Z1) is only
* active with Transaction code XK01, XK02, XK03
*-----------------------------------------------------
  IF I_SCREEN_GROUP = 'Z1'.
    IF SY-TCODE = 'XK01' OR
       SY-TCODE = 'XK02' OR
       SY-TCODE = 'XK03'.
      E_ADD_ON_ACTIVE = 'X'.
```

```
    ENDIF.
  ENDIF.

endmethod.
```

Listing 1.4 Example for Method `CHECK_ADD_ON_ACTIVE`

The result of the preceding steps is that at that point, a new function with the name **Additional License data,** as shown in Figure 1.26, appears in the vendor master.

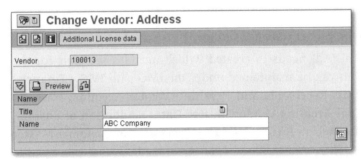

Figure 1.26 Additional License Data Function

Step 3: Append Tables (LFA1, LFB1, or LFM1)

In the third step, the database tables need to be appended by the user-defined fields. Depending on whether the new screen should appear under the General, Company Code, or Purchasing maintenance, either Table LFA1 (General Vendor Data), LFB1 (Company Code Dependent Data), or LFM1 (Purchasing Data) need to be appended with the new fields. In our example, Table LFM1 is extended by two fields, `ZZLICENSE` and `ZZEXP_DATE`, as shown in Figure 1.27.

Transp. Table	LFM1			Active				
Short Description	Vendor master record purchasing organization data							

	Attributes	Delivery and Maintenance	Fields	Entry help/check	Currency/Quantity Fields			

					Srch Help	Predefined Type		
Field	Key	Initi...	Data element	Data Ty...	Length	Deci...	Short Description	
.APPEND	☐	☐	ZLICENSE_DATA	STRU	0	0	Additional License Data	
ZZLICENSE	☐	☐	ZZLICENSE	CHAR	12	0	Licence Number	
ZZEXP_DATE	☐	☐	ZZEXP_DATE	DATS	8	0	Expiration date	

Figure 1.27 Append Structure in Table LFM1

74

Step 4: Create Customer Subscreens

In the next step, the customer subscreen needs to be created, including the screen flow logic with Transaction SE51. The subscreen shown in Figure 1.28 is called ZZ_LFM1_LICENSE with screen number **9000**.

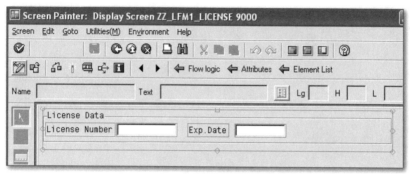

Figure 1.28 Subscreen ZZ_LFM1_LICENSE 9000

Every screen within SAP requires a main program and a screen flow logic. Listings 1.5 through 1.7 show the main program ZZLFM1_LICENSE, as well as the ZZ_LFM1_LICENSE_TOP and ZZ_LFM1_LICENSE_PBO includes.

```
*&--------------------------------------------------*
*& Module Pool    ZZ_LFM1_LICENSE
*&--------------------------------------------------*
PROGRAM  ZZ_LFM1_LICENSE.

INCLUDE ZZ_LFM1_LICENSE_TOP.
INCLUDE ZZ_LFM1_LICENSE_PBO.
```

Listing 1.5 Example Program ZZ_LFM1_LICENSE

```
*&--------------------------------------------------*
*&  Include    ZZ_LFM1_LICENSE_TOP
*&--------------------------------------------------*
TABLES: LFM1, T020.

DATA:    g_activity       TYPE aktyp.
```

Listing 1.6 Example Include ZZ_LFM_LICENSE_TOP

```
*-------------------------------------------------------*
***INCLUDE ZZ_LFM1_LICENSE_PBO .
*-------------------------------------------------------*
*&------------------------------------------------------*
*&      Module  FIELD_STATUS_9000   OUTPUT
*&------------------------------------------------------*
*------------------------------------------------------
* The screen fields are not input fields, if the
* Activity is A (Display)
*------------------------------------------------------
MODULE FIELD_STATUS_9000 OUTPUT.
  g_activity = T020-aktyp.
  LOOP AT SCREEN.
    IF screen-name = 'LFM1-ZZLICENSE'.
      IF g_activity = 'A'.
        screen-input = 0.
      ELSE.
        screen-input = 1.
      ENDIF.
    ENDIF.
    IF screen-name = 'LFM1-ZZEXP_DATE'.
      IF g_activity = 'A'.
        screen-input = 0.
      ELSE.
        screen-input = 1.
      ENDIF.
    ENDIF.
    MODIFY SCREEN.
  ENDLOOP.
ENDMODULE.                    " FIELD_STATUS_9000  OUTPUT
```

Listing 1.7 Example Include ZZ_LFM1_LICENSE_PBO

Listing 1.8 shows the flow logic of screen ZZ_LFM1_LICENSE 900.

```
PROCESS BEFORE OUTPUT.
* MODULE STATUS_9000.
  MODULE FIELD_STATUS_9000.

PROCESS AFTER INPUT.
* MODULE USER_COMMAND_9000.
```

Listing 1.8 Screen Flow Logic of Subscreen ZZ_LFM1_LICENSE 900

Step 5: Create Customer Subscreens

In the next step, a BAdI needs to be created that calls the customer subscreen created in the prior step. This can be maintained under the IMG path **IMG • Financial Accounting • Accounts Receivable and Payable • Vendor Accounts • Master Data • Preparation for Creating Vendor Master Data • Adoption of Customer's Own Master Data Fields • Business-Add-In: Customer Subscreen.** This BAdI includes a variety of methods that allow you to execute different functions, such as the following:

- Data transfer
  Method: SET_DATA or GET_DATA

- Hide add-on tab pages
  SUPPRESS_TAXI_TABSTRIPS

- However, only method GET_TAXI_SCREEN is required. This method defines which subscreen is called. In our example, we created subscreen 9000 in program ZZ_LFM1_LICENSE. Listing 1.9 shows example code for method GET_TAXI_SCREEN. This method was created under implementation Z_LICENSE_ADD_DATA.

```
method IF_EX_VENDOR_ADD_DATA_CS~GET_TAXI_SCREEN.

* Call the customer subscreen
  IF FLT_VAL = 'Z1'.
    IF I_TAXI_FCODE = 'Z1_LNCS'.
      E_SCREEN   = '9000'.
      E_PROGRAM = 'ZZ_LFM1_LICENSE'.
      E_HEADERSCREEN_LAYOUT = ' '.
    ENDIF.
  ENDIF.

endmethod.
```

Listing 1.9 Example for Method GET_TAXI_SCREEN

The result of all prior steps is a new user-defined screen as shown in Figure 1.29 in the vendor master data.

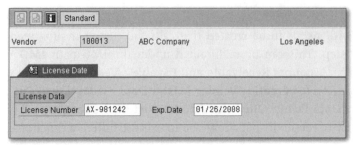

Figure 1.29 User-Defined Screen

1.7.4 Vendor Master Substitution Using BAdI VENDOR_ADD_DATA

In the previous section, the creation of additional vendor screens was described, with BAdI VENDOR_ADD_DATA. BAdI VENDOR_ADD_DATA however, has two methods, which can be used to default company-code dependent or purchasing vendor master data fields, even if no additional screens are created:

▶ Method `PRESET_VALUES_CCODE` (Company-code dependent fields)

▶ Method `PRESET_VALUES_PORG` (Purchasing fields)

As an example, the following substitution rule is created (Listing 1.10):

1. Default automatically the Vendor Reconciliation account '220200' for company code '1000'.

```
method IF_EX_VENDOR_ADD_DATA~PRESET_VALUES_CCODE.
*-------------------------------------------------
* Default Reconciliation account 220200 for company
* code 1000
*-------------------------------------------------
  IF I_ACTIVITY = 'H' OR           "Create Vendor
     I_ACTIVITY = 'V'.             "Change Vendor
    CASE E_LFB1-BUKRS.
      WHEN '1000'. E_LFB1-AKONT = '0000220200'.
      WHEN OTHERS.
    ENCASE.
  ENDIF.

endmethod.
```

Listing 1.10 Vendor Substitution Example for BAdI VENDOR_ADD_DATA

1.7.5   Personnel Number Validation Using User-Exit HRPBAS01

User-exit HRPBAS01 is an enhancement which allows user-defined validation for the personnel number, entered in the Personnel Number field. It is also possible to switch off the personnel number validation at all. This allows the utilization of the field, even if HR master data are not implemented. The user-exit is triggered at the time the personnel number is entered with rules defined in function module EXIT_SAPLRPIN_001.

In the following example, the SAP standard validation check is switched off (Listing 1.11).

```
*&---------------------------------------------------------*
*&  Include      ZXP02U01
*&---------------------------------------------------------*
*---------------------------------------------------------*
* The field RET (Return code) specifies, the result of the user-
* defined validation rule:
* RET = 0; All validation were successful
* RET = 1; Personnel number not active
* RET = 2; Personnel number unknown
* RET = 3; Personnel number not valid for this date
* RET = 4; Use SAP standard validation
*---------------------------------------------------------*

* No validation of the personnel number
  RET = '0'.
```

Listing 1.11 Personnel Number Validation Using User-exit HRPBAS01

1.7.6   Other Enhancements

In the prior sections, the most commonly used enhancements for vendor master data were described in detail. In addition, SAP delivers a variety of additional enhancements:

▸ **Publish & Subscribe BTE 00001450**
Vendor master data: Individual duplication check.

▸ **User-exit FARC0002**
Vendor master checks during archiving.

1.8 Vendor Master Data Search Helps

Search helps are also knows as matchcode searches. Search helps are used to find vendor account numbers without specifying the vendor account number. If you don't know the account number, for example, you can search for the account via other specifications, such as the name or the city. When defining the search help, you need to specify which fields of a master record can be used for the search.

In addition, a search help shouldn't be case sensitive, which means the search results should be the same whether you enter *SMITH* or *Smith* in the name field. SAP delivers three matchcode fields for vendor master data. The values for these matchcode fields are always stored in uppercase in the database. These fields can be maintained under the IMG path **IMG • Financial Accounting • Accounts Receivable and Payable • Vendor Accounts • Master Data • Matchcode • Check Search Fields for (Vendor) Matchcodes.** Table 1.9 shows the delivered matchcode fields and assigned field names.

Matchcode Field	Field Name	Description
MCOD1	NAME1	Name
MCOD2	NAME2	Name 2
MCOD3	ORT01	City

Table 1.9 Parameters for BTE 00001460

A common mistake in user-defined search helps is to use the fields NAME1, NAME2, or ORT01. Instead, you should use the corresponding matchcode fields, that is, MCOD1 instead of NAME1. This ensures that the search results are not dependent on whether the user enters the search values in uppercase or lowercase.

1.9 Vendor Master Data Table Structure

Table 1.10 lists the most commonly used vendor master data tables. These tables can be useful for either programmers or users who want to create their own queries to display vendor master data.

Table Name	Description
LFA1	Vendor Master (General Section)
LFB1	Vendor Master (Company Code)
LFBK	Vendor Master (Bank Details)
LFM1	Vendor Master (Purchasing Organization)
LFM2	Vendor Master (Purchasing Data)
LFZA	Vendor Master (Permitted Payee)

Table 1.10 Vendor Master Data Tables

1.10 Deleting Vendor Master Data

If vendor master data are created by mistake, and no transactional data, such as invoices or purchasing documents, are created for this vendor, the vendor master data can be deleted with Transaction OBR2. SAP developed this transaction to delete test data, however, this transaction code can also be used in a production environment on an exceptional basis by authorized users.

Deletion of Vendor Master Data with Transaction OBR2

Vendor master data can only be deleted with Transaction OBR2, if the following is true:

▶ No transactions were posted to these vendors.

▶ No purchasing view data exist for these vendors. In this case, the vendor master data needs to be archived.

1.11 Vendor Master Data Reporting

The standard delivered reports for vendor master data are limited. SAP delivers the following reports:

▶ Transaction: S_ALR_87012086: Vendor List

▶ Transaction: S_ALR_87012087: Address List

▶ Transaction: S_ALR_87012089: Display Changes to Vendors

1.12 Summary

In this Chapter the functionality of the vendor master data, the central master data with AP, were described. Vendor master data are necessary to create transactions within AP and Purchasing. Vendors are grouped by organization and by business purpose (vendor account group). The maintenance of the vendor master data can be done centrally or decentralized, depending on your organizational business requirements. Many SAP software enhancements are available which allow user-defined validations, additional screens, or field substitutions.

In Chapter 2, we will explore the SAP software Accounting Principles, such as document types, and posting keys.

A variety of different business transactions can be processed within Accounts Payable (AP). All transactions within the SAP system are based on the same accounting document principles, such as document types and postings keys.

2 Accounting Document Principles

Before we explore the details of the different business transactions within AP, it's important to understand the accounting document principles within SAP. Every posting in SAP, such as Journal Entry, Accounts Payable Invoice, Credit Memo, or Payment, results in an accounting document. Every accounting document looks the same and includes the following at a minimum:

▸ One document header

▸ Two line items

The following sections describe these principles in detail.

2.1 Document Header

The *document header* contains information valid for the entire financial document. The most important document header fields include the following:

▸ Document type

▸ Document number

▸ Posting date

▸ Document date

▸ Invoice receipt date

▸ Reference

2.1.1 Document Type

The *document type* is a key used to classify accounting documents and distinguish between business transactions to be posted. The document type is either entered during document entry in the document header or determined automatically via configuration settings and applies to the whole document. The document type has the following functions:

▶ The document type differentiates between business transactions. It tells you instantly what sort of business transaction is processed, such as invoice, credit memo, or payment. This is useful when analyzing the posted business transactions for an account.

▶ The document type determines which account types can be posted with a document type, such as vendors, customers, or GL accounts.

▶ A number range is assigned to every document type. The numbers for the documents you create are taken from this number range.

SAP delivers a list of preconfigured document types as shown in Table 2.1.

Document Type	Description
KR	Vendor Invoice
RE	Vendor Invoice (Logistic Invoice Verification)
KG	Vendor Credit Memo
KZ	Vendor Payment
KN	Vendor Net Invoice and Credit Memo

Table 2.1 Preconfigured Document Types

From an end-user and change-management perspective, it's important that document types are clearly defined and the two-character key is meaningful and easy to understand. From a best-practice perspective, you should create user-defined document types. Table 2.2 lists sample document types that follow these principles.

The document types can be maintained under the navigation path **IMG • Financial Accounting • Accounts Receivable and Payable • Business Transactions • Incoming Invoices/Credit Memos • Carry Out and Check Document Settings • Define Document Types.**

Document Type	Description
VI	Vendor Invoice
VC	Vendor Credit Memo
VR	Vendor Document Reversal
VP	Vendor PO Invoice
VM	Vendor PO Credit Memo
ZC	Vendor Check Payment
ZA	Vendor ACH Payment
ZW	Vendor Wire Payment

Table 2.2 Sample Document Types

Figure 2.1 shows the different configuration options for document types.

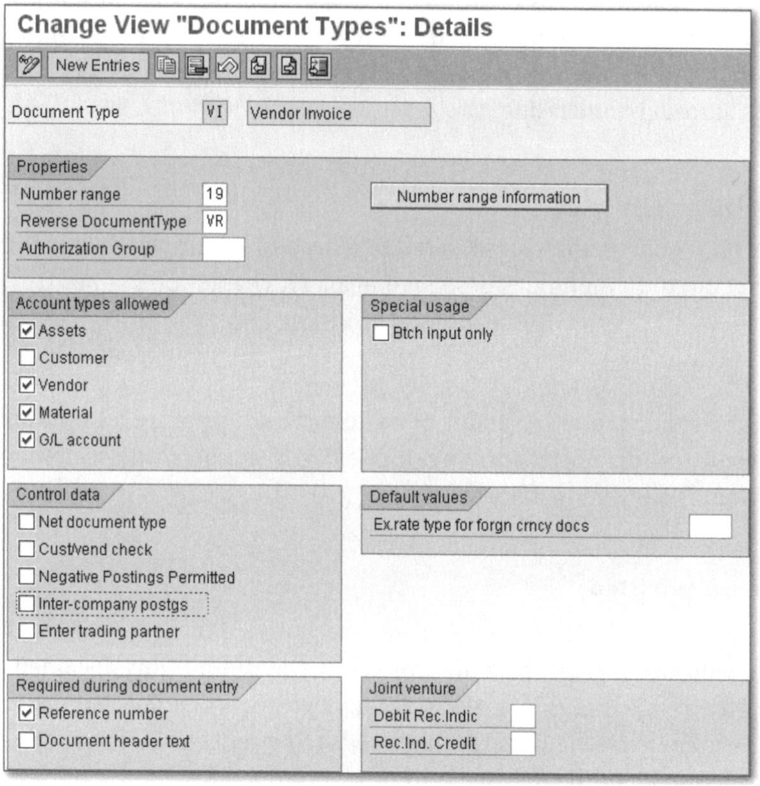

Figure 2.1 Detail Screen of Document Type Configuration

Number Range

Every document is posted with a document number. The assigned number range determines the number range interval of the document. Document number ranges are discussed in more detail in the next section of this chapter.

Reverse Document Type

The **Reverse Document Type** field defines which document type is used if a document is reversed. If no reversal document is specified, the reverse document is assigned the document type of the original document.

Account Types Allowed

Account types allowed specifies to which account types the document type can be posted. For AP as a minimum, **Vendor** and **G/L account** need to be set because every invoice and payment is posted against a vendor and one or multiple GL accounts. If inventory postings need to be allowed in PO-related invoices, **Material** also needs to be set. **Assets** only needs to be set if your company allows direct asset acquisitions through purchasing.

Net Document Type

If you use the net discount method for invoices, you need to set the **Net document type** flag. The net discount method is described in a later chapter of this book.

Cust/Vend Check

This flag defines whether multiple vendor or customer line items are allowed in the same document for this document type. If this flag is set, only one customer or vendor line item is allowed in a document.

Negative Postings Permitted

After a document is posted, the system updates the transaction figures, such as total debit and credit postings. If this indicator is set, you can use this document type to reverse incorrect postings by making negative postings and thus eliminate their effect on the transaction figures. This flag needs to be set in both the reversal and in the document type of the document to be reversed.

For example, an invoice over $100 is posted to a vendor, reversed, and entered again. The document types don't allow negative postings. In this case, the vendor total credit transactions show $200. If the **Negative Postings Permitted** flag would have been set, the reversal would have been posted with positive $100 as a credit posting, and only $100 would show as the total of all credit transactions.

Reference Number Required

If you require, the **Reference number** to be a required field, then you need to set this flag. Within AP, the **Reference number** usually represents the invoice number from your vendor and is therefore required.

Document Header Text Required

If the **Document header text** is required upon data entry, then you need to set this flag.

2.1.2 Document Number

The document number or number range identifies which number is assigned to a document. There are two types of number assignments possible for a document:

▸ **External**
The document number is entered manually during document entry. This number range type isn't commonly used if transactions are entered in SAP.

▸ **Internal**
The system automatically assigns the next sequential number of the number range. This method is usually used for vendor invoices.

Another important principle is that the document number by itself doesn't uniquely identify a document in SAP. A unique document is identified by the following:

▸ Document number

▸ Fiscal year

▸ Company code

This is due to the fact that document number ranges can be defined as year dependent, and the same number range can also be used in multiple company codes.

For example, you decide that your vendor invoices are within the 1900000000 – 1999999999 number range interval and are year dependent. Year dependent means that the invoice numbers start again with 190000000 every year. After two fiscal years, you have two invoices with 1900000000 but in two different fiscal years.

The number ranges can be maintained within Transaction FBN1 or under the navigation path **IMG • Financial Accounting • Financial Accounting Global Settings • Document • Document Number Ranges • Documents in Entry View • Define Document Number Ranges for Entry View.**

Figure 2.2 shows document number ranges for company code 1000. For year independent number ranges, enter "9999" in the year column; otherwise, enter the fiscal year for which the interval is valid. If you choose year-dependent number ranges, make sure that you have the number ranges defined before the start of every fiscal year.

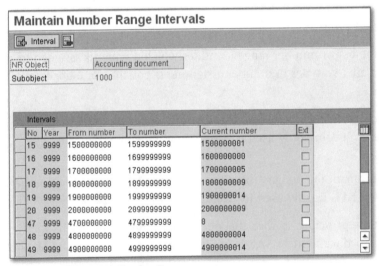

Figure 2.2 Document Number Ranges

2.1.3 Posting Date

The *posting date* determines in which fiscal year and period the document is posted. The system defaults the current date as the default date, however, you can manually overwrite this date as long as the period is permitted for postings.

2.1.4   Document Date (Invoice Date)

In AP transactions such as Invoice Entry or Credit Memo Entry, the *document date* represents the invoice date. The invoice date is the date printed on the vendor invoice. Based on the invoice date, the due date of an invoice is usually determined. The calculation of the due date is covered in the "Payment Terms" section of Chapter 5, Outgoing Payment Processing.

2.1.5   Invoice Receipt Date

For public-sector organizations, the Invoice Receipt Date field is available to enter the date when the invoice was received in the organization. This field is especially important to public-sector organizations that have to comply with the Prompt Payment Act.

2.1.6   Reference

The Reference field represents the invoice number of your vendor and is usually submitted to your vendor during payment processing either on a check or electronically. It's recommended to have the Reference field set as required for a document type.

2.2   Document Line Item

In every accounting document, at least two line items have to exist, and a document has to be in balance, which means that the total of all debit amounts has to equal the total of all credit amounts. A document can have multiple debit and credit lines. As long as the totals of all debit and credit lines are the same, the document is correct.

2.2.1   Posting Key

Within SAP, the *posting key* is a two-character key that serves as the main control key for the line item. The posting key determines the following:

- ▶ Debit or credit entry
- ▶ Allowed account types

▶ Layout of the entry screen

▶ Sales related

▶ Special GL transaction

▶ Reversal posting key

▶ Payment transaction

SAP delivers standard posting keys. It's not recommended to change these keys which can be maintained or displayed within Transaction OB41 or under the navigation path **IMG • Financial Accounting • Financial Accounting Global Settings • Document • Line Item • Control • Define Posting Keys.**

Figure 2.3 shows **Posting Key 31**, which represents the vendor invoice line item.

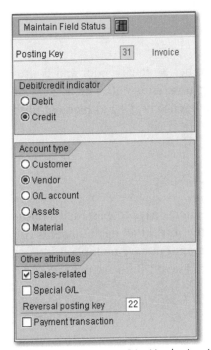

Figure 2.3 Posting Key 31 – Vendor Invoice

Debit/Credit Indicator

The **Debit/credit indicator** determines whether the line item posted with this posting key is either a debit or a credit line.

Account Type

The **Account type** determines whether this posting key can be used with a customer, vendor, GL account, asset, or material account number. Using the preceding example, **Posting Key 31** can only be posted with a vendor.

Posting Key Is Sales-Related

Sales-related means that the amounts posted with this posting key are used to calculate the total of sales and purchases for customers or vendors. For example, if you want to know the total of all purchases of a vendor, you need to ensure that the invoices are posted with a posting key where the **Sales-related** indicator is set. By doing that, the Sales/Purchase column is updated in the Vendor Balance Display – Transaction FK10N.

Special G/L

SAP refers to **Special G/L** transactions for vendor or customer postings, which have a special business function, such as down payments or security deposits. These postings are usually posted to reconciliation accounts other than the one defined in the vendor or customer master data. The line items have to be posted with a posting key, which has the **Special G/L** indicator set.

Reversal Posting Key

The **Reversal posting key** defines which posting key is used if a line item is reversed.

Payment Transaction

The **Payment transaction** indicator is set for all posting keys that are relevant for payments such as incoming payments, outgoing payments, payment differences (residual items), or payment clearings.

Table 2.3 lists the most important posting keys used within AP.

Posting Key	Name	Debit/ Credit	Account Type	Sales-Relevant	Payment
40	Debit Entry	Debit	GL Account		
50	Credit Entry	Credit	GL Account		
01	Invoice	Debit	Customer	X	
11	Credit Memo	Credit	Customer	X	
21	Credit Memo	Debit	Vendor	X	
31	Invoice	Credit	Vendor	X	
25	Outgoing Payment	Debit	Vendor		X
35	Incoming Payment	Credit	Vendor		X
70	Debit Asset	Debit	Asset		
75	Credit Asset	Credit	Asset		

Table 2.3 Standard List of Posting Keys

Tip: Remember the Correct Posting Key

Especially if you just started working with SAP, you might have difficulties remembering the correct posting key for a line item. Here are two tips that will help you remember the correct key:

▶ SAP always has a debit posting key and a corresponding credit posting key for the same business transaction. The lower of these postings keys is always the debit posting key. For example, 40 is a debit posting with a GL account, and 50 is a credit posting.

▶ In most cases, except assets, the credit posting key is 10 higher than the corresponding debit posting key. For example, a credit memo is posted to a vendor with posting key 21, and an invoice is posted with posting key 31.

2.3   Summary

Now that you understand the principles of accounting documents, let's take a look at the different posting transactions available with AP.

Within Accounts Payable (AP), a variety of different business transactions can be processed. These business processes include invoices, credit memos, document parking, and recurring entries.

3 Business Transactions in Accounts Payable

In this chapter, we'll discuss the different business transactions within AP. We'll explore the configuration steps, transactions, and available enhancements.

Business transactions with regards to payments and purchase order invoices are covered in later chapters of this book.

3.1 Invoice/Credit Memo Processing

Within AP, invoices and credit memos can be processed in different ways. SAP delivers multiple transactions to process invoices and credit memos. Since the earliest releases, the General Invoice and Credit Memo transactions were available. As of Release 4.6, the Enjoy transactions were added. The following different transactions are available:

- ▶ FB60: Invoice – Enjoy Transaction
- ▶ FB65: Credit Memo – Enjoy Transaction
- ▶ F-43: Invoice – General Transaction
- ▶ F-41: Credit Memo – General Transaction
- ▶ FB10: Invoice/Credit Memo East Entry Transaction

The difference between the Enjoy and the General transaction is, that the Enjoy transactions are single screen transactions with multiple tabs, which allow you to enter, hold, park, or post a transaction. For General transactions, multiple screens have to be processed.

However, the Enjoy transactions have some functional limitations compared to the General transactions:

▸ No line items against assets can be processed.

▸ Account assignment models can't be used, only account assignment templates. An account assignment model can use equivalence numbers, which allows you to distribute amounts automatically.

▸ Only invoices against one vendor can be processed.

Bottom line is that you'll process the majority of your transactions with the Enjoy transactions, but occasionally you'll have to use the General transactions because of the limitations of the Enjoy transactions.

3.2 Invoice/Credit Memo – Enjoy Transaction

There is basically no difference between the Invoice and Credit Memo Enjoy transactions, except that the business transaction is defaulted to invoice or credit memo. All other functions and screens are the same. Therefore, only the Invoice transaction is covered in detail in this chapter.

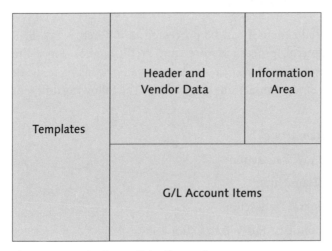

Figure 3.1 Invoice Entry – Enjoy Transaction

As shown in Figure 3.1, the Enjoy transaction screen is divided into four screen areas:

▸ **Templates**
▸ **Header and Vendor Data**

- ▸ **Information Area**
- ▸ **G/L Account Items**

3.2.1 Templates

The **Templates** area includes folders for screen variants for line items, account assignment templates, and held documents.

Screen Variants

A *screen variant* refers to the column layout of the **G/L acct items** area. You can create your own column layout by hiding columns, changing the column sequence, or changing default values. The screen variant can be maintained with Transaction SHD0. Within the folder, you can add or remove a screen variant by right-clicking on the **Screen-Variants** node or by single-clicking **Screen Variant**.

Account Assignment Templates

Account assignment templates are default values for the **G/L Acct items** area. For example, if you post on a regular basis the same invoice to the same GL accounts and cost centers, you can create an account assignment template with the different GL account and cost center combinations. The following functions are available for account assignment templates:

- ▸ Save Account Assignment Template
- ▸ Delete Account Assignment Template
- ▸ Add Account Assignment Template
- ▸ Remove Account Assignment Template
- ▸ Empty Folder

To save or create an account assignment template, you need to enter the GL account line items first, and then go to the header menu and select **Edit • Acct Assignment Templates • Save Account Assignment Templates**. Enter the name of the account assignment template, and the template will be saved in your folder. If the amount values in the template change on a regular basis, make sure that you save the template without the amount values filled.

The *Delete Account Assignment Template* function will delete a selected template globally, which means it will be deleted from the system. To delete a template, select the template in the node, right-click, and select **Delete acct assignment template**. The *Remove Account Assignment Template* function will just remove the template from your folder; it won't be deleted from the system.

To add an account assignment template to your folder that was created by another user, select the **Account assignment templates for items** folder, right-click, and select **Add Account Assignment Template.**

The *Empty Folder* function removes all account assignment templates from your folder.

To use an account assignment template, just double-click on the template you want to use, and the saved values are defaulted into the **G/L acct items** area.

Hold Documents

The *Hold Document* function allows you to save and complete invoices at a later point. For example, you might need additional information for the invoice to be completed, or you were interrupted and want to save your work. To save a document, go to the header menu, and select **Hold (F5)**. Enter a **Temporary document number,** and click **Hold document**. The temporary document number can be numeric or alphanumeric. The document is then saved in the **Held documents** folder. To complete a held document, just select the document, and complete the document. After it's complete and posted, the held document number disappears from your folder.

Held Documents
If you receive message F5 410: "Held documents must be converted; read long text" when you select the hold document function, Program RFTMPBLU needs to be executed with Transaction SA38. This program needs to be executed once in every client.

Figure 3.2 shows a sample template area with **Screen variants for items**, **Account assignment templates for items**, and **Held documents** folders.

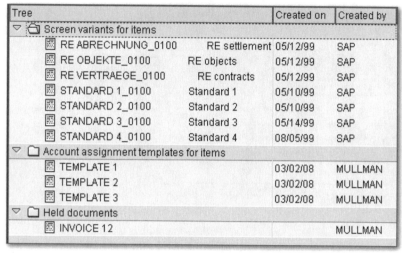

Figure 3.2 Sample Template Area

3.2.2 Header and Vendor Data

The Header and Vendor data area includes different tabs for the document header information as well as the vendor line item. The following tabs are available:

▸ **Basic data**

▸ **Payment**

▸ **Details**

▸ **Tax**

▸ **Withholding tax**

▸ **Amount split**

▸ **Notes**

Basic Data Tab

The **Basic data** tab includes the vendor number as well as the main invoice information, such as dates, invoice reference, invoice amount, and tax amount as shown in Figure 3.3.

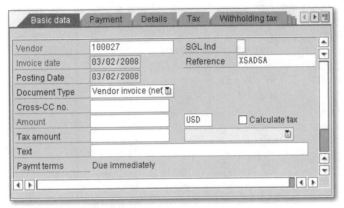

Figure 3.3 Basic Data Screen

The **Text** field allows you to enter additional information about the invoice. The text can be used internally or externally. To distinguish between these, you must begin the text for external use with "*". These texts can then be printed on correspondences, such as checks or payment advice notes. The asterisk is removed when the text is printed.

Payment Tab

The **Payment** tab includes all of the information relevant for payment of an invoice, such as **Payt Terms**, **Discount**, **Pmt Method**, **Pmnt Meth.Sup.**, and **Pmnt Block** as shown in Figure 3.4.

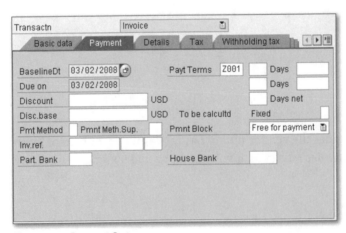

Figure 3.4 Payment Screen

If the payment terms are entered in the vendor master data in the **Payment Transaction** screen of the company data view (see Section 1.3.2 "Payment Transaction" in Chapter 1), these payment terms are defaulted during invoice entry. The payment terms are described in more detail in Chapter 5, Outgoing Payment Processing.

With regards to discounts, you can either let the system calculate the discount based on the percentages entered in the payment terms, for example, 15 days 1% Discount – 30 days net, or you can enter a fixed discount amount in the **Discount** field. If both a percentage and a discount amount are entered, the system always uses the fixed discount amount. The **Disc. base** field allows you to enter a different base amount to be used for calculating the discount. This could be the case if a discount is granted for only part of the invoice amount. Table 3.1 shows calculation examples of the discount, with an invoice amount of $100 and different discount fields used. The Result column shows the calculated discount amount.

Invoice Amount	Discount Percentage	Discount Amount	Discount Base	Result
$100	10%			$10
$100	10%	$20		$20
$100	10%	$5		$5
$100		$10		$10
$100	10%		$50	$5
$100	10%	$20	$50	$20

Table 3.1 Discount Calculation Example

In a later section of this chapter, the difference between the gross and net discount method is described in detail.

Details Tab

The **Details** tab shown in Figure 3.5 includes additional informational fields, such as **Assign.** or **Header Text**. Other country-specific fields and additional reference fields, such as Reference 1 or Reference 2, can be made available for data entry as well.

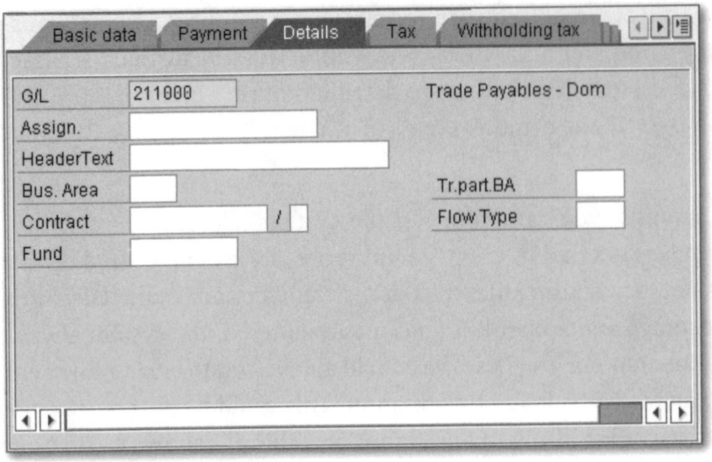

Figure 3.5   Details Screen

Tax Tab

The **Tax** tab is filled after you select the **Calculate tax** field in the **Basic data** tab. Taxes within AP are covered in detail in a later chapter.

Withholding Tax Tab

If a vendor is subject to withholding tax, the withholding tax information is filled in this screen. Withholding tax reporting is covered in detail in Chapter 10.

Amount Split

Amount split is a function that allows you to split an invoice into multiple payments. For example, you receive an invoice for over $100 and want to pay $80 immediately and $20 in 30 days. The amount split function allows you then to split the entire invoice amount into different line items with separate payment methods, payment terms, withholding tax terms, and payment supplement. You can activate amount split in the IMG via the navigation path **IMG • Financial Accounting • Financial Accounting Global Settings • Company Code • Enter Global Parameters.** You need to set the flag for **Enable amount split** in the company code global data (this screen is not shown in the figure).

Figure 3.6 shows an example of an invoice split into two separate line items. If you use the split functionality, the document type of the invoice must not be a document type with a net method.

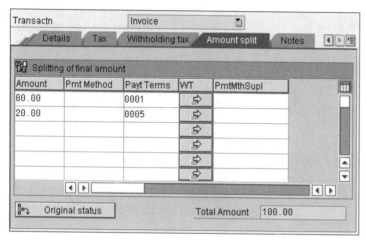

Figure 3.6 Invoice Amount Split Screen

Notes Tab

The **Notes** tab allows you to enter unlimited additional long text information for the invoice. The entered text can later be accessed via the long text function in the vendor line items.

3.2.3 Information Area

The information area shows the address and bank information of the vendor entered. From the information area, you can display the vendor master data by choosing the function **Display Vendor**. In addition, you can drill down to the open items of the vendor by selecting the **List of open items** function. If an alternative payee or permitted payee is entered, the address information doesn't change to the address of the alternative or permitted payee.

3.2.4 GL Accounts Item Area

The **G/L acct** item area includes a table for all account line items of this invoice. Up to 999 line items can be posted per invoice. The total of all account line items has to correspond with the total invoice amount. Figure 3.7 shows an invoice entered with two GL account line items.

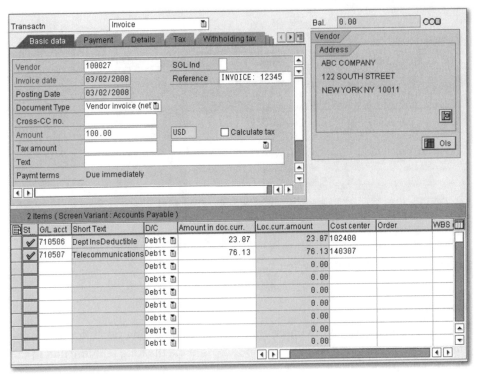

Figure 3.7   Invoice with Two GL Account Line Items

Within the **G/L acct** item area, several functions are available that allow you to insert, copy, delete, or sort the lines.

3.2.5   Invoice Simulation

After the invoice details have been entered, the invoice can be simulated. During the simulation process, the system calculates any automatic line items, such as tax or net discount line items. This allows the user to verify the correctness of these automatic line items. To execute the simulation, select the **Simulate** button or go to **Document • Simulate** in the header menu. Figure 3.8 shows a simulated invoice with a vendor net discount line item.

```
Doc.Type : RN ( Invoice - net ) Normal document
Doc. Number                Company code   1000     Fiscal year  2007
Doc. date      03/05/2008   Posting date   03/16/2008 Period       09
Calculate Tax  ☐
Doc.currency   USD
```

Itm	PK	Account	Account short text	Assignment	Tx	Cost Ctr	Amount
1	31	100013	ABC Company				100.00-
2	40	630010	Electricity	January 2008		210	98.00
3	40	217500	Clearing Vendor Disc				2.00

Figure 3.8 Simulated Invoice Example

If you want to return to the entry screen of the invoice, you receive the information message F5 257: "Automatically created line items will be deleted." This message means that the automatic line items created during the simulation, such as taxes or net discounts, will be deleted. This is necessary because these terms will be re-created anytime the simulation or posting is executed.

3.2.6 Simulate General Ledger

If you're on SAP Release level ECC 5.0 or ECC 6.0, and you have the new GL active in your company, you can also simulate the GL entries. The difference to the simulate function is that you can verify the postings in the different ledgers as well as any splitting rules for your company code. To execute the Simulate General Ledger function, go to **Document • Simulate General Ledger** in the header menu. Figure 3.9 shows the simulated GL line item for an invoice.

```
Document Date 05.03.2008     Posting Date    16.03.2008   Fiscal Year      2007
Reference                    Cross-co. code no.           Posting Period   9
Currency       USD           Ledger Group                 Ledger           0L
```

C...	Fund	Itm	L.item	PK	...	G/L Account	G/L account name	Amount	Curr.
1000	1100100	1	000001	31		211000	Trade Payables - Dom	100.00-	USD
	1100100	2	000002	40		630010	Electricity	98.00	USD
	1100100	3	000003	40		217500	Clearing Vendor Disc	2.00	USD

Figure 3.9 Simulate General Ledger Screen

3.2.7 Invoice Posting

After the invoice is complete, and all details are entered correctly, just click the **Post** button in the menu header, and the system will generate a document number.

3.3   Invoice/Credit Memo – General

There is basically no difference between the Invoice and Credit Memo – General transaction, except that the document type and posting key in the initial screen are defaulted with different values. All other functions and screens are the same. Therefore, only the Invoice transaction is covered in detail.

The General transaction is also known as the Complex Invoice Posting transaction because additional functionality compared to the Enjoy transaction is available. The following is a list of additional functions:

▶ Invoices with postings against assets or customers are possible.

▶ Invoices against multiple vendors can be processed.

▶ Account assignment models can be used. An account assignment model can use equivalence numbers, which allows you to distribute amounts automatically.

▶ The Post with Reference function allows you to copy prior posted invoices or generate reverse postings.

When you enter an invoice through the General transaction, you need to understand the meaning of the posting keys (described in Section 2.2.1 "Posting Keys" of Chapter 2) because the correct debit and credit posting keys for the vendor, GL accounts, assets, or customer line items have to be entered. This requires more accounting knowledge from the users than in the Enjoy transaction, where the posting keys are defaulted in the background and do not have to be entered. Table 3.2 list the most commonly used posting keys within AP.

Posting Key	Name	Debit/Credit	Account Type
40	Debit Entry	Debit	GL Account
50	Credit Entry	Credit	GL Account
01	Invoice	Debit	Customer
11	Credit Memo	Credit	Customer
21	Credit Memo	Debit	Vendor
31	Invoice	Credit	Vendor
25	Outgoing Payment	Debit	Vendor
35	Incoming Payment	Credit	Vendor
70	Debit Asset	Debit	Asset
75	Credit Asset	Credit	Asset

Table 3.2 List of Posting Keys

To enter an invoice with a vendor and one GL line item, you have to process at a minimum three screens:

▸ Vendor Invoice: Header Data

▸ Vendor Invoice: Add Vendor Item

▸ Vendor Invoice: Add G/L Account Item

3.3.1 Vendor Invoice: Header Data

The **Header Data** screen shown in Figure 3.10 includes all document header fields, such as **Document Date**, **Posting Date**, **Reference**, and **Doc. Header Text**.

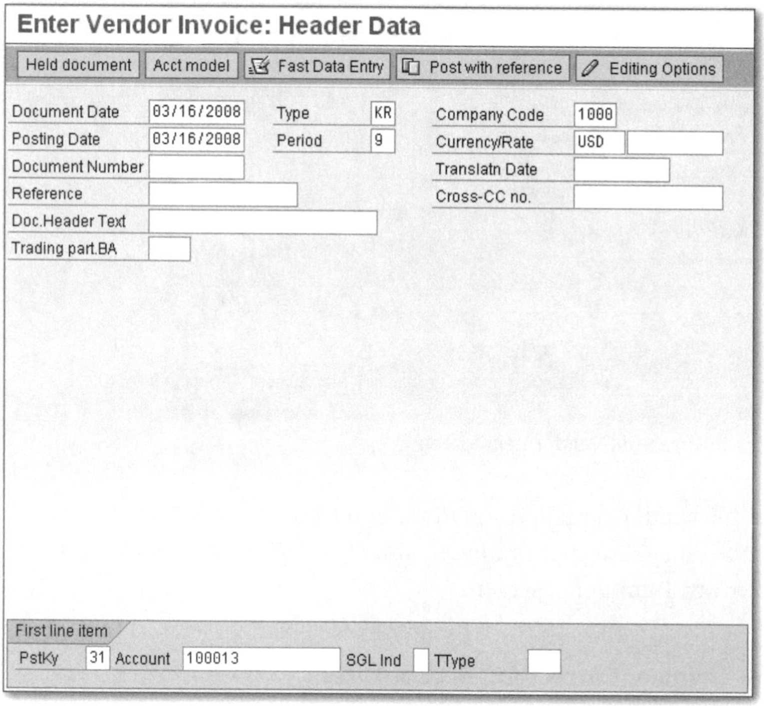

```
┌──────────────────────────────────────────────────────────────────────────┐
│ Enter Vendor Invoice: Header Data                                          │
│ ┌────────────┬───────────┬──────────────────┬───────────────────┬───────────────┐
│ │Held document│ Acct model│ ⬚ Fast Data Entry│ ⬚ Post with reference│ ⬚ Editing Options│
│ └────────────┴───────────┴──────────────────┴───────────────────┴───────────────┘
│ Document Date   03/16/2008   Type    KR    Company Code  1000
│ Posting Date    03/16/2008   Period   9    Currency/Rate USD
│ Document Number                             Translatn Date
│ Reference                                   Cross-CC no.
│ Doc.Header Text
│ Trading part.BA
│
│ First line item
│ PstKy  31  Account  100013     SGL Ind   TType
└──────────────────────────────────────────────────────────────────────────┘
```

Figure 3.10 Vendor Invoice: Header Data screen

To enter an invoice, you need to use posting key "31" for the first line item, and enter a vendor number in the **Account** field. After you've entered the invoice header information and the vendor, press the **Enter** key to access the **Add Vendor Item** detail screen.

3.3.2 Vendor Invoice: Vendor Item

The **Add Vendor Item** screen shown in Figure 3.11 includes all vendor line item details, such as amount, payment term, payment method, assignment, and text information.

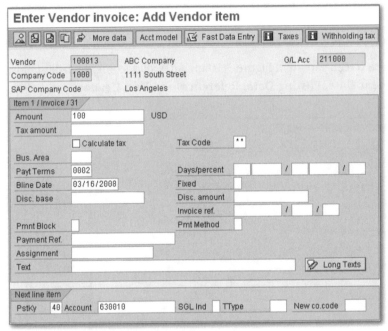

Figure 3.11 Vendor Invoice: Add Vendor Item Screen

After you enter all vendor detail information, enter posting key "40" for the GL account item, enter the GL account number, and press the **Enter** key to access the **Correct G/L Account Item** detail screen.

3.3.3 Vendor Invoice: Correct GL Account Item

The **Correct G/L account item** screen shown in Figure 3.12 includes all GL line item details, such as amount, assignment, text, and account assignment. Account assignments can be cost centers, internal orders, or WBS elements. Depending on your organization, additional fields such as business area, fund, grant, functional area, or commitment item are visible as well.

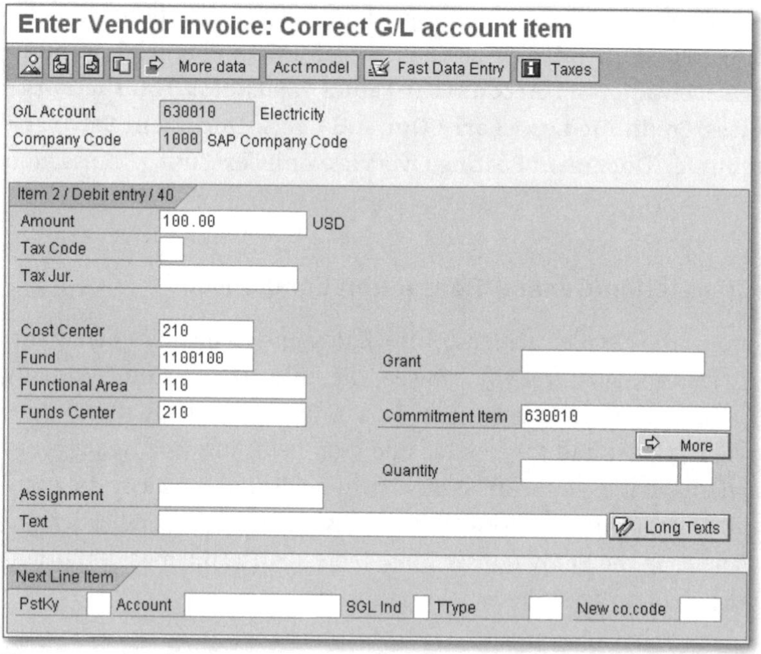

Enter Vendor invoice: Correct G/L account item

More data | Acct model | Fast Data Entry | Taxes

G/L Account   630010   Electricity
Company Code   1000 SAP Company Code

Item 2 / Debit entry / 40

Amount	100.00	USD
Tax Code		
Tax Jur.		

Cost Center	210		
Fund	1100100	Grant	
Functional Area	110		
Funds Center	210	Commitment Item	630010

More

Quantity

Assignment

Text   Long Texts

Next Line Item

PstKy   Account   SGL Ind   TType   New co.code

Figure 3.12   Vendor Invoice: Correct G/L Account Item Screen

After you enter the complete invoice, you can execute the same functions as described in the Enjoy transaction. You'll be able to simulate GL or post the document. In addition, you can display the document overview by selecting the **Display Document Overview** button, or go to **Goto • Document Overview** in the header menu. Figure 3.13 shows the document overview of the entered invoice with all line items.

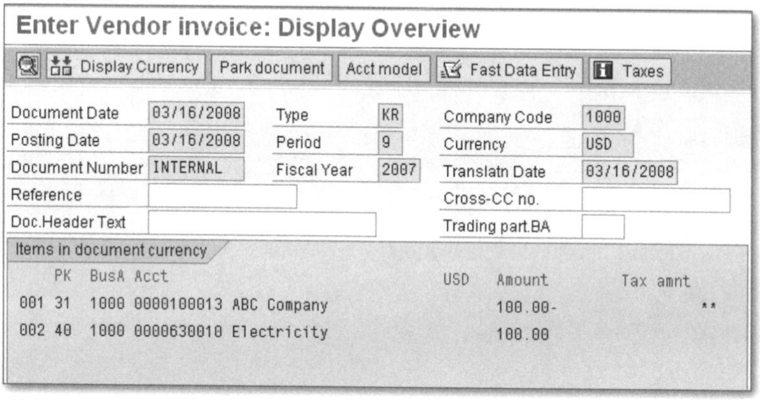

Enter Vendor invoice: Display Overview

Display Currency | Park document | Acct model | Fast Data Entry | Taxes

Document Date	03/16/2008	Type	KR	Company Code	1000
Posting Date	03/16/2008	Period	9	Currency	USD
Document Number	INTERNAL	Fiscal Year	2007	Translatn Date	03/16/2008
Reference				Cross-CC no.	
Doc.Header Text				Trading part.BA	

Items in document currency

PK	BusA	Acct		USD	Amount	Tax amnt
001	31	1000	0000100013 ABC Company		100.00-	**
002	40	1000	0000630010 Electricity		100.00	

Figure 3.13   Display Overview Screen

To select a different line layout, go to **Settings • Line Layout.** Additional line layouts can be configured in the IMG via navigation path **IMG • Financial Accounting • Accounts Receivable and Accounts Payables • Business Transactions • Incoming Invoices/Credit Memos • Carry Out and Check Document Settings • Define Line Layout for Document Posting Overview** or by executing Transaction O7Z2.

3.3.4 Enjoy Transaction/General Transaction Comparison

In the prior sections, the detailed screens of the Enjoy and General Invoice transaction were described in detail. As you can see, the Enjoy transaction is visually more appealing than the General transaction. This is due to the fact that SAP combined the document header and the vendor line item fields into the **Header and Vendor data** section and moved the most important fields into the **Basic data** tab. However, it's sometimes confusing to end users to distinguish between header and vendor line item fields in the Enjoy transactions. Table 3.3 lists the most important header and vendor item fields in the Enjoy transaction.

Field	Document Header/ Vendor item	Enjoy Tab	Comment
Vendor	Vendor item	Basic data	
Document Date	Document header	Basic data	Document Date is called Invoice Date in the Enjoy transaction.
Posting Date	Document header	Basic data	
Reference	Document header	Basic data	
Amount	Vendor item	Basic data	
Text	Vendor item	Basic data	
Payment term	Vendor item	Payment	
Payment Method	Vendor item	Payment	
Assignment	Vendor item	Details	
Document Header Text	Document header	Details	

Table 3.3 Enjoy Transaction Fields

3.4   Invoice/Credit Memo – Fast Entry

The third option to enter invoices or credit memos manually is the Fast Entry transaction. The Fast Entry transaction allows you to specify individually by user which fields are available in the vendor line item. For the GL line items, different line item templates can be configured.

The Fast Entry transaction is processed in two steps. In the first step, field values are specified that are valid for all invoices. After the values are specified, the invoices can be posted from one single screen. The Fast Entry transaction has multiple shortcomings compared to the Enjoy and General transactions:

▶ As in the Enjoy transaction, only postings to GL accounts can be processed. No postings against assets or customers are possible.

▶ Not all fields are available in the GL item templates, such as grant.

3.4.1   Fast Entry: Header Data

The **Header Data** screen shown in Figure 3.14 has multiple sections with different functionality.

Specifications for the Following Documents

This section includes all fields that can't be changed in the individual invoices. These fields include the **Company Code, Document Type, Posting Date**, and **Posting Period** for the invoices to be entered. If one of these fields needs to be changed, the user has to navigate back to this screen and change the value.

Default Data for the Following Documents

This section includes all fields that are defaulted for the individual invoices and can be changed. These fields include **Currency** and **Document Date**.

Additional Input Fields for Document Header and Vendor Item

This section includes fields that can be made available for data entry in the vendor and document header.

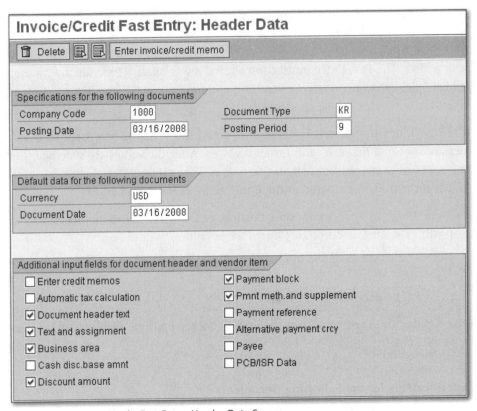

Figure 3.14 Invoice/Credit Fast Entry: Header Data Screen

After the correct information is selected, select the **Enter Invoice/credit memo** button.

3.4.2 Fast Entry: Enter Items

The **Enter items** screen shown in Figure 3.15 combines all header, vendor item, and GL line item details in a single screen. Additional header and vendor item fields can be displayed be selecting the **All Fields** button. If any of the default specifications, such as company code, document type, posting date, or period, need to be changed, you can navigate back to the **Header** screen be selecting the **Specifications** button.

Invoice/Credit Fast Entry Enter items

| | Last item | Mask | All Fields | Specifications | Acct model | Fast Data Entry |

| Document Date | 03/16/2008 | Curr./ex.rt/date | USD | | 03/16/2008 |
| Reference | | Doc.Header Text | | |

Vendor posting / ABC Company / Los Angeles

Account	100013	Business Area	
Amount	100.00	Discount amount	
Tax amount		
Payt Terms	0001	
Baseline Date	03/16/2008	Days/percentage		/	/
Payment Block		Payment Method	
Text/assignment		/	

Offsetting item (1-6)

Account	Amount	Tx	Cost Ctr	Order	CoCd	S
630010	100.00		210		1000	☐
						☐
						☐
						☐
						☐
						☐

Figure 3.15 Invoice/Credit Fast Entry: Enter Items Screen

To select a different line template, go to **Settings • Input Template.** Additional templates can be configured in the IMG via navigation path **IMG • Financial Accounting • Accounts Receivable and Accounts Payables • Business Transactions • Incoming Invoices/Credit Memos • Invoice/Credit Memo Fast Entry • Define Screen Templates for G/L Account Items** or by executing Transaction O7E6.

3.5   Invoice Entry Configuration Steps

The configuration steps for the Invoice/Credit Memo processing is minimal. Besides the configuration steps already discussed, the only missing configuration steps are setting default values for the Enjoy, General, and Fast Entry transactions.

3.5.1   Define Default Values for Enjoy Transactions

For the Invoice and Credit Memo Enjoy transactions, the document types and posting keys values have to be defaulted.

Default Document Type

The document type defaults can be maintained in the IMG via navigation path **IMG • Financial Accounting • Accounts Receivable and Accounts Payables • Business Transactions • Incoming Invoices/Credit Memos • Incoming Invoices/ Credit Memos - Enjoy • Define Document Types for Enjoy Transaction.** Figure 3.16 shows the default document types for **Invoice** and **Credit Memo**.

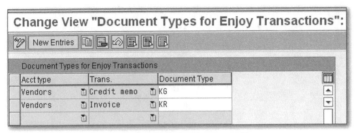

Figure 3.16 Enjoy Transaction Default Document Types

Default Posting Keys

The posting keys have to be defaulted for the vendor line items, GL line items, and vendor special GL transactions. The posting keys can be defaulted in the IMG via navigation path **IMG • Financial Accounting • Accounts Receivable and Accounts Payables • Business Transactions • Incoming Invoices/Credit Memos • Incoming Invoices/Credit Memos - Enjoy • Define Posting Key for Incoming Invoices/ Credit Memos.** Table 3.4 shows the recommended posting keys for the different transaction types.

Transaction	Description	Debit	Credit
EGK	Vendor item in incoming invoice	21	31
EGS	GL item in incoming invoice	40	50
EGX	Vendor item with special GL indicator	29	39

Table 3.4 Posting Key Default Values

3.5.2   Define Default Values for General Transactions

For the Invoice and Credit Memo General transactions, the document types and posting keys values have to be defaulted. The document type and posting key can be maintained in the IMG via navigation path **IMG • Financial Accounting • Accounts Receivable and Accounts Payables • Business Transactions • Incoming Invoices/Credit Memos • Carry Out and Check Document Settings • Define Default Values** or by executing Transaction OBU1. To change the default document type and posting key, double-click on the transactions codes for invoices (F-43) and credit memos (F-41).

3.5.3 Define Default Values for Fast Entry Transaction

For the Fast Entry transaction, the posting keys values have to be defaulted, which can be maintained in the IMG via navigation path **IMG • Financial Accounting • Accounts Receivable and Accounts Payables • Business Transactions • Incoming Invoices/Credit Memos • Invoice/Credit Memo Fast Entry • Define Posting Keys for Fast Entry** or by executing Transaction OBXJ. The configuration values are identical to the posting key for the Enjoy transaction.

3.6 Document Parking

The *park invoice* function allows users to enter an invoice but not post it. There are different reasons for parking an invoice, such as an invoice that isn't yet complete or an invoice requires additional information. The following transaction codes can be used to park an invoice:

- FV60: Park Invoice – Enjoy Transaction
- FV65: Park Credit Memo – Enjoy Transaction
- F-63: Park Invoice – General Transaction
- F-66: Park Credit Memo – General Transaction

The parking transactions are similar to the transactions for entering invoices. After an invoice is entered, the user has to decide whether an invoice should be parked or saved as complete. The following list shows the differences in the functionality between parking and saving as complete:

- A parked document can be incomplete, which means the document doesn't need to be in balance.
- FI substitutions and validations are only executed after a document is saved as complete.

▸ If you're using a workflow approval process, the Park function does not start the workflow. Only after you choose the Save as Complete function, is the workflow process executed.

3.7 Discount Methods

SAP provides two different discount methods for AP: gross discount method and net discount method.

3.7.1 Gross Discount Method

In the *gross discount method*, the discount terms are entered during the invoice posting. During the payment process, the system determines whether the discount terms are met and posts the calculated discount to a discount account.

Financial Documents for the Gross Discount Method		
For example, an invoice over $100 is entered with a 2% discount. During the payment, a discount of $2 is calculated and posted to a discount account.		
Document 1: Invoice Posting		
Debit	Expense Account	$100
Credit	AP Reconciliation Account	$100
Document 2: Payment Posting		
Debit	AP Reconciliation Account	$100
Credit	Cash Account	$98
Credit	Cash Discount Account	$2

The Cash Discount account is determined automatically during the payment processing and can't be entered manually. It can be maintained in the IMG via navigation path **IMG • Financial Accounting • Accounts Receivable and Accounts Payables • Business Transactions • Outgoing Payments • Outgoing Payments Global Setting • Define Accounts for Cash Discount Taken** or by executing Transaction OBXU.

If the Cash Discount account is defined as a cost element in the Controlling component (CO), the discount has to be posted to a CO account assignment as well. A CO account assignment can be a cost center, internal order, or WBS element. Because the CO assignment can't be entered manually, it has to be determined automatically during the payment processing. This assignment can be maintained in the IMG via navigation path **IMG • Controlling • Cost Center Accounting • Actual Postings • Manual Actual Postings • Edit Automatic Account Assignment** or by executing Transaction OKB9. Within Transaction OKB9, a default cost center or internal order has to be entered for the Cash Discount Account. If your organization uses multiple business areas, but you want to default the same cost center or internal order for all business areas, the **BArIn** flag (account assignment business area has priority) has to be set within Transaction OKB9. Otherwise, one cost center or internal order per business area has to be defaulted.

Within SAP, the CO account assignment can also be determined automatically with a CO substitution or directly entered in the cost element as a default value. However, the described configuration setting is the most common method.

3.7.2 Net Discount Method

In comparison to the gross discount method, the *net discount method* calculates and posts the discount at the time of the invoice entry to a Net Discount account. The expenses are reduced by the discount amount immediately upon invoice entry.

During the payment processing, it's determined whether the discount terms are met. If the discount terms are met, the vendor payment is reduced by the net discount amount.

If the discount terms are not met, the vendor is paid with the full invoice amount. Because the expense account is reduced by the discount amount during invoice entry, lost discount is posted to offset the Net Discount account.

Financial Documents for the Net Discount Method		
For example, an invoice over $100 is entered with a 2% discount. The discount terms are met during the payment processing.		
Document 1: Invoice Posting		
Debit	Expense Account	$98
Debit	Net Discount Account	$2
Credit	AP Reconciliation Account	$100

Document 2a: Payment Posting (Discount terms met)

Debit	AP Reconciliation Account	$100
Credit	Net Discount Account	$2
Credit	Cash Account	$98

If the discount terms were not met during the payment processing, the following document will be posted:

Document 2b: Payment Posting (Discount terms not met)

Debit	AP Reconciliation Account	$100
Credit	Cash Account	$100
Debit	Lost Discount Account	$2
Credit	Net Discount Account	$2

The net discount method is used in AP if you choose a document type where the **Net document type** flag is set in the configuration of the document (see Section 2.1.1 "Document Type" in Chapter 2).

The Net Discount account is determined automatically during the invoice processing and can't be entered manually. It can be maintained in the IMG via navigation path **IMG • Financial Accounting • Accounts Receivable and Accounts Payables • Business Transactions • Incoming Invoices/Credit Memos • Define Account for Net Procedure** or by executing Transaction OBXA.

The Net Discount account is usually defined as a balance sheet account. You should also define this account as open item managed within the account master data. Open item managed accounts allow you to clear debit and credit transactions of an account. The remaining balance is always the open transactions.

The Lost Discount account is also determined automatically via navigation path **IMG • Financial Accounting • Accounts Receivable and Accounts Payables • Business Transactions • Outgoing Payments Global Settings • Define Account for Lost Discount** or by executing Transaction OBXV.

Similar to the Discount account, the Lost Discount account also needs to be posted to a CO account assignment if the Lost Discount account is defined as a cost element in the CO module. This assignment can be maintained in the IMG via navigation path **IMG • Controlling • Cost Center Accounting • Actual Postings • Manual**

Actual Postings • Edit Automatic Account Assignment or by executing Transaction OKB9. Within Transaction OKB9, a default cost center or internal order has to be entered for the Lost Discount account.

3.7.3 Discount Method Differences

Besides the different financial postings generated by the discount methods as shown previously, the discount method chosen depends on your company's business requirements. If you're required to report discounts to be taken, you want to opt for the net discount method. The net discount method also allows you to report the discount to be taken by business area, segment, profit center, or fund. In this case, you need to be on the new GL and have document splitting active in your company code.

If you choose the net discount method, keep in mind that amount split during invoice entry isn't possible. The amount split function was covered in the "Invoice Entry Enjoy Transaction" section of this chapter.

3.8 Alternative Payees

The alternative payee functionality allows you to remit the payment to a vendor or address that is different from the vendor you entered in the invoice. Within the AP application, SAP delivers a variety of different options to process payments to alternative payees. The following options are currently available:

- Alternative payee
- Alternative payee in document
- Permitted payee

3.8.1 Alternative Payee

The **Alternative payee** field is available within the vendor master data screen on two different tabs, on the general **Payment transactions** tab as shown in Figure 3.17 and on the company code specific payment tab of the vendor.

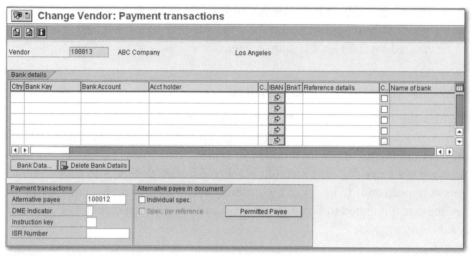

Figure 3.17 Alternative Payee Field in General Payment Transactions Tab

If the **Alternative payee** is entered, all payments to a vendor are issued to the alternative payee. If the alternative payee is filled in both tabs, the company code specific payee has priority.

Upon invoice entry, whether an alternate payee is assigned to the vendor isn't visible to the user. Because the vendor address on the screen does not change, the alternate payee option can only be used if all payments with no exceptions are issued to the alternate payee.

3.8.2 Alternative Payee in Document

This option is similar to the one-time vendor invoice and payment functionality in AP. In comparison to one-time vendor transactions, the user has the option to enter an alternate address or bank information in the invoice, whereas for one-time vendors, this information always has to be filled in.

To allow alternate payee in document information to be entered, the **Individual spec.** checkbox has to be selected in the general **Payment transactions** tab of the vendor master data as shown in Figure 3.18.

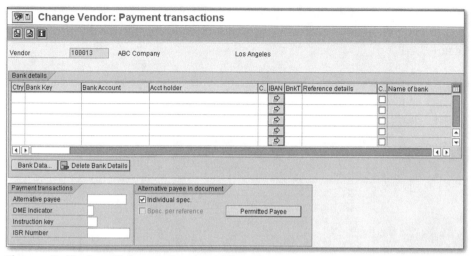

Figure 3.18 Vendor with Payee in Document Allowed

After the alternate payee in document information is allowed for a vendor, the **Individual payee** checkbox is available during invoice entry on the **Payment** tab of the invoice as shown in Figure 3.19.

Enter Vendor Invoice: Company Code 1000

| Tree on | Company Code | Hold | Simulate | Park | Editing options |

Transactn: Invoice   Bal. 0.00

Basic data | Payment | Details | Tax | Withholding tax

BaselineDt 03/23/2008
Due on 03/23/2008
Discount   USD
Disc.base   USD   To be calcultd   Fixed
Pmt Method
Inv.ref.
Part. Bank

Payt Terms 0001   Days
                   Days
                   Days net
Pmnt Block   Free for payment

House Bank
Payment Ref.

□ Individual payee

Vendor
Address
ABC Company
1111 South Street
Los Angeles CA 12345

Bank account
Bank Number
Not available

OIs

Figure 3.19 Invoice Entry with Payee in Document

If you click on the **Individual payee** checkbox, a new screen pops up that allows you to enter alternative address or bank information specific for this invoice (see Figure 3.20).

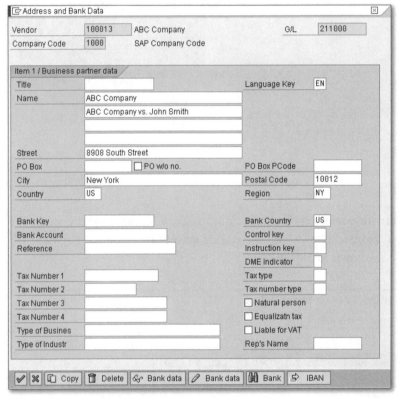

Figure 3.20 Payee in Document Screen

This option usually raises security concerns within an AP department because payments can be issued to payee addresses that are different from the vendor master data. These concerns can be mitigated be using payments blocks for vendors with payee in documents allowed. These invoices have to be released first by a second user before payment issuance.

One example where it's recommended to use the payee in documents functionality is payments to lawyers, where case or settlement information are entered in the second name line, because this information has to appear on the issued check.

3.8.3   Permitted Payee

The permitted payee option allows the assignment of multiple permitted payees to the same vendor. In the first step, the permitted payees need to be assigned in the vendor master data. During invoice entry, the correct alternative payee is chosen from the list of permitted payees assigned to this vendor.

Permitted payees can be assigned in the general **Payment transactions** screen in the vendor master data or company code specific on the company code payment tab of the vendor. After you click on the **Permitted payee** button, a second screen as shown in Figure 3.21 appears that allows assigning multiple permitted payees to this vendor.

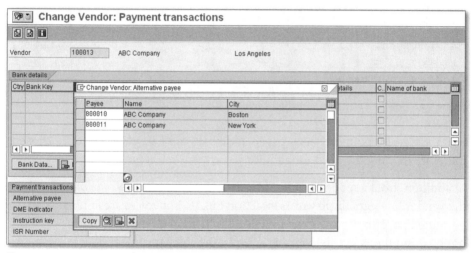

Figure 3.21   Assignment of Permitted Payee

If at least one permitted payee is assigned to a vendor, the **Payee** field is available during invoice entry, and the user can choose from the assigned permitted payees. Because the user intentionally has to choose the correct payee address from the permitted payee list as shown in Figure 3.22, in comparison to the alternative payee option, issuance of payments to wrong payee addresses can be avoided.

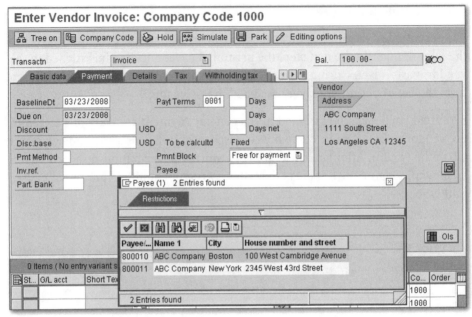

Figure 3.22 Invoice Entry with Permitted payees

From a security point of view, payee addresses can't be changed, only chosen, therefore limiting the need for additional payment releases.

In addition, from a reporting point of view, the alternative payee is only visible in the vendor line item display of Transaction FBL1N if invoices are entered with the permitted payee option. Figure 3.23 lists three invoices posted with the different options, and the **Payee** field is only filled in the third invoice.

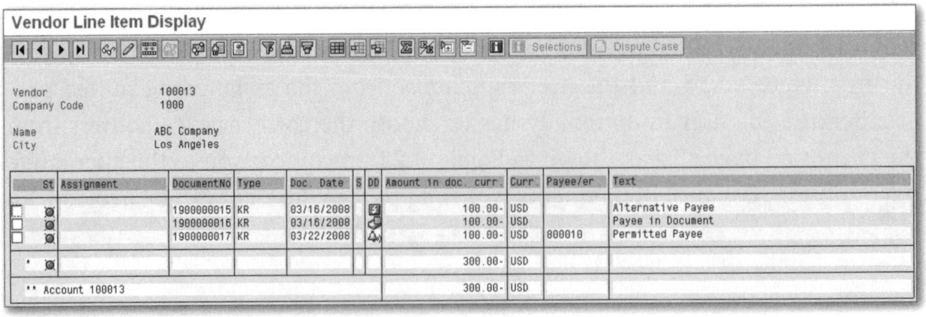

Figure 3.23 Line Item Display with Transaction FBL1N

3.8.4   Recommendation

As shown in the preceding examples, the same results can be achieved with all three options. However, the main difference lies is in the security and reporting capabilities. The recommendation is usually to use payee in document and permitted payees, which often fits the needs of a company. To use all three options in combination is usually too confusing for the users and is only needed if alternate payee transactions have to be processed with automated invoice creation processes, such as Evaluated Receipt Settlements (ERS) or invoicing plans, where the users can't enter a permitted payee.

In addition, the permitted payee option allows you to structure your vendor master data where you have one main vendor and multiple permitted payees. This makes it possible to have all invoices posted to one vendor and payments remitted to multiple alternative addresses. From a configuration point of view, the following configurations are recommended:

▶ Create a separate vendor account group with different number range assignment for your permitted payees, that is, REMT – Remittance vendors

▶ Hide the reconciliation account field in this vendor account group. This prevents remittance vendors from being chosen directly during invoice entry.

▶ Do not create the purchasing views for these vendors. Otherwise, these vendors can be used in purchasing for requisitions or purchase orders.

3.9   Recurring Entries

The recurring entries functionality allows the automatic creation of invoices on a recurring basis. Recurring basis means that the date intervals and frequency of the recurring entries have to be defined for each recurring entry. Using this functionality is only recommended if the invoice line items, such as accounts, CO account assignments, or amounts don't change during the recurring entry time frame. Examples for recurring entries are rent payments or subscriptions, where the amounts do not change on a regular basis.

In this chapter, only the AP recurring entry functionality is discussed. In a later chapter, the invoicing plan functionality is described, which allows recurring entries for purchase orders.

Recurring entries are processed in two steps. In the first step, the recurring entries are created, and in the second step, the actual invoices are created based on the recurring entries.

> **Note**
>
> The Recurring Entry transactions are shared in GL, AP, and AR. It's therefore not possible to restrict the authorizations by recurring entry type.

3.9.1 Recurring Entry Creation

Recurring entries can be created with Transaction FBD1 or by using the navigation path **SAP Menu • Accounting • Financial Accounting • Accounts Payable • Document Entry • Reference Documents • Recurring Entry Document**. Figure 3.24 shows the header data of a recurring entry for quarterly rent payments.

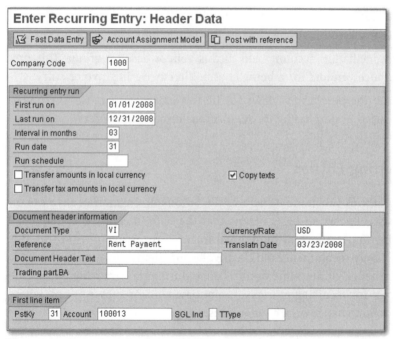

Figure 3.24 Enter Recurring Entry: Header Data Screen

The **Header Data** screen is divided into three sections:

- ▸ **Recurring entry run**
- ▸ **Document header information**
- ▸ **First line item**

Recurring Entry Run

The **Recurring entry run** section defines the time frame and the frequency of the recurring entry. You can either define the intervals and frequency directly in the document, or you can assign a **Run schedule** to the recurring entry.

First Run On/Last Run On

The **First run on** field identifies the date when the first recurring entry is to be created. The **Last run on** date is when the final recurring entry is created.

Intervals in Months

The **Intervals in months** field defines the interval between the recurring documents. For example, enter "1" for a monthly recurring entry. A quarterly document recurring entry has the value "3".

Run Date

The **Run date** field defines on which date of a month the recurring document is created. If a recurring document is created on the last date of the month, enter "31". If no value is entered, the calendar day of the **First run on** date field is used.

Table 3.5 shows examples of different recurring entry intervals.

First Run On	Last Run On	Intervals in Months	Run Date	Description
01/01/2008	12/31/2008	1	31	Monthly document on the last day of a month. First document on 1/31/2008. Last document on 12/31/2008.
01/31/2008	12/31/2008	1		Monthly document on the last day of a month. First document on 1/31/2008. Last document on 12/31/2008.

Table 3.5 Recurring Entry Interval Examples

First Run On	Last Run On	Intervals in Months	Run Date	Description
04/01/2008	12/31/2020	12	15	Yearly document on the 15th day of a month. First document on 4/15/2008. Last document on 4/15/2020.
06/01/2008	12/31/2009	3	1	Quarterly document on the first day of a month. First document on 6/1/2008. Last document on 10/1/2009.

Table 3.5 Recurring Entry Interval Examples (Cont.)

If recurring entries need to be created on dates other than monthly intervals and frequency, such as weekly schedules or different dates in every month, a separate **Run Schedule** is necessary.

The run schedules have to be maintained in the IMG via navigation path **IMG • Financial Accounting • Financial Accounting Global Settings • Document • Recurring Entries • Define Run Schedule**. In a second step, the actual dates need to be assigned to the run schedule in the IMG via navigation path **IMG • Financial Accounting • Financial Accounting Global Settings • Document • Recurring Entries • Enter Run Dates**.

Document Header Information

The **Document header information** section defines invoice header information, such as **Document Type** or **Reference** number. The document date and posting date are not available because they are determined automatically during the execution of the recurring entry described later in this section.

First Line Item

The screens for line item information are the same as in the General Invoice entry, which were described in Section 3.3 "Invoice – General Transaction." The **First line item** includes the **Posting key** and the **Account**. If you want to enter a vendor invoice, use "31" as the posting key and the vendor number in the **Account** field.

The recurring invoice needs to be completed by creating additional line items as described in Section 3.3.

3.9.2 Recurring Entry Execution

The recurring entry execution process creates the actual documents with Transaction F.14 or using the navigation path **SAP Menu • Accounting • Financial Accounting • Accounts Payable • Periodic Processing • Recurring Entries • Execute**.

This program selects any recurring entry documents whose next run data is the same as the date of the settlement period or falls within the interval for the settlement period. It does not include recurring entry documents that are marked for deletion.

As a result, a batch input session is created that contains all accounting documents to be created. To post the accounting documents and update the recurring entry documents, you have to process the batch input session with Transaction SM35.

Create Posting Documents from Recurring Documents

Company code	1000	to	
Document Number		to	
Fiscal Year		to	

General selections

Document type	VI	to	
Posting date		to	
Entry date		to	
Reference number		to	
Reference Transaction		to	
Reference key		to	
Logical system		to	

Further selections

Settlement period	01/01/2008	to	03/31/2008
Run schedule		to	
User		to	

Output control

Batch input session name	REC_INVOICE
User name	MULLMANN
Blocking date for BI session	
☐ Hold processed session	

Figure 3.25 Recurring Entry Execution – Selection Screen

Figure 3.25 shows the selection of recurring entries with document type **VI** and recurring documents to be created with run dates between 1/1/2008 and 3/31/2008. The result will be a batch invoice session with the name **REC_INVOICE**. This batch input session needs to be processed with Transaction SM35.

3.9.3 Additional Recurring Transactions

To maintain and list recurring entries, the following additional transactions are available:

- ▶ **F.15: ALV list of recurring entries**
  This program can be used to determine which documents will be created in a particular time period.

- ▶ **FBD2: Change Recurring Entry**
  This transaction allows changes to the recurring entry. In particular, the recurring entry data, such as intervals or run schedules, can be changed. It isn't possible to change accounts or amounts. If a recurrent entry isn't valid anymore, the deletion flag can be set in this transaction via the header menu by selecting **Goto • Recurring Entry Data.**

- ▶ **FBD3: Display Recurring Entry**
  Single recurring entry documents can be displayed.

- ▶ **FBD4: Display Changes**
  All changes to a particular recurring entry documents can be displayed.

- ▶ **F.56: Delete Recurring Entry**
  Recurring entry documents, which are marked for deletion with Transaction FBD2, can be deleted with this transaction.

3.10 Account Assignment Models

Account assignment models are used as invoice entry templates for invoices or credit memos, which have the same line item details. The account assignment models described in this section can only be used in general invoice transactions, such as the following:

- ▶ F-43: Invoice – General
- ▶ F-41: Credit Memo – General

▸ FB10: Invoice/Credit Memo East Entry

▸ FBD1: Recurring Entries

Within the Enjoy transactions, account assignment templates can be created, which were described in Section 3.2 and are only visible within the Enjoy transactions.

The account assignment models have the following advantage over the account assignment templates:

▸ The maintenance of account assignment models can be controlled by authorization with Transaction FKMT and for each single model by using the authorization group.

▸ Account assignment models with amounts or equivalence numbers can be created.

3.10.1 Account Assignment Models Maintenance

Account assignment models can be maintained with Transaction FKMT or using the navigation path **SAP Menu • Accounting • Financial Accounting • Accounts Payable • Document Entry • Reference Documents • Account Assignment Model**.

In the account assignment model header as shown in Figure 3.26, the model name, currency, and chart of accounts are entered.

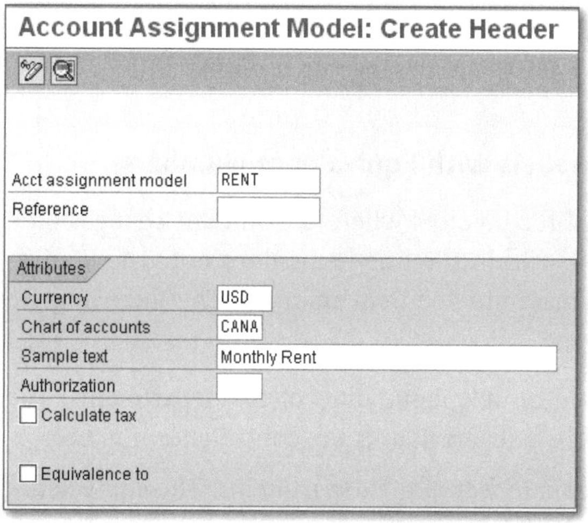

Figure 3.26 Account Assignment Model: Create Header Screen

3.10.2 Account Assignment Models with Amounts

If the **Equivalence to** checkbox is not set, the **Amount** field is available in the line item screen as shown in Figure 3.27.

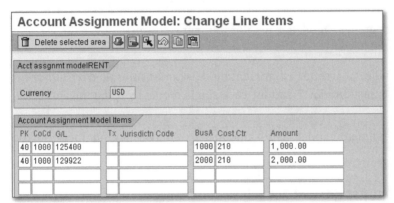

Figure 3.27   Account Assignment Model: Line Items with Amounts

During invoice entry, the amounts in the account assignment model are copied into the invoice and used as default values. All values can be changed during the invoice entry.

For example, an invoice is posted with Transaction F-43 and the preceding account assignment model. Within the transaction, enter the document header information and the vendor line first. Then click the **Acct model** button, and select the account assignment template. Click **Post,** and the invoice is posted.

3.10.3 Account Assignment Models with Equivalence Numbers

The equivalence numbers are used for invoices where the amount changes on a recurring basis, however, the ratio within the line items does not. The equivalence number is then used to calculate the line item amounts. The following are examples for these types of invoices:

▶ Post the telephone invoice based on telephone lines of the departments. The number of telephone lines within a department is the equivalence number.

▶ Post the rent invoice based on square feet of the departments. The equivalence numbers are the square feet of the departments.

If the **Equivalence to** checkbox is set in the model header, instead of the **Amount** field, an **Equivalence Number** field is displayed as shown in Figure 3.28.

Account Assignment Model: Change Line Items

| 🗑 Delete selected area | | | | | | |

Acct assgnmt modelTELEPHONE

Monthly Telephone Invoice

Currency | USD

Account Assignment Model Items

PK	CoCd	G/L	Tx	Jurisdictn Code	BusA	Cost Ctr		Equiv
40	1000	125400			1000	210		23
40	1000	129922			1000	230		17
40	1000	125400			1000	122		64

Figure 3.28 Account Assignment Model: Line Items with Equivalence Numbers

Equivalence Number Calculation Example

For example, a telephone invoice has to be posted. The expense line items need to be posted to three different departments based on the number of telephone lines. Department 210 has 23 lines, Department 230 has 17 lines, and Department 122 has 64 lines.

Because the invoice is received on a monthly basis, and the number of telephone lines doesn't change, an account assignment model with the name TELEPHONE and three line items are created.

▶ An invoice over $2,345.76 is received. During the invoice entry, the account assignment model TELEPHONE is chosen, and the invoice amount is divided into the three departments based in the number of lines.

▶ The following amounts are calculated per department:

▶ Department 210: $518.78

▶ Department 230: $383.44

▶ Department 122: $1,443.54

For example, an invoice is posted with Transaction F-43, and the preceding account assignment model. Within the transaction, enter the document header information and the vendor line first. Then click the **Acct model** button, and select the account assignment template. Enter the invoice amount in the **Debit distribution** field as shown in Figure 3.29. The **Amount** is then calculated based in the equivalence numbers. To post the invoice, click the **Post** button.

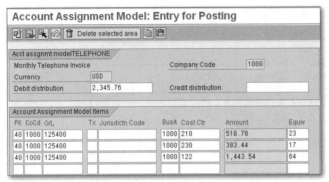

Figure 3.29 Invoice Entry with Account Assignment Model

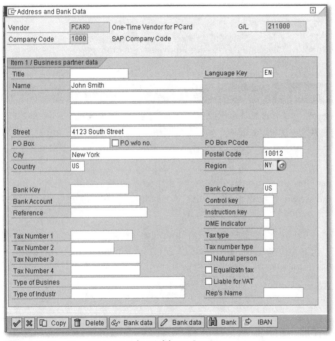

Figure 3.30 One-Time Vendor Address Screen

3.11 One-time Vendor Invoices

The characteristic of one-time vendor invoices is that all invoices are posted against the same one-time vendor. However, the address for each invoice is different. During invoice entry, you select a one-time vendor, and an address screen as shown in Figure 3.30 appears. Within the address screen, the name and address of the one-time information needs to be entered. After the one-time information is complete, the invoice needs to be completed with the same steps as shown in the invoice entry sections in this chapter.

3.12   New GL and Document Splitting

This section doesn't provide a detailed overview of the new GL functionality or document splitting, but instead, the intention is to introduce you to the concepts of the new GL and document splitting within AP.

3.12.1   The New GL

The splitting functionality was introduced by SAP with Release 4.7 or SAP Enterprise. The splitting functionality was available in this release only within the Special Ledger module. As of release ECC 5.0, SAP introduced the new GL functionality and enhanced the existing splitting functionality.

The new GL is a way to combine multiple ledgers, such as GL, Profit Center Ledger, or Cost of Sales Ledger into one single application.

3.12.2   Document Splitting

As an organization, you always have to be able to answer the question "How many open APs do we have by business area, fund, or profit center?" In the past, this question could not be answered easily because the vendor line items are posted without business area, fund, or profit center, especially if an invoice against multiple different elements is entered. As a workaround, balance sheet adjustments with Program SAF180 had to be posted to reflect payables by business area, for example.

The introduction of the splitting functionality solved this issue, due to the fact that invoices can be split by certain splitting criteria on a real-time basis. Currently, the following splitting criteria are available:

▶ Business area

▶ Segment (new field as of ECC 5.0)

▶ Profit center

- ▸ Functional area
- ▸ Fund
- ▸ Grant
- ▸ Funded program

After an invoice is posted, the invoice is visible in the **Entry View**. The **Entry View** shows how the invoice is entered in your system.

In addition, the invoice is also posted into the new GL and split in real-time based on the splitting criteria. It can be posted to one or multiple ledgers and is visible in the **General Ledger View**.

For example, I chose a public sector invoice, where the invoice is split by fund. Figure 3.31 shows the **Entry View,** and Figure 3.32 shows the **General Ledger View**. As you can see, within the **General Ledger View**, the AP line item is split based on the funds posted in the expense lines. This makes it possible now to answer the question "How many open APs do we have by business area, fund, or profit center?" on a real-time basis.

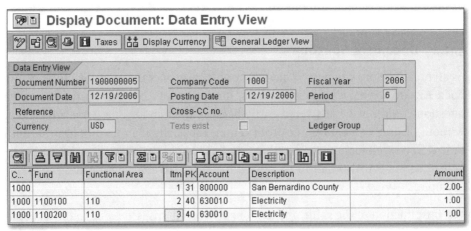

Figure 3.31 Entry View of an Invoice

SAP PRESS released a new book *New General Ledger in SAP ERP Financials*, which covers the new GL and the splitting functionality in detail.

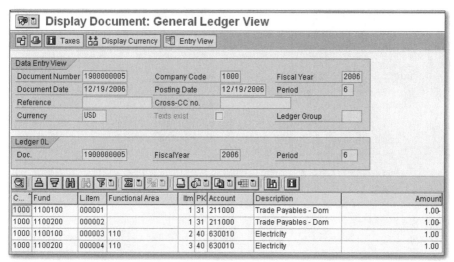

Figure 3.32 General Ledger View of an Invoice

3.13 Enhancements

In the previous sections, we discussed configuration and the transaction codes for AP business transactions. This chapter describes enhancements with coding examples. SAP delivers three types of enhancements:

▶ User-exits

▶ Business Transaction Events (BTE)

▶ Business Add-Ins (BAdI)

Appendix A through C explains how each of these different types of enhancements needs to be implemented.

3.13.1 One-Time Vendor Address Validation Using User-Exit SAPLFCPD

User-exit SAPLFCPD allows you to validate the vendor address screen for one-time vendors or payees in documents. This ensures that all address information is entered correctly such as name, street, or city information. The entered data are validated against rules defined in function module EXIT_SAPLFCPD_001.

For example, the following validation rules are created:

▶ Either the street information or a PO box needs to be entered. Otherwise, issue an error message (see Listing 3.1).

```
*&---------------------------------------------------------------*
*&  Include          ZXCPDU01
*&---------------------------------------------------------------*
*----------------------------------------------------------------*
* Rule 1: Validate if the address information are entered
*         completely. Either a Street address or a PO Box needs
*         to be entered.
*         Message 012 is created in message class ZFI with
*         Transaction SE91
*----------------------------------------------------------------*
if i_bsec-stras is INITIAL and
   i_bsec-pfach is INITIAL.
  MESSAGE e012(ZFI).
endif.
```

Listing 3.1 Validation Example for User-exit SAPLFCPD

3.13.2 Duplicate Invoice Check via Process BTE 00001110

The standard SAP duplicate invoice check issues a message if an invoice is already entered with the same values in the following fields:

▶ BUKRS: Company code
▶ LIFNR: Vendor
▶ WAERS: Currency
▶ XBLNR: Reference (invoice reference)
▶ BLDAT: Document date (invoice date)
▶ WRBTR: Amount

Process BTE 00001110 Document Posting: Check on Invoice Duplication allows the creation of user-defined rules for checking duplicate invoices. For example, you can use function module FI_DUPLICATE_INVOICE_CHECK, which uses the SAP standard duplicate invoice validation rule. If you set the export parameter E_NOSTD = X in the BTE, the standard rules are not executed.

3.13.3 Exclude OK-codes in Enjoy Transactions via Public & Subscribe BTE 00001140

Public & Subscribe BTE 00001140 Post Document: Exclude OK-codes (Enjoy), allows deactivating pushbuttons or menu options in invoice posting transactions such as FV60 or FB60. This might be useful, if certain functions should not be allowed during the execution of a transaction. The deactivated OK-codes are appended to table T_EXCTAB within function module Z_INTERFACE_00001140.

As an example, the following rule is created:

1. If an invoice is entered using the Parked document transaction FV60, the "Post" pushbutton (OK-code "BU") should not appear on the screen (see Listing 3.2).

```
*-------------------------------------------------------------*
* Rule 1: Hide the "Post" pushbutton in transaction FV60.
*-------------------------------------------------------------*
  IF sy-tcode = 'FV60'.
    t_exctab-okcode = 'BU'.
    append t_exctab.
  ENDIF.
```

Listing 3.2 Example code for BTE 00001140

3.14   FI Substitutions and Validations

The SAP Financial Accounting component contains FI substitutions and FI validations. A *substitution* allows defaulting of values for certain fields, whereas a *validation* checks the data entry and issues messages if the validation isn't fulfilled.

The substitutions and validations are executed anytime a financial transaction is created at different call-up points. The call-up point defines at what point during data entry of the transaction the substitution or validation is executed. Table 3.6 lists the different call-up points available.

Description	FI Substitution	FI Validation
Document Header	Call-up point 1	Call-up point 1
Line Item	Call-up point 2	Call-up point 2
Complete Document	N/A	Call-up point 3

Table 3.6 Validation and Substitution Call-Up Points

The document header substitution and validation is executed after all required document header information is filled, such as document date, posting date, or document type. At that point, the substitution and validation is called.

The line item substitution and validation are called after the line item information is entered, such as amount and account.

At call-up point 3, a complete document can be validated. The validation is executed at the time a document is saved. A FI substitution isn't possible for a complete document but can be achieved with Process BTE 00001120 – Document Posting: Field Substitution Header/Line Item.

As a rule, substitutions are always executed before the validations. This allows the validation of substituted field values. Appendix D describes the creation of FI substitutions and validations. For additional information, look up the following notes in OSS:

- **48121:** User-Exits in Validations/Substitutions
- **42615:** Substitution in FI

Program: RGUGBR00

If you have problems with substitutions or validations after client copies or transports, you can regenerate the substitutions or validations with Program RGUGBR00.

3.14.1 Document Header Validation – Call-Up Point 1

During the document header validation, all document header fields (Table BKPF) and selected system fields, such as user name, transition code, or system date, are available. It's therefore possible to validate different combination of header and system fields. Following is a list of examples of possible document header validation rules:

- The invoice date must not be greater than the posting date of the invoice.
- The posting date can't be a future date.
- Only document type VM can be used in Transaction FB60.

3.14.2 Document Line Item Validation – Call-Up Point 2

During the document line item validation, all fields from call-up point 1 as well as all line item fields (Table BSEG) are available. This allows you to create validation rules with document line item and document header fields.

For example, Figure 3.33 shows a line item validation, where the line item text (BSEG-SGTXT) is required for vendor line items (BSEG-KOART = 'K').

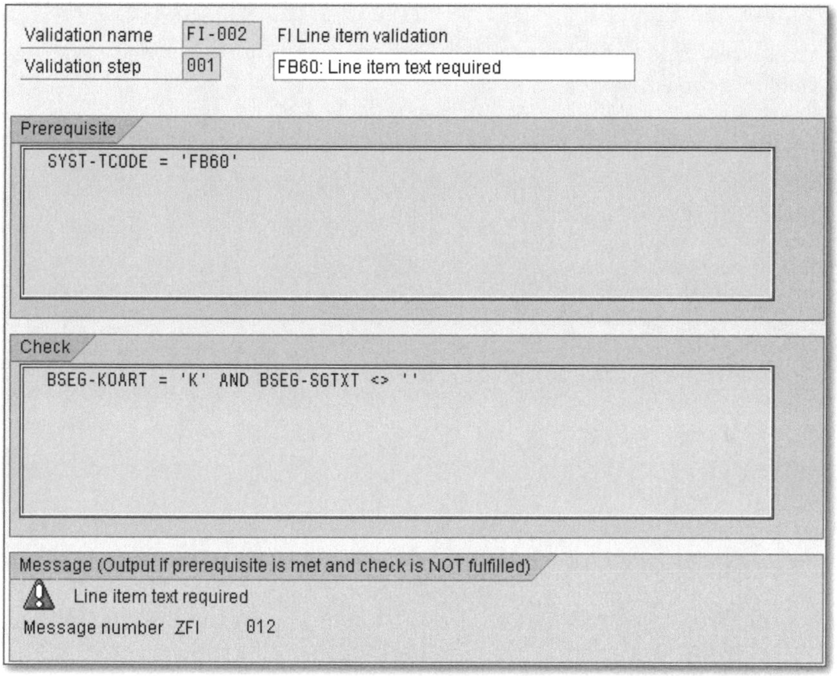

Figure 3.33 FI Line Item Sample Validation Rule

If a validation requires more complicated rules that can't be fulfilled with configuration, a user-exit can be created and executed with a FI validation.

3.14.3 Document Line Item Validation with User-Exit– Call-Up Point 2

Using a user-exit allows you to validate the entered information against information in SAP, which isn't available in the FI validation fields, such as vendor master data.

For example, we use the preceding validation rule, where the line item text is required but only for vendor account group KRED. Because the vendor account group field (LFA1-KTOKK) isn't available in the FI validation fields of Tables BKPF and BSEG, a user-exit has to be used. The following example shows the sample code for this requirement (see Listing 3.3). Appendix D describes the creation of a FI validation or FI substitution with user-exit in more detail.

```
*------------------------------------------------------------------*
*         FORM UF01
*------------------------------------------------------------------*
*         Line item text is required for vendor postings with
*         vendor account group 'KRED'
*------------------------------------------------------------------
*   ←  BRESULT    T = True   F = False                            *
*------------------------------------------------------------------*
FORM uf01 USING b_result.
  TABLES LFA1.

  B_RESULT  = B_TRUE.
  CHECK BESG-KOART = 'K'.                   "Vendor Line item
  SELECT SINGLE * FROM LFA1 WHERE LIFNR = BSEG-LIFNR.
  IF SY-SUBRC = 0.
    CHECK LFA1-KTOKK = 'KRED'.
    IF BSEG-SGTEXT IS INITIAL.
      B_RESULT = B_FALSE.
    ENDIF.
  ENDIF.


ENDFORM.
```

Listing 3.3 Example FI Validation User-Exit

3.14.4   Complete Document Validation – Call-Up Point 3

If you require the information of the entire document, such as document header and all document line items, for the validation, call-up point 3 has to be used. The validation for call-up point 3 requires the use of a user-exit. Following are examples for these types of validations (see Listing 3.4):

▶ Invoices against one-time vendor REFUND have to be posted with GL account 501110 and cost center 100345.

▶ Invoices with cross business area line items are not allowed.

```
*----------------------------------------------------------------*
*   FORM UF02
*----------------------------------------------------------------*
*   For Vendor 'REFUND', all line items need to be posted with
*   G/L account '501110' and cost center '100345'
*----------------------------------------------------------------*
*   <-- B_RESULT    T = True  F = False                          *
*----------------------------------------------------------------*
FORM uf02 USING    bool_data    TYPE GB002_015
         CHANGING b_result.
DATA: H_REFUND_VENDOR(1) TYPE C.

  B_RESULT = B_TRUE.
  H_REFUND_VENDOR = 'N'.
  LOOP AT BOOL_DATA-BSEG INTO BSEG
                         WHERE KOART = 'K'.
    IF BSEG-LIFNR = 'REFUND'.
      H_REFUND_VENDOR = 'Y'.
    ENDIF.
  ENDLOOP.

  CHECK H_REFUND_VENDOR = 'Y'.
  LOOP AT BOOL_DATA-BSEG INTO BSEG
                         WHERE KOART = 'S'.
    IF NOT BSEG-KOSTL = '0000100345' OR
       NOT BSEG-SAKNR = '0000501110'.
      B_RESULT = B_FALSE.
    ENDIF.
  ENDLOOP.

ENDFORM.
```

Listing 3.4 Example for Complete Document Validation

3.14.5 Substitutions

Substitutions allow defaulting values in document header or line item fields. Not all fields are currently allowed to be substituted because some fields may depend on values of other fields and can therefore not be substituted. An example is the business area because the business area value is defaulted based on the business area value in the cost center and is therefore not allowed to overwrite this value with a substitution.

SAP, however, allows the opening of additional fields for substitutions. A number of these fields are listed in OSS Note 42615. For example, a substitution is created to substitute the payment block value *A*, if a vendor invoice is posted with more than $100,000.

The substitution has to be created in the following steps:

1. Open the payment block field (BSEG-ZLSPR) for substitution.

2. Regenerate the substitution rules with Program RGUGBR00.

3. Create the substitution rule.

Open the Payment Block Field (BSEG-ZLSPR) for Substitution

All allowed substitution fields are stored in Table GB01. This table can be maintained with view VWTYGB01 using Transaction SM30. To allow a field to be substituted, the **Exclude** indicator has to be removed from this field. Figure 3.34 shows the maintenance of Table GB01 for the payment block field (BSEG-ZLSPR).

Change View "Maintenance View for GB01": Overview

New Entries

Maintenance View for GB01

	Class	Typ	Table	Field	Exclude
	9	Refers to fields… 🗎	BSEG	ZLSCH	☑
	9	Refers to fields… 🗎	BSEG	ZLSPR	☐
	9	Refers to fields… 🗎	BSEG	ZOLLD	☑
	9	Refers to fields… 🗎	BSEG	ZOLLT	☑

Figure 3.34 Maintenance of Table GB01

Regenerate the Substitution Rules with Program RGUGBR00

The second step is the regeneration of the substitution and validation rules. Program RGUGBR00 regenerates the rules. After the regeneration, the field can be used in the substitution. Select all indicators for application FI and call-up point 2 as shown in Figure 3.35.

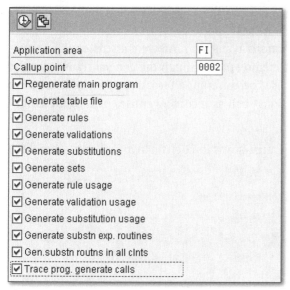

Figure 3.35 Regeneration of Substitutions and Validations

Substitution Rule Creation

In the last step, the substitution rule needs to be created. Figure 3.36 shows the substitution rule for the preceding requirement.

Substitution	FI-S02	New substitution
Step	001	Payment Block for Invoices

Prerequisite

```
BSEG-KOART = 'K' AND BSEG-SHKZG = 'H' AND BSEG-WRBTR >=
'100000.00'
```

Substitutions (if prerequisite is met)

Field	is substituted by:	
Pmnt Block	Constant value	A

Figure 3.36 Sample Substitution Rule

3.15 Summary

In this Chapter all business transactions available in AP were discussed. These processes include invoice and credit memo entry through the general transactions as well as through enjoy transactions. The different alternative payee options were discussed as well as special functions such as recurring entries or account assignment models.

In the next Chapter the available transactions in Logistic Invoice Verification (LIV) are discussed in detail.

Purchasing-related invoices and credit memos are executed through Logistics Invoice Verification (LIV), which is part of materials management (MM). This chapter covers the integration points, configuration steps, and execution of the different processing options within LIV.

4 Logistic Invoice Verification

In this chapter, we'll discuss the different business transactions within LIV. LIV is part of the materials management (MM) component within SAP, even thought invoicing is a business function within Accounts Payable (AP). The reason is because LIV allows the processing of purchasing-related invoices, and purchasing is the main function of the material management application.

The manual LIV invoicing and credit memo process will be covered in detail as well as the automated processes, such as Evaluated Receipt Settlement (ERS), invoicing plans, and consignment materials.

Before we discuss the different configuration steps of LIV, we need to take a closer look at the different goods-receipt (GR) and invoice receipt (IR) settings available in purchasing. Depending on these purchase order settings, the processing of good receipts and invoices is different. In the following sections, these processes are described:

- Three-way match
- Two-way match
- Non-valuated goods receipts (GR)
- GR-based Invoice Verification

4.1 Three-Way Match Invoice Verification

Three-way match is the classic invoicing process of matching incoming invoices on price against the purchase order and on quantity against the GR made for the purchase order in question. The system always performs a three-way match, as long as two flags are set within a purchase order:

- **Goods Receipt** flag
- **Inv. Receipt** flag

The **Goods Receipt** flag can be found in the purchase order line item in the **Delivery** tab as shown in Figure 4.1.

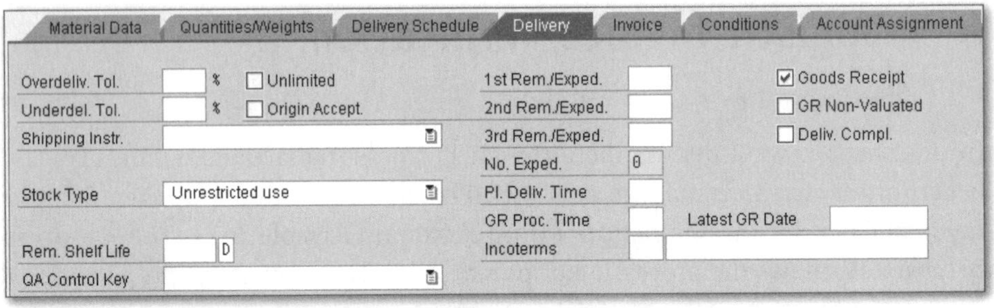

Figure 4.1 Goods Receipt Flag in a Purchase Order

The **Goods Receipt** flag specifies that a GR is expected. A GR is posted with Transaction MIGO for inventory purchases or nonmaterial purchases. For external services, a GR is posted with Transaction ML81N – Maintain Service Entry Sheets.

The invoice receipt (**Inv. Receipt**) flag is the second flag relevant for the three-way match. This flag can be found in the purchase order line item in the **Invoice** tab as shown in Figure 4.2.

Figure 4.2 Inv. Receipt Flag in a Purchase Order

If the **Inv. Receipt** flag isn't set, the goods are delivered free of charge.

It's important to note that the sequence in which the GR and invoice document are entered is irrelevant, which means that the invoice can be entered before the GR document or the other way around. This allows the AP department to post invoices before the goods are delivered. To avoid paying invoices without a GR, the invoices are usually blocked automatically for payment until the GR document is processed. The process is covered in the "Invoice Block" section of this chapter.

4.1.1 Accounting Entries During Three-Way Match

SAP uses the *GR/IR accounting concept* for the three-way match process. Goods Receipt/Invoice Receipt (GR/IR) means that both the GR document and the IR document are posted against a GR/IR balance sheet clearing account. The balance in this GR/IR account represents either the goods receipted but not yet invoiced (credit balance) or the goods invoiced but not yet received (debit balance). The following example illustrates this principle.

GR/IR Accounting Concept

For example, a purchase order is created for 10 books with a price of $50 per book. In the purchase order, the books are assigned to GL account 510100 – Books. The GR/IR account is 211200, and the vendor account number is 10000.

The vendor delivers 7 books, and a GR document is created. During the GR, the purchased items are expensed, and the GR/IR account is credited.

Document 1: GR document

Debit:	510100 – Books	$350
Credit:	211200 – GR/IR Account	$350

In the next step, the vendor sends an invoice over 7 books, and AP posts an invoice:

Document 2: IR document

Debit:	211200 – GR/IR Account	$350
Credit:	Vendor 10000	$350

After the invoice is posted, the balance in the GR/IR account is zero, which means that all GRs are invoiced.

The GR/IR account has to be defined as a balance sheet account with *Line item display* and *Open item management* in the GL account master. Open item management allows documents to be offset with other documents in the same account. For the GR/IR account, GR documents are offset with invoices. This ensures that at any time, you can analyze whether invoices have been received for the goods received for a specific purchase order.

In addition, the sort key should be defaulted with the value "14" for purchase orders. This setting supports the automatic GR/IR clearing process, which is described in Chapter 14.

Figure 4.3 shows the relevant settings for the GR/IR account in the GL master data.

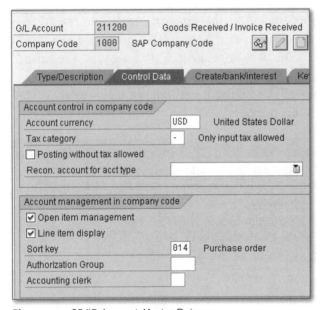

Figure 4.3 GR/IR Account Master Data

Now that you understand the GR/IR accounting concept, let's look at how the system processes variations of this concept using price differences. The system processes price differences differently, depending on whether the GR document or the invoice document is posted first.

4.1.2 Price Differences (Goods Receipt Document Posted First)

If the GR document is posted before the invoice document, the amount in the GR document is always the received quantity multiplied by the purchasing price. Any price difference is posted during the invoice entry. The following example illustrates the accounting entries.

> **Price Differences (Goods Receipt Document Posted Before Invoice Document)**
>
> For example, a purchase order is created for 10 books with a price of $50 per book. In the purchase order, the books are assigned to GL account 510100 – Books. The GR/IR account is 211200, and the vendor account number is 10000.
>
> The vendor delivers 7 books, and a GR document is created. During the GR, the purchased items are expensed, and the GR/IR account is credited.
>
> Document 1: GR document
>
> Debit: 510100 – Books $350
>
> Credit: 211200 – GR/IR Account $350
>
> The vendor sends an invoice with the amount of $315 for 7 books. The price of a single book is only $45 compared to $50 in the purchase order. AP posts an invoice:
>
> Document 2: IR document
>
> Debit: 211200 – GR/IR Account $350
>
> Credit: 510100 – Books $35
>
> Credit: Vendor 10000 $315
>
> After the invoice is posted, the balance in the GR/IR account is zero. The book expense account 510100 is credited with $35, which represents the reduced price of the books.

During the posting of the invoice, the amount field is first defaulted with $350 and needs to be changed to $315 manually. The price difference is always posted to the purchase order account assignments, such as GL account, cost center, internal order, or WBS element.

4.1.3   Price Differences (Invoice Document Posted First)

In the next example, the invoice is posted before the GR document with a different unit price than in the purchase order. This type of posting usually causes some confusion because the GR document is posted with the invoiced price per unit rather than the purchasing price. The following example illustrates the accounting entries.

> **Price Differences (Invoice Document Posted Before Goods Receipt Document)**
>
> For example, a purchase order is created for 10 books with a price of $50 per book. In the purchase order, the books are assigned to GL account 510100 – Books. The GR/IR account is 211200, and the vendor account number is 10000.
>
> The vendor sends an invoice with the amount of $364 for 7 books. The price of a single book is $52 compared to $50 in the purchase order. AP posts an invoice:
>
> Document 1: IR document
>
> Debit: 211200 – GR/IR Account $364
>
> Credit: Vendor 10000 $364
>
> The vendor delivers all 10 books, and a GR document is created.
>
> Document 2: GR document
>
> Debit: 510100 – Books $514
>
> Credit: 211200 – GR/IR Account $514
>
> Because an invoice was already entered for 7 books with a price of $52 per book, 7 books are valuated with $52 per book. The remaining 3 books are valuated with the purchasing price of $50 because no invoice was posted for these books. Therefore, the total amount is $364 + $150 = $514.

In this section, we covered the standard three-way match and its accounting entries and variation due to price differences. In the next section, two-way match invoices are described.

4.2   Two-Way Match Invoice Verification

Two-way match is an invoicing process of matching incoming invoices on price and quantity against the purchase order. No GR documents are entered. The system performs a two-way match, as long as the **Goods Receipt** flag is *not* set in the purchase order and the **Inv. Receipt** flag *is* set.

The accounting entries in the two-way match process are much more simplified compared to the accounting entries in the three-way. Because no goods-receipt document is entered, all purchased items are expensed during invoice entry and not at the time of the GR. The following example illustrates the accounting entries during a two-way match.

> **Accounting Entry (Two-Way Match)**
>
> For example, a purchase order is created for 10 books with a price of $50 per book. No GR is required. In the purchase order, the books are assigned to GL account 510100 – Books. The GR/IR account is 211200, and the vendor account number is 10000.
>
> The vendor sends an invoice with the amount of $350 for 7 books. AP posts the following invoice:
>
> Document 1: IR document
>
> Debit: 510100 – Books $350
>
> Credit: Vendor 10000 $350

4.2.1   Blanket Purchase Orders

Blanket purchase orders are set up in procurement as framework orders (Order type FO) and with amount limits (Item category B). These types of purchase orders only contain an amount limit as well as a validity date range. No quantities are specified in the purchase order.

During invoice processing, the invoice posting date has to fall within the validity period of the blanket purchase, and the total of all invoice amounts must not exceed the total limit of the purchase order to process an invoice.

4.3   Non-Valuated Goods Receipt

The *non-valuated GR* process is a variation of the three-way match process. Incoming invoices are matched on the price against the purchase order and on quantity against the GR made for the purchase order in question. The difference is that no accounting document is created during the GR, therefore, it's called *non-valuated GR*.

The system performs a non-valuated three-way match when the following flags are set within a purchase order:

► **Goods Receipt** flag

► **GR Non-Valuated**

► **Inv. Receipt** flag

The **Goods Receipt** and **GR Non-Valuated** flags can be found in the purchase order line item in the **Delivery** tab as shown in Figure 4.4.

Material Data	Quantities/Weights	Delivery Schedule	Delivery	Invoice	Conditions	Account Assignment

Overdeliv. Tol.	% ☐ Unlimited	1st Rem./Exped.		☑ Goods Receipt
Underdel. Tol.	% ☐ Origin Accept.	2nd Rem./Exped.		☑ GR Non-Valuated
Shipping Instr.		3rd Rem./Exped.		☐ Deliv. Compl.
		No. Exped.	0	
Stock Type	Unrestricted use	Pl. Deliv. Time		
		GR Proc. Time		Latest GR Date
Rem. Shelf Life	D	Incoterms		
QA Control Key				

Figure 4.4 Goods Receipt and GR Non-Valuated Flags

Non-valuated GR must be used if multiple account assignments are used within a purchase order line. Multiple account assignment allows multiple accounts, cost centers, or internal orders to be assigned to one purchase order line item. The total purchase order line item quantity can be distributed by quantity or percentage to the different account assignments.

Another common example of using non-valuated GR is the direct purchase of assets. In this case, the delivery of the assets is confirmed during the GR, however, the asset values are posted during the invoicing process.

The accounting entries for the non-valuated GR process are the same as for the two-way match process.

4.4   GR-Based Invoice Verification

GR-based Invoice Verification is a variation of the three-way match invoicing process. A common misconception is that the **GR-Bsd IV** flag must be switched on in the purchase order to perform three-way match-based Invoice Verification. However, this isn't true. As described in the prior sections, SAP always performs the three-way match for purchase orders if the **Goods Receipt** and **Inv. Receipt** flags are set.

The **GR-Bsd IV** flag can be found in the purchase order line item in the **Invoice** tab as shown in Figure 4.5.

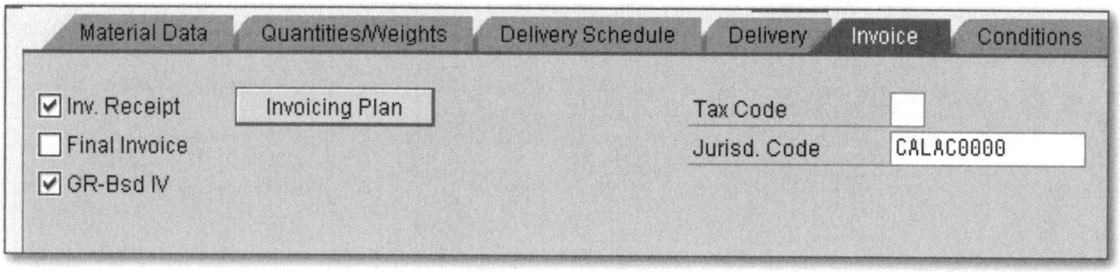

Figure 4.5 GR-Bsd IV Flag in Purchase Order

Although the **GR-Bsd IV** setting does not trigger or activate the three-way match process, the importance of this flag is the level of detail in the GR document that is presented to the user entering the invoices.

Purchase orders with this flag switched on capture and retain information about every GR document that is entered against a specific purchase order item. During invoice entry, the user sees all GRs entered for a purchase order line and has to match the invoice against the individual GRs. This may be very useful if the vendor requires that deliveries are matched to invoices. Therefore, GR-based Invoice Verification is more like *delivery-based invoice verification*. For purchase orders with a large number of GR documents, however, the invoice entry could end up tedious and time consuming.

Purchase orders that have this flag switched off still capture all information in the GR documents but don't keep track of the details in each individual GR document. Instead, all of the GR documents are summarized by purchase order item during invoice entry. The result is that individuals who enter an invoice see information about each GR document that was entered for the purchase order item, but they see only summarized information, that is the sum of the quantities in all GR documents for that PO item.

4.4.1 Invoice Verification Examples

To illustrate the differences, two purchase orders are created for 10 books with a price of $50 per book. For both purchase orders, three individual GRs are entered with the quantities of 5, 3, and 2 books.

In Figure 4.6, the invoice entry screen is shown if GR-based Invoice Verification is set in the purchase order line. Because three GR documents are entered, three separate lines are shown during the invoice entry. In addition, the **Del. Note** column shows the delivery note entered during GR, and the **Received** column displays the individual GR quantity.

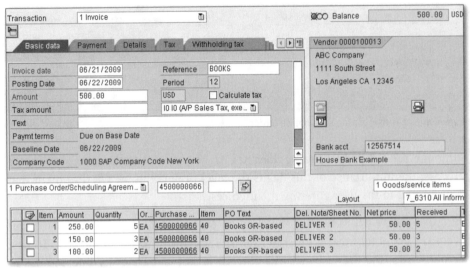

Figure 4.6 GR-Based Invoice Verification Example

In comparison, Figure 4.7 shows the invoice entry screen if GR-based invoice verification is *not* set in the purchase order line. All three GR documents are displayed in a summarized form, and the **Received** column displays the total quantity of all GR documents. The **Del. Note** column, on the other hand, is blank because the line represents multiple GR documents.

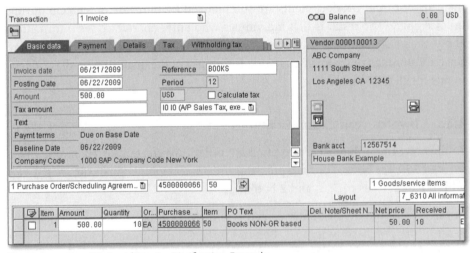

Figure 4.7 Non-GR-Based Invoice Verification Example

Besides the appearance of the GR documents during invoice processing, there are additional differences that need to be taken into consideration when deciding if GR-based Invoice Verification should be used.

4.4.2 GR-Based Invoice Verification Flag Set On

The main difference between having the GR-based invoice verification flag set or not is that GR-based Invoice Verification requires the GR document to be posted before the invoice can be processed. This business process constraint causes a lot of issues in organizations because the invoice needs to be handled multiple times if the GR isn't entered at the time of the invoice entry. On the other side, the invoice could be parked and processed later, however, this also requires that the invoice document is processed again.

Another potential problem is reconciliation with vendors. If a dispute arises with a vendor regarding a purchase order, reconciling your records with the vendor's could become a very difficult task if you have a large number of GRs and invoices for a purchase order. In addition, if credit memos need to be processed, assigning them to the correct GR documents could become a difficult task.

In summary, GR-based Invoice Verification allows you to track invoices and credit memos against individual GR documents in greater detail. On the other hand, this decision may needlessly complicate the job of the AP clerks.

4.4.3 GR-Based Invoice Verification Flag Set Off

It's also a misperception to assume that not choosing GR-based Invoice Verification would increase the risk of paying vendors for non-delivered items. The reason is because invoices without deliveries are blocked automatically if the tolerances are configured correctly. In addition, blocked invoices can be released automatically using the *Release Blocked Invoice* functionality with Transaction MRBR. This process allows invoices to be entered prior to the GR document. After the GR document is entered, the invoice is matched with the GR, and the invoice is released automatically for payments.

Tolerances and Transaction MRBR are covered in a later section of this chapter.

4.4.4 GR-Based Invoice Verification Conclusion

Universal guidelines as to when the flag should be set are impossible because vendors don't all use the same invoicing process. Setting the GR-based invoice verification flag gives more detailed information during the invoice processing but also adds complexity to the entire business process.

Therefore, the only rule is that this setting has to be evaluated on a case-by-case basis. Although some vendors invoice individual deliveries, meaning they list each delivery on the invoice, most vendors don't. It's therefore recommended to only set this flag if the vendor absolutely requires GR-based Invoice Verification.

4.5 Invoice Entry Process with Transaction MIRO

After discussing the different purchase order settings, let's take a look at the invoice entry process within LIV. The most commonly used process is the online invoice entry through Transaction MIRO. This transaction can be accessed via the SAP menu path **SAP Menu • Logistics • Material Management • Logistic Invoice Verification • Document Entry • Enter Invoice**. This transaction allows the processing of the following:

► Invoices

► Credit memos

► Subsequent debit/credit

There's basically no difference between the invoice and credit memo entry, except that the business transaction is defaulted to invoice or credit memo. All other functions and screens are the same. Therefore, only the invoice transaction and subsequent debit/credit are covered in detail.

As shown in Figure 4.8, the transaction screen is divided into four screen areas:

► **Worklist/PO Structure**

► **Header and Vendor Data**

► **Information Area**

► **Purchase order items**

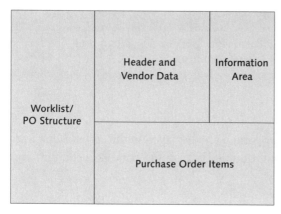

Figure 4.8 Invoice Entry Screen

4.5.1 Worklist/PO Structure

The *Worklist/PO Structure* area allows switching between a worklist folder structure and a purchase order structure.

Worklist

The worklist contains different folders that allow the user to see which invoice documents aren't completely posted. The worklist contains three folders for the different statuses of a document:

▸ Held documents

▸ Parked documents

▸ Documents completed for posting

Held Documents
The *Hold Document* function allows you to save and complete invoices at a later point. For example, you might need additional information for the invoice to be completed, or you might get interrupted and want to save your work. To save a document, go to the header menu, and select **Hold (F5)**. The system assigns a document number and saves the document in the *Held documents* folder. To complete a held document, just select the document, and complete the document. After it's complete and posted, the held document number disappears from your folder.

Held Documents

If you receive message F5 410: "Held documents must be converted; read long text" when you select the hold document function, Program RFTMPBLU needs to be executed with Transaction SA38. This program needs to be executed once in every client.

Parked Documents

Any documents that were previously parked are displayed in the *Parked Documents* folder. To access a parked document, double-click on the parked document, and complete the invoice.

Documents Completed for Postings

Documents completed for posting refers to parked documents that were saved as complete. A document with status Saved as Complete is technically still a parked document, however, the invoice document is completely entered and ready to be posted.

PO Structure

After a purchase order is entered for invoice processing, the PO Structure area shows the entire purchase order history for this purchase order, including GR documents and previously posted invoices.

4.5.2 Header and Vendor Data

The Header and Vendor Data area includes different tabs for the document header information as well as for the vendor line item. The following tabs are available:

- Basic Data
- Payment
- Details
- Tax
- Withholding Tax
- Amount Split
- Contacts
- Notes

The different tabs were already described in Section 3.2.2 of Chapter 3. The document header and vendor line item information to be entered are the same as for an AP invoice using Transaction FB60.

4.5.3 Information Area

The Information area shows the address and bank information of the vendor entered. From the information area, you can display the vendor master data by choosing the function **Display Vendor**. In addition, you can drill down to the open items of the vendor by selecting the **List of open items** function. If an alternative payee or permitted payee is entered, the address information doesn't change to the address of the alternative or permitted payee.

4.5.4 Purchase Order Items Area

The *Purchase Order Items* area shown in Figure 4.9 contains a table of the purchase order details. During invoice entry, the invoice needs to be matched against the line item details. Depending on the purchase order flags, such as GR-based invoice verification, the detailed information is displayed differently.

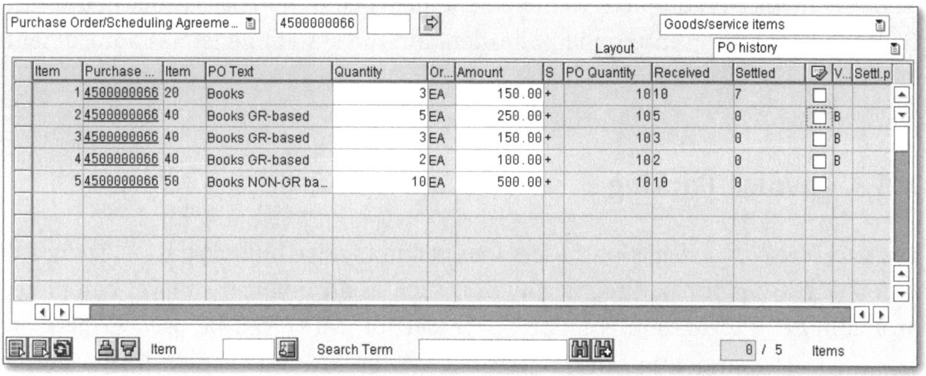

Figure 4.9 Purchase Order Item Area

Reference Document Category

Different *Reference Document Categories* allow you to select the items by categories, such as purchase order, delivery note, or service entry sheet. The most commonly used category is "Purchase order."

Indicator: Goods/Delivery Cost

In the invoice entry, you have to specify what the invoice you are posting is for:

▶ Goods/service items

▶ Planned delivery costs

▶ Both goods/service items and planned delivery costs

Depending on your selection, the system calculates the values and defaults them.

Layout

Different invoice *layouts* are predefined by SAP. Based on the layout selected, the information is displayed differently. Columns are hidden, or the information is displayed in a different column sequence. The layout *All information* displays all available fields, for example. To configure your own layout, maintain the layout in the IMG via the navigation path **IMG • Materials Management • Logistic Invoice Verification • Incoming Invoice • Maintain Item List Variants.**

4.5.5   Invoice Posting

After the invoice is completely entered and matched to purchase order items, just click the **Post** button in the menu header, and the system generates a document number.

4.6   Invoice Parking

The *park invoice function* allows users to enter an invoice but not post it. There are different reasons for parking an invoice, such as an invoice isn't yet complete, or additional information is missing. Transaction MIR7 can be used to park an invoice. This transacting can be accessed via the SAP menu path **SAP Menu • Logistics • Material Management • Logistic Invoice Verification • Document Entry • Park Invoice.**

The parking transaction is similar to the transactions for entering invoices. After an invoice is entered, the user has to decide whether an invoice should be parked or saved as complete. The following list shows the differences in the functionality between parking and saving as complete:

▶ A parked document can be incomplete, which means the document does not need to be in balance.

▶ FI substitutions and validations are only executed after a document is saved as complete.

▶ If you are using a workflow approval process, the Park function does not start the workflow. Only after you choose the Save as Complete function is the workflow process executed.

4.7 Incoming Invoice Configuration

In this section, the main configuration steps for incoming invoices are described. Throughout this chapter, you can find additional functions such as Evaluated Receipt Settlement (ERS) or tolerances. The specific configuration steps related to each function are described within their respective sections.

The following configuration items can be found in the IMG via the navigation path **IMG • Materials management • Logistic Invoice Verification • Incoming Invoice.**

4.7.1 Define Attributes of System Messages

Message control is a feature within SAP that allows you to change the standard message type provided by SAP. Different specifications are possible for the online mode and for batch input sessions processed in the background. You can make the specifications globally or individually by user. If you enter a user name, then the specifications only apply to this particular user. If you leave the user name blank, then the settings apply to all users.

Figure 4.10 shows an example where Message **298** is changed from information (I) in the standard to an error (E) message. SAP predefines which messages and which message types can be changed.

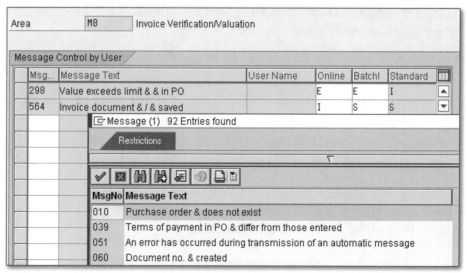

Figure 4.10 Define Attributes of System Messages Screen

4.7.2 Define Tax Jurisdiction

This configuration step is only relevant if your company code uses a jurisdiction-based tax calculation procedure, such as TAXUSJ. In this case, the jurisdiction code per plant needs to be defined. Within the configuration, select **Edit address** to maintain the jurisdiction code.

4.7.3 Automatic Account Assignment

The *automatic account assignment* configuration is the main integration configuration step between materials management and financial accounting. In this configuration step, the GL accounts are defined, which are used in the different materials management processes.

Within the automatic account assignment, three main sections can be found:

- ▶ Account Assignment
- ▶ Simulation
- ▶ GL Accounts

The *Account Assignment* section contains the configuration steps of the automatic account assignments, which will be the focus of this section.

The *Simulation* section allows the simulation of accounting entries after the configuration is completed. The simulation function executes a specific transaction type, such as posting of freight costs, and displays all configured GL accounts for this transaction type as shown in Figure 4.11.

Transaction								
Transactn Type	Posting of freight costs							

Posting Lines								
Posting Lines Text	VIGCd	AM		De	G/L Acct	Cr	G/L Acct	
Gain/loss from revaluation		-e-		83	--Missing-	93	--Missing-	
Inventory posting		-e-		89	--Missing-	99	--Missing-	
Purchase offsetting account		-e-		40	--Missing-	50	--Missing-	
Purchasing freight account	-e-	-e-	-e-	40	510998	50	510998	
Materials management exch.rate	-e-	-e-	-e-	83	700400	93	700400	
Cost (price) differences		-e-		86	--Missing-	96	--Missing-	
Inventory posting		-e-		89	--Missing-	99	--Missing-	

Figure 4.11 Simulation of Account Assignment

The *GL Accounts* section is a report that lists all GL accounts used in automatic account assignment and where these GL accounts are used. In other words, with this report, you can determine if a GL account is used in the correct transactions.

Account Assignment

The Account Assignment configuration is probably one of the most complicated configuration steps within SAP because the terminology isn't very intuitive.

The configuration is basically done in two steps. In the first step, the correct *transaction/event key* has to be chosen. In the second step, the GL accounts for every key have to be defined based on your organization's requirements.

Transaction/Event Key

During the execution of a transaction within materials management, different event keys are processed. The system then determines the GL accounts based on the configured event keys. Figure 4.12 shows a list of the event keys.

Group RMK Materials Management postings (MM)

Procedures

Description	Transaction	Account determ.
Rev.from agency bus.	AG1	☑
Sales fr.agency bus.	AG2	☑
Exp.from agency bus.	AG3	☑
Expense/revenue from consign.mat.consum.	AKO	☑
Expense/revenue from stock transfer	AUM	☑
Subsequent settlement of provisions	B01	☑
Subsequent settlement of revenues	B02	☑
Provision differences	B03	☑
Inventory posting	BSD	☑
Change in stock account	BSV	☑

Figure 4.12 Transaction/Event Keys Screen

In this configuration step, all event keys for materials management are listed. First, only the relevant keys for LIV need to be determined. The following list gives an overview of the transactions and event keys relevant in LIV:

- **Inventory posting (BSX)**
  This transaction is used for all postings to inventory accounts. Such postings are affected, for example:
  - In inventory management, for GRs to own stock and goods issues from own stock
  - In Invoice Verification, if price differences occur in connection with incoming invoices for materials valuated at moving average price and there is adequate stock coverage
- **Materials management small differenes (DIF)**
  This transaction is used in Invoice Verification if you define a tolerance for minor differences, and the balance of an invoice does not exceed this tolerance.
- **Freight clearing (FR1), Freight provisions (FR2), Customs clearing (FR3), Customs provisions (FR4)**
  These transactions are used to post delivery costs for GRs against purchase orders and incoming invoices. Which transaction is used for which delivery cost depends on the condition types defined in the purchase order.
- **External service (FRL)**
  The transaction is used for GR and IR in connection with subcontract orders.

▶ **Price differences (PRD)**
Price differences can arise in the case of materials with moving average price if there isn't enough stock to cover the invoiced quantity. For goods movements in the negative range, the moving average price isn't changed. Instead, any price differences arising are posted to a price difference account.

▶ **Invoice reductions in Logistics Invoice Verification (RKA)**
This transaction/event key is used in LIV for the interim posting of price differences for invoice reductions.

▶ **Unplanned delivery costs (UPF)**
Unplanned delivery costs are delivery costs that were not planned in a purchase order, such as freight or customs duty. Instead of distributing these unplanned delivery costs among all invoice items in LIV, the unplanned delivery costs can be posted to a special account.

▶ **GR/IR clearing account (WRX)**
Postings to the GR/IR clearing account occur for GR and IR against purchase orders.

After the relevant transaction is determined, the GL accounts can be defined. Double-click on the transaction, and the account assignment screen as shown in Figure 4.13 is displayed.

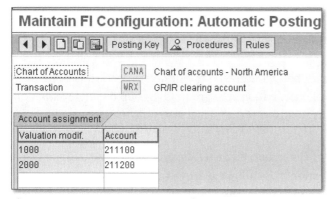

Figure 4.13 Account Assignment Configuration

Within every key, the *rules* for the account assignment need to be defined. The rules specify how granular the account determination has to be within your organization. By choosing the **Rules** button, the different rules allowed for a key are displayed. For example, Figure 14.14 shows the allowed rules for **Transaction WRX**.

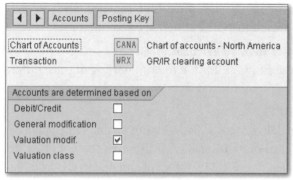

Figure 4.14 Rules Configuration Screen

Up to four rules can be allowed for an event key:

▶ **Debit/Credit**
If this flag is on, differents accounts for debit and credit entries can be defined.

▶ **General modification**
This flag is used for the account modifier. The account modifier is usually used to identify movement types with materials management and isn't relevant for LIV.

▶ **Valuation modifi.**
This flag controls whether the account assignment determination is done on a valuation area group level. A valuation area group is a group of single valuation areas. Usually a valuation area is a "plant" witin materials management.

▶ **Valuation class**
In the accounting view of the material master data, materials are assigned to a valuation class. The valuation class allows different GL account determination within the automatic account assignment.

In the preceding example, the GR/IR account needs to be determined by plant. Therefore, only the **Valuation modif.** flag is set.

4.7.4   Number Assignment

LIV is a function within materials management. The system therefore creates two documents for every invoice posted in LIV — one MM document and one FI document. Along with the different modules comes a problem, which especially causes headaches and frustration in an AP department. The document numbers of an invoice in MM and FI aren't the same! This especially causes a problem when a posted invoice need to be reversed.

In this section, the configuration steps are described to have the same document numbers in MM and FI. The key lies in the number range assignment of the MM and FI document. The MM document number assignment has to be configured as internal, and the assignment must be external for the FI documents. In this case, the MM document number is passed on to the FI document, which means that the number of the FI document is identical to the MM document.

Because the document number assignment in MM isn't company-code specific, in contrast to the FI document, the following points have to be taken into consideration before using external document number assignments for FI documents:

▸ Continuous number assignments for FI documents aren't guaranteed, especially if your organization has more than one company code.

▸ The document number rages in MM and FI have to be the same for all company codes.

▸ You have to use a different number range assignment for FI invoice posting (FB60).

▸ If you use document parking, and the number range intervals are fiscal year dependent, you can't change the posting date of the document, if the fiscal year is different from that determined for the previous posting date. In this case, you have to delete the document and re-enter it. There are no restrictions for fiscal year independent number rages

---

Tip: Scenarios in Which You're Already Live with SAP

If you've already posted thousands of invoices in your system, and the numbers are already different, you need to find unused number range intervals in MM and FI. Because most companies don't change the SAP number ranges during the original implementation, number range interval "52" is usually available in MM and FI. The number ranges can be changed immediately or at the beginning of the next fiscal year.

In the following customizing steps, a new number range "52" for LIV invoices is created. The customizing consists of five steps:

1. Maintain the FI document number range.

2. Assign an FI number range to FI document types.

3. Assign document types in Invoice Verification.

4. Maintain MM document number ranges.

5. Update the MM number range assignment.

Maintain the FI Document Number Range

In Section 2.1.2 of Chapter 2, the maintenance of the number range in FI was described. Alternatively, use Transaction OMR4, and go to Number range for document types in FI. Insert a new document number range by clicking the Insert button at the top of the screen. Create number range interval "52" with the document numbers **5200000000 – 5299999999**. The external number range flag (**Ext**) needs to be set as shown in Figure 4.15.

Intervals					
No	Year	From number	To number	Current number	Ext
47	9999	4700000000	4799999999	0	☐
48	9999	4800000000	4899999999	4800000004	☐
49	9999	4900000000	4999999999	4900000014	☐
50	9999	5000000000	5099999999	5000000042	☐
51	9999	5100000000	5199999999	5100000018	☐
52	9999	5200000000	5299999999		☑
X1	9999	9100000000	9199999999	9100000002	☐
X2	9999	9200000000	9299999999	0	☐

Figure 4.15   FI Number Range Configuration

Assign an FI Number Range to FI Document Types

The second step is to assign a number range to the FI document type for invoices. Use Transaction OMR4, and go to Document type. Double-click on the document type that is used for LIV invoices. In this example, the SAP standard **Document Type** RE is used. In the **Number range** field, assign the new number range interval "52" as shown in Figure 4.16.

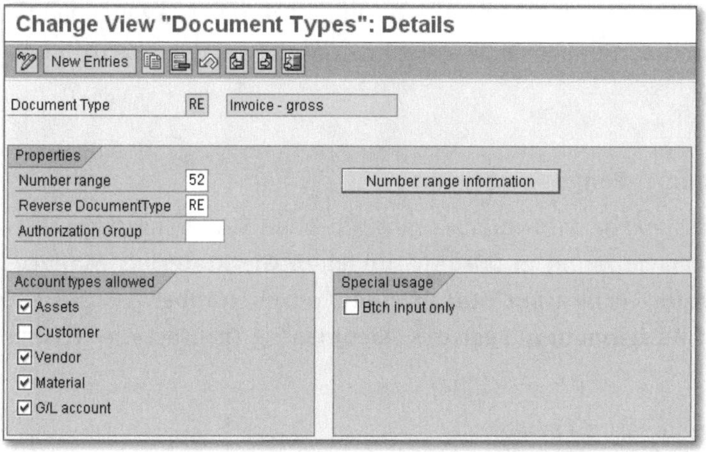

Change View "Document Types": Details

New Entries

| Document Type | RE | Invoice - gross |

Properties
Number range	52		Number range information
Reverse DocumentType	RE
Authorization Group	

Account types allowed
- ☑ Assets
- ☐ Customer
- ☑ Vendor
- ☑ Material
- ☑ G/L account

Special usage
- ☐ Btch input only

Figure 4.16 Number Range Assignment in FI Document Type

Assign Document Types in Invoice Verification

The next step is the assignment of the document type "RE" to the (LIV) transaction. Use Transaction OMR4, and go to Document types in Invoice Verification. Double-click on Transaction Code MIRO, and enter the document type "RE" to be used as shown in Figure 4.17.

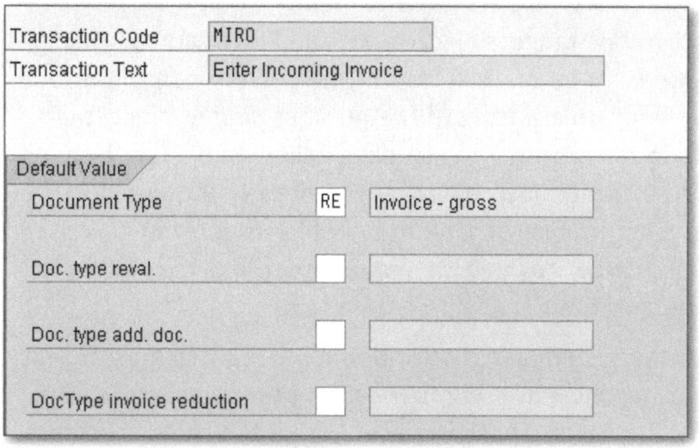

| Transaction Code | MIRO |
| Transaction Text | Enter Incoming Invoice |

Default Value
Document Type	RE	Invoice - gross
Doc. type reval.		
Doc. type add. doc.		
DocType invoice reduction		

Figure 4.17 Document Type Assignment

Maintain MM Document Number Ranges

Use Transaction OMRJ, and click Change Intervals. Insert a new document number range by clicking the Insert button at the top of the screen. For MM documents,

169

create number range interval "52" with the document numbers **5200000000 – 5299999999**. For internal number range assignment, don't set the external number range (**Ext**) checkbox.

Update the MM Number Range Assignment

The last step is to assign the MM number range to your MM transaction. This configuration step can be found in the IMG under **IMG • Materials Management • Logistic Invoice Verification • Incoming Invoice • Number Assignment • Maintain Number Assignment in Logistics Documents • Transaction – Assign Number Ranges**.

Two different transactions are available:

▸ **RD**
Manual Invoice entry (MIRO).

▸ **RS**
Cancel, reverse invoice, ERS, EDI IR, invoicing plan, and revaluation.

Update Transaction RD with number range interval 52.

Tip: Skipped Document Numbers in LIV

All master data or transactional data in SAP are assigned to number range objects. For LIV invoices, the corresponding number range object is RE_BELEG. If number range buffering is switched on, an interval of numbers is stored in the shared memory of the application server. The interval depends on a setting of the number range object, called **No. of numbers that must be held in the buffer**. The standard delivered SAP setting for number range object RE_BELEG is 10, which means that at the time of the first posting of a LIV invoice, the system assigns an interval of 10 numbers to a user. After this user posts 10 invoices, and therefore all numbers of this interval are used up, the system assigns the next interval of 10 numbers to this user.

Why are numbers then skipped, if the system assigns continual intervals to a user? The reason is that multiple users are using the same number range object in parallel, and different intervals are assigned to these users. Another reason is that the shared memory is deleted, if the system gets shut down, for example, through regular offline system backups.

You should switch off number range buffering for LIV invoices using Transaction SNRO and object RE_BELEG. To switch off buffering, select **Edit • Set up Buffering • No Buffering** within Transaction SNRO.

4.7.5   Tax Treatment in Invoice Reduction

This configuration is relevant if your organization uses the invoice reduction process (see Section 4.8.3). The system creates two accounting documents for invoice reduction. The first document, the original document, contains the invoice data sent by the vendor. The second document, the complaint document, contains information about the invoice reduction.

▶ If the tax reduction is carried out in the complaint document, the taxes in the original document correspond to those in the vendor invoice. The tax amount for the invoice reduction is credited in the complaint document.

▶ If the tax reduction is carried out in the original document, the taxes in the original document are reduced by the tax amount for the invoice reduction. In this case, the complaint document does not contain any tax postings. This procedure is recommended if the system calculates the taxes automatically.

4.7.6   Maintain Default Values for Tax Code

In this configuration step, the default values for the tax code when entering an invoice are defined. In addition, the tax code and jurisdiction code for unplanned expenses are defined if these expenses are posted to a separate account. Figure 4.18 shows the configuration screen for the default tax codes.

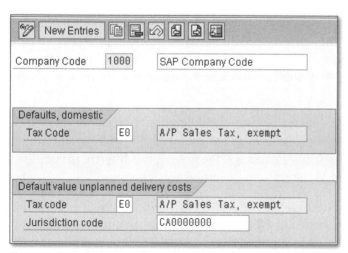

Figure 4.18   Default Tax Codes and Jurisdiction Code

4.7.7 Configure the Treatment of Exchange-Rate Differences

This configuration step specifies how exchange rate differences should be calculated for invoices in foreign currencies. Three options are available:

- ▶ The exchange rate differences are calculated from the exchange rate at the time of the GR, and the exchange rate is calculated at the time of the IR.
- ▶ The exchange rate differences are calculated from the exchange rate at the time of the IR and the assumed exchange rate, which is valid for a specific period of time, such as a year or a season.
- ▶ No exchange rate differences are calculated. Instead, the differences from exchange rate fluctuations are considered price differences and posted to a price difference account.

4.7.8 Determine Mail to Purchasing When Price Difference Occur

This configuration step specifies whether a message is sent to purchasing if a price variance occurs between the purchase order and invoice. The *message-determination* also needs to be configured by defining the message details, such as form, text, and message medium.

4.7.9 Define Vendor-Specific Tolerances

Vendor-specific tolerance groups can be defined for LIV. These tolerances are used during invoice processing and automatic invoice reduction. Within the vendor master data, these tolerance groups can be assigned to a vendor in the **Payment transaction** tab. Figure 4.19 shows the configuration screen for vendor-specific tolerance groups.

During invoice entry, the system calculates the difference between the net invoice amount (gross invoice amount less taxes and unplanned delivery costs) and the net total of the line. If the net invoice amount is the greater, the difference is positive; if the net invoice amount is the smaller, the difference is negative.

If the difference is within the tolerance range for negative or positive differences, the system automatically generates a difference line in a small differences account. The small difference account is specified in automatic account determination for transaction/event key DIF.

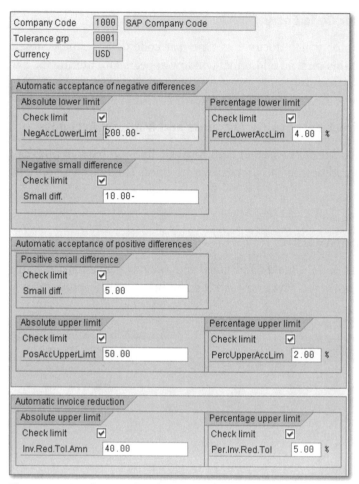

Figure 4.19 Vendor-Specific Tolerance Configuration

If the difference is within the tolerance range for automatic invoice reduction, the system posts the difference to a clearing account and generates a credit memo in a second document to clear this. For invoice reduction postings, the clearing account is defined in the automatic account assignment with transaction/event key RKA.

If no tolerance group is assigned to a vendor, or if no tolerances have been specified for the assigned tolerance group, the system creates a difference line if the difference is smaller than the tolerance defined for tolerance key BD (see Section 4.11).

4.7.10 Maintain Bar Code Entry

This activity specifies for which documents type, bar code details can be stored within the system. In this case, an additional window appears for entering the bar code.

4.7.11 Activate Direct Entry to GL Accounts and Material Accounts

This configuration step specifies whether additional GL lines or material lines can be entered in LIV in addition to the purchase order lines. The following options are available:

▶ Dir.posting to G/L = active

▶ Dir.posting to material = active

The activation of these options makes additional entry tabs available for data entry in LIV. Figure 4.20 shows the data entry tab if an additional GL account entry is activated.

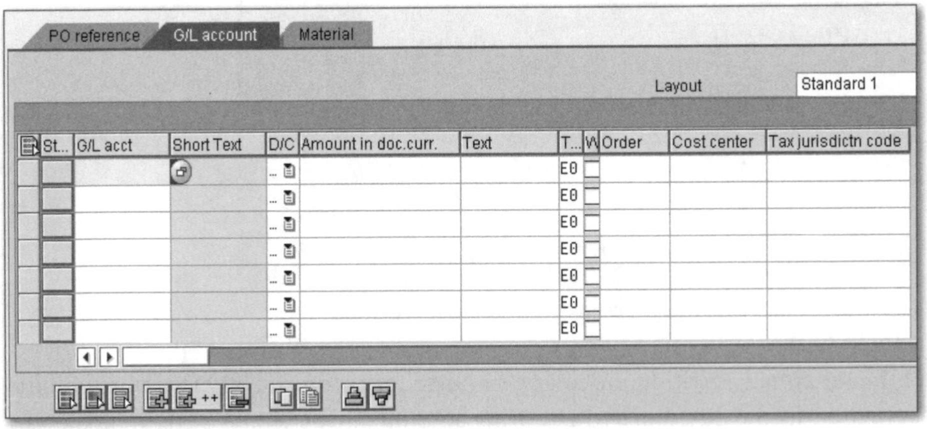

St...	G/L acct	Short Text	D/C	Amount in doc.curr.	Text	T...	W	Order	Cost center	Tax jurisdictn code
			...			E0				
			...			E0				
			...			E0				
			...			E0				
			...			E0				
			...			E0				
			...			E0				
			...			E0				

PO reference | G/L account | Material

Layout: Standard 1

Figure 4.20 Additional GL entry tab

4.7.12 Maintain List Variants

Additional *list variants* or *layouts* of the line item display can be defined in this configuration step. You should create a new layout rather than change the SAP predefined layouts. The following layout editing options are available:

► Change the column sequence.

► Change the column width.

A single column can be set as hidden, required entry, display only, or with a default value.

4.7.13 Aggregation

The *aggregation* function controls the way the items can be aggregated. In the first configuration step, the layouts need to be maintained with the *Maintain Variants for Aggregation List* function. This configuration steps works the same as the *Maintain List Variants*.

In the second step, the aggregation criteria, such as delivery note, plant, or material, are specified for each variant in the *Preset Aggregation Criteria* configuration.

4.7.14 Define Start Logo

In this step, a logo can be specified per company code. This configuration step might be useful if invoices for different company codes are entered to allow users to identify entry errors in the correct company code.

4.7.15 Set Check for Duplicate Invoices

The **Duplicate Invoice Check** configuration shown in Figure 4.21 specifies which criteria the system uses to identify duplicate invoices.

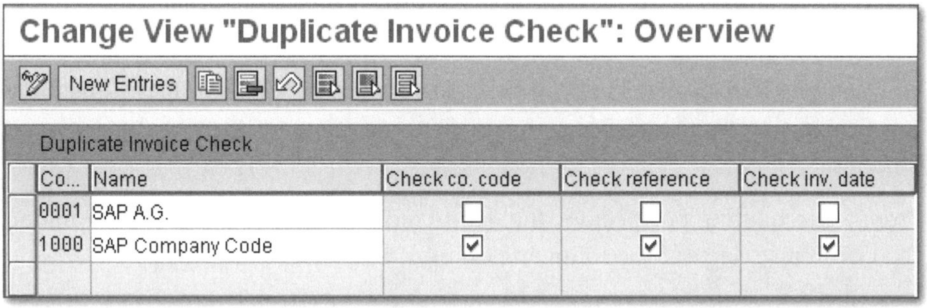

Change View "Duplicate Invoice Check": Overview

New Entries

Duplicate Invoice Check

Co...	Name	Check co. code	Check reference	Check inv. date
0001	SAP A.G.	☐	☐	☐
1000	SAP Company Code	☑	☑	☑

Figure 4.21 Duplicate Invoice Check Configuration

The system checks whether an invoice for a specific vendor with the same invoice amount is already entered. The duplicate check is only executed if a reference number is entered during invoice entry. In addition, the **Check double Inv.** flag has to be set in the **Payment transaction** tab of the vendor master data.

If a duplicate invoice is found, Message M8 108"Check if invoice already entered under accounting doc. no. & &" is issued. In the standard format, this is an information message (I) only. To change the message type to an error message (E), adjust the attributes for system messages as described earlier in Section 4.7.1 for Message class M8 and Message number 108.

4.8 Special Functions During Invoice Entry

In the prior sections, the "normal" invoice entry process and its configuration steps were described. In this section, some special invoice entry features and additional configuration for the LIV process are explained.

4.8.1 Subsequent Debit/Credit

Subsequent debit/credit is a function within LIV, which allows posting of additional debit or credit amounts to previously posted invoices. This function is used to correct the invoiced amounts without affecting the quantity posted. Following are some examples where this function should be used:

▶ A vendor sends you an additional invoice for additional charges, such as custom charges. The charges affect the value of the previously entered invoice but not the quantity. To process this invoice, enter a *subsequent debit*.

▶ A vendor gives you a rebate for delivered items. To process this rebate, enter a *subsequent credit* because only the value should be affected. It isn't possible to enter a credit memo because this would involve a return of the delivered items.

From an accounting perspective, the debit/credit amounts are distributed among the line items selected. The following example illustrates this principle.

> ### Subsequent Debit Example
>
> A purchase order is created with one line item for 10 books with a price of $50 per book. In the purchase order, the books are assigned to GL account 510100 – Books. The GR/IR account is 211200, and the vendor account number is 10000.
>
> The vendor delivers 7 books, and a GR document is created. During the GR, the purchased items are expensed, and the GR/IR account is credited.
>
> Document 1: GR document
>
> Debit: 510100 – Books $350
>
> Credit: 211200 – GR/IR Account $350
>
> In the next step, the vendor sends an invoice over 7 books, and AP posts an invoice:
>
> Document 2: IR document
>
> Debit: 211200 – GR/IR Account $350
>
> Credit: Vendor 10000 $350
>
> The vendor realizes that additional charges of $20 for all 10 books should have been invoiced. AP posts a subsequent debit:
>
> Document 3: Subsequent debit
>
> Debit: 510100 – Books $20
>
> Credit: Vendor 10000 $20

Processing Subsequent Debit/Credit

To process a subsequent debit or credit, select the correct transaction within LIV as shown in Figure 4.22.

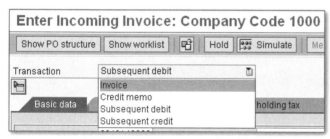

Figure 4.22   Subsequent Debit/Credit Selection

After the subsequent debit/credit transaction is selected for a specific purchase order, the system defaults all prior invoiced quantities. At that point, the subsequent debit/credit amount needs to be entered in the **Amount** field, and the **Quantity** adjusted to reflect the quantity of the debit/credit amount.

4.8.2 Purchase Order Text

The *purchase order text* function can be used to alert the AP clerk of special conditions that pertain to a specific purchase order. A business process is established that the buyer enters these conditions into the **Terms of payment** text in the purchase order header as shown in Figure 4.23.

Figure 4.23 Purchase Order Header Text

Upon invoice entry in LIV, the user gets informed that the buyer entered special conditions into the **Terms of payment** text field and now has the ability to display this text.

The configuration for purchase order texts can be found in the IMG via the navigation path **IMG • Materials Management • Logistic Invoice Verification • Incoming Invoice • Edit PO Supplement Text in Invoice Verification**. Within this step, two activities need to be configured:

1. Activate PO text for the company code under **Order text: general**.
2. Specify the text-IDs for which the user will be informed in LIV under **Notifiable order text types**.

4.8.3 Invoice Reduction

For an incorrect invoice, you usually contact the vendor and ask for a correction invoice. Upon the receipt of the corrected invoice, the invoice is then entered, and the vendor paid.

Invoice reduction however, can automate this process by automatically creating a credit entry, if the vendor invoice amount is higher than the invoice amount due.

In this case, the system would automatically generate a second document with the credit value.

Invoice Reduction Processing

An invoice is processed the usual way using LIV. To use the invoice reduction process, choose the line item layout **Invoice reduction**. In this layout, three additional fields relevant for invoice reduction are visible.

▶ **Correction ID**

▶ **Invoice Amount according to Vendor**

▶ **Quantity according to Vendor**

During data entry, first choose the value **Vendor error: reduce invoice** from the available values in the **Correction ID** field. With the selection of a **Correction ID**, the fields **Invoice Amount according to Vendor** and **Quantity according to Vendor** become available for data entry. Enter the amount and quantity of the incorrect invoice in these fields.

The default values in the **Amount** and **Quantity** fields should not be changed because they represent the correct values. The total amount of the invoice is then entered in the **Amount** field in the **Basic** tab, and the invoice can be posted successfully.

The following example explains the process and the accounting documents.

Invoice Reduction

A total of 10 books are ordered for a unit price of $50 per book. In the purchase order, the books are assigned to GL account 510100 – Books. The GR/IR account is 211200, and the vendor account number is 10000. Account 211300 is defined as the clearing account for invoice reduction.

The vendor delivers 10 books, and a GR document is created.

Document 1: GR document

Debit: 510100 – Books $500

Credit: 211200 – GR/IR Account $500

The vendor sends an incorrect invoice of $510. You contact the vendor, and the vendor agrees to have the invoice reduced by $10. The invoice is posted in AP with the invoice reduction function:

Document 2: IR document

Debit: 211200 – GR/IR Account $500

Debit: 211300 – Invoice Reduction $10

Credit: Vendor 10000 $510

The system automatically generates the following credit document.

Document 2: Invoice Reduction document

Debit: Vendor 10000 $10

Credit: 211300 – Invoice Reduction $10

Invoice Reduction Configuration

To configure invoice reduction, a balance sheet clearing account needs to be specified in the automatic account assignment for transaction/event key RKA (refer to Section 4.7.3).

In addition, a document type needs to be specified for invoice reduction in the document type assignment for Invoice Verification using Transaction OMR4. This configuration step was described in Section 4.7.4.

4.8.4   Prepayment

The *prepayment* feature is a new function in ECC 6.0. Prepayments allow your organization to process invoices and vendor payments independently of GR or invoice checks. Therefore, prepayments should only be used if you have built a good vendor relationship to avoid issues with your vendor in the case of unjustified prepayments.

Prepayment Processing

In the **Payment** tab of the vendor master, it's specified whether prepayment is required, is possible, or isn't permitted. The prepayment process is done in three steps.

1. An invoice is entered in one of the following ways:

   ▶ In a background process, using BAPI `BAPI_INCOMINGVOICE_SAVE` or `BAPI_INCOMIGINVOICE_PARK`

> ▶ With EDI

> ▶ Parking an incoming invoice via Transaction MIR7

2. During entry, the document is marked as a prepayment document. This prepayment document is posted against the vendor and a prepayment clearing account.

3. The prepayment is then paid via the standard payment process using F110.

4. The prepaid invoice is posted. This step creates the offsetting entry to the prepayment clearing account as well as the entry in the GR/IR account.

Prepayment Configuration

The following three steps are involved in the configuration prepayments:

1. Account assignment configuration

2. Field control configuration

3. Company code configuration

Account Assignment Configuration

A balance sheet clearing account needs to be specified in the automatic account assignment for transaction/event key PPX (refer to Section 4.7.3).

Field Control Configuration

The prepayment field control configuration specifies which fields can be changed in the prepayment document. This configuration can be found in the IMG via the navigation path **IMG • Materials Management • Logistic Invoice Verification • Incoming Invoice • Prepayment • Configure Field Control for Payment.**

Company Code Configuration

In the prepayment configuration on a company code level, the document type, reversal code, and field control from step 2 is specified. In addition, the circumstances are specified under which prepayment documents are created. This configuration can be found in the IMG via the navigation path **IMG • Materials Management • Logistic Invoice Verification • Incoming Invoice • Prepayment • Prepayment Control on a Company Code Level.**

> **Restrictions**
>
> The following restrictions apply for prepayments:
>
> ▶ Prepayments can't be used for U.S. tax jurisdiction codes.
>
> ▶ Prepayments can't be used for one-time vendors.
>
> ▶ Prepayments can't be used in connection with sales/purchase tax or acquisition tax.
>
> In addition, several other restrictions apply with regards to the new GL, cash discounts, or exchange differences. Read the SAP IMG for details on these restrictions.

4.8.5   PO History Categories

SAP delivers the PO history categories that are language dependent with a short text and long text. These categories are used in the PO history tab of a purchase order. Depending on the log-on language, such as English or French, the corresponding short text is displayed. If all categories aren't translated properly, these texts can be maintained with Transaction SM30 using view V_163B_T. Figure 4.24 show the current categories, short and long text in English.

POHist.Cat.	Short Text	Long text
1	AAf	Down Payment Req.
2	AAfV	DP Request Clearing
3	AnzV	Down Payt Clearing
A	DPyt	Down payment
B	NAbr	Subseq. settlement
C	NeuR	Miscell. provision
D	SEnt	Service entry
E	GR	Goods receipt
F	DCGR	Delivery costs
G	DCIR	Delivery costs
I	DCAM	Del.costs acct.maint
J	RLfs	Return delivery
K	AccM	Account maintenance
L	DINt	Delivery note
M	DCIn	Del. costs log. inv.

Figure 4.24   Sample PO History Category

4.8.6 Variance Types

Variance types is a new field added to the line items with ECC 6.0. The variance types allow displaying variances between GRs and invoices immediately before data entry. Different variance types can be configured in the IMG under navigation path **IMG • Materials Management • Logistic Invoice Verification • Incoming Invoice • Variance types • Maintain Variance Types.**

If you define a new variance type, BAdI `MRM_VARIANCE_TYPE` needs to be implemented to fill the variance type field appropriately.

4.9 Delivery Costs

For purchases, the vendor may charge additional delivery costs such as freight, custom charges, or insurance costs. Depending on whether these costs are known at the time of the creation of the purchase order, these costs are classified as one of the following:

- Unplanned delivery costs
- Planned delivery costs

4.9.1 Unplanned Delivery Costs

Unplanned delivery charges aren't known at the time of the creation of the purchase order and are entered directly in LIV. Depending on your businesses requirements, there are basically three ways to enter unplanned delivery charges entered:

- Unplanned Delivery costs field in LIV
- Direct Posting to GL account in LIV
- Subsequent debit posting

Unplanned Delivery Cost Field

SAP provides a separate field for unplanned delivery costs (**Unpl. Del. Csts**) as shown in Figure 4.25. The additional costs can be entered directly in this field and either distributed among the invoice items or posted to a separate GL account.

Note that the costs are distributed over all invoice items posted to date and not the current invoice only. This posting option is configuration in the IMG under navigation path **IMG • Materials Management • Logistic Invoice Verification • Incoming Invoice • Configure How Unplanned Delivery Costs Are Posted.**

If a separate GL account is chosen, the account has to be maintained in the automatic account assignment under transaction/event key UPF (Unplanned delivery costs). In addition, a tax code has to be defaulted for unplanned delivery costs as described in Section 4.7.6.

If your organization requires the unplanned delivery costs to be distributed based on your own requirements, BAdI MRM_UDC_DISTRIBUTE can be used to change the distribution of the costs.

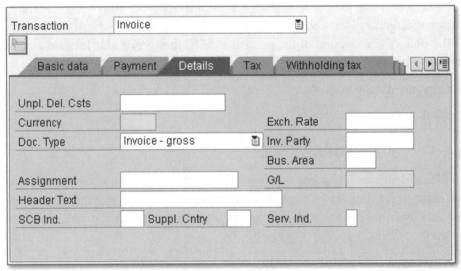

Figure 4.25 Unplanned Delivery Cost Field

Direct Posting to a GL Account

A second posting option for unplanned delivery charges is the direct posting to GL accounts, if direct entry to GL accounts is activated (refer to Section 4.7.11). In this case, the costs have to be charged manually to specific GL accounts.

Subsequent Debit Posting

The third posting option is entering separate documents using the subsequent debit function within LIV. With this option, the charges are also distributed manually over the already invoiced items.

4.9.2 Planned Delivery Costs

Planned delivery costs use the condition technique within purchasing. SAP delivers a variety of predefined condition types for planned delivery costs that can be value, percentage, or a value by quantity based:

- FRA1: Freight %
- FRB1: Freight (Value)
- FRC1: Freight/Quantity

These conditions are manually assigned to a purchase order line item in the **Conditions** tab shown in Figure 4.26.

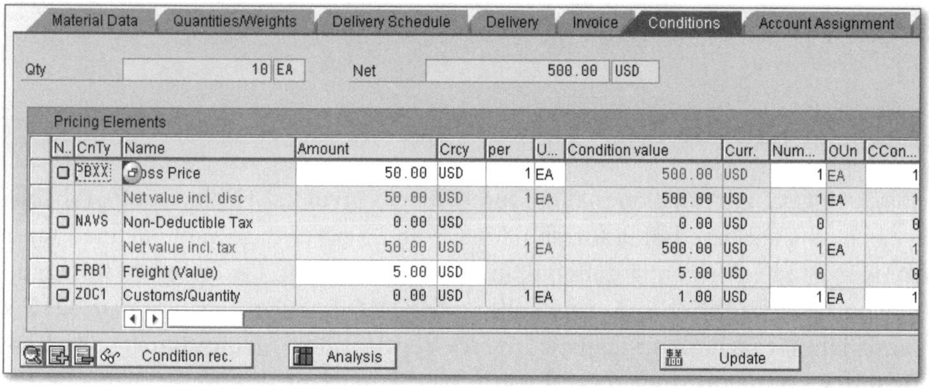
Material Data
Quantities/Weights
Delivery Schedule
Delivery
Invoice
Conditions
Account Assignment
Qty
10 EA
Net
500.00 USD
Pricing Elements
N.. CnTy Name Amount Crcy per U... Condition value Curr. Num... OUn CCon...
PBXX Gross Price 50.00 USD 1 EA 500.00 USD 1 EA 1
Net value incl. disc 50.00 USD 1 EA 500.00 USD 1 EA 1
NAVS Non-Deductible Tax 0.00 USD 0.00 USD 0 0
Net value incl. tax 50.00 USD 1 EA 500.00 USD 1 EA 1
FRB1 Freight (Value) 5.00 USD 5.00 USD 0 0
ZOC1 Customs/Quantity 0.00 USD 1 EA 1.00 USD 1 EA 1
Condition rec.
Analysis
Update

Figure 4.26 Planned Delivery Costs in Purchase Order

The planned delivery costs are posted to balance sheet clearing accounts during GR. The GL accounts are assigned through the automatic account assignment as described in Section 4.7.3.

During the invoice entry in LIV, you need to choose **Goods/service items + planned delivery costs** to enter both goods/service and planned delivery costs as shown in Figure 4.27.

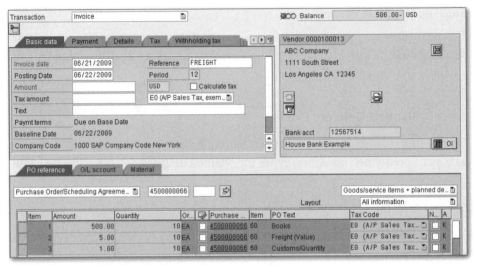

Figure 4.27 Invoice Entry with Planned Delivery Costs

You should use the planned delivery costs option instead of the unplanned options because the costs are correctly posted to the materials, and tolerances are taken into consideration correctly.

4.10 Stochastic Block

Stochastic block is a function that randomly blocks invoices. The blocking probability is calculated based on a threshold value and a percentage value defined for a company code. The configuration is a two-step process. In the first step, stochastic block is activated for a company code in the IMG under navigation path **IMG • Materials Management • Logistic Invoice Verification • Invoice Block • Stochastic Block • Activate Stochastic Block.**

The second step is the specification of the threshold value and percentage per company code as shown in Figure 4.28 in the IMG under navigation path **IMG • Materials Management • Logistic Invoice Verification • Invoice Block • Stochastic Block • Set Stochastic Block.**

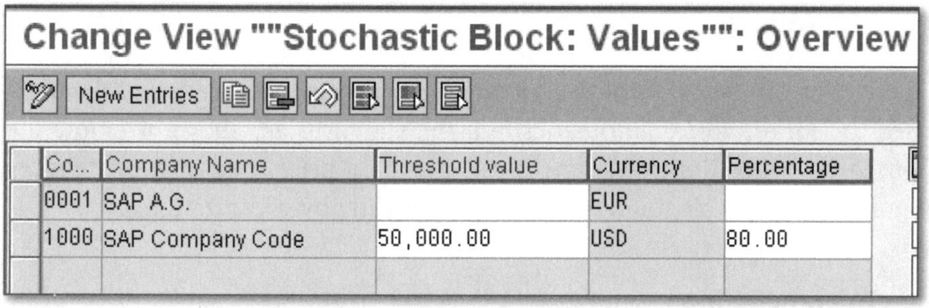

Figure 4.28 Stochastic Block Threshold and Percentage Value

The result of these configuration steps is that the blocking probability of every invoice document is calculated. Based on this probability, the invoices will be blocked. If the invoice amount is higher than the **Threshold value**, the probability is always equal to the **Percentage** specified. If the invoice amount is lower than the **Threshold value**, the probability is calculated based on the following formula:

*Probability = Invoice Amount / Threshold Amount * Percentage*

The following example illustrate this calculation.

Stochastic Block Example

Your organization requires 80% of all invoices over $50,000 to be randomly blocked for manual review.

Invoice Amount:

60,000 — Probability = 80%

50,000 — Probability = 80%

40,000 — Probability = 40,000 / 50,000 * 80% = 64%

25,000 — Probability = 25,000 / 50,000 * 80% = 40%

100 — Probability = 100 / 50,000 * 80% = 0.16%

A stochastically-blocked invoice can be released using Transaction MRBR, which is described in the next section.

4.11 Tolerances

SAP delivers many types of tolerances related to Invoice Verification. Tolerances are used to block invoices automatically if the variances are above or below the configured tolerance limits. Variances can occur on price, quantity, or delivery dates, and the acceptable tolerance limits vary greatly by organization.

4.11.1 Tolerance Keys

Within SAP, the different tolerance types are defined as *tolerance keys*. Each tolerance key can have up to four limit values:

▶ Absolute upper limit

▶ Upper percentage limit

▶ Absolute lower limit

▶ Lower percentage limit

Following is a list of all available tolerance keys and their purposes.

AN – Amount for Item Without Order Reference

If the item amount check is activated for lines that are added without reference to a purchase order, the systems checks against the absolute upper limit. If the amount is higher than the limit, the invoice will be blocked.

AP – Amount for Item with Reference Check

If the item amount check is activated, lines with reference to a purchase order are checked against the absolute upper limit. This limit is usually set very high. If the amount is higher than the limit, the invoice will be blocked.

BD – Form Small Differences Automatically

The main purpose of tolerances is to ensure that the vendors aren't getting overpaid. On the other side, it doesn't make economical sense to disallow overpayments in the case of small differences. The time to resolve the variance will probably cost more than the variance itself. The limits for small differences are usually set at a small absolute value. Within the automatic account assignment, a small difference account has to be configured under transaction/event key DIF.

BR – Percentage OPUn Variance (IR Before GR)

This tolerance checks the order price unit, which is an alternative unit of measure used in purchasing for ordering purposes. For example, 10 gallons are purchased at a price of $10 per gallon. One gallon contains 3.6 liters. If the invoice, however, contains a liter price different from $2.78, then there is an OPUn difference.

BW – Percentage OPUn Variance (GR Before IR)

This tolerance is calculated the same way as tolerance key BR.

DQ – Exceed Amount: Quantity Difference

This tolerance controls quantity differences. If a GR has been defined for an order item, and a GR has already been posted, the system multiplies the net order price by (quantity invoiced - (total quantity delivered - total quantity invoiced)).

If no GR has been defined, the system multiplies the net order price by (quantity invoiced - (quantity ordered - total quantity invoiced)).

The system compares the result with the absolute upper and lower limits defined. This allows relatively high quantity variances for invoice items for small amounts but only small quantity variances for invoice items for larger amounts.

DW – Quantity Variance GR Quantity = Zero

If a GR is defined for an order item, but none has as yet been posted, the system multiplies the net order price by (quantity invoiced + total quantity invoiced so far). The system then compares the outcome with the absolute upper tolerance limit defined.

If you haven't maintained tolerance key DW for your company code, the system blocks an invoice for which no GR has been posted yet. If you want to prevent this block, then set the tolerance limits to **Do not check**.

KW – Variance from Condition Value

This tolerance calculates the difference in invoiced delivery costs compared to the planned delivery costs in the purchase order. If the limits are exceeded, the invoice will be blocked.

LA – Amount of Blanket Purchase Order

The system calculates the sum of the value invoiced so far for the purchase order item and the value of the current invoice and compares it with the value limit of the purchase order. It then compares the difference with the upper percentage and absolute tolerances defined.

LD – Blanket purchase Order Time Limit Exceeded

The system determines the number of days by which the invoice is outside the planned time interval. If the posting date of the invoice is before the validity period, the system calculates the number of days between the posting date and the start of the validity period. If the posting date of the invoice is after the validity period, the system calculates the number of days between the posting date and the end of the validity period. The system compares the number of days then with the absolute upper limit defined.

PP – Price Variance

The system determines by how much each invoice item varies from the quantity invoiced multiplied with the order price. It then compares the variance with the upper and lower limits defined.

PS – Price Variance: Estimated Prices

If the price in an order item is marked as an estimated price, the system then calculates the difference between the invoice value and the quantity invoiced multiplied with the order price and compares the variance with the upper and lower tolerance limits defined.

ST – Date Variance – Value X Days

For each item, the system calculates the invoice value multiplied with (scheduled delivery date - date invoice entered) and compares the result with the absolute upper limit defined. This allows relatively high schedule variances for invoice items for small amounts but only small schedule variances for invoice items for large amounts.

VP – Moving Average Price (MAP) Variance

When a stock posting line is created as a result of an invoice item, the system calculates the new moving average price that results from the posting. It compares the percentage variance of the new moving average price to the old price using the percentage tolerance limits defined. The same tolerance is also checked at the time of a GR to highlight large changes in the MAP.

4.11.2 Invoice Block Configuration

Invoice blocks are configured with the following steps:

► Determine payment block.

► Set tolerance limits.

► Activate workflow template.

► Perform item amount check.

► All configuration steps can be found in the IMG under navigation path **IMG** · **Materials Management** · **Logistic Invoice Verification** · **Invoice Block**.

Determine Payment Block

SAP predefines payment block "R" for tolerance blocks and statistical blocks within Invoice Verification. Only the description can be changed for this payment block. Additional manual payment blocks can be defined as needed.

Set Tolerance Limits

The tolerance limits for all of the previously described tolerance keys can be defined in this step. For example, Figure 4.29 shows the configuration screen for **Tolerance key PP**.

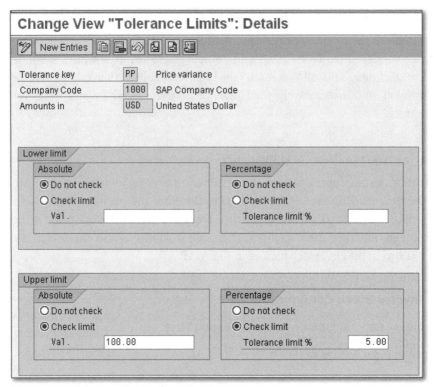

Figure 4.29 Tolerance Key Configuration Screen

4.11.3 Activate Workflow Template

For a price variance, a workflow template can be activated that sends a workflow message to the buyer to inform him of a price difference. The buyer then checks on the correct price and adjusts the purchase order price if necessary. After the price in the purchase is adjusted, the invoices can automatically be released using Transaction MRBR.

4.11.4 Item Amount Check

By activating the item amount check, the system checks the tolerance keys AP and AN. This is useful if you want all items above certain amounts to be reviewed before payment.

In the first step, the item amount check has to be activated for the company code globally under **Activate Item Amount Check**. In the next step, the purchase order item category for which item amount check should be executed needs to be specified as shown in Figure 4.30. The **Goods Receipt** flag allows you to specify whether the item amount check should only be executed for items with or without GR. This might be helpful if the item amount check should be executed for two-way match invoices only.

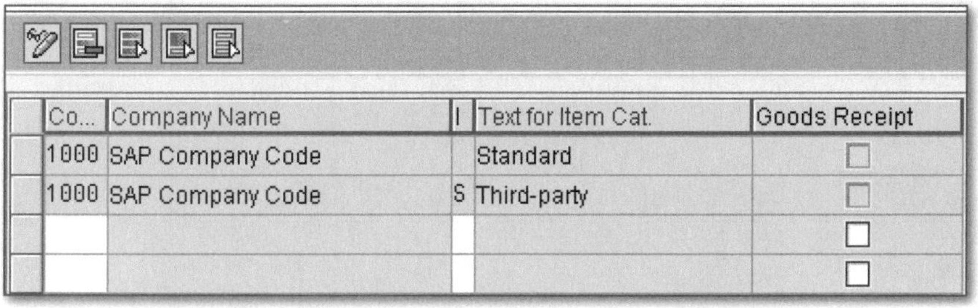

	Co...	Company Name	I	Text for Item Cat.	Goods Receipt
	1000	SAP Company Code		Standard	☐
	1000	SAP Company Code	S	Third-party	☐
					☐
					☐

Figure 4.30 Item Amount Check by Purchase Order Line Item Category

The different tolerance keys were described in this section. The next section covers Transaction MRBR, which allows the release of blocked invoices.

4.12 Release Blocked Invoices (MRBR)

Before blocked invoices in LIV can be paid, these invoices have to be released in a separate step. With Transaction MRBR, invoices can be released manually or automatically. This transaction can be found in the SAP menu path **SAP Menu • Logistics • Material Management • Logistic Invoice Verification • Further processing • Release Blocked Invoices.** The selection screen of this transaction as shown in Figure 4.31 is divided into four sections:

▶ **Selection of Blocked Invoices**

▶ **Processing**

▶ **Blocking Procedure**

▶ **Display Options**

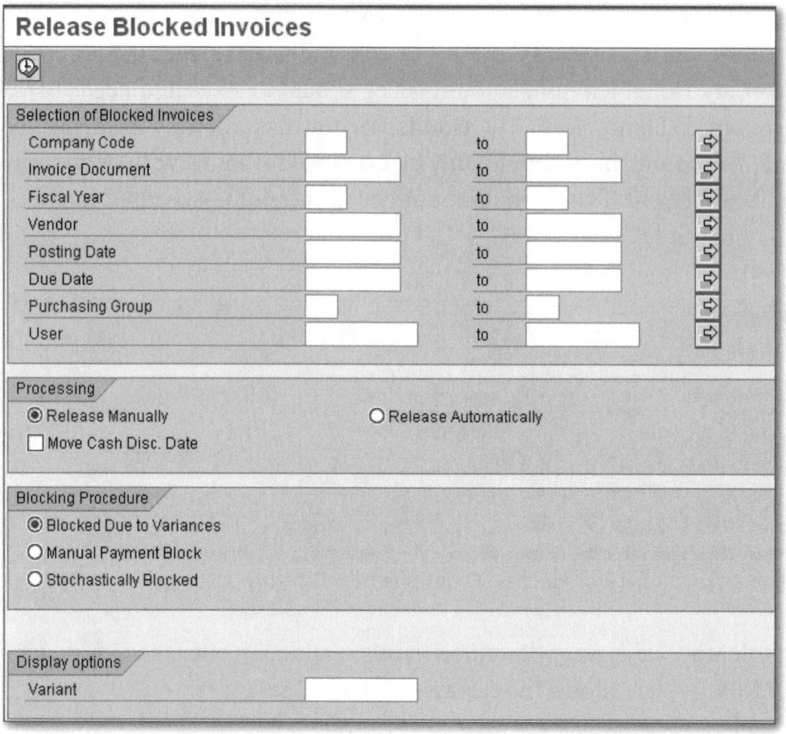

Figure 4.31 Release Blocked Invoices

Selection of Blocked Invoices

In this section, the blocked invoices can be selected based on certain selection criteria, such as company code, vendor, posting date, or user.

Processing

Blocked invoices can be released manually or automatically.

Release Manually

Manual blocked invoices or stochastically blocked invoices have to be released manually. In this case, the blocking reason can either be deleted, or the invoice can be released. It isn't recommended to manually release invoices blocked due to variances because the blocking occurred due to exceeding a tolerance limit. It's rather recommended to correct the reason for the blocking of the invoice.

Release Automatically

It's recommended to schedule a job with the flag **Release Automatically** on a daily basis. This flag performs a check of all blocked invoices, where the block reason doesn't apply anymore, for example, a missing GR was posted or purchasing adjusted the price in a purchase order line item. These blocked invoices are then released.

Move Cash Discount Date

If the **Move Cash Disc. Date** field is selected, the system moves the discount terms to take advantage of a discount.

Blocking Procedure

In the **Blocking Procedure** section, the types of blocked invoices that will be processed are specified, such as **Blocked due to Variances**, **Manual Payment Block**, or **Stochastically Blocked**.

Display options

In the **Display options** section, the variant of the ALV layout can be specified, that is displayed, if the invoices are released manually.

4.13 Enhancements During Invoice Entry

Within Invoice Verification, SAP delivers a variety of BAdIs to enhance the standard functionality. The implementation of a BAdI is described in Appendix C.

4.13.1 Default Transaction Values with BAdI MRM_TRANSACT_DEFAULT

BAdI `MRM_TRANSACT_DEFAULT` allows defaulting of specific transaction fields anytime Invoice Verification is executed. These fields include the transaction/event, such as invoice or credit memo, line item layouts, or the worklist and PO structure. This BAdI is executed at the start of Transactions MIRO or MIR7 or after a document is posted in LIV.

For example, Listing 4.1 shows the following default rule:

▶ The default transaction/event should be set to Invoice, and the reference document category to purchase order/scheduling agreement.

> **Note**
>
> Within the BAdI, double-click the domain values to find the SAP internal values for the transaction/event or reference document category.

```
method IF_EX_MRM_TRANSACT_DEFAULT~TRANSACTION_DEFAULT_SET.
*----------------------------------------------------------
*  Default transaction/event 'Invoice'
*----------------------------------------------------------
  E_VORGANG = '1'.          " 1 = Invoice
                            " 2 = Credit memo
                            " 3 = Subsequent Debit
                            " 4 = Subsequent Credit


*----------------------------------------------------------
*  Default reference document category
*----------------------------------------------------------
  E_REFERENZBELEGTYP = '1'. " 1 = PO / Service Agreement
                            " 2 = Delivery Note
                            " 3 = Bill of Lading
                            " 4 = Service Entry Sheet

endmethod.
```

Listing 4.1 Sample BAdI MRM_TRANSACT_DEFAULT

4.13.2 Default Header Fields: MRM_HEADER_DEFAULT

BAdI MRM_HEADER_DEFAULT allows defaulting of specific document header fields, such as document type, reference number, or document date. This BAdI works similar to BAdI MRM_TRANSACT_DEFAULT and is executed at the start of Transactions MIRO or MIR7 or after a document is posted in LIV.

For example, Listing 4.2 shows the following default rule:

▶ Set the current date as the default date for the document date.

```
method IF_EX_MRM_HEADER_DEFAULT~HEADER_DEFAULT_SET.
*----------------------------------------------------------
* The default value for the Document date is the
* current date
```

```
*-------------------------------------------------------
  E_BLDAT = SY-DATUM.
endmethod.
```

Listing 4.2 Example BAdI MRM_HEADER _DEFAULT

4.13.3 Default Payment Terms: MRM_PAYMENT_TERMS

BAdI MRM_PAYMENT_TERMS allows the payment terms to be defaulted, such as base-line date, discount terms, or payment block. This BAdI is executed after the purchase order is entered. All purchase order information is available at that time.

4.13.4 Validate Document Header: MRM_HEADER_CHECK

BAdI MRM_HEARDER_CHECK allows the validation of the document header data during Invoice Verification.

For example, Listing 4.3 shows the following validation rule:

▶ If a credit memo is entered, display a warning message if the document type isn't CR.

```
method IF_EX_MRM_HEADER_CHECK~HEADERDATA_CHECK.
*-----------------------------------------------
* Document type must be 'CR' for Credit memos
*-----------------------------------------------
  IF I_RBKPV-XRECHL = 'H'.      "Credit memo entry
    IF I_RBKPV-BLART <> 'CR'.
      MESSAGE w012(ZFI).
    ENDIF.
  ENDIF.
endmethod.
```

Listing 4.3 Example Code for BAdI MRM_HEADER_CHECK

4.13.5 Complete Document Validation: INVOICE_UPDATE

BAdI INVOICE_UPDATE and method CHANGE_AT_SAVE allow the validation of the complete invoice document, including all header data and line item data. The validation is executed at the time the document is saved.

For example, Listing 4.4 shows the following validation rule:

▶ If a document is entered with a vendor that has multiple payment methods assigned in the vendor master data, the payment method needs to be specified in the document.

```
method IF_EX_INVOICE_UPDATE~CHANGE_AT_SAVE.
DATA: T_LFB1     TYPE LFB1,
      H_ZWELS    TYPE I.
*-------------------------------------------------------
* The payment method has to be specified if the vendor
* has more than one payment method assigned in the
* vendor master data
*-------------------------------------------------------
  IF S_RBKP_NEW-ZLSCH = SPACE.
    SELECT SINGLE * FROM LFB1 INTO T_LFB1 WHERE
                                BUKRS = S_RBKP_NEW-BUKRS AND
                                LIFNR = S_RBKP_NEW-LIFNR.
    IF SY-SUBRC = 0.
      H_ZWELS = 0.
      COMPUTE H_ZWELS = STRLEN( T_LFB1-ZWELS ).
      IF H_ZWELS > 1.
        MESSAGE E012(ZFI).
      ENDIF.
    ENDIF.
  ENDIF.
endmethod.
```

Listing 4.4 Example Code for BAdI INVOICE_UPDATE Method CHANGE_AT_SAVE

4.13.6 Additional BAdIs During Invoice Verification

In addition to the preceding examples, the following BAdIs are available during Invoice Verification:

▶ MRM_UDC_DITRIBUTE
This BAdI allows you to distribute unplanned delivery costs based on user-defined rules.

▶ MRM_WT_SPLIT_UPDATE
Change of withholding tax data and data for vendor split.

▶ MRM_TOLERANCE_GROUP
Default of a vendor-specific tolerance group.

▶ MRM_ITEM_CUSTFIELDS
Integration of customer fields in Invoice Verification.

4.14   Evaluated Goods Receipt Settlement (ERS)

ERS is a function within LIV that is usually performed within AP. With ERS, invoices are created automatically, based on GR documents. This reduces the number of invoices entered manually. If an invoice is already posted and goods are returned, the system automatically posts a credit memo during the next ERS run. In addition, for reducing the manual effort in posting invoices, ERS has the following advantages:

▶ No price or quantity variances occur in Invoice Verification.

▶ Invoices are posted more quickly, and therefore discounts are more likely to be taken.

▶ The vendor is paid faster.

Not every process is suitable for ERS. From experience, ERS works best if the following factors are taken into consideration:

▶ Your organization established a good vendor relationship.

▶ Internal approval and control procedures are in place to avoid overpayments.

▶ The vendor is informed and agrees on using ERS.

For example, the following processes fit well with ERS.

▶ Your organization established purchase orders for temporary employee services with a fixed hourly rate during the time of the agreement. The purchase order line items are created with line item category D, for external services. Every week, a service entry sheet is created with reference to the purchase order, specifying the time worked. Upon approval of the service entry sheet, the GR document is created automatically. On a daily basis, AP runs the ERS process, and invoices are created based on the approved service entry sheets.

▶ Your organization has a quantity agreement with a vendor for vehicle parts. The prices are fixed over the duration of the agreement. The vendor delivers the parts, and GR documents are posted. Again, on a daily basis, AP runs the ERS process, and invoices are created automatically based on the GR documents.

4.14.1   How to Avoid Pitfalls

The following bullet points are guidelines that your organization should take into consideration when implementing ERS:

- ▶ Communicate changes to vendors before ERS is implemented.

  - ▶ Explain the meaning of ERS to vendors and that the vendors are getting paid in the future based on agreed prices on services/goods delivered.

  - ▶ Obtain approval of the changes and conditions before implementing ERS.

  - ▶ Inform the vendors when the first ERS invoice and payment is expected.

  - ▶ If your organization experiences resistance from the vendors, explain the advantages, such as faster payments and simplified paper flow.

- ▶ Don't be too ambitious at the beginning.

  - ▶ Start with a small number of vendors and purchase orders.

  - ▶ Slowly increase the number of vendors.

  - ▶ Build a comfort level internally and externally.

4.14.2 Configuration Steps

ERS requires minimal configuration. Following are the configuration steps for ERS:

- ▶ Maintain FI accounting document number ranges.
- ▶ Assign FI document types.
- ▶ Maintain the MM document number range.
- ▶ Update the MM number range assignment.

All of these configuration steps can be found in the IMG under navigation path **IMG • Materials management • Logistic Invoice Verification • Incoming Invoice • Number Assignment,** which were covered in Section 4.7.4 "Number Assignment."

> **Document Type Recommendation**
>
> You should create a separate document type, that is, EV, for invoices created through ERS. This allows the AP clerk to distinguish manually created documents from automatically created documents.

4.14.3 Master Data Settings

To allow ERS for a vendor and a specific purchase order, the ERS flags need to be set in the vendor master as well as in the purchase order.

Vendor Master Maintenance

In the *purchasing view* of the vendor master data, two ERS-relevant flags are available as shown in Figure 4.32. It's recommended to set both flags.

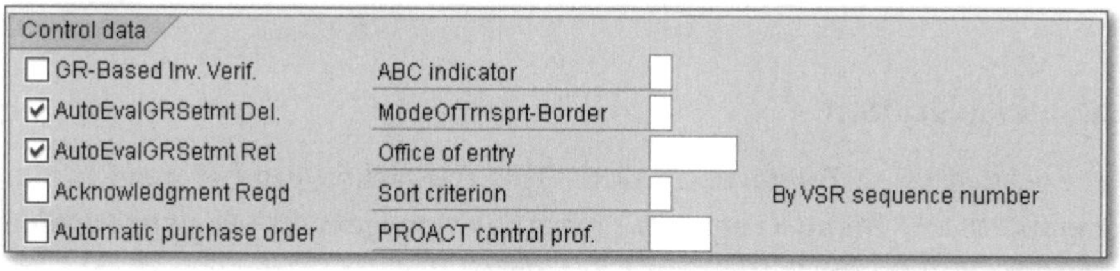

Figure 4.32 ERS Flag in the Purchasing View of the Vendor Master Data

AutoEvalGRSetmt Del.

This flag specifies that ERS settlements are allowed for this vendor for deliveries or GRs.

AutoEvalGRSetmt Ret.

This flag specifies that a credit memo for returns is created during the ERS processing.

Purchase Order Maintenance

After the ERS flags in the vendor master data are maintained, the ERS flag in the purchase order line item needs to be set. This flag is available in the **Invoice** tab of the purchase order line item as shown in Figure 4.33.

Figure 4.33 ERS Flag in Purchase Order Line Item

Besides setting the **ERS** flag, the **GR-Bsd IV** flag should also be set because a GR is required before an invoice can be created automatically. In addition, the system requires a valid **Tax Code** because no tax code can be entered manually during invoice creation.

ERS Flag in Purchase Order

After these ERS flags are set in the vendor master data, all new purchase orders for this vendor are created with the **ERS** flag, unless the **No ERS** flag is set in the info records in purchasing.

4.14.4 ERS Execution

ERS is executed using Transaction MRRL. This transaction can be found in the SAP menu path **SAP Menu • Logistics • Material Management • Logistic Invoice Verification • Automatic Settlement • Evaluated Receipt Settlement (ERS)**. The selection screen of this transaction as shown in Figure 4.34 is divided into three sections:

▶ **Document Selection**

▶ **Processing Options**

▶ **Display Options**

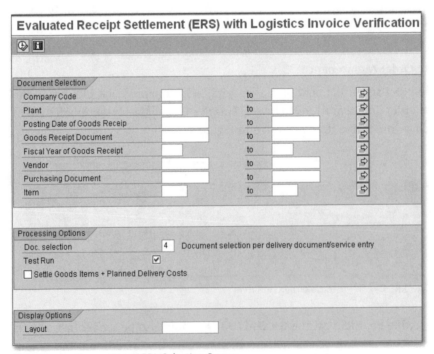

Figure 4.34 Transaction MRRL Selection Screen

Document Selection

In this section, the posted GR documents relevant for ERS can be selected based on certain criteria, such as company code, vendor, posting date, or purchase order.

Processing Options

ERS can be executed in four different processing options. Based on the processing option, invoices are getting created with different detail levels. Table 4.1 shows the processing option and the level of invoices created.

Option	Document Selection	Explanation
1	Vendor	The system sums up all GR documents by vendor and posts one invoice. If the purchase orders have different payment terms, it creates one invoice for every vendor/payment term combination.
2	Purchase order	The system creates one invoice per purchase order.
3	Purchase order item	The system creates one invoice per purchase order line item
4	Delivery document/Service entry	Each GR document/service entry sheet is created as a single invoice document.

Table 4.1 ERS Processing Options

Settle Goods Items + Planned Delivery Costs

The **Settle Goods Items + Planned Delivery Costs** flag is a new function in ECC 6.0, which allows the settlement of planned delivery costs for ERS invoices. Within Transaction MRRL, delivery costs can only be settled if the processing options 1, 2, or 3 are chosen. If planned delivery costs need to be settled per delivery document/service entry sheet (option 4), Transaction MRDC need to be executed. This transaction is covered in the next section.

Display Options

In the **Display Options** section, you can specify the ALV list layout of the processed invoices.

4.14.5 Planned Delivery Cost Settlement

Planned delivery cost settlement using Transaction MRDC is a new function in ECC 6.0. The system creates one invoice for every condition type for the quantity delivered. This transaction can be found in the SAP menu path **SAP Menu • Logistics • Material Management • Logistic Invoice Verification • Automatic Settlement • Automatic Delivery Costs Settlement.** The selection screen of this transaction is shown in Figure 4.35.

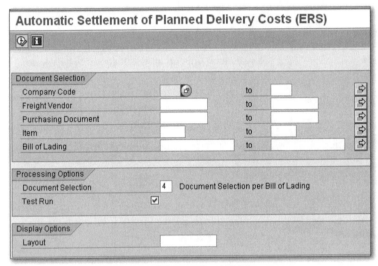

Figure 4.35 Selection Screen of Transaction MRDC

Independent of whether planned delivery costs are settled through Transaction MRRL or MRDC, only the freight vendors for which planned delivery settlement is activated are settled. These vendors need to be specified in the IMG via navigation path **IMG • Materials Management • Logistic Invoice Verification • Evaluated Receipt Settlement (ERS) • Specify Automatic Settlement of Planned Delivery Costs.**

4.14.6 ERS Enhancements

SAP delivers multiple enhancements for ERS. For creation of ERS documents using Transaction MRRL, enhancement MRMH0001 could be used to change header fields or line item information for ERS invoices.

For the creation of invoices for planned delivery costs, two BAdIs are available:

- **Change Header data:** MRM_ERS_HDAT_MODIFY
- **Change Line Item data:** MRM_ERS_IDAT_MODIFY

Enhancement MRMH001

Listing 4.5 shows the implementation of enhancement MRMH0001 with the following requirements:

- The document date is the execution date.
- For service entry sheets, move the "External number in the service entry sheet" to the reference number.
- For GR documents, move the "Goods-receipt reference" to the reference number.

```
*&--------------------------------------------------------------*
*&  Include            ZXM08U20
*&--------------------------------------------------------------*
DATA: T_ESSR LIKE ESSR,
      T_MKPF LIKE MKPF.

  LOOP AT T_SELWENR.
    MOVE-CORRESPONDING I_RBKPV TO E_RBKPV_ERS_CHANGE.
*-----------------------------------------------------
* 1. Document date is the ERS execution date
*-----------------------------------------------------
    E_RBKPV_ERS_CHANGE-BLDAT = SY-DATUM.



*-----------------------------------------------------
* 2. Service Entry Sheets
* Move the external number to the reference number
*-----------------------------------------------------
    SELECT SINGLE * FROM ESSR INTO T_ESSR WHERE
                            LBLNI = T_SELWENR-LFBNR.
    IF SY-SUBRC = 0.
      E_RBKPV_ERS_CHANGE-XBLNR = T_ESSR-LBLNE.
    ENDIF.


*-----------------------------------------------------
* 3. Goods Receipt Documents
```

```
* Move Goods-receipt reference to the reference number
*-------------------------------------------------
   SELECT SINGLE * FROM MKPF INTO T_MKPF WHERE
                           MBLNR = T_SELWENR-LFBNR AND
                           MJAHR = T_SELWENR-LFGJA.
   IF SY-SUBRC = 0.
     E_RBKPV_ERS_CHANGE-XBLNR = T_MKPF-XBLNR.
   ENDIF.
 ENDLOOP.
 E_CHANGE = 'X'.
```

Listing 4.5 Example Code for MRMH0001

4.15   Invoicing Plans

The *invoicing plans* function within LIV allows the creation of invoices based on due dates and amounts specified in a purchase order, similar to recurring entries covered in Section 3.9 in Chapter 3.

This function works similar to ERS where invoices are created automatically based on information in the purchase order line item. However, for invoicing plans, no GRs are necessary.

Two different invoicing plan types are available:

▶ Periodic invoicing plans
▶ Partial invoicing plans

Periodic invoicing plans are designed for fixed-value payments on a regular basis, such as monthly or quarterly. Examples are rent agreements or lease agreements.

For *partial invoicing plans*, the payment amounts are based on the percentage of the overall purchase order line item amount.

4.15.1   Configuration Steps

To configure invoicing plans, use the same steps for the number assignments as described in the "Evaluated Goods Receipt Settlement (ERS)" section. All of these configuration steps can be found in the IMG under navigation path **IMG • Materials Management • Logistic Invoice Verification • Incoming Invoice • Number Assignment**, which were covered in Section 4.7.4 "Number Assignment."

Document Type Recommendation

You should create a separate document type, that is, IP, for invoices created through invoicing plans. This allows the AP clerk to distinguish manually created documents from automatically created documents.

In addition to the number assignment configuration, the invoicing plan types need to be configured in the IMG under navigation path **IMG • Materials Management • Purchasing • Purchase Order • Incoming Plan • Invoicing Plan Types**. Figure 4.36 shows the invoicing plan type configuration for a monthly invoicing plan.

Inv. Pl. Ty.	ML	Monthly on Last day of Month		
Origin of General Data				
Start Date	11	Contract Start Date		
End Date	09	Contract End Date		
Horizon	52	Horizon 1 Year		
Dates from				
Dates until				
Invoice Data: Suggestion for Dates				
Per. Inv. Date	51	Monthly on Last of Month	DDateCat.	P1
Var. Inv. Date				
No. Days Year		Days in Month	Calendar ID	
Control Data: Generate Dates				
Dialog Pur. Order	X	☐ In Advance		

Figure 4.36 Invoicing Plan Configuration Screen

Within the invoicing plan type, the start date, end date, and time horizon are specified. In addition, the suggested invoice dates are defined. The **Dialog Pur. Order** flag sets whether the dates are determined automatically in the purchase order or manually.

4.15.2 Master Data Settings

To allow invoicing plans for a vendor and a specific purchase order, the ERS flags need to be set in the vendor master as well as in the purchase order.

Vendor Master Maintenance

In the purchasing view of the vendor master data, the **AutoEvalGRSemtmt. Del.** flag needs to be set as shown earlier in Figure 4.32.

Purchase Order Maintenance

After the ERS flag in the vendor master data is maintained, the ERS flag in the purchase order line item needs to be set. This flag is available in the **Invoice** tab of the purchase order line item as shown earlier in Figure 4.33.

Besides setting the **ERS** flag, the invoicing plan needs to be specified in the purchase order line item in the **Invoice** tab. Figure 4.37 shows an invoicing plan for a monthly payment of $10,000 with an invoice date on the last date of a month.

Invoice plan								
Inv. plan ty.	10 Sample periodic inv…		51 Monthly on Last of Month	In Advance ☐				
Start date	08/01/2008			Dates from				
End date	06/01/2009			Dates until				
Horizon	08/31/2009 52 Horizon 1 Year				Cal-Id			

Deadlines							
Start of settl.	AcctSettlm…	Invoice date	Invoice value	Crcy	RS	R	DCat
08/01/2008	08/31/2008	08/31/2008	10,000.00	USD		A	P1
09/01/2008	09/30/2008	09/30/2008	10,000.00	USD		A	P1
10/01/2008	10/31/2008	10/31/2008	10,000.00	USD		A	P1
11/01/2008	11/30/2008	11/30/2008	10,000.00	USD		A	P1
12/01/2008	12/31/2008	12/31/2008	10,000.00	USD		A	P1
01/01/2009	01/31/2009	01/31/2009	10,000.00	USD		A	P1
02/01/2009	02/28/2009	02/28/2009	10,000.00	USD		A	P1
03/01/2009	03/31/2009	03/31/2009	10,000.00	USD		A	P1
04/01/2009	04/30/2009	04/30/2009	10,000.00	USD		A	P1
05/01/2009	05/31/2009	05/31/2009	10,000.00	USD		A	P1
06/01/2009	06/01/2009	06/30/2009	10,000.00	USD		A	P1
	☑						
	☑						

Figure 4.37   Sample Invoicing Plan

For the invoicing plan, the **GR-based IV** flag as well as the **Goods Receipt** flag must not be set in the purchase order line item. On the other side, the system requires a valid **Tax Code** because no tax code can be entered manually during invoice creation.

4.15.3 Invoicing Plan Settlement Execution

Invoicing plan settlement is executed using Transaction MRIS. This transaction can be found in the SAP menu path **SAP Menu • Logistics • Material Management • Logistic Invoice Verification • Automatic Settlement • Invoicing Plan Settlement.** The selection screen of this transaction as shown in Figure 4.38 is divided into three sections:

- **Document Selection**
- **Processing Options**
- **Display Options**

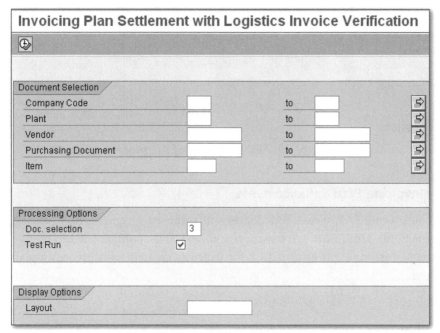

Figure 4.38 Invoicing Plan Settlement Transaction

Document Selection

In this section, the purchase order line items relevant for invoicing plan settlement can be selected based on certain criteria, such as company code, vendor, or purchase order.

Processing Options

Invoicing plan settlement can be executed in three different processing options. Based on the processing option, invoices are created with different detail levels. Table 4.2 shows the processing option and the level of invoices created.

Option	Document Selection	Explanation
1	Vendor	The system sums up all GR documents by vendor and posts one invoice. If the purchase orders have different payment terms, it creates one invoice for every vendor/payment term combination.
2	Purchase order	The system creates one invoice per purchase order.
3	Purchase order item	The system creates one invoice per purchase order line item

Table 4.2 Invoicing Plan Settlement Processing Options

Display Options

In this section, you can specify the ALV list layout of the processed invoices.

4.15.4 Invoicing Plan Enhancements

Depending on your SAP release, SAP delivers different enhancements for invoicing plan settlements. Until ECC 5.0, enhancement MRMH0001 could be used to change header fields or line item information for invoices created with invoicing plan settlement.

As of Release ECC 5.0, two new BAdIs are available:

▶ **Change Header data:** MRM_MRIS_HDAT_MODIFY

▶ **Change Line Item data:** MRM_MRIS_IDAT_MODIFY

The BAdIs work similar to the enhancement described in the "Evaluated Goods Receipt Settlement (ERS)" section.

4.16   Consignment/Pipeline Stock Settlement

The invoice settlement for pipeline materials is the same as for consignment materials. Conceptually, your organization pays for the consumption of these items. After the items are consumed, an invoice is created automatically using Transaction MRKO. This transaction can be found in the SAP menu path **SAP Menu • Logistics • Material Management • Logistic Invoice Verification • Automatic Settlement • Consignment and Pipeline Settlement.** Figure 4.39 shows the selection screen of Transaction MRKO.

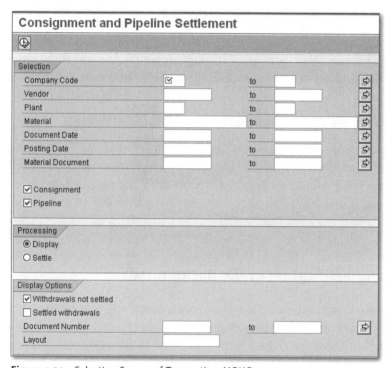

Figure 4.39   Selection Screen of Transaction MRKO

4.16.1   Consignment Stock

Consignment stock remains the property of the vendor until it's used. No financial transactions occur until its use. At the time of a goods movement, such as goods issue, a consignment stock liability account is credited with the consumed value of the stock. The invoices are created for all stock used until the last settlement date.

At that time, the unsettled consignment value is transferred from the consignment liability account to the vendor account, and the vendor is paid.

Even purchase orders are created for consignment materials; these purchases orders are usually used for replenishment of the consignment stock only and should be set to **Non-valuated GR.**

4.16.2 Pipeline Stock

Pipeline stock is a special material type used for materials that are available in unlimited quantity, such as water or electricity. These materials are then used in Bills of Materials (BOM) and can be consumed like normal materials. From an accounting perspective, the consumption and invoice settlement for pipeline stocks work the same way as consignment stock. A pipeline liability account is credited at the time of the consumption and debited at the time of the invoice settlement.

4.16.3 Enhancements for Consignment and Pipeline Settlement

Depending on your SAP release, SAP delivers different enhancements for consignment and pipeline settlement. Until ECC 5.0, enhancement RMVKON90 could be used to change header fields for invoices created with Transaction MRKO. As of Release ECC 5.0, a new BAdI MRM_MRKO_HDAT_MODIFY is available to change the header data.

4.17 Invoicing Verification in the Background

Invoicing verification in the background via Transaction MIRA is a process that can be used for mass amounts of data for which no item check is required. During invoice entry, only the document header information, invoice amount, and tax information are entered.

In a second step, the entered invoices are allocated in the background using Program RMBABG00.

This process isn't commonly used.

4.18 GR/IR Account Maintenance

In Section 4.1, the traditional three-way match invoicing process was described. As shown, SAP uses the GR/IR accounting concept for the three-way match process. In GR/IR, both the GR document and the IR document are posted against a GR/IR balance sheet clearing account. The balance in this GR/IR account represents either the goods receipted but not yet invoiced (credit balance) or goods invoiced but not yet received (debit balance). In a perfect process, the ordered quantity is delivered and invoiced, and the balance in the GR/IR account is zero. The automatic GR/IR clearing process then clears the open items in the GR/IR account (see Section 14.3 in Chapter 14).

Many times, however, you'll end up with amount discrepancies in the GR/IR account that result from one of the following:

▸ Delivery surplus

▸ Invoice surplus

Delivery surplus means that the delivered quantity is larger than the invoiced quantity. *Invoice surplus*, on the other hand, means a larger invoiced quantity than quantity delivered.

> **Note: GR/IR Difference Isn't the Result of a Price Difference**
>
> A common misunderstanding of a GR/IR difference is that this difference is the result of a net price difference in the invoice and GR. This is not correct. As illustrated in Section 4.1.1 "Accounting Entries During Three-Way Match," price differences are distributed to the purchase order line account assignments, such as GL account and cost center, as long as the delivered quantity is equal to the invoice quantity.
>
> A difference in the GR/IR account is therefore the result of a quantity difference between the GR and invoice.

What are the steps to resolve a difference in the GR/IR account? The first step is a manual analytical step that investigates whether all GR documents and invoice documents are completely posted.

If all documents are posted, the difference in the GR/IR account has to be resolved manually in a second step using Transaction MR11 (Maintain GR/IR Clearing Account). This transaction lists all quantity differences of a purchase order in the GR/IR account and posts adjusting accounting entries.

The following examples show the accounting entries for a delivery surplus and an invoice surplus.

Accounting Entries for Delivery Surplus

A purchase order is created for 10 books with a price of $50 per book. In the purchase order, the books are assigned to GL account 510100 – Books. The GR/IR account is 211200, and the vendor account number is 10000.

The vendor delivers 10 books, and a GR document is created. During the GR, the purchased items are expensed, and the GR/IR account is credited.

Document 1: GR document

Debit: 510100 – Books $500

Credit: 211200 – GR/IR Account $500

The vendor sends an invoice with the amount of $400 for 8 books. AP posts an invoice:

Document 2: IR document

Debit: 211200 – GR/IR Account $400

Credit: Vendor 10000 $400

After the invoice is posted, the credit balance in the GR/IR account is $100 because the vendor invoiced only 8 books but delivered 10 books.

After a manual analysis, it's decided that the vendor won't invoice the remaining 2 books. The delivery surplus in the GR/IR account has to be cleared manually using Transaction MR11.

Document 3: Manual GR/IR clearing

Debit: 211200 – GR/IR Account $100

Credit: 510100 – Books $100

The result of the manual GR/IR clearing is that the account assignments in the purchase order are credited with the adjustment amounts because the expense posting in the GR document was too high. The balance in the GR/IR account is zero after the adjustment.

In the next example, the accounting entries for an invoice surplus posting are illustrated.

Accounting Entries for Invoice Surplus

A purchase order is created for 10 books with a price of $50 per book. In the purchase order, the books are assigned to GL account 510100 – Books. The GR/IR account is 211200, and the vendor account number is 10000.

The vendor delivers 10 books, and a GR document is created. During the GR, the purchased items are expensed, and the GR/IR account is credited.

Document 1: GR document

Debit: 510100 – Books $500

Credit: 211200 – GR/IR Account $500

The vendor sends an invoice with the amount of $550 for 11 books. AP posts an invoice:

Document 2: IR document

Debit: 211200 – GR/IR Account $550

Credit: Vendor 10000 $550

After the invoice is posted, the debit balance in the GR/IR account is $50 because the vendor invoiced 11 books but delivered only 10 books.

After a manual analysis, it's decided that no additional GR will be entered. The invoice surplus in the GR/IR account has to be cleared manually using Transaction MR11.

Document 3: Manual GR/IR clearing

Debit: 510100 – Books $50

Credit: 211200 – GR/IR Account $50

The result of the manual GR/IR clearing is that the account assignments in the purchase order are debited with the adjustment amounts because the vendor was paid, but the expenses were never posted. The balance in the GR/IR account is zero after the adjustment.

4.18.1 GR/IR Clearing Configuration Steps

The only configuration step for the manual GR/IR clearing is the specification of the document type and number ranges in the IMG via navigation path **IMG • Materials management • Logistic Invoice Verification • Clearing Account Maintenance.** The same steps apply as previously described in Section 4.7.4 "Number Assignment."

4.18.2 Execution of Transaction MR11

Transaction MR11 can be found in the SAP menu path **SAP Menu • Logistics • Material Management • Logistic Invoice Verification • GR/IR Account Maintenance • Maintain GR/IR Clearing Account.** The selection screen of this transaction is divided into three sections:

- ▶ **Document Header Data**
- ▶ **Choose Section**
- ▶ **Processing**

Document Header Data Section

In the **Document Header Data** section shown in Figure 4.40, the document header information of the GR/IR clearing posting are specified.

Figure 4.40 MR11 – Document Header Section

Company Code
The **Company Code** field specifies in which company code the clearing documents are posted.

Posting Date
The posting date of the clearing documents is entered in the **Posting Date** field.

Reference/Document Header Text
Additional references of the posted documents can be entered in the **Reference** or **Document Header Text** fields.

Choose Section

In the **Choose** section shown in Figure 4.41 the selection options for the GR/IR differences are specified. In the first part, purchase order relevant information, such as vendor, purchase order, or plant, can be specified.

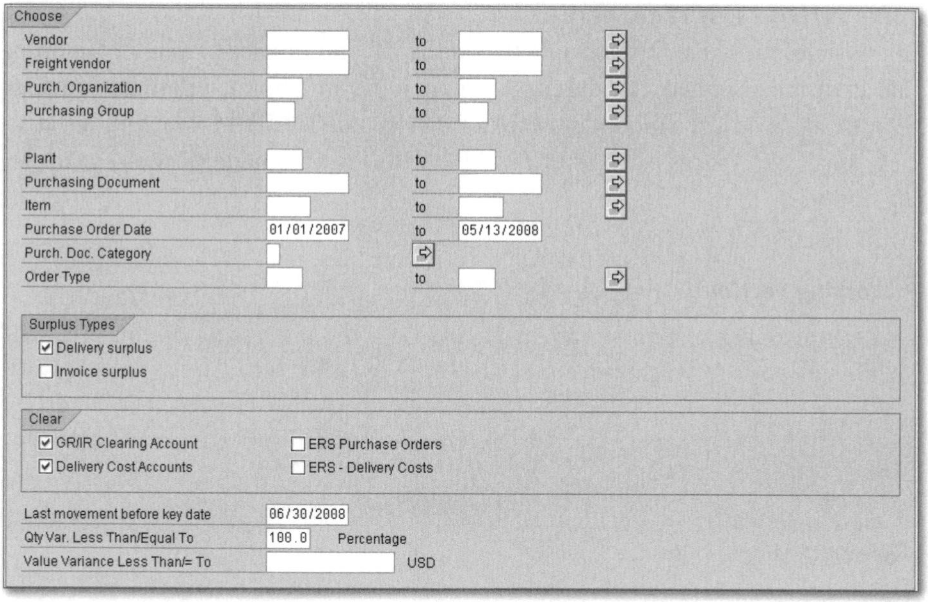

Figure 4.41 MR11 – Choose Section

Surplus Types

In this section, you specify differences due to **Delivery surplus**, **Invoice surplus**, or both.

Clear

You can clear differences in the **GR/IR Clearing Account**, **Delivery Cost Account**, or **ERS Purchase Orders**. The accounts to be cleared need to be selected here.

Last Movement Before Key Date

The **Last movement before key date** field specifies the posting date of the GR and invoice documents up to which the items are selected. This field is used to select only items that have differences over a certain time.

Qty Var. Less Than/Equal to

This field is used to specify the percentage value of the quantity variance of the delivered and invoiced quantity of a purchase order. All purchase orders with a percentage smaller than or equal to the percentage specified are selected.

Value Variance Less Than/= to

In this field, the value difference between the GR and invoice of a purchase order line item are specified. All purchase orders with an amount difference smaller than or equal to the amount specified are selected. This field is mainly used to clear small differences, such as under $10, with the automatic clearance processing option.

Processing Section

In the **Processing** section shown in Figure 4.42, the processing option of GR/IR maintenance has to be chosen.

Figure 4.42 MR11 – Processing Section

If **Automatic clearance** is selected, the differences are cleared in the background automatically. This option should only be used to clear small differences automatically. The **Prepare List** option of the other side lists all purchase orders with differences in a selection screen as shown in Figure 4.43.

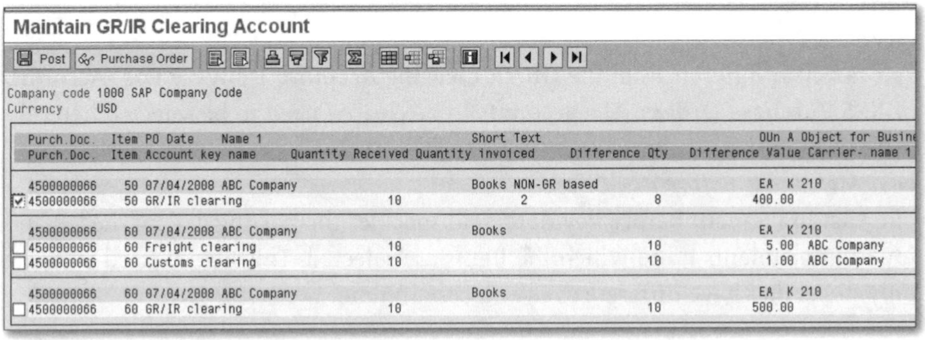

Maintain GR/IR Clearing Account

Purch.Doc.	Item	PO Date	Name 1		Short Text		OUn A Object for Busine
Purch.Doc.	Item	Account key name	Quantity Received	Quantity invoiced	Difference Qty	Difference Value Carrier- name 1	
4500000066	50	07/04/2008 ABC Company			Books NON-GR based		EA K 210
☑ 4500000066	50	GR/IR clearing	10		2	8	400.00
4500000066	60	07/04/2008 ABC Company			Books		EA K 210
☐ 4500000066	60	Freight clearing	10			10	5.00 ABC Company
☐ 4500000066	60	Customs clearing	10			10	1.00 ABC Company
4500000066	60	07/04/2008 ABC Company			Books		EA K 210
☐ 4500000066	60	GR/IR clearing	10			10	500.00

Company code 1000 SAP Company Code
Currency   USD

Figure 4.43 MR11 – GR/IR Clearing Screen

To manually clear the differences, select the items, and click **Post**. The system calculates the adjustment values and creates one financial document for all items selected.

4.18.3 Transaction MR11SHOW

To display and cancel previously posted clearing documents with Transaction MR11, use Transaction MR11SHOW. This transaction can be found in the SAP menu path **SAP Menu • Logistics • Material Management • Logistic Invoice Verification • GR/IR Account Maintenance • Display/Cancel Account Maintenance Documents.**

4.19 Invoice Overview

The *Invoice Overview* function with Transaction MIR6 has a dual function that is often not used to its full potential:

▶ It can be used as a display transactions for posted documents.

▶ It can be used as a worklist to display not fully posted transactions and continue processing within this worklist.

To illustrate the second option, Figure 4.44 shows the selection screen of Transaction MIR6.

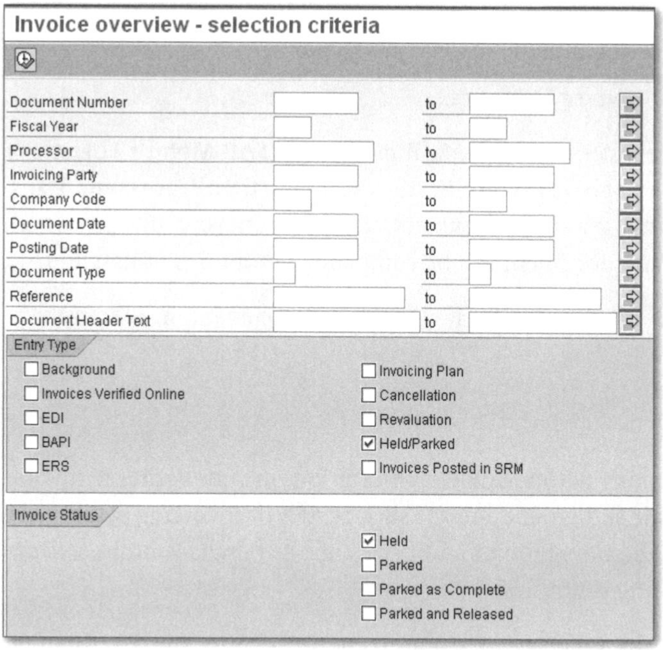

Figure 4.44 Selection Screen of Transaction MIR6

All held invoices are selected by choosing the **Entry Type Held/Parked** and the **Invoice Status Held**. The result is a worklist of all held invoice documents as shown in Figure 4.45.

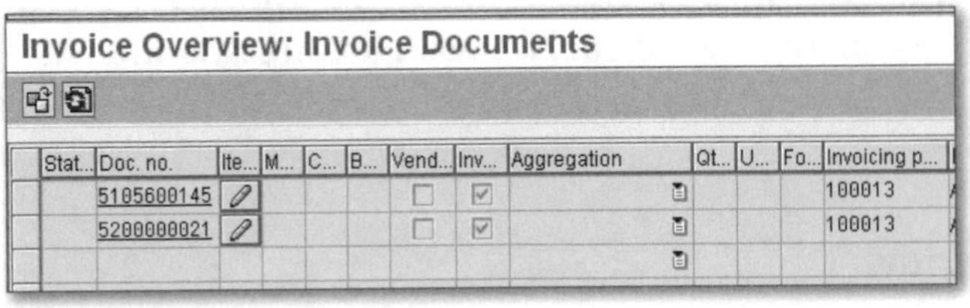

Figure 4.45 Worklist of Held Documents

Within this worklist, the documents can be further processed by clicking the **Change Items** button next to the document number. The systems jumps to Transaction MIR4, and the invoice document can be completed.

4.20 Invoice Display

Within Invoice Verification, two transactions are available to display posted documents:

▶ **MIR4:** Display Invoice Document

▶ **MIR5:** Display List of Invoice Documents

Both transactions can be accessed via the SAP menu path **SAP Menu • Logistics • Material Management • Logistic Invoice Verification • Further Processing.** Transaction MIR4 allows displaying a single document. If a document isn't fully processed, such as held or parked, the document can be completed within this transaction.

Transaction MIR5, on the other hand, displays the selected documents in a list format.

4.21 Summary

In this chapter, all functions within Invoice Verification, including online invoice entry as well as automatic settlement options such as ERS or invoicing plans, were described. In addition, the integration and importance of purchase order settings were illustrated on posting examples.

This chapter concludes the invoice entry options within AP. In the next chapter, the outgoing payment options are described.

Within Accounts Payable (AP), payments can be processed through different processes and different payment media. Based on the different processes, different payment methods, terms, supplements, or grouping need to be defined.

5 Outgoing Payment Processing

In this chapter, we'll discuss the different terms and configuration steps that apply to all payments within AP. Independent of the payment medium, such as check, wire, or ACH payment, the same payment principles apply.

The following payment process and payment medium terms are described in this chapter:

► Payment method

► Payment method supplement

► Payment term

► Payment grouping

► Payment block reason

5.1 Payment Method

The *payment method* describes the procedure by which payments are made to a vendor, such as check, bank transfer, bill of exchange, or wire transfer. The payment method is defined as a one-character, alphanumeric field value. Table 5.1 shows typical examples of payment methods.

The payment methods are defined in two steps:

1. All of the specifications that are required for each payment method in each country need to be defined. This is necessary for the payment methods used by your organization in each country. If you have company codes in Germany,

France, and the United States, for example, you define the payment method for each country.

2. The payment methods for each company code are defined, which includes the use of the payment method.

Payment Method	Description
C	Check Payment
A	ACH Payment
S	Separate Check
W	Wire transfer
P	Personnel Check
B	Bill of Exchange

Table 5.1 Example of Payment Methods

5.1.1 Country-Specific Definitions for the Payment Method

The country-specific details for the payment method can be configured in the IMG via navigation path **IMG • Financial Accounting • Accounts Receivable and Accounts Payables • Business Transactions • Automatic Outgoing Payments • Payment Method/Bank Selection for Payment Program • Set up Payment Methods per Country for Payment Transactions**. The configuration screen is divided into four sections:

► **Payment Method for**

► **Payment method classification**

► **Required master record specifications and Posting details**

► **Payment medium**

Payment Method for

In the **Payment Method for** section shown in Figure 5.1, the payment method is defined with a description. The payment method has to be classified to be used for **Outgoing payments** or **Incoming payments**. The outgoing payments method is used for AP-related payments. For Accounts Receivable (AR) transactions, the payment methods are defined as incoming payment methods.

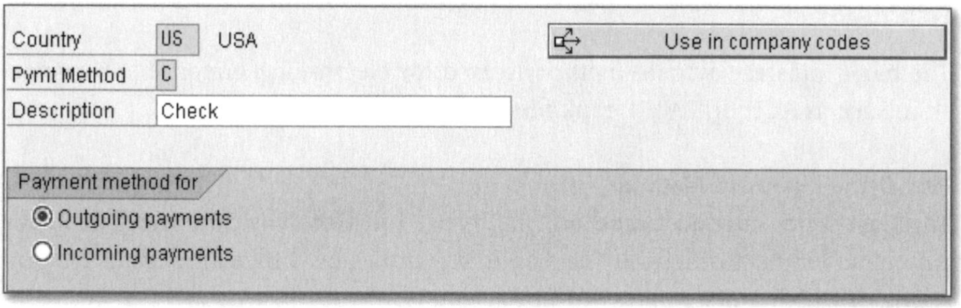

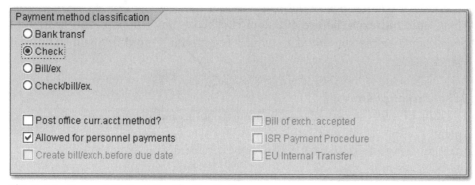

Figure 5.1 Payment Method For Section

Payment Method Classification

In the **Payment Method Classification** section shown in Figure 5.2, the payment method is assigned to a specific payment method type.

Figure 5.2 Payment Method Classification Section

Payment Types

Four different outgoing payment method types are available.

▶ Bank transfers

▶ Check

▶ Bill of Exchange

▶ Check/Bill of Exchange

The most commonly used payment types are bank transfers and payments by check. Bill of exchange (**Bill/ex**) or the Check/Bill of Exchange (**Check/bill/ex.**) payment types are mainly used in European countries such as Spain, Italy, and France.

The bank transfer payment method is used for electronic payment file transmission, such as ACH or SWIFT bank file transfers.

Post Office Curr.Acct Method?

The **Post office curr.acct method?** flag is used in Germany and Switzerland for payments via post offices. If the flag is set, only post office bank branches are selected, which are set up as current accounts. The bank accounts can be maintained with Transaction FI02.

Allowed for Personnel Payments

If the **Allowed for personnel payments** flag is set, the payment method can be used within SAP HR Payroll for payment issuance.

Create Bill/Exchange Before Due Date

The **Create bill/exch. before due date** checkbox allows the creation of the bill of exchange before the due date, which is commonly used in Spain, Italy, and France.

Bill of Exchange Accepted

The **Bill of exch. accepted** flag is used in some European countries, such as Spain.

ISR Payment Procedure

The **ISR Payment Procedure** flag indicates that this payment method uses the payment order procedure used by the Swiss Postal Service for companies located in Switzerland. The vendor needs to be assigned to an ISR number in the Payment Transactions screen.

EU Internal Transfer

The **EU Internal Transfer** flag is used for payments within the member countries of the European Union (EU).

Required Master Record Specifications/Posting Details

In the **Required master record specifications** section shown in Figure 5.3, you specify which vendor master data values are checked during the payment issuance for this payment method

Required master record specifications	Posting details	
☑ Street,P.O.box or P.O.box pst code	Document type for payment	ZP
☐ Bank details	Clearing document type	ZV
☐ SWIFT Code and IBAN	Sp.G/L ind.b/ex. / b/ex.pmnt req.	
☐ Collection authorization	☐ Payment order only	

Figure 5.3 Required Master Record Specifications/Posting Details Section

Street, P.O.box or P.O box pst code
If this flag is set, the system validates whether the address of the vendor or alternative payee is complete. This ensures that no payments are issued to vendors with incomplete addresses, which is important for payments via checks. If the address is incomplete, an error message is issued during the payment run.

Bank Details
If this flag is set, the system validates whether the bank information is completely entered in the vendor master data in the Payment Transaction tab. This ensures that no payments are issued to vendors with incomplete bank information, which is necessary for payments via bank transfers. If the bank details are incomplete, an error message is issued during the payment run.

SWIFT Code and IBAN
If you set this flag, then the payment method is only used if both the SWIFT code and the IBAN of the account number have been maintained for the business partner's bank details. This check is particularly useful for intra-European payment transactions. The SWIFT code needs to be maintained in the bank details with Transactions FI02 and FI12.

Collection Authorization
Only payments are issued via bank transfers if the **Collection authorization** flag is maintained in the bank details of the vendor master data. This is helpful if you want to have the bank information validated before a payment is issued.

Document Type for Payment
Any payment documents with this payment method are created with this document type during the payment issuance.

Clearing Document Type
The **Clearing document type** specifies which document type the payment program uses to post the clearing document that is created with cross-company code payments.

Payment Order Only
If the **Payment order only** flag is set, the payment program does not issue a payment document, and the invoices are not cleared. Instead, a payment order is generated, which contains the information used to clear the items at a later date. The payment is posted when it appears on the bank statement, and the relevant open items are selected when the payment order is entered. The paid items remain blocked for other clearing transactions and further payment runs until the payment has been posted.

Payment Medium

In the **Payment medium** section shown in Figure 5.4, the payment medium tool is specified that will be used to issue the payments to the vendors. SAP uses the generic term *payment medium* for all types of payment output during the payment run, such as checks, remittance advices, or bank transfer files.

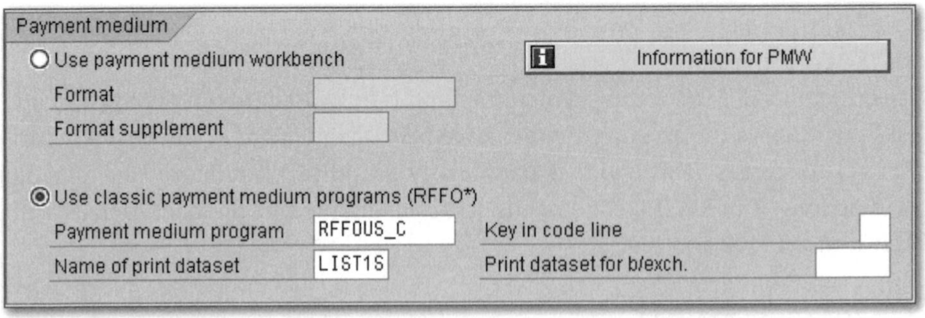

Figure 5.4 Payment Medium Section

Use Payment Medium Workbench

The Payment Medium Workbench (PMW) was introduced in Release 4.6. PMW is a generic payment medium program for all payment medium formats for which different variants are defined in configuration. The configuration steps for ACH transfer with PMW are described in Chapter 9.

Use Classic Payment Medium Programs

Prior to Release 4.6, SAP delivered payment programs specific to the payment format, that is, RFFOUS_C - Check printing program or RFFOM100 – International Bank transfers. These programs had to be executed after the payment run to create the payment details in the correct payment formats.

SAP delivers a large variety of predefined country-specific electronic payment formats for both the classic payment medium programs and PMW. The available payment formats are listed in OSS Note 101440 for the classic payment medium programs and in OSS Note 395679 for the PMW.

5.1.2 Company Code Specific Definitions for the Payment Method

The company code specific details for the payment method can be configured in the IMG via navigation path **IMG • Financial Accounting • Accounts Receivable and Accounts Payables • Business Transactions • Automatic Outgoing Payments • Payment Method/Bank Selection for Payment Program • Set up Payment Methods per Company Code for Payment Transactions.** The configuration screen is divided into four sections:

▶ **Amount limits/Grouping of items**

▶ **Foreign payments/Bank selection control**

▶ **Forms**

▶ **Payment advice note control**

Amount Limits/Grouping of Items

In the **Amount limits** section shown in Figure 5.5, the amount limits are specified for this payment method. In the **Grouping of items** section, you specify how open items are grouped during the payment run.

Amount limits			Grouping of items	
Minimum amount	1.00	EUR	☐ Single payment for marked item	
Maximum amount	500,000.00	EUR	☐ Payment per due day	
Distribution amnt		EUR		

Figure 5.5 Amount Limits/Grouping of Items Section

Minimum Amount

Minimum amount defines the lower amount limit for which payments are issued. If the payment method is explicitly assigned to the invoice, which means you entered the payment method in the invoice, the lower amount limit does not apply.

Maximum Amount

Maximum amount defines the upper amount limit for which payments are issued. If the payment method is explicitly assigned to the invoice, which means you entered the payment method in the invoice, the upper amount limit does not apply.

Distribution Amount

Payments exceeding the **Distribution amnt** are analyzed to see if it's possible to split them into several payments totaling a maximum of this amount. The payment method check is made, unlike the minimum or maximum amount, independently of the payment method specification in the invoice or credit memo. This field is useful if an upper amount limit exists for a specific payment method. For example, in Europe, the upper amount limit for EU internal bank transfers is 12,500 EUR.

Single Payment for Marked Item

If the **Single payment for marked item** flag is set, all items, where the payment method is entered explicitly in the invoice or credit memo, are paid individually. If the payment program selects the payment method, the items are grouped together. You should set this flag for check payments so that if a single check is required, the payment method is then entered directly into the invoice.

Payment Per Due Day

The **Payment per due day** flag specifies that only items due on the same day will be paid with a single payment. This might be useful if the due date has to be submitted to the bank for every payment because the due date is stored in the header record of the payment.

Foreign Payments/Bank Selection Control Section

In the **Foreign payments/foreign currency payments** section shown in Figure 5.6, you specify whether foreign payments are allowed for this payment method. The **Bank selection control** section allows you to optimize the bank selection during the payment run.

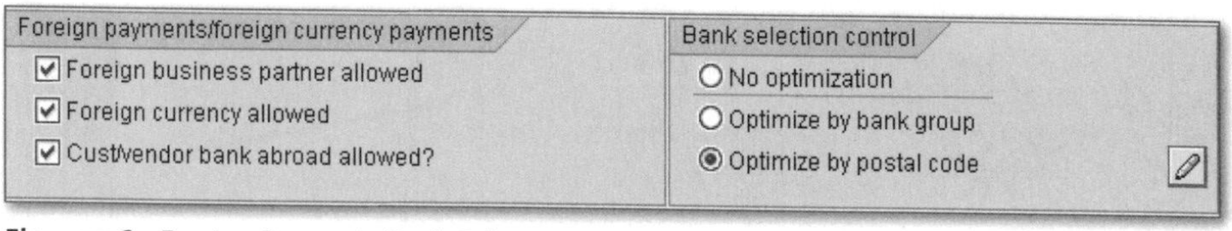

Figure 5.6 Foreign Payments/Bank Selection Control Section

Foreign Business Partner Allowed

If you need to issue payments to vendors abroad with this payment method, you need to select the **Foreign business partner allowed** flag. A vendor is classified as foreign if the country in the vendor master data address screen is different from the country of your company code.

Foreign Currency Allowed

If you select the **Foreign currency allowed** flag, payments can be submitted in a foreign currency for this payment method. The foreign currencies allowed for this payment method are maintained for the payment methods in the country. If no permitted foreign currency has been defined there, every currency is permitted.

Cust/Vendor Bank Abroad Allowed?

If the **Cust/vendor bank abroad allowed?** flag is set, foreign banks can be selected from the vendor master data for payments.

Bank Selection Control

With the help of the **Bank selection control** section, your company can group payments by bank. You'll be able to group payments by groups of banks or regionally by postal code, for example, if you have one house bank on the East Coast and another on the West Coast. By selecting the **Optimize by postal code** option, you can group the payments by postal code as shown in Figure 5.7.

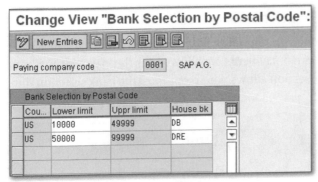

Figure 5.7 Bank Selection by Postal Code

By selecting the **Optimize by bank group** option, you can group the payments by bank. The system checks whether your company's bank group belongs to the same bank group as your vendor's bank group. In this case, the payments are grouped together. In bank master data, you determine the bank group to which a bank belongs (Transaction FI02).

Forms

The **Forms** section shown in Figure 5.8 specifies which output forms are created during the payment medium execution. In addition, the forms can be sorted during printing (Correspondence) and the information within the form can be sorted as well (Line items). For specific payment medium formation, the company address information needs to be maintained.

Forms		
Form for the Payment Medium	SAPscript	F110_PRENUM_CHCK
Next form	SAPscript	
	Form	

Drawer on the form	Sorting of the	
Testname 1	Correspondence	
Testname 2	Line items	
D-12345 Testort		

Figure 5.8 Forms Section

Form for the Payment Medium

Form for the Payment Medium specifies which form is used during the payment medium execution. Forms are usually used for payments by check or bill of exchange. The forms can be created in two formats, SAPscript and PDF (Adobe). Table 5.2 shows a list of sample forms provided by SAP.

Form	Description	Format
F110_PRENUM_CHCK	Check with check number	SAPscript
F110_D_SCHECK_A4	Check in German A4 format	SAPscript
F110_US_AVIS	Payment advice	SAPscript
F110_AVIS_INT	Payment advice note	PDF
FI_PAYM_DE_CHECK	Check with check number	PDF

Table 5.2 List of SAP sample forms

All sample SAPscripts can be found in Transaction SE71 and Transaction SFP for Adobe forms.

Next Form

If a payment method requires a second form to the payment medium form, for example, for Bill of Exchange payments, a second form is specified in the **Next form** field.

Drawer on the Form

In these four fields, you need to specify the address information for your company, which is then transferred to the payment medium. Which information is required depends on the forms and payment medium formats. For ACH payments, for example, the first line should contain your company name, which is then transferred to the bank transfer file.

Sorting of the Correspondence

In this field, you can specify how the output of your correspondence for your payments is sorted by specifying a sort variant. For example, you can define that your checks are sorted by vendor name, postal code, or payment method supplement. The correspondence sort variant can be configured in the IMG via navigation path **IMG • Financial Accounting • Accounts Receivable and Accounts Payables •**

Business Transactions • Automatic Outgoing Payments • Payment Media • Sort Variants • Payment Media: Define Sort Variants.

Sorting of the Line Items

In this field, you can specify how the line items on your correspondence are sorted by specifying a line item sort variant. For example, you can define that line items on your payment advice or checks are sorted by document date or reference number. The line item sort variant can be configured in the IMG via navigation path **IMG • Financial Accounting • Accounts Receivable and Accounts Payables • Business Transactions • Automatic Outgoing Payments • Payment Media • Sort Variants • Payment Media: Define Sort Variants for Line Items.**

Payment Advice Note Control

The **Payment advice note control** section shown in Figure 5.9 defines, how the payment medium should handle note to payee lines and payment advices for your forms.

Note to Payee Lines

A *note to payee* refers to additional information submitted to your vendor, so payments can be identified by invoice date or invoice number.

For check payments, every invoice counts as two lines on a check stub because a second line can be printed, if an invoice is entered with additional external information in the text field of the invoice or credit memo. External text information must begin with "*". The asterisk is removed during printing.

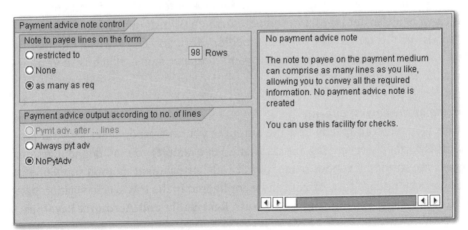

Figure 5.9 Payment Advice Control Section

For example, a check payment process is used with multiple invoices. On your check stub, you have enough space for 20 lines. If a payment is created for more than 20 lines, you have multiple options:

▶ Overflow checks should be created and marked as VOIDED.

▶ A payment advice should be created with all additional lines.

▶ A separate check should be created every 20 lines, which means that a maximum of 10 invoices or credit memos are paid with the same check.

Table 5.3 lists all possible payment advice note options with an explanation of the effect as well as examples. The note to payee lines is restricted to 20 lines.

Note to Payee Lines on the Form	Payment Advice Output According to No. of Lines	Explanation
Restricted to 20 lines	Pymnt adv. after 20 lines	A separate payment advice is created if the number of lines exceeds the number of lines specified. **Example:** A separate payment advice is created for check payments if more than 20 lines are required on the check stub. The payment advice can be printed on a different printer than the checks.
Restricted to 20 lines	Always pyt adv	A separate payment advice is always created independently from the number of note to payee lines.
Restricted to 20 lines	No Pyt Adv. Pymnt mthd valid to 20 lines	No payment advice note created. Only a restricted number of lines is allowed for the note to payee on the payment medium. The payment program chooses another payment method if more space is required for the note to payee information.
Restricted to 20 lines	No Pyt Adv. Distribute items, 20 lines per payment	No payment advice note is created. Only a restricted number of lines is provided for the note to payee on the payment medium. The payment program splits the open items over several payments. **Example**: A separate payment and check will be created every 20 lines. This may be desired of you don't want to deal with overflow checks or payment advices.

Table 5.3 Payment Advice Note Control Options

Note to Payee Lines on the Form	Payment Advice Output According to No. of Lines	Explanation
None	Always pyt adv	There is no note to payee information on the payment medium. A payment advice is always created. **Example**: A payment advice will always be printed for payments via bank transfer, such as ACH payments
As many as required	Always pyt adv	The note to payee on the payment medium can comprise as many lines as necessary. In addition, a payment advice note is created.
As many as required	No Pyt Adv.	The note to payee on the payment medium can comprise as many lines as necessary. No payment advice note is created. **Example**: Overflow checks are created if 20 lines are exceeded. The overflow checks are VOIDED.

Table 5.3 Payment Advice Note Control Options (Cont.)

5.2 Payment Method Supplements

Payment method supplements allow you to classify invoices or credit memos that have special handling requirements, such as in-house checks, attachments, or foreign country checks.

This supplement is then used to group payments. Payments are separated according to payment method supplements and can be printed separately by these supplements or sorted by them for printing. The payment method supplement can also be defaulted in the vendor master data in the company code specific Payment transaction tab. In this case, it's defaulted during document entry and can be overwritten there.

To allow payment method supplements, the payment method supplement needs to be activated for your company code in the IMG via navigation path **IMG • Financial Accounting • Accounts Receivable and Accounts Payables • Business Transactions • Automatic Outgoing Payments • Payment Method/Bank Selection for Payment Program • Set up All Company Codes for Payment Transactions.**

As shown in Figure 5.10, set the **Pyt meth suppl.** flag in the **Control data** section to activate payment method supplement.

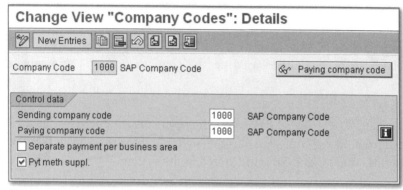

Figure 5.10 Activation of Payment Method Supplement

In the second step, the different payment method supplement types have to be defined in the in the IMG via navigation path **IMG • Financial Accounting • Accounts Receivable and Accounts Payables • Business Transactions • Automatic Outgoing Payments • Payment Method/Bank Selection for Payment Program • Define Payment Method Supplement.**

Figure 5.11 shows examples of typical payment method supplements for check payments.

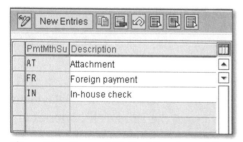

Figure 5.11 Payment Method Supplement Examples

5.3 Payment Terms

Payment terms define rules with which the system can determine the required terms of payment automatically. The rules are stored under a four-character key.

5.3.1 Baseline Date and Net Due Date

Within the payment term context, SAP uses the terms *baseline date* and *net due date*. The following overview lists the different dates and their definitions:

▶ **Baseline date**
The baseline date is the base date from which the payment terms apply. The baseline date can be defaulted based on the configuration of the payment term.

▶ **Net due date**
The net due date is a calculated date when the payments are due. The due date is calculated from the baseline date plus the highest number of days within the payment terms. The net due date isn't stored in the system.

5.3.2 Defaulting of Payment Term Values

The payment terms can be defaulted automatically during invoice or credit memo entry, based on values in the vendor master data. However, the behavior is different for invoices, credit memos, or invoices in LIV.

Invoice Entry in Accounts Payable

If an invoice is entered in AP using transactions such as FB60, FV60, or F-43, the payment terms are copied from the **Payment terms** field in the **Payment transaction** tab of the company code data view of the vendor. If no payment terms are entered, the payment terms have to be entered manually.

Credit Memo Entry in Accounts Payable

If a credit memo is entered in AP using transaction such as FB65, FV65, or F-41, the payment terms are copied from the **Credit memo term** field in the **Payment transaction** tab of the company code data view of the vendor. If no terms are entered, "*" can be entered in the **Payment term** field during credit memo entry, and the invoice payment term will be defaulted.

Invoice Entry in LIV

Within the purchasing view of the vendor master data, the field **Terms of Payment** is used for purchasing. During the creation of a purchase order, the payment term value in the purchasing view is copied into the purchase order, which can be changed then directly in the purchase order, if different payment terms apply for a specific purchase order.

During the invoice entry then in LIV using Transaction MIRO or MIR7, the payment terms from the purchase order are copied into the invoice.

5.3.3 Payment Term Configuration

The payment terms can be configured under the navigation path **IMG • Financial Accounting • Accounts Receivable and Payable • Business Transactions • Incoming Invoices/Credit Memos • Maintain Terms of Payment.**

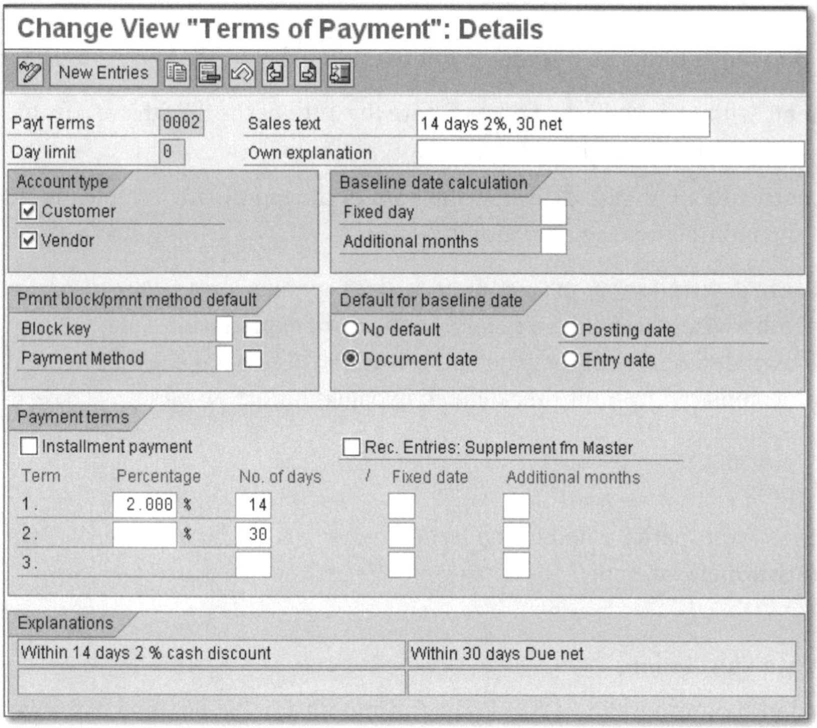

Figure 5.12 Payment Term Configuration Screen

SAP delivers a large number of sample payment terms. You can either use these terms as delivered or configure your own terms. The payment term configuration screen shown in Figure 5.12 is divided into different sections:

- ▸ Payment terms, Day limit, and description
- ▸ Account type
- ▸ Baseline date calculation
- ▸ Payment block/payment method default
- ▸ Default for baseline date
- ▸ Payment terms

Payment Terms, Day Limit, and Description

The payment term is a four-character key. The payment term can also be day limited, which means you can define the same payment term key with different day limits.

The following terms of payment require you to enter a day limit:

- ▸ Documents with an invoice date on or before the 15th of the month are payable on the last day of the next month.
- ▸ Documents with an invoice date after the 15th of the month are payable on the 15th of the month after the next month.

The **Sales text** description is only required if the payment term is also used for customers; otherwise, this field isn't filled. In the **Own explanation** field, you can enter your own description of the payment terms. In this case, the SAP-generated explanation is replaced by your user-defined explanation.

Account Type

In this section, you specify whether the term of payment can be used in AP (**Vendor**), AR (**Customer**), or both.

Baseline Date Calculation

In this section, you can define a fixed day and month for the baseline date. For example, the baseline date is always on the last day of a month by entering the value **31** into the **Fixed day** field. By entering a value into the **Additional months** field, the system adds additional calendar months to the baseline date. For example, if you want to have the baseline date defined as the 15th of next month, enter the value "15" in the **Fixed day** field and the value "1" in the **Additional months** field.

Default Values for Payment Block and Payment Method

This section allows you to default a payment block and payment method for a payment term. By selecting the checkbox next to the payment block or payment term, the payment block and payment method values are also transferred into the document, if the payment terms are changed directly in the document.

Default for Baseline Date

If the **Fixed day** field and **Additional months** field are not filled, the baseline date is defaulted based on the posting date, document date, or entry date, or it isn't defaulted at all. The most common default value is the document date, which usually represents the invoice date.

Payment Terms

In the **Payment terms** section, up to three different terms can be defined. You can build simple term such as pay immediately up to terms with discounts and different due dates. Use the SAP-delivered sample payment terms as a reference.

If the **Installment payment** flag is set, the invoiced amount will be broken down into partial amounts with different due dates, based on installment terms. The installment payment terms are configured under the navigation path **IMG • Financial Accounting • Accounts Receivable and Payable • Business Transactions • Incoming Invoices/Credit Memos • Define Terms of Payment for Installment Payments**. The total percentage of the installments has to be 100%.

5.4 Payment Grouping

Payment grouping keys allow paying items with the same values in the key fields together. The grouping key can have up to three fields from the database Tables BSIK (vendors). The grouping key is entered in the vendor master data in the **Pay-**

ment transaction screen into the field **Key for Payment Grouping.** The payment groups are configured under the navigation path IMG • Financial Accounting • **Accounts Receivable and Accounts Payables** • **Business Transactions** • **Automatic Outgoing Payments** • **Payment Method/Bank Selection for Payment Program** • **Define Payment Groupings.** For example, you could group payments for invoices with the same document type into single payments.

5.5 Payment Block Reasons

Using *payment blocking reasons*, you can differentiate why invoices are to be blocked for payment. The defined payment block key is used to block an open item or a vendor account for payment transactions. During the automatic payment transactions, the block key affects open items if it's, stored in the vendor master data in the payment transaction tab or entered directly in the invoice or credit memo during data entry.

Some of the payment block reasons in SAP have special meanings and should only be used for these purposes:

▶ If the "*" payment block key is entered in the vendor master data, none of the items in this account are included in the automatic payment process.

▶ If the "+" payment block key is entered in the vendor master data, only those items for which a payment method is explicitly defined are included in the automatic payment process.

▶ The **"A"** block key is generally set automatically when a down payment is entered. For this reason, you should neither delete the "A" nor use it for other purposes.

The payment block reasons are configured under the navigation path IMG • Financial Accounting • **Accounts Receivable and Accounts Payables** • **Business Transactions** • **Outgoing Payments** • **Outgoing Payment Global Settings** • **Payment Block Reasons** • **Define Payment Block Reasons.** Figure 5.13 lists sample payment block reasons.

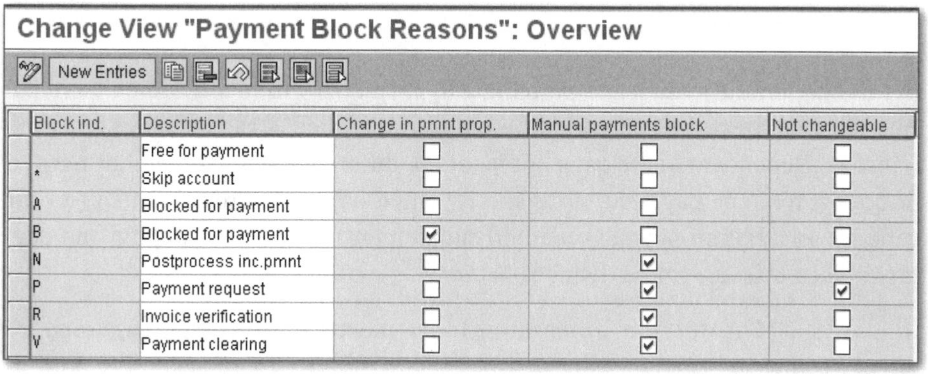

Block ind.	Description	Change in pmnt prop.	Manual payments block	Not changeable
	Free for payment	☐	☐	☐
*	Skip account	☐	☐	☐
A	Blocked for payment	☐	☐	☐
B	Blocked for payment	☑	☐	☐
N	Postprocess inc.pmnt	☐	☑	☐
P	Payment request	☐	☑	☑
R	Invoice verification	☐	☑	☐
V	Payment clearing	☐	☑	☐

Change View "Payment Block Reasons": Overview

New Entries

Figure 5.13 Payment Block Reasons

In the payment block configuration, additional flags can be set for each payment block.

Indicator: Change in Payment Proposal Permitted

This flag specifies whether a change of the payment block key is allowed in the payment proposal of the automatic payment program. If the flag isn't set, the block reason can neither be set nor deleted when a payment proposal is processed.

Indicator: Blocked for Manual Payments

This flag specifies whether documents with this payment block key can be cleared manually during an incoming invoice processing. Vendor master data with this payment block key don't have any effect on the manual entry of incoming invoices, only documents such as invoices or credit memos.

Payment Blocked Not Changeable

This flag specifies that the payment block can't be changed with dialog transactions, such as change document using Transaction FB02. A nonmodifiable payment block is relevant for the payment release workflow. In this case, a blocked item must be released for payment within the workflow. After the payment release, the payment block is automatically reset in the background. Only one payment block for the payment release workflow can be designated as not modifiable.

5.6   Summary

In this Chapter the main terms pertaining to payments within SAP were described. Payments can be processed with different payment media, such as checks or bank transfers. Dependent of the payment medium, different payment methods need to be configured. The payment terms specify when payments are submitted to your vendors. In addition payment method supplements, payment grouping and payment block reasons can be defined.

In the next Chapter the different manual payment processing options are discussed.

Within Accounts Payable (AP), payments can be processed manually or automatically via the automatic payment program. This chapter describes the manual payment transactions.

6 Manual Payment Processing

In this chapter, we'll discuss the different transactions for manual outgoing payments. Most of the payments are usually processed using the automatic payment program, which is covered in Chapter 7. The manual payment transactions are used on an exception basis. Reasons for using these transactions are listed here:

▶ Creating ad-hoc payments via check

▶ Partial payment processing

▶ Debit memo postings

▶ Vendor refunding (incoming payment)

The following manual payment transactions are described in this chapter:

▶ **F-53:** Post Outgoing Payments

▶ **F-58:** Post Outgoing Payments + Print Forms

▶ **F-52:** Post Incoming Payments

6.1 Post Outgoing Payments

Manual outgoing payments can be created with Transaction F-53 or using the navigation path **SAP Menu • Accounting • Financial Accounting • Accounts Payable • Document Entry • Outgoing Payment • Post**. This transaction can be used to record vendor payments manually. For example, a wire transfer payment is created and posted in your system. In a subsequent step, the vendor payment is posted manually.

Within Transaction F-53, the payments are posted in a two-step process:

1. Enter header data.

2. Select open items, and post the payment.

6.1.1 Header Data

The Header data screen is divided into three sections:

▶ **Document Header** section

▶ **Bank data** section

▶ **Open item selection** section

Document Header Section

The **Document Header** section shown in Figure 6.1 contains the payment header details information such document type, document date, posting date, reference information, and company code information.

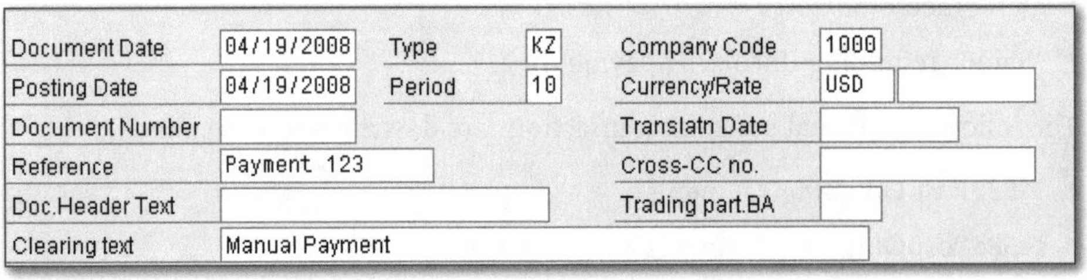

Document Date	04/19/2008	Type	KZ	Company Code	1000
Posting Date	04/19/2008	Period	10	Currency/Rate	USD
Document Number				Translatn Date	
Reference	Payment 123			Cross-CC no.	
Doc.Header Text				Trading part.BA	
Clearing text	Manual Payment				

Figure 6.1 Document Header Section

Clearing Text
In the **Clearing text** field, a description can be specified, which is then copied automatically into the text field of all cleared line items.

Bank Data Section

The **Bank data** section shown in Figure 6.2 contains the account information, amounts, and account assignments of the payment posting.

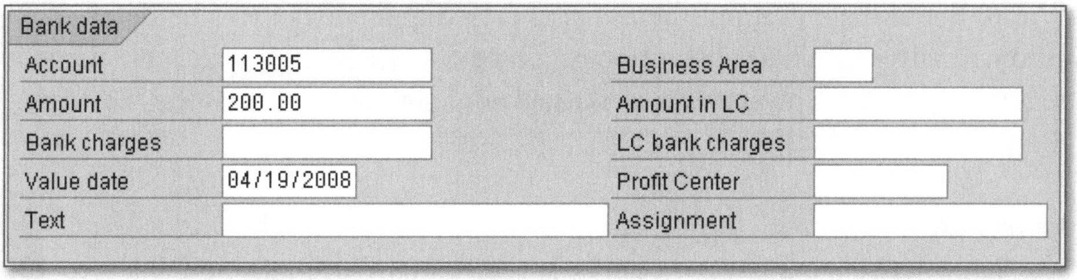

Figure 6.2 Bank Data Section

Account

The **Account** field contains the GL account of the outgoing payment. Usually, this GL account is a cash or bank account within your chart of accounts.

Amount

The **Amount** field contains the amount value of the payment.

Bank Charges

If additional bank charges apply for this payment, the **Bank charges** field will contain the bank charge amount. The bank charges are posted to a separate bank charge account. The charges are entered as positive amounts, and the system automatically determines the correct postings key.

This account can be configured in the IMG via navigation path **IMG • Financial Accounting • Accounts Receivable and Accounts Payables • Business Transactions • Outgoing Payments • Outgoing Payments Global Settings • Define Accounts for Bank Charges (Vendors)** or via Transaction OBXK. In this configuration step, the posting keys and the GL account for the bank charges must be defined.

If the bank charge account is defined as a cost element in the Controlling module (CO), the bank charge must be posted to a CO account assignment as well. A CO account assignment can be a cost center, internal order, or WBS element. Because the CO assignment can't be entered manually, it has to be determined automatically during payment processing. This assignment can be maintained in the IMG via navigation path **IMG • Controlling • Cost Center Accounting • Actual Postings • Manual Actual Postings • Edit Automatic Account Assignment** or by executing Transaction OKB9. Within Transaction OKB9, a default cost center or internal order has to be entered for the bank charge account.

Within the SAP application, the CO account assignment can also be determined automatically with a CO substitution or can be directly entered in the cost element as a default value. However, the described configuration setting is the most common method.

Value Date
The **Value date** of your payment can be specified in this field, if your bank accounts require a value date.

Text/Assignment
Additional payment information can be entered in the **Text** and **Assignment** fields as required.

Open Item Selection Section

In the **Open item selection** section shown in Figure 6.3, all information to preselect the vendor open items are entered.

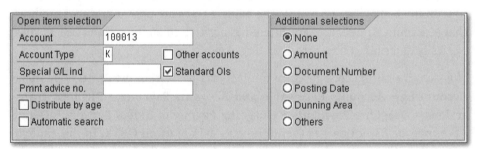

Figure 6.3 Open Item Selection Section

Account/Account Type
The **Account** field contains the account from which the open items are selected. Depending on the **Account type** field value, the **Account** field contains different account values. Table 6.1 shows the **Account type/Account** combinations.

Account Type	Account
K	Vendor
D	Customer
S	GL account

Table 6.1 Account Type/Account Combinations

Within Transaction F-53, the account type K for vendor accounts is defaulted and a vendor number needs to be entered in the account field.

Other Accounts

If the **Other accounts** checkbox is selected, a pop-up screen appears that allows you to enter additional vendor accounts. This function may be helpful if you have several vendor accounts for the same vendor and need to search for open items in all these vendor accounts.

Special G/L Indicator

The **Special G/L ind** field allows the selection of open items, which are posted with a special G/L indicator, such as guarantees or retention. In this case, you have to enter the special G/L indicator key.

Standard OIs

If the **Standard OIs** checkbox is selected, all regular vendor open items, which are not posted with a special G/L indicator, are selected.

Distribute by Age

If the open items should be selected by age or days in arrears, the **Distribute by age** flag needs to be selected. The selection of items to be cleared is carried out automatically, with the items with the most days in arrears being selected first. If there are open items with the same number of days in arrears, then credit postings have priority over debit postings. If the amount can't be distributed completely, then a posting on account of the remaining amount is created.

Automatic Search Indicator

If this flag is set, the system tries to find a combination of open items whose total amount corresponds with the amount entered in the bank data amount field. If the amount is found, then the items are selected. If only a near amount is found, then a window appears in which you can accept or reject the proposal.

Additional Selections

Additional selections allows you to search the vendor open items by other selection criteria, such as posting date or document number. You can configure the criteria, which appear in the **Additional selections** screen, in the IMG via navigation path **IMG • Financial Accounting • Accounts Receivable and Accounts Payables**

• **Business Transactions** • **Outgoing Payments** • **Manual Outgoing Payments** •
Make Settings for Processing Open Items • **Choose Selection Fields.**

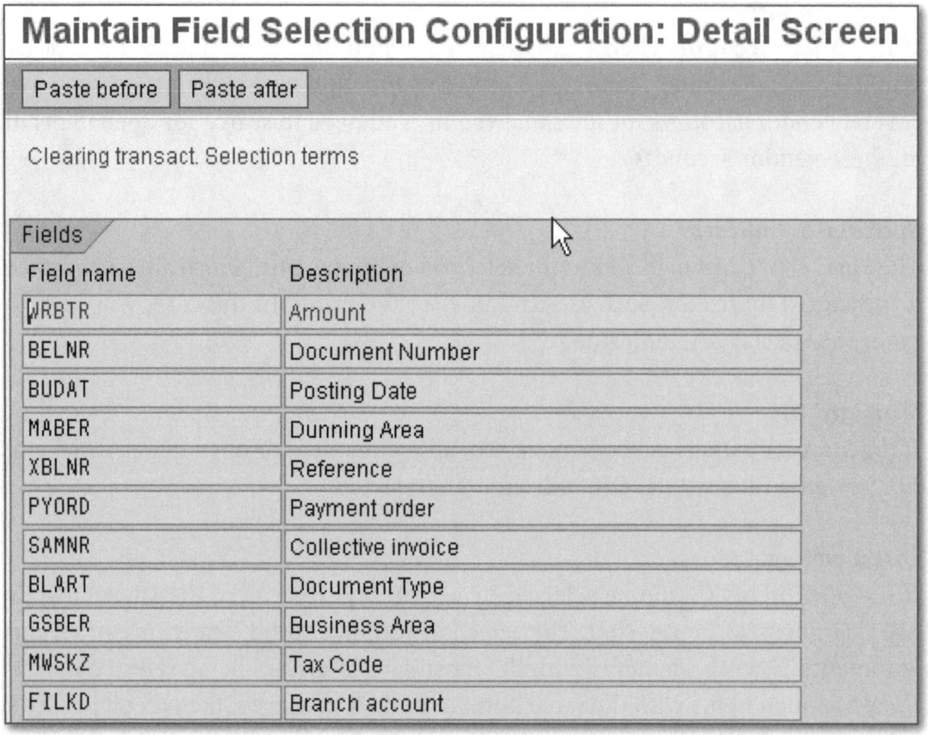

Maintain Field Selection Configuration: Detail Screen	
Paste before	Paste after

Clearing transact. Selection terms

Fields

Field name	Description
WRBTR	Amount
BELNR	Document Number
BUDAT	Posting Date
MABER	Dunning Area
XBLNR	Reference
PYORD	Payment order
SAMNR	Collective invoice
BLART	Document Type
GSBER	Business Area
MWSKZ	Tax Code
FILKD	Branch account

Figure 6.4 Additional Selection Configuration Screen

If you want to include other fields in the **Additional selections** screen, such as
the **Reference** field, the sequence of the fields can be changed. The first four fields
shown in Figure 6.4 will appear in the **Additional selections** section. All other
fields can be chosen by selecting the **Others** option.

6.1.2 Select Open Items

When all header data are entered, select the **Process Open Item** button, and all
open vendor items will be displayed as shown in Figure 6.5.

In this screen, the items to be paid need to be selected by double-clicking on a
specific line item. The **Amount entered** field shows the payment amount entered
from the previous screen, whereas the **Assigned** field shows the total of all selected

items. Any amount difference can be entered into the **Difference postings** field and will be posted to the vendor account either as a debit or credit line, depending on the sign of the difference.

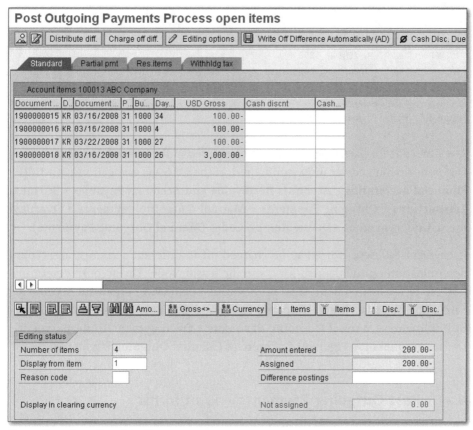

Figure 6.5 Open Item Selection

The **Not assigned** field always shows any amount difference and has to be zero before the payment can be posted.

Partial Payments/Residual Items

By selecting the **Partial Payments** or **Residual items** tab, invoices can be partially paid. As shown in Figure 6.6, the first line item is paid partially.

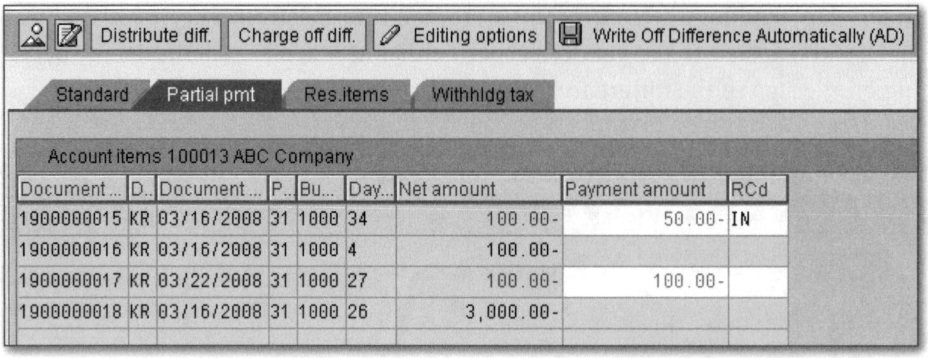

Figure 6.6 Partial Payment Screen

A reason code for partial payments can be entered in the **Reason Code (RCd)** field. Different reason codes can be configured in the IMG via navigation path **IMG • Financial Accounting • Accounts Receivable and Accounts Payables • Business Transactions • Outgoing Payments • Manual Outgoing Payments • Overpayment/Underpayment • Define Reason Codes (Manual Outgoing Payments)**.

If payment differences need to be charged off to different accounts, an account determination can be defined for a specific reason code. The account determination can be configured in the IMG via navigation path **IMG • Financial Accounting • Accounts Receivable and Accounts Payables • Business Transactions • Outgoing Payments • Manual Outgoing Payments • Overpayment/Underpayment • Define Accounts for Payment Differences (Manual Outgoing Payments)**.

6.2   Post Outgoing Payments + Print forms

Ad-hoc or *immediate checks* can be created with the Outgoing Payments + Print form functionality via Transaction F-58 or by using the navigation path **SAP Menu • Accounting • Financial Accounting • Accounts Payable • Document Entry • Outgoing Payment • Post + Print Forms**.

Within Transaction F-58, the payments are posted in a three-step process:

1. Enter header data.
2. Enter header document date.
3. Select open items, and post the payment.

6.2.1   Header Data

The Header data screen contains information relevant for selecting the correct bank information, payment method, and output information. The screen is divided into two sections:

- ▶ **Payment Method and Form Specifications**
- ▶ **Output control**

Payment Method and Form Specifications

This section, as shown in Figure 6.7, contains information on how and from which account the payments are issued, such as company code, payment method, and bank information.

Payment method and form specifications		Processing type	
Company Code	1000	☑ Calculate pmnt amnt	
Payment method	C		
House Bank	BANK		
Check lot number	1		
Alternative form			
Padding Character	*		

Figure 6.7   Payment Method and Form Specification Section

House Bank

In the **House bank** field, the bank, such as Citibank or Deutsche Bank, from where the payments are issued is specified. The bank account number is determined via the bank account determination, which is covered in Chapter 7.

Check Lot Number

If checks have to be printed, a **Check lot number** needs to be entered. A check lot represent a batch of checks, which may or may not be prenumbered. The system determines the last check number within this batch and creates a check with the next available check number.

Alternative Form

Within the configuration of the payment method (see Chapter 5), a specific form is assigned to the payment method. In the **Alternative form** field, a different form can be entered, in case the payment needs to be printed on a different form.

Padding

The payment amount can be printed in words on the payment forms, such as checks. Blank spaces are replaced with a padding character that can be selected using this parameter.

Calculate Payment Amount

By selection the **Calculate pmnt amnt** flag, the payment amount does not to be entered but is rather calculated by selecting the items to be paid. You should select this flag.

Output Control

In the **Output Control** section shown in Figure 6.8, all information relevant for printing must be specified, such as printers.

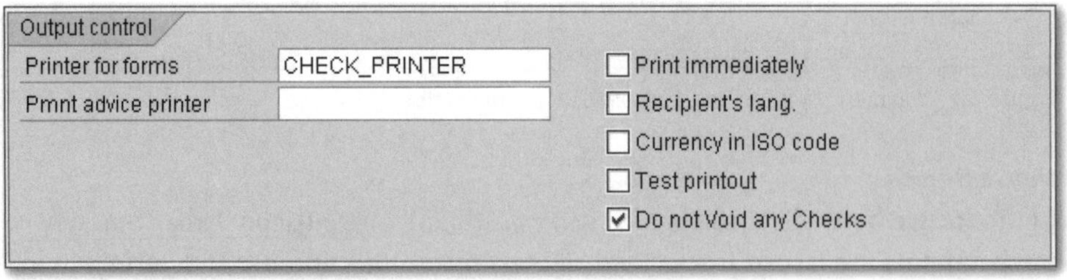

Figure 6.8 Output Control Section

Print Immediately

The output forms are printed immediately if this flag is set. Otherwise, the forms have to be printed later via the spool request Transaction SP02.

Recipient's Language

The forms are printed in the recipient's language, if this flag is set.

Test Printout

If the **Test printout** flag is set, the actual form is printed in a test mode to be able to adjust the printer.

Do Not Void Any Checks

This flag is only relevant for check printing because it specifies how the system should react in a check overflow.

If pre-numbered checks are used, you should not set this flag because the system creates a new check number with each single page. If there is a check overflow, the overflow checks are recorded in the check register and voided as overflow checks.

If the check number is not printed on the check, that means no prenumbered checks are used and you should deselect this flag. If there is a check overflow, no overflow check numbers are issued by the system.

After all header information is entered, click the **Enter payments** button to go to the Header document data screen.

6.2.2 Header Document Data

The **Header Document data** screen shown in Figure 6.9 contains the document header, bank posting details, payee, and open item selection specifications.

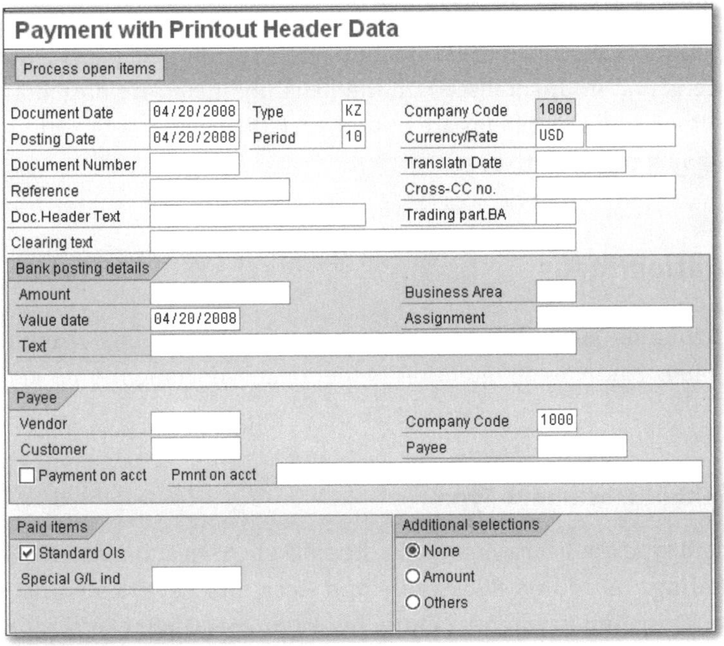

Payment with Printout Header Data

Process open items

Document Date	04/20/2008	Type	KZ	Company Code	1000	
Posting Date	04/20/2008	Period	10	Currency/Rate	USD	
Document Number				Translatn Date		
Reference				Cross-CC no.		
Doc.Header Text				Trading part.BA		
Clearing text						

Bank posting details

Amount		Business Area	
Value date	04/20/2008	Assignment	
Text			

Payee

Vendor		Company Code	1000
Customer		Payee	
☐ Payment on acct	Pmnt on acct		

Paid items
☑ Standard OIs
Special G/L ind

Additional selections
◉ None
◯ Amount
◯ Others

Figure 6.9 Header Document Data Screen

The screen sections are structured in a similar way as in the post outgoing payment transaction. Also the required field information is the same as described in the previous section.

The main difference is that in this transaction, only one vendor can be paid at one time, and the **Amount** field doesn't have to be entered with the payment amount if **Calculate pmnt amnt** is selected in the **Header Document data** screen. At a minimum, the document header information, such as document date, posting date, document type, and vendor account number, is required.

By clicking the **Process open items** button, the open items for this vendor are selected for payment. The screen and the functions are the same as described in the post outgoing payment transaction.

6.3 Post Incoming Payments

Incoming payments can be created with Transaction F-52 or by using the navigation path **SAP Menu • Accounting • Financial Accounting • Accounts Payable • Document Entry • Other • Incoming Payment**. This transaction can be used to record incoming vendor payments, for example, for vendor refunds.

The screens are the same as described in Transaction F-53 Post Outgoing Payment. The main difference is that in this transaction, the bank line items are posted as debit postings, and the vendor line items are posted as credits, which is the opposite of the post outgoing payment transaction.

6.4 Configuration Steps

The required configuration steps for the transactions described in this chapter are minimal. The only required configuration is the default document type per transaction.

6.4.1 Define Default Document Type

The default document type can be maintained in the IMG via navigation path **IMG • Financial Accounting • Accounts Receivable and Accounts Payables • Business Transactions • Outgoing Payments • Outgoing Payments Global Settings •**

Carry out and Check Document Settings • **Define Default Values** or by executing
Transaction OBU1.

F-48	Post Vendor Down Payment	KZ	
F-49	Customer Noted Item	DA	09
F-51	Post with Clearing	AB	
F-52	Post Incoming Payments	KZ	
F-53	Post Outgoing Payments	KZ	
F-54	Clear Vendor Down Payment	KA	
F-55	Enter Statistical Posting	KA	39
F-56	Reverse Statistical Posting	KA	
F-57	Vendor Noted Item	KA	39
F-58	Payment with Printout	KZ	
F-59	Payment Request	AB	
F-63	Park Vendor Invoice	KR	31
F-64	Park Customer Invoice	DR	01
F-65	Preliminary Posting	SA	40
F-66	Park Vendor Credit Memo	KG	21

Figure 6.10   Set Default Values Configuration Screen

To change the default document type as shown in Figure 6.10, double-click on the
transaction codes for **Post Incoming Payments (F-52)**, **Post Outgoing payments
(F-53)**, and **Payment with Printout (F-58)**.

6.5   Summary

On an exception basis, payments within AP have to be processed manually. In this
Chapter, the manual payment processing transactions were described.

In the next Chapter, the Automatic Payment process is explained in detail.

Within Accounts Payable (AP), payments can be processed manually or automatically via the automatic payment program. This chapter describes the automatic payment process.

7 Automatic Payment Processing

In this chapter, we'll discuss the automatic payment execution with the payment program via Transaction F110, which is used for the majority of the AP payments.

The payment program is capable of processing both outgoing payments (AP) and incoming payments (AR). The payment program processes domestic and foreign payments for vendors and customers. It creates payment documents and supplies data to the payment medium programs. These payment medium programs print either a payment list or payment forms such as checks, or create data carriers such as magnetic tape or floppy disks.

The standard system contains payment medium programs and forms for the most common payment methods. It can also create payments on disk. Payment forms and file formats vary from country to country and sometimes also from bank to bank.

The payment medium program stores data in the SAP print administration and in the Data Medium Exchange (DME) administration. From there, data is picked up separately per form/data carrier and output to the printer or data carrier.

The following topics will be discussed in detail:

▶ Payment program process flow

▶ Executing the payment program

▶ Configuration of the payment program

▶ Payment media programs

▶ Enhancements of the payment program

7.1 Payment Program Process Flow

Before we cover the execution steps of the payment program, we'll take a look at the process flow of the payment program. Figure 7.1 shows the entire process flow graphically from the proposal run to the generation of the payment media.

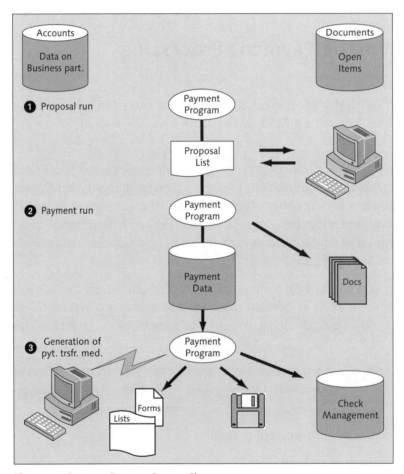

Figure 7.1 Payment Program Process Flow

During the proposal run, all specified vendor accounts and open items are analyzed if they are relevant for payment. The result is a payment proposal list that lists items to be paid as well as exceptions. The proposed items can be edited after the proposal run.

In the payment run, the payment documents are created in Financial Accounting (FI) based on the accepted items in the proposal run.

In the last step, the payment media formats are created. Payment media formats can be forms or different files for data transfer.

7.2 Executing the Payment Program (F110)

This section describes a general overview of the processing steps that need to be taken to execute a payment run.

1. **Planning and parameter specifications**
   Before every payment run, you need to specify which company codes, account types, and accounts to include in the payment run. Furthermore, you need to enter the desired posting date, possible payment methods, and the date of the next payment run.

2. **Creating the payment proposal**
   After the specifications for the payment run are complete, the payment proposal can be scheduled. You either enter the desired start date and time or arrange for immediate execution. The status display shows which step the job is at currently.

   If the payment proposal is created, the system first checks the results, reading the proposal log and recording any exceptions in it. This includes reading the proposal log in which all exceptions are recorded.

   By displaying or printing the payment proposal list or by editing the payment proposal, you can get an overview of the payments proposed by the program.

3. **Editing the payment proposal**
   The payment proposal processing can be divided between the clerks responsible. To do this, the accounting clerk ID needs to be stored in the vendor master data.

   It's possible to make changes when editing the payment proposal. Changes to the payment (payment method, house bank) and the items paid (block indicator, cash discount) can be made. All changes affect only the documents in the payment proposal. No changes are made to the source documents.

4. **Executing the payment run and payment medium programs**
   After the payment proposal is accepted, the payment run can be scheduled. The

job created for the payment run will contain either only the payment program as one step or an extra step for each payment medium program and each variant. In the latter case, the variants to use for each payment medium program have to be specified prior to scheduling the payment run. In scheduling the run, you select the desired start time and select the print programs option.

If you want to run only the payment program first, you can schedule the print programs for a different time in a separate job.

7.2.1 Creation of a Payment Run

The payment program can be executed via Transaction F110 or by using the navigation path **SAP Menu • Accounting • Financial Accounting • Accounts Payable • Periodic Processing • Payments**. Figure 7.2 shows the initial screen of the payment program.

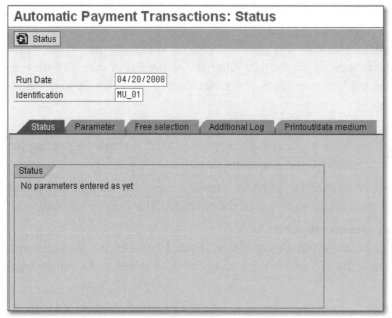

Figure 7.2 Payment Program: Initial Screen

Within the payment program, all information and results, such as parameters, proposals, or payments, are stored within the system by a unique key. This key is the **Run Date** together with the **Identification** field.

Run Date

For every payment run, a run date has to be entered. The run date is usually the date on which the payment run will be carried out. However, a program run at an earlier or later date is also possible.

Identification

Identification is a five-character alphanumeric key that further specifies your payment run. This may be necessary if multiple payment runs are executed on the same day or multiple users throughout your organization have the authorization to create payment runs. This key can be freely defined; however, you should create a procedure that establishes a naming convention for the identification key for your organization. For example, the first two characters could be the initials of the person who created the payment run followed by a sequential number of the payment run.

Status

The **Status** window informs you of the current status of the payment run. The status changes after each processing step. Table 7.1 shows the most common status messages within the payment program and their meaning.

Status	Meaning
No parameters entered as yet	This is the initial status when a payment run is created.
Parameters have been entered	The payment run parameters have been entered. The payment proposal run can be executed.
Payment proposal has been created	The payment proposal is created. The proposal can be edited or the payment run can be executed.
Payment run has been carried out	The payment run is executed.
Posting orders: X generated, X completed	The payment run generated and completed X number of payments.

Table 7.1 Payment Program Status Messages

261

7.2.2 Planning and Parameter Specifications

Before the start of the payment run, the payment parameters have to be specified. These payment parameters define which period, which company code, and which vendors or customers the payment program should consider.

The following tabs are available to enter the parameters:

- **Parameter** tab
- **Free selection** tab
- **Additional Log** tab
- **Printout/data medium** tab

Only the **Parameter** tab is mandatory; the **Free selection** tab and the **Additional Log** tab are optional. The **Printout/Data Medium** tab is only required if data medium outputs, such as checks or payment advices, are required.

Parameter Tab

Figure 7.3 shows the **Parameter** tab of the payment run. The information in this tab is mandatory.

Posting Date

The **Posting Date** field specifies the posting date of the payment documents as well as the posting date printed in the payment media, such as checks.

Docs Entered Up To

This date specifies the entry date of documents up to which documents should be considered in the payment run. Open items entered after this date aren't processed in the payment run.

Customer Items Due By

This field is the date by which a customer open item must be due to be considered in the payment run. If a date isn't specified, the posting date counts as the due date.

Company Code

This field contains the list of company codes to be paid.

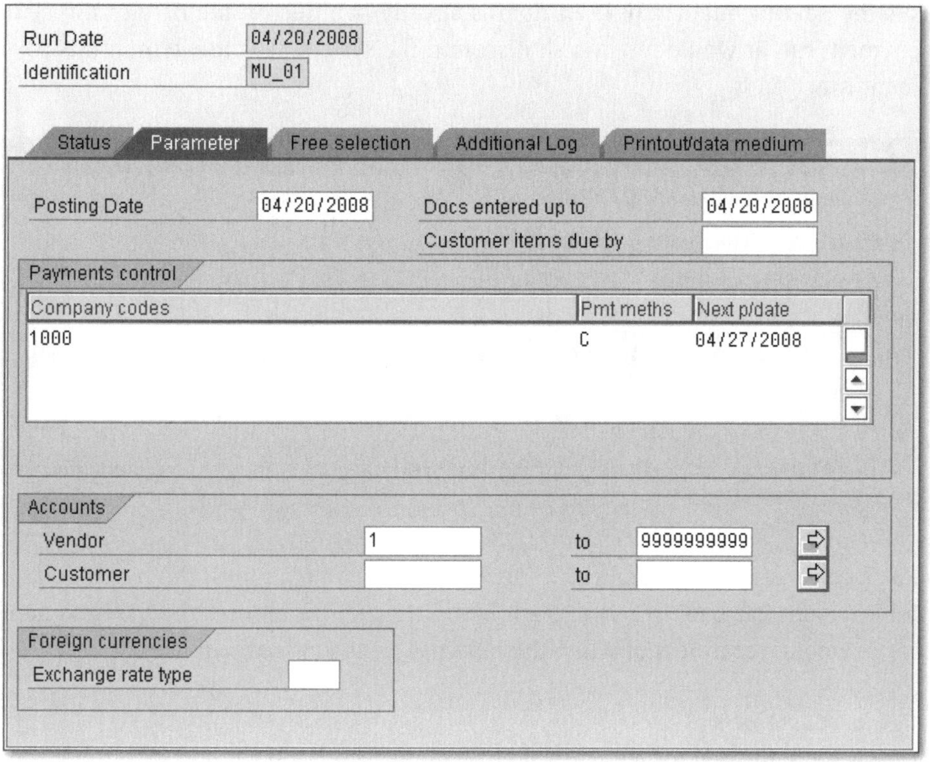

Figure 7.3 Parameter Tab Screen

Payment Methods

The **Pmt meths** field contains the payment methods used in the payment run. Enter the required payment methods without any extra separators between the letters.

The payment methods are selected by the system in the order in which they are specified. For example, the payment run should use the payment methods S and U. If both of these are permitted for a certain payment, payment method S is selected first if the methods are entered in the order SU. If, however, the methods are entered US, payment method U will be selected first.

Next P/Date

The **Next p/date** field (posting date of the next payment run) is very important because it determines which open items should be paid in this payment run versus the next payment run. If an item is already overdue on the date of the next payment run or would lose a cash discount, the system pays the item in this payment run.

Example

The following documents are open:

▶ Item 1: $100 due date 4/15/2008

▶ Item 2: $150 due date 4/30/2008

▶ Item 3: $200 due date 4/20/2008 2% discount. Full amount due on 4/30/08.

The posting date is entered with 4/15/2008 and the next payment date of 4/22/2008. The following items will be paid in this payment run:

▶ Item 1 because this item in due.

▶ Item 3 because the cash discount will be lost if it's paid in the next payment run on 4/22/2008.

For receivables, the general rule is that they can't be paid until the baseline date for payment has been reached. Such items are paid on or after the baseline date for payment, regardless of when the next payment run is scheduled.

Vendor/Customers

In this field, the vendor and customer accounts to be paid need to be entered.

Exchange rate type

The **Exchange rate type** field contains the rate type for the payment amounts translated from the foreign currency to the local currency during the payment run. If no rate type is specified, the average rate (rate type M) is used.

Free Selection Tab

The **Free selection** tab shown in Figure 7.4 contains field names and values that allow you to further restrict the selection of the open items.

Up to three additional field names can be selected from the document, vendor, or customer master data tables. For example, in Figure 7.4, the open item selection is restricted to the document types **VM** and **RE**.

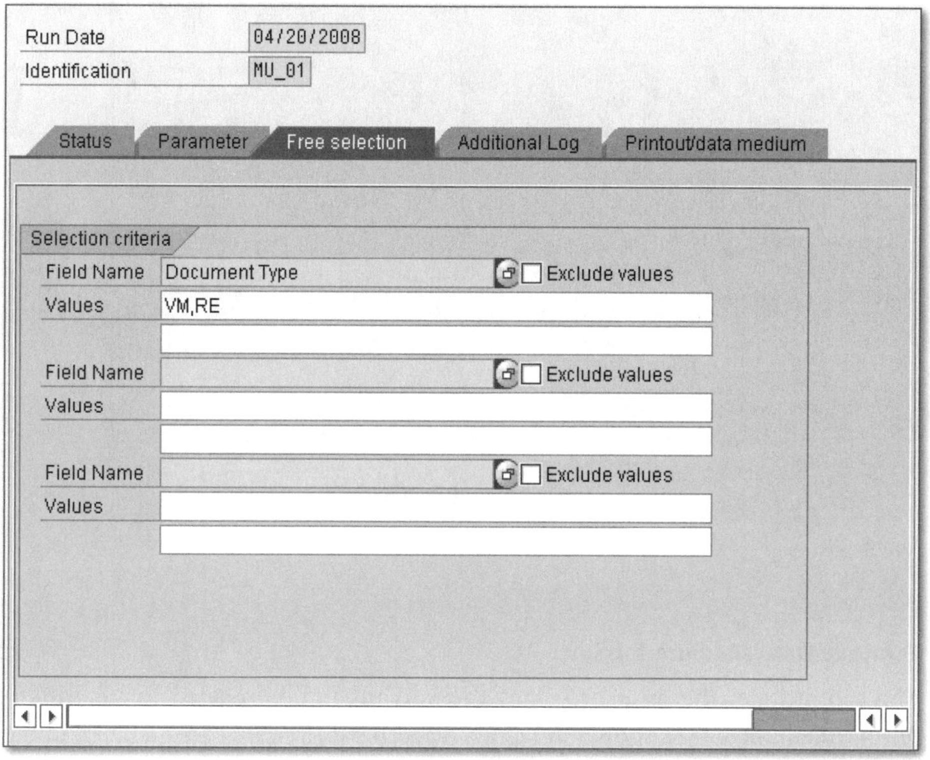

Figure 7.4 Free Selection Tab Screen

Additional Log Tab

The **Additional Log** tab shown in Figure 7.5 allows you to have additional log information displayed in the proposal log. The proposal log can be displayed after the proposal run. Additional log information is optional.

In this tab, you specify the vendors for which the additional log information should be displayed.

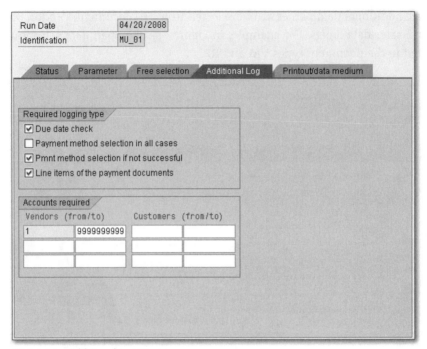

Figure 7.5 Additional Log Screen

Printout/Data Medium Tab

This tab includes the print programs and variants to be executed for the different payment media. As shown in Figure 7.6, program variants are assigned to the different programs. The variants contain the selection and output details for each payment medium.

SAP delivers a large variety of predefined country-specific electronic payment formats for both the classic payment medium programs as well as the Payment Medium Workbench (PMW). The available payment formats are listed in OSS Note 101440 for the classic payment medium programs and in OSS Note 395679 for PMW.

The execution and configuration steps for check printing and file transfer via ACH are covered in detail in Chapters 8 and 9.

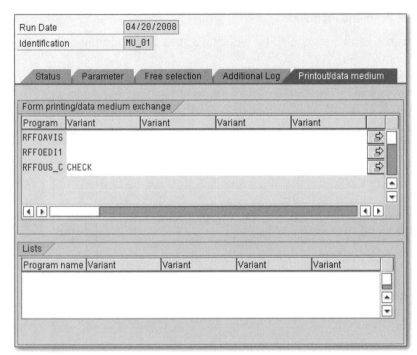

Figure 7.6 Printout/Data Medium Screen

Authorized Users

If it's required that only certain users can change the payment parameters, additional authorized users can be entered under **Edit • Authorized Users**.

7.2.3 Payment Proposal Run

After all parameters for the payment run are specified, the payment proposal can be created. The payment proposal displays the open items whose payment is proposed by the payment program.

The following list shows the different procedures during the proposal run:

▶ User schedules the payment proposal.

▶ Payment proposal runs automatically and creates the proposal list, payment proposal log, and exception list.

▶ User edits the payment proposal.

Schedule the Payment Proposal

The proposal run can be scheduled by entering a start date and time or immediately as shown in Figure 7.7.

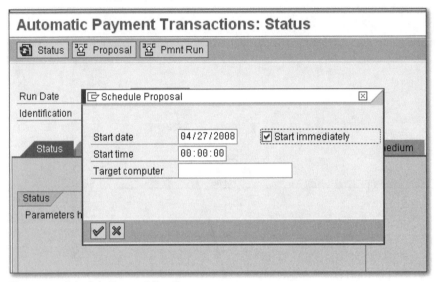

Figure 7.7 Schedule Payment Run Screen

After the proposal is finished, several options are available for displaying, editing, or listing the results of the proposal run. Table 7.2 shows the different options available with a description of the option. All options can be accessed via the header menu **Edit • Proposal.**

Option	Description
Display Proposal	Displays the results of the proposal run; no editing options are available.
Edit Proposal	Allows you to edit the proposal. Items can be included or excluded, and payments can be changed.
Delete Proposal	Deletes the proposal run, and allows the payment run parameters to be changed again.
Proposal List	Displays all payments and exceptions via the execution of Report RFZALI20.
Exception List	Displays all exceptions via the execution of Report RFZALI10.

Table 7.2 Proposal Run Options

Option	Description
Display Proposal Log	Informs of any configuration errors or reasons why open items were not selected for payments. The detail of the log depends on the specifications in the **Additional log** screen in the payment run parameters.

Table 7.2 Proposal Run Options (Cont.)

Vendor Lock During Proposal Run
During the payment proposal run, the selected vendors are locked for further selection in other proposal runs. These vendors can't be selected until a payment proposal is either deleted or the payment run is completed.
If the payment run parameters need to be changed, delete the proposal run, change the payment run parameters, and run the proposal again.
Always delete a proposal run if you decide that the selected open items should not be paid.

Editing the Payment Proposal

The payment proposal can be edited online after it is created. Both payments and line items can be processed and edited. Accounting clerks can process the payment proposal, which allows several users to process extensive proposals in parallel. The system records all changes, which can be accessed in the Display Proposal function under header menu **Environment • Payment changes** or **Environment • Line Item Changes**.

All changes made when editing the payment proposal affect only the payment proposal and not the source documents, such as invoices or credit memos. For example, an invoice is blocked for payment in the proposal. By setting the payment block in the proposal, the original invoice document won't be blocked. The invoice will just be blocked in this payment proposal.

Figure 7.8 shows the results of a payment proposal. Vendor payments with a green value in the **Type** column will be paid with this payment run. In this case, the **Payment** column is also filled with an internal payment number, such as **F110000002**. Every payment number results in a separate payment document. All exceptions are shown with a red value in the **Type** column and won't be paid.

For items that can be paid, the payments as well as the line item can be edited. For exceptions, only the line items are allowed for editing.

269

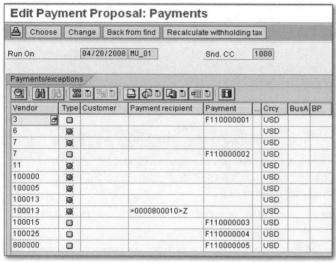

Figure 7.8 Payment Proposal Results

Payment Changes

To change a payment, select the payment row, and click on **Change**. It's possible to change the payment method, payment method supplement, bank assignment, instruction key, and due date as shown in Figure 7.9.

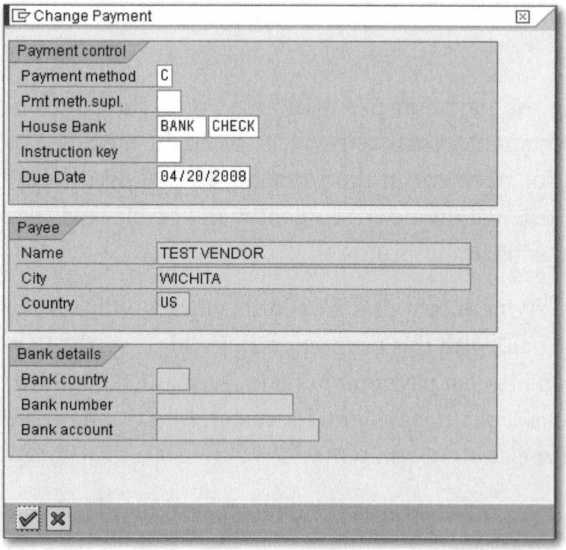

Figure 7.9 Change Payment Screen

Line Item Changes

To change the line items, double-click on the payment to see all line items for this payment. For example, Figure 7.10 shows three line items for one payment.

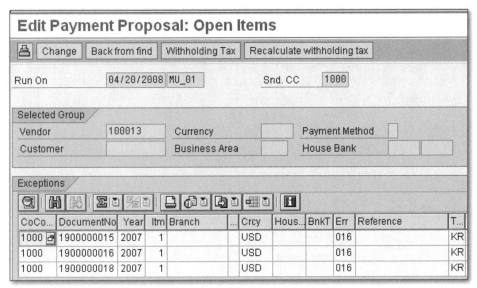

Figure 7.10 Line Items Within the Payment Proposal

To change a particular line item, select the payment row, and click on **Change**. You can change the block, change the discount term, or reallocate the item as shown in Figure 7.11.

The block within a payment proposal can only be set or deleted if the payment block is allowed to be changed within a payment proposal (see Section 5.5 "Payment Block Reasons" in Chapter 5).

To change the cash discount amount, click in the **Cash discount %** field or the **Days** field and change the amount.

The *Reallocate* function allows you to remove line items from one payment and assign them to another one. If there are other payments for this vendor in the proposal, the system lists the payments to which the items can be assigned in a new screen. (This screen is not shown in the figure.) Select one of the displayed payment methods by selecting **Choose**. A new payment for the item can also be created by choosing **Newpayment** and entering the payment method, house bank, and account into the fields provided.

If no other payment exists for the vendor, a new payment always has to be created.

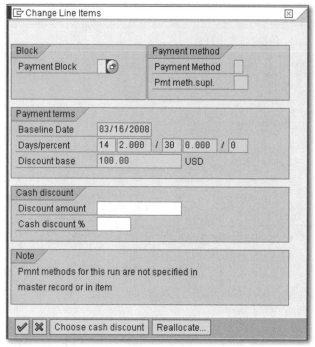

Figure 7.11 Change Line Items Screen

After all editing options are completed, the payment proposal needs to be saved to make the changes effective.

Schedule the Payment Run

After the proposal is edited and accepted, the payment run can be scheduled by entering a start date and time or immediately as shown in Figure 7.12.

Several programs are used in creating the payments:

▶ The payment program creates the payment documents and prepares the data for printing the forms or creating the tape or disk.

▶ Various payment medium programs use the data prepared by the payment program to create forms or files for the data media.

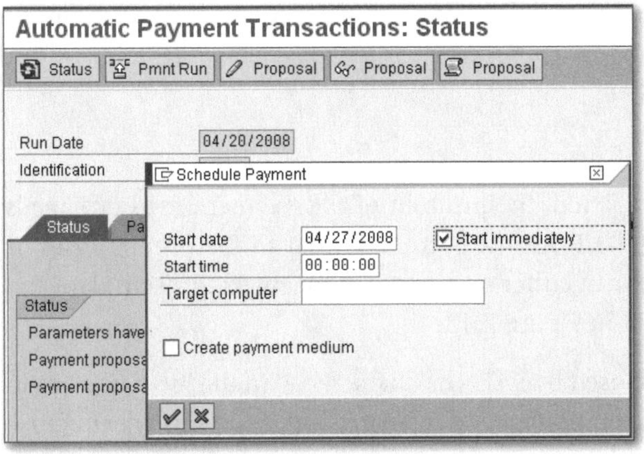

Figure 7.12 Payment Run Schedule Screen

By selecting the **Create payment medium** flag, the payment media such as checks or files are created at the same time. Otherwise, the payment medium formats have to be created in a separate run. This flag is only visible if print variants are specified in the **Printout/data medium** tab of the payment run.

After the payment run is finished, several options are available for displaying the results of the payment run. Table 7.3 shows the different options available with a description of the option. All options can be accessed via the header menu **Edit • Payments.**

Option	Description
Schedule Print	Allows you to schedule a job for printing the payment media. The same function is available by choosing the **Printout** button.
Display	Displays all payments within the payment proposal that were paid.
Payment List	Displays all payments via the execution of Report RFZALI20.
Exception List	Displays all exceptions in the payment run via the execution of Report RFZALI10.
Display Log	Displays a log during the payment run. All error and warning message are listed in this log.
Delete Output	Deletes the payment data. The creation of payment media data is then impossible.
Termination of Postings	Allows you to analyze which postings are abandoned if a system termination happened during the payment run.

Table 7.3 Payment Run Options

After the successful execution of the payment, the creation of payment mediums have to be scheduled if necessary.

Schedule the Printout

After the payment run is completed, the printout of the payment medium needs to be scheduled by choosing the **Printout** button. Similar to the proposal run or payment run, the printout run can either be scheduled by entering a start date and time or immediately as shown in Figure 7.13.

In addition, a job name is proposed by SAP. The character '**?**' in the job name has to be replaced by another character, that is, 1 or A. SAP is designed this way because multiple printout job names might be necessary for the same payment run.

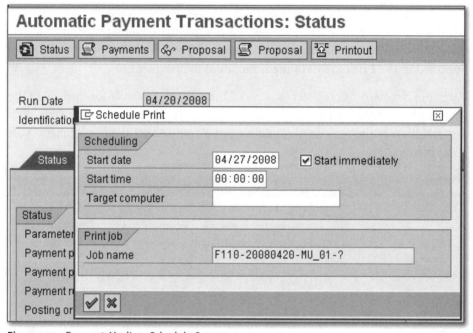

Figure 7.13 Payment Medium Schedule Screen

After the printout is scheduled and executed, the spools can be displayed under the header menu **System • Own Spool Requests**.

7.3   Executing the Payment Program Periodically (F110S)

In the prior section, the execution of the payment program via Transaction F110 was described in detail. If the payment program needs to be scheduled automatically, Transaction F110S allows payments to be scheduled in a background process. Transaction F110S can be executed via the navigation path **SAP Menu • Accounting • Financial Accounting • Accounts Payable • Periodic Processing • Schedule Payment Program Periodically.**

Transaction F110S has essentially the same selection parameters available as Transaction F110. After the parameters are entered, payments can be scheduled to be executed in the background

7.4   Payment Program Configuration

This section describes the configuration steps of the payment program. Payment program configuration involves determining the following:

▶ What is to be paid? To do this, you specify rules used to select the open items to be paid and group them for payment.

▶ When payment is carried out. The due date of the open items determines when payment is carried out.

▶ To whom the payment is made by specifying the payee.

▶ How the payment is made. You determine rules that are used to select a payment method.

▶ From where the payment is made. You determine rules that are used to select a bank and a bank account for the payment.

The preceding rules and conditions must be defined if the payment program is to determine the previously mentioned information automatically.

Following are the configuration steps:

1. Set up all company codes for payment transactions.
2. Set up paying company codes for payment transactions.
3. Set up payment methods per country for payment transactions.
4. Set up payment methods per company code for payment transactions.

5. Set up bank determination for payment transactions.

Steps 3 and 4 were already covered in Section 5.1 "Payment Methods" in Chapter 5.

7.4.1 Set Up All Company Codes for Payment Transactions

The company code details for all company codes from which payment can occur have to be configured in the IMG via navigation path **IMG • Financial Accounting • Accounts Receivable and Accounts Payables • Business Transactions • Automatic Outgoing Payments • Payment Method/Bank Selection for Payment Program • Set up All Company Codes for Payment Transactions.** The configuration screen is divided into three sections:

▶ **Control data**

▶ **Cash discount and tolerances**

▶ **Vendors and Customers**

Control data

The **Control data** section shown in Figure 7.14 contains main specifications for the company code.

Figure 7.14 Control Data Section

Sending Company Code

The sending company code is the company code in which transactions such as invoice or credit memos are entered.

When making cross-company code payments, specify the sending company code as well as the paying company code. If the sending company code is different from the paying company code, the system notes the sending company code in the payment transfer medium or payment advice.

Furthermore, the sending company code affects how the system groups items from different company codes into one payment. Items are only grouped into one payment for company codes with the same paying company code and the same sending company code.

If the sending company code isn't specified, the system automatically regards the paying company code as the sending company code.

Paying Company Code

The **Paying company code** field specifies from which company code the payments are processed. The bank accounts are selected from the paying company code.

Separate Payment per Business Area

If this flag is set, a separate payment per business area is generated. To do that, the business area needs to be entered in the line item details of the invoice or credit memo upon data entry.

Payment Method Supplement

After the **Pyt meth suppl.** flag is set, payment method supplements can be used within the company code (see Section 5.2 "Payment Method Supplement" in Chapter 5).

Cash Discount and Tolerances

The **Cash discount and tolerances** section shown in Figure 7.15 contains information specifications for calculating the due date and discount information.

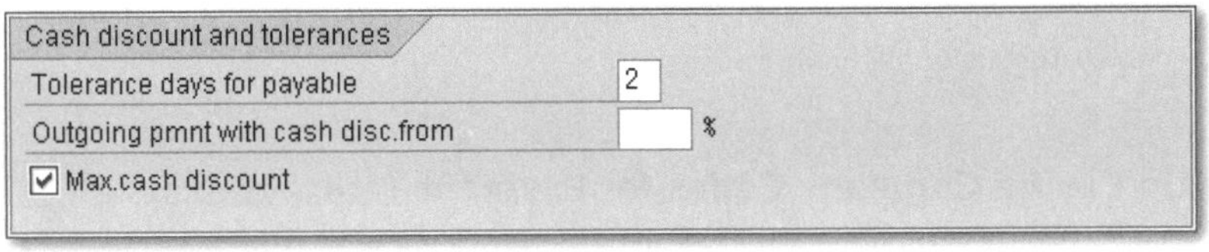

Figure 7.15 Cash Discount and Tolerances Screen

Tolerance Days for Payable

In Section 7.2.2, the importance of the **Posting date of the next payment run** was discussed and how the system would use this date to select items to be paid. To complicate matters further, the **Tolerance days for payable** field specifies the number of tolerance days allowed for the due date of payments. To determine the due date, the system adds the number of days specified in this field to the due date of the item. This date is also known as the grace period.

Outgoing Pmnt with Cash Disc. From

In this field, the lower limit for payments with cash discount deductions is specified. Only items that have a cash discount percentage rate greater than or equal to the one specified here are paid with the cash discount deducted. If the percentage rate is less than the one specified here, payment is made at the due date for net payment.

Max Cash Discount

If the **Max.cash discount** flag is set, the cash discount is always deducted, even if the payment is made after the due date eligible for cash discount.

Vendors/Customers

If special GL postings, such as down payments, are selected during the proposal run, these special GL indicators need to be specified in the fields shown in Figure 7.16.

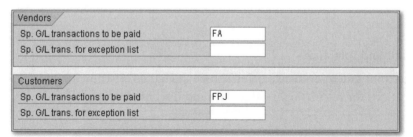

Figure 7.16 Vendor/Customers Configuration Screen

7.4.2 Set Up Paying Company Codes for Payment Transactions

The paying company code details are configured in the IMG via navigation path **IMG • Financial Accounting • Accounts Receivable and Accounts Payables • Business Transactions • Automatic Outgoing Payments • Payment Method/ Bank Selection for Payment Program • Set up Paying Company Codes for Payment Transactions.** The configuration screen is divided into three sections:

- ▶ **Control Data**

- ▶ **Forms**

- ▶ **Sender Details for SAPscript Forms**

Control Data

The **Control Data** section shown in Figure 7.17 contains the control specifications for the paying company code.

Minimum Amounts for Payment

The **Minimum amount for outgoing payment** field defines the minimum amount for which payments are created. This prevents payments generated for amounts that don't justify the expenses incurred. The field **Minimum amount for incoming payment** is used within AR for incoming payment methods.

Control Data		
Minimum amount for incoming payment	1.00	USD
Minimum amount for outgoing payment	1.00	USD
☐ No exchange rate differences		
☐ No Exch.Rate Diffs. (Part Payments)		
☐ Separate payment for each ref.		
☐ Bill/exch pymt		

Figure 7.17 Control Data Screen

No Exchange Rate Differences

This flag ensures that no exchange rate differences are posted by the payment program. If the flag is set, no exchange rate difference posting is generated. The amount in the bank posting in local currency doesn't result from translating the foreign currency amount at the current rate but from the total of the local currency amounts from the paid items.

If the indicator isn't set, the difference between the exchange rate at the time of posting and the exchange rate at the time of payment is determined for items that are posted in foreign currency. The exchange rate differences that have been determined are automatically posted for each payment. The exchange rate difference accounts can be configured in the IMG via navigation path **IMG • Financial Accounting • Accounts Receivable and Accounts Payables • Business Transactions • Outgoing Payments Global Settings • Define Accounts for Exchange rate differences.**

No Exch. Rate Diffs. (Part Payments)

This flag ensures that no exchange rate differences are posted for partial payments using Transaction F-59. The system behavior is the same as with payments within the payment program.

Separate Payment for Each Ref.

If this flag is set, invoices and credit memos with the same reference will be paid with the same payment. This specification is usually used in countries where a payment reference is required for each single payment, such as Norway or Finland.

Bill/Exch Pymt

The **Bill/Exch pymt** flag needs to be set if the payment method is a bills of exchange or a bill of exchange payment request. This flag causes additional configuration options for bills of exchange to be displayed.

Forms

The **Forms** section as shown in Figure 7.18 contains the forms to be used for payment advices as well as payments submitted via EDI.

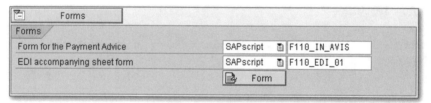

Figure 7.18 Forms Screen

The forms can be created using *SAPscript* or in *PDF* format. Table 7.4 lists sample forms delivered by SAP. The SAPscript forms can be maintained using Transaction SE71, and the SAP Interactive Forms by Adobe with Transaction SFP.

Forms	Format
F110_IN_AVIS	SAPscript
F110_AVIS_INT	PDF
F110_EDI_01	SAPscript
FI_PAYM_INT_EDI	PDF

Table 7.4 Sample Forms

Sender Details for SAPscript Forms

The **Sender Details for SAPscript Forms** section shown in Figure 7.19 specifies the text modules used in the payment advice or EDI forms for printing header, footer signature, or sender information.

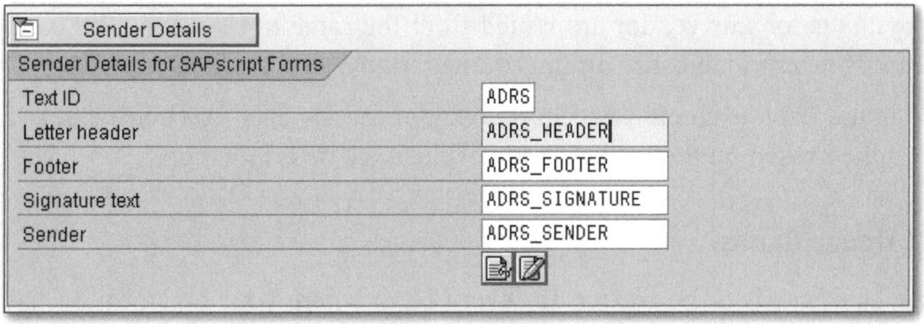

Sender Details	
Sender Details for SAPscript Forms	
Text ID	ADRS
Letter header	ADRS_HEADER
Footer	ADRS_FOOTER
Signature text	ADRS_SIGNATURE
Sender	ADRS_SENDER

Figure 7.19 Sender Details for SAPscript Forms Screen

The text modules can be maintained by choosing the **Change text module** button or with Transaction SO10.

7.4.3 Set Up Payment Methods per Country for Payment Transactions

The configuration settings for this step were described in detail in Section 5.1 "Payment Methods" in Chapter 5.

7.4.4 Set Up Payment Methods per Company Code for Payment Transactions

The configuration settings for this step were described in detail in Section 5.1 of Chapter 5.

7.5 Set Up Bank Determination for Payment Transactions

The payment program needs to determine during the payment run the bank details from where payments are issued. Within SAP, the bank details are defined by *house bank* and *bank account*. The house banks are banks with which your company code maintains bank accounts. The bank accounts are the single bank accounts within a house bank.

The house bank selection depends on whether the bank details are specified within the vendor master data or are determined automatically by the payment program.

▶ The house bank can be specified within the vendor master data in the **Payment Transaction** tab of the company code data view. If the house bank is entered, all payments for this vendor are issued from the same house bank. The bank account is determined based on the configuration of the bank determination.

▶ If no house bank is entered within the vendor master data, the house bank is determined based on the configuration of the bank determination.

7.5.1 House Banks

A house bank needs to be created for every bank where your organization has bank accounts and payments may be issued. Each house bank of a company code is represented by a *House Bank ID* in the SAP system. The house banks can be maintained within the IMG via navigation path **IMG · Financial Accounting · Bank Accounting · Bank Accounts · Define House Banks** or via Transaction FI12.

House Bank
The **House bank** field is a short key or ID for your House bank (see Figure 7.20). Table 7.5 shows examples of House bank ID's.

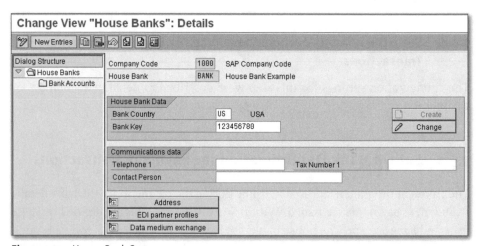

Figure 7.20 House Bank Screen

House Bank IDs	Description
CITI	Citibank
DBANK	Deutsche Bank
BOFA	Bank of America

Table 7.5 House Bank ID Examples

Bank Country
The **Bank Country** specifies in which country the bank resides.

Bank Key
The routing number or ABA number needs to be entered in the **Bank Key** field. The bank key format is validated based on the length and checking rule in your country-specific checks. The rules can be configured under the navigation path **IMG • SAP NetWeaver • General Settings • Set Countries • Set Country-Specific Checks.**

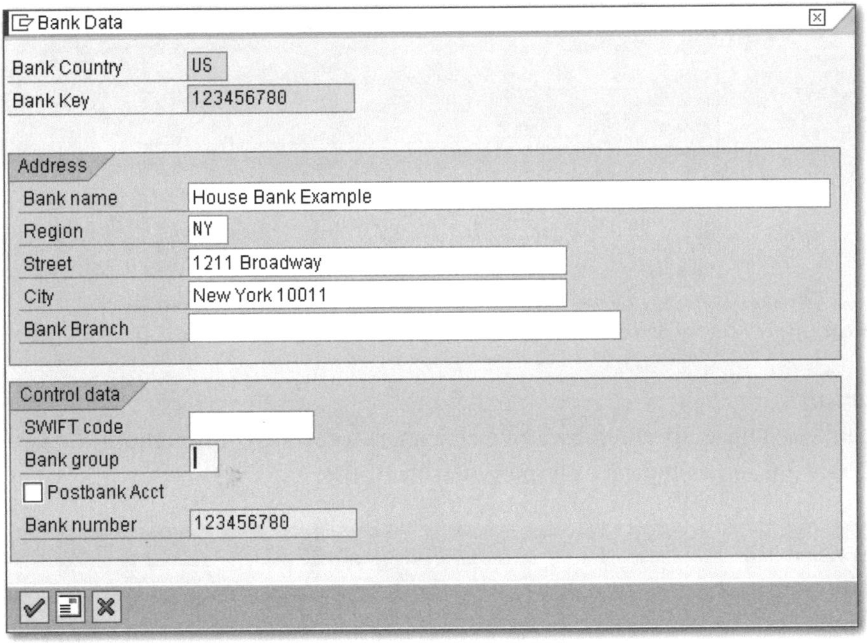

Figure 7.21 Bank Address Screen

In addition, for each bank key, a *bank master* has to be defined. The bank master contains the address information of the bank (see Figure 7.21). This can be done either directly within this configuration by clicking the **Create** button or via Transaction FI01.

The bank master maintenance transaction codes can be found using the navigation path **SAP Menu • Accounting • Financial Accounting • Banks • Master Records • Banks Master Record.**

7.5.2 Bank Accounts

A bank account needs to be created for every bank where payments may be issued. One house bank can have multiple bank accounts, such as checking or savings accounts. Each bank account is represented by an **Account ID** in the SAP system. The bank accounts are maintained in the same IMG path and transaction code as the house banks. Within the house bank configuration, select the **Bank Accounts** node to see all bank accounts for a specific house bank. Figure 7.22 shows the configuration screen of the bank account.

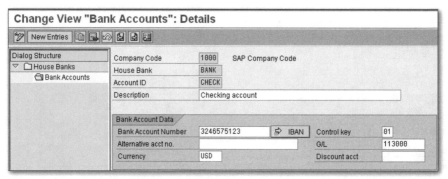

Figure 7.22 Bank Account Screen

Account ID

The bank account is specified by a five-character **Account ID** throughout the system. Table 7.6 shows typical examples of account IDs.

Account IDs	Description
CHECK	Checking Account
SAVNG	Saving Account
PAYRL	Payroll Account
EUR	EURO account

Table 7.6 Account ID Examples

Description

The **Description** field contains the description of the bank account.

Bank Account Number

The **Bank Account Number** field contains the account number under which the bank account is managed at the bank. The bank account number format is validated based on the length and checking rule in your country-specific checks. The rules can be configured under the navigation path **IMG • SAP NetWeaver • General Settings • Set Countries • Set Country-Specific Checks.**

Control Key

The bank **Control key** is country specific and identifies the type of bank account, that is, checking or savings account. This field isn't relevant for all countries.

Alternative Acct No.

The **Alternative acct no.** is used for distinguishing bank accounts with identical account numbers. This can occur if a house bank manages accounts in different currencies using the same account number.

G/L

The **G/L** field specifies the GL account within your company code that contains the balance for the bank account.

Discount Acct

Credit memos resulting from discounting bills of exchange at this bank account are posted to the discount account specified in this field.

Currency

The **Currency** field specifies the currency of the bank account.

7.5.3   Bank Account Selection Logic

The payment program determines the house bank in the following sequence:

1. First, it determines the house banks based on the payment method and currency. If it finds no entry for the combination, it checks the bank for payment methods without currency specification, if such an entry exists.

2. It determines the account ID on the basis of the house bank, the payment method, and the currency.

3. Finally, it checks whether sufficient amounts are available for both the bank ID and account ID.

During the payment run, the payment program attempts to determine a house bank and a bank account that has a sufficient amount available for payment. This may result in the following possibilities:

▸ No house bank is found that fulfills all conditions. The payment can't be made with the payment method. If no bank is determined, the payment method can't be used. If another method is available, it will then be checked as well. This is noted in the log for the payment run.

▸ One house bank only is determined. The payment is made via this house bank.

▸ The program produces a list of house banks. The payment is made from the house bank with the highest priority according to the defined ranking order of the banks. This isn't the case if payment optimization has been specified. Payment optimization was covered in Section 5.1.2 "Company Code Specific Definitions for the Payment Method" in Chapter 5.

7.5.4 Configuration Steps for Bank Determination for Payment Transactions

This section describes how to specify the configuration that the payment program uses to select the banks or bank accounts from which payment is to be made.

If your organization has several house banks that can be used for payment transactions and has limited funds in these accounts, the available cash balances have to be planned for each bank account, and the ranking order by which the payment program uses these accounts has to be defined. In addition because there are several house banks available to the payment program, the order in which the bank accounts are selected has to be specified.

The following settings need to be configured:

▸ **Ranking order of banks**
Specify which house banks are permitted and rank them in a list.

▶ **Bank accounts**

For each house bank and payment method, specify the bank accounts to be used for payments.

▶ **Available amounts**

For each account at a house bank, specify the amounts that are available for the payment run. Enter separate amounts for incoming and outgoing payments. Specifying available amounts enables you to control which bank account is used for payments.

▶ **Value date**

Specify how many days elapse between the posting date of the payment run and the value date at the bank, dependent on the payment method, bank account, payment amount, and currency. The system can determine the value date, taking into account the bank calendar and any individual arrangements made with the bank.

▶ **Fees/charges**

Define charges that are printed on the bill of exchange forms.

The bank selection for payment transactions can be configured in the IMG via navigation path **IMG • Financial Accounting • Accounts Receivable and Accounts Payables • Business Transactions • Automatic Outgoing Payments • Payment Method/Bank Selection for Payment Program • Set Up Bank Determination for Payment Transactions.**

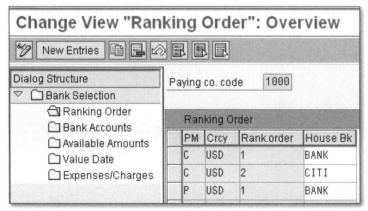

Figure 7.23 Ranking Order Screen

Ranking Order

If multiple house banks are available for payment of a payment method, the ranking order of the house bank needs to be defined.

As shown in Figure 7.23, two house banks are allowed for payment method C. During the payment program, the system first checks whether the payment can be made with House Bank. If an error occurs, the system will check whether House Bank CITI would be possible for the payment.

Bank Accounts

As shown in Figure 7.24, for every combination of house bank, payment method, and currency, bank account specifications have to be defined.

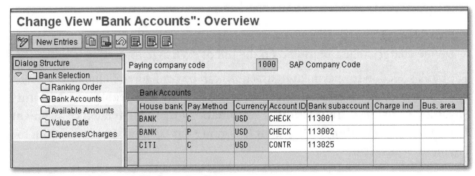

Figure 7.24 Bank Account Configuration Screen

Account ID

The **Account ID** represents the bank account of the house bank from which the payments are made.

Bank Subaccount

The **Bank subaccount** field specifies the GL account that is used to post the payments.

Charge Ind

If charges have to be printed on the bill of exchange forms, a charge scale can be defined. In this field, the **Charge ind** of the charge scale needs to be entered. The charges are configured in the *Expenses/Charges* step.

Bus. Area

The **Bus. Area** field is only used if payments aren't separated according to business areas. Otherwise, the bank posting receives the unique business area of payment.

Available Amounts

The payment program checks whether the selected bank accounts have sufficient funds for payment. The available amounts can be specified for the bank accounts at the house banks separately for incoming payments and outgoing payments as shown in Figure 7.25.

For outgoing payments, the amount that can be paid needs to be defined. If this limit is exceeded, the payment program selects another bank. If your organization has only restricted funds available in a bank account, you should ensure that these amounts are up-to-date before every payment run. The available amounts can be changed before every posting run with Transaction S_ALR_87001486 or by using the navigation path **SAP Menu • Accounting • Financial Accounting • Accounts Payable • Environment • Enter Available Amounts for the Payment Program.**

In addition, the payment program doesn't carry out amount splitting. If the amount on a bank account isn't sufficient for a payment, the payment program selects another bank account. If it finds no bank account from which it can post the entire amount for a payment, it doesn't carry out the payment.

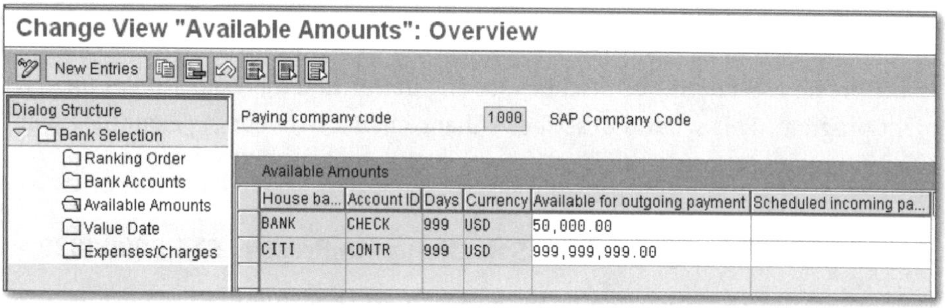

Figure 7.25 Available Amounts Screen

Days

The *number of days until charge/value date* is only used for bill of exchange payments and defines the number of days before a bill of exchange payment is posted before the due date. In all other cases, enter "999" in the **Days** field.

Value Date

The **Value Date** field shown in Figure 7.26 defines the probable number of days before a payment is carried out to the bank account. The number of days is added to the posting date and results in the date relevant for cash management and forecasts when the payment is to be expected on the bank account.

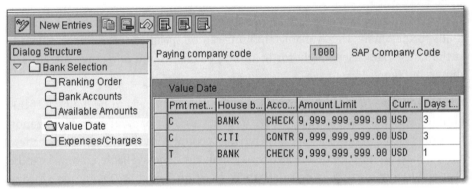

Figure 7.26 Value Date Configuration Screen

Expenses/Charges

In the last configuration step, charges can be defined that are printed on the bill of exchange forms.

7.6   Enhancements

In the previous sections, we discussed configuration and the execution of the payment program. This section describes enhancements with coding examples available during the payment run.

7.6.1   Payment Program: Item Selection with Process BTE 00001820

This BTE (Business Transaction Event) provides an opportunity to change the payment block or payment method in an open vendor item directly after the selection and before the output in the payment proposal.

The function module receives the data from Table BSIK for the open vendor item. The posting date, date of the next payment run, and the date to which open customer items are to be considered are also available.

Status messages (message type S) can be output in the function module. The log options from the payment run parameters in the structure I_TRACE are given to decide which messages are required in the payment run log.

The free selections maintained in the payment run parameters are given in Table T_FLDTAB_1820. By setting the export parameter E_NO_FREE_SELECTIONS = 'X', the standard checks on the free selections can be deactivated.

The payment block from the open item is given in the transfer parameter C_ZLSPR, which can be changed before it is returned. Each payment block can be set and the item appears on the exception list. The payment block "*" has a special role. If it's set, the item is no longer taken into account, and it's no longer visible in the exception list. You can use parameter C_ZLSCH to change the payment method of the item selected.

Sample Code

Listing 7.1 shows an example with the following requirements:

▶ During the execution of the payment program, all blocked open items are displayed in the exception list. To shorten the exception list, all line items with payment block A should not be listed in the exception log.

▶ If the vendor has the payment block A set in the vendor master data, no items should appear in the exception list for this vendor.

```
FUNCTION Z_PROCESS_00001820.

DATA: h_lfb1 like lfb1.
*----------------------------------------------------------------
* Requirement 1: All line items with payment block 'A'
*                should not appear in the exception list.
*----------------------------------------------------------------
  IF i_bsik-zlspr = 'A'.
    c_zlspr = '*'.
  ENDIF.


*----------------------------------------------------------------
* Requirement 2: If the vendor is blocked for payment with
*                payment block 'A', all line item should
*                not appear in the exception list.
*----------------------------------------------------------------
  SELECT SINGLE * from lfb1 INTO h_lfb1
```

```
                    WHERE lifnr = i_bsik-lifnr AND
                          bukrs = i_bsik-bukrs.
  IF h_lfb1-zahls = 'A'.
    c_zlspr = '*'.
  ENDIF.

ENDFUNCTION.
```

Listing 7.1 Sample Code for BTE 00001820

All changed documents during the execution of this BTE are listed in the proposal log.

7.6.2 Payment Program: Individual Bank Determination with Process BTE 00001810

The purpose of this BTE is to provide a way of individually determining which of its own bank details and which partner bank details should be used for a payment. The authorized bank details are transferred in Table T_HBANK. If you don't want to use some of the banks determined, you can set the indicator XCUSF on the relevant line.

Sample Code

Listing 7.2 shows an example with the following requirement:

▶ Your company has two banks configured for payments with payment method C. If the payment amount is greater than $100,000, house bank CITI should be used, otherwise, house bank BANK. Note that the payment amount field I_RWBTR has a negative value for outgoing payments.

```
FUNCTION Z_PROCESS_00001810.

-------------------------------------------------------------------
* Requirement 1: Use house bank 'CITI' for payments over
*                USD 100,000 Other wise use house bank 'BANK'
*------------------------------------------------------------------
* Note: For outgoing payments, the payment amount field
*       I_RWBTR has a negative value.
*------------------------------------------------------------------

  CHECK i_waers = 'USD'.
```

```
 CHECK i_rzawe = 'C'.

 IF i_rwbtr <= -100000.
   LOOP AT t_hbank.
     CASE t_hbank-hbkid.
       WHEN 'CITI '.
       WHEN OTHERS. t_hbank-xcusf = 'X'.
     ENDCASE.
     MODIFY t_hbank.
   ENDLOOP.
 ELSE.
   LOOP AT t_hbank.
     CASE t_hbank-hbkid.
       WHEN 'BANK '.
       WHEN OTHERS. t_hbank-xcusf = 'X'.
     ENDCASE.
     MODIFY t_hbank.
   ENDLOOP.
 ENDIF.

ENDFUNCTION.
```

Listing 7.2 Sample Code for BTE 00001810

7.6.3 Payment Program: Edit Groups with Process BTE 00001830

This BTE enables you to exclude individual items from a group or to exclude an entire group from payment after the items have been grouped.

The function module receives information about the group in structure C_REGUH and its line items in Table T_REGUP. The posting date, date of the next payment run, and the date to which open customer items are to be considered, are available as well.

By setting the field XIGNO in C_REGUH to the value 'X', the entire group can be excluded, which means that all items in this group appear on the exception list.

If the field XIGNO is set at item level, that is, in a line in Table T_REGUP, only this item is excluded from payment and appears on the exception list.

7.6.4 Payment Proposal: Maintenance Authorization Check with Process BTE 00001860

This BTE enables you to check additional authorizations during the proposal change. By setting the field C_NOCHANGE to the value 'X', line items can't be changed within the proposal change functionality.

Listing 7.3 shows an example with the following requirement:

▶ If a payment is made with payment method T, it isn't allowed to change the item in the proposal.

```
FUNCTION Z_PROCESS_00001860.

---------------------------------------------------------------
* Requirement 1: The payment proposal can't be edited for
*                payments with payment method 'T'
*---------------------------------------------------------------
  IF i_reguo-rzawe = 'T'.
    c_nochange = 'X'.
  endif.
ENDFUNCTION.
```

Listing 7.3 Sample Code for BTE 00001860

7.7 Summary

The majority of the payments in AP are paid via the automatic payment program. In this Chapter the execution, configuration and available enhancements of the automatic payment program were discussed.

In the next Chapter, AP payments via Check processing is described in detail.

Within Accounts Payable (AP), payments can be issued in different payment media formats. One of the most common formats is check printing.

8 Check Processing

Even in the electronic age, check printing is a common form of issuing AP payments in the United States, the United Kingdom, France, Canada, and Australia.

Two different types of checks forms are commonly used, however, the processing is slightly different:

▶ Prenumbered check forms

▶ Blank check forms

Prenumbered checks have the check numbers and MICR codes already printed on the check forms. In this case, the SAP software determined check number during check printing needs to match the preprinted check numbers.

For *blank check forms*, no check information is preprinted on the check, and the check number as well as the MICR code are determined by the SAP software and printed on the check.

The main advantage of using blank check forms is a more simplified check-management process because the check numbers are automatically determined by the SAP software and printed on the checks, thereby ensuring that the check register is always correct.

On the other side for prenumbered checks, before every check-printing run, you need to ensure that the check numbers match the SAP software determined check numbers. Otherwise, the check numbers in the check register won't match with the issued checks, which will cause issues during check reconciliation.

Prenumbered checks, however, do have a cost advantage over blank check forms because blank check forms require a special MICR code enabled printer as well as special ink.

This chapter covers all aspects of check management with SAP software, including the following:

▶ Check Management Configuration

▶ Check Printing

▶ Check Management

▶ Positive Pay

▶ Check Problems and Resolutions

8.1 Check Management Configuration

Besides the configuration steps within the payment methods as well as the payment program, minimal additional configuration steps for check printing are required.

8.1.1 Check Lot

A *check lot* or *check batch* is a check number range predefined in the system. A bank usually assigns a check lot to your organization, which identifies the issued checks from your organization. During check printing, the SAP software determines the next available check number, assigns the check number to the payment, and updates the check register. The check lots can be configured in the IMG via navigation path **IMG • Financial Accounting • Accounts Receivable and Accounts Payables • Business Transactions • Automatic Outgoing Payments • Payment Media • Check Management • Define Number Ranges for Checks** or via Transaction FCHI.

A check lot needs to be defined for every paying company code, house bank, and bank account ID combination, where checks need to be issued. It's possible to create multiple check lots within the same bank. This might be useful if different locations issue checks from the same bank account, however, the check numbers must be segregated by location. Figure 8.1 shows the creation screen of a check lot.

Lot Number

The **Lot number** is a four-digit identifier of a check number range. During check printing, this check lot needs to be specified to assign the correct check numbers.

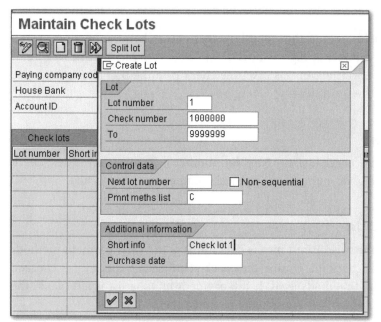

Figure 8.1 Check Lot Creation Screen

Check Number

The **Check number** field contains the lower number of the check number range. A check number can have up to 13 characters, which are usually numeric. However an alphanumber prefix or suffix is also allowed, for example, CK100000 – CK199999.

Check Number and Electronic Banks Statements (EBS)
If your organization uses Electronic Bank Statement (EBS) to clear issued checks automatically, the check numbers submitted by your bank have to match the exact length of the numbers in the check lot.
For example, your bank submits the check numbers with leading zeros in the EBS file, such as 0000123456. In this case, the check lot needs to be defined with leading zeros as well, such as 0000100000 – 0000199999.
If you want to avoid leading zeros, the check numbers in the bank file needs to be changed during the EBS upload via BAdI FIEB_CHANGE_BS_DATA.

To Number

The **To** number field contains the highest number of the check number range. You should make this number as high as possible to avoid running out of check numbers during check printing. In this case, the check printing program issues error messages during check printing.

Next Lot Number

If you have multiple check lots, the **Next lot number** field contains the next check to be used if the highest number of the check number range is reached.

Payment Method List

The payment method list (**Pmnt meths list**) contains the valid payment methods to be used for this check lot. During the check printing, the check lot is checked against the payment methods used. If the payment method list is left blank, the check lot can be used with every suitable payment method.

Short Info/Purchase Date

The **Short info** and **Purchase date** fields contain a short description as well as a date of the check lot for information purposes only.

8.1.2 Void Reasons

The second configuration step is to specify void reasons for checks. A *void reason* is required when a check needs to be voided. The void reasons shown in Figure 8.2 can be configured in the IMG via navigation path **IMG • Financial Accounting • Accounts Receivable and Accounts Payables • Business Transactions • Automatic Outgoing Payments • Payment Media • Check Management • Define Void Reason Codes** or via Transaction FCHV.

The void reason is a two-digit numeric code that can be defined based on your organization's requirements. However, certain void reasons are reserved for the print program and have special functions. These codes can't be changed. Table 8.1 lists the void reason codes with special functions.

```
Change View "Check Void Reason Codes": Overview

  New Entries

  Check Void Reason Codes
  | Reason | Void reason cde              | Reserved for print programs  |
  |        |                             |                             |
  | 1      | Test printout               | 1 Sample printout           |
  | 2      | Page overflow               | 2 Page overflow             |
  | 3      | Form closing                | 3 Form closing              |
  | 4      | Ripped during printing      |                             |
  | 5      | Printed incorrectly         |                             |
  | 6      | Destroyed/unusable          |                             |
  | 7      | Stolen                      |                             |
  | 8      | Incorrect lot inserted      |                             |
  | 9      | Reversed check payment      |                             |
  | 10     | Check voided after printing |                             |
  | 99     | Zero net check              | 4 Zero net check            |
```

Figure 8.2 Check Void Reason Code Screen

Void Reason Codes	Description	Function
1	Sample printout	During the check printing, sample checks can be printed. These checks are voided with reason code 1. It's possible to avoid sample checks via a parameter in the check printing program.
2	Page overflow	Page overflow or check overflow checks are voided with reason code 2. Voiding overflow checks is only necessary for preprinted check forms. It's possible to avoid voiding overflow checks via a parameter in the check printing program.
3	Form closing	A form summary section can be printed at the end of a check printing run. This check is voided with reason code 3. It's possible to avoid a form summary section via a parameter in the check printing program.

Table 8.1 Reserved Void Reason Codes

In addition, a special void reason code for *zero net checks* can be defined, which is used in countries such as the United States and Canada.

8.2 Check Printing Program

The most commonly used check printing program with check management is RFFOUS_C. If a different check printing program is required, all available payment formats are listed in OSS Note 101440 for the classic payment medium programs.

8.2.1 RFFOUS_C Print Program sections

The check printing program RFFOUS_C is divided into five sections:

- ▶ Company code selection
- ▶ Further selections
- ▶ Print control
- ▶ Output control
- ▶ Reprint checks

Payment run/Company Code Selection Section

In the **Payment run/Company code selection** section shown in Figure 8.3, the payment run and company code selections are defined.

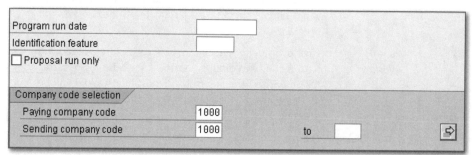

Figure 8.3 Company Code Selection Section

Payment Run Selection

The payment run selection consists of the **Program run date** and the **Identification feature** fields. These fields only have to be filled out if checks have to be printed manually by directly executing the check printing program. Usually, these fields are filled automatically during the print program execution during the payment run.

Paying Company Code
In the **Paying company code** field, the company code from where the payments are made has to be specified. This field is mandatory.

Sending Company Code
The **Sending company code** field specifies the origin company codes of the items to be paid. Multiple company codes can be entered.

Further Selections Section

The **Further selections** section shown in Figure 8.4 specifies the payment method and bank selections for check printing. The following fields always have to be specified:

▶ **House Bank**

▶ **Account ID**

▶ **Check lot number**

It's also recommended to specify the **Payment method**, if your organization uses multiple payment methods.

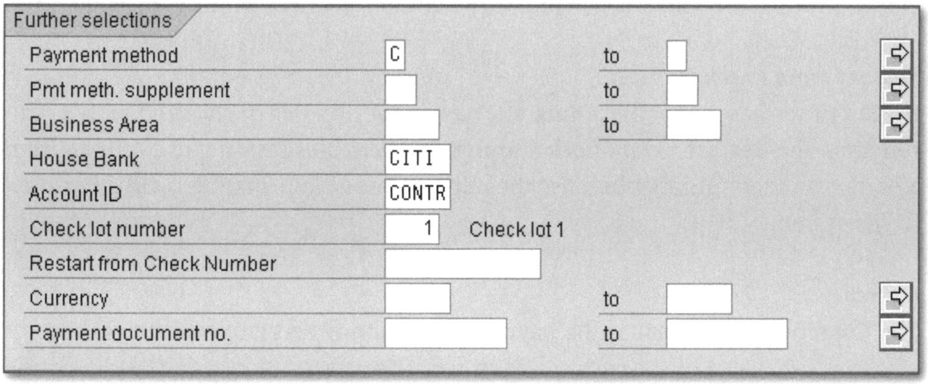

Figure 8.4 Further Selections Section

Payment Method

The **Payment method** field specifies the payment methods for which the checks need to be printed (it's recommended to specify the payment methods).

Payment Method Supplement

The **Pmt meth. supplement** field allows the selection of specific payment method supplements. Payment method supplements were covered in Chapter 5.

Business Area

Payment can also be selected by business area using the **Business Area** field. In this case, it's recommended to have payments separated by business area.

House Bank

The **House Bank** field specifies the house bank from which the payments are made. This field is a mandatory field in the check printing program.

Account ID

The **Account ID** field specifies the bank account ID of the house bank from which the payments are made. This field is a mandatory field in the check printing program.

Check Lot Number

The **Check lot number** field identifies the check lot of the bank to be used during check printing. This field is a mandatory field in the check printing program.

Restart from Check Number

If the printer has stopped printing after a certain number of checks due to a malfunction, the **Restart from Check Number** field enables printing to continue from a particular check number because the relevant check information is already stored in the system.

Currency

The **Currency** field specifies the payment selection for certain currencies only.

Payment Document Number

In the **Payment document no** field, only specific document numbers can be selected for printing.

Print Control Section

In the **Print control** section, specifications of the output and printers are made during check printing (see Figure 8.5).

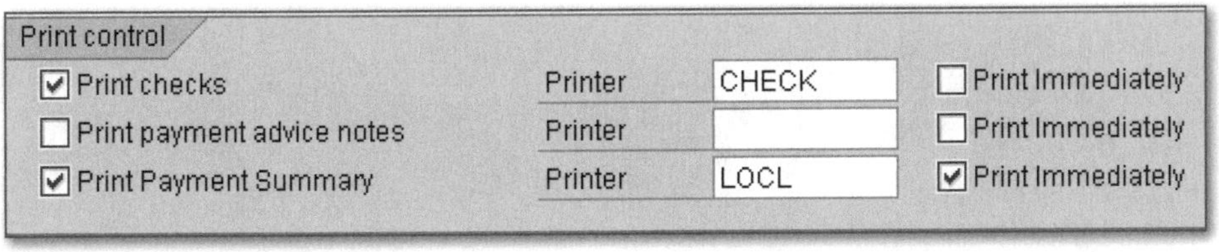

Figure 8.5 Print Control Section

Print Checks
The **Print checks** flag needs to be set if checks need to be printed.

Print Payment Advice Notes
The **Print payment advice notes** flag needs to be set if payment advices need to be printed. Payment advices are needed if the note to payee information is printed on a payment advice (see Section 5.1.2 in Chapter 5).

Print Payment Summary
The **Print Payment Summary** flag needs to be set if a payment summary needs to be printed after the check printing run. The payment summary lists all payments and totals by bank account.

Printer
Specify a **Printer** for each of the selected outputs. Usually, the payment advice notes and the payment summary are printed on a different printer than the checks.

Print Immediately
The **Print Immediately** flag needs to be set if the printout should be executed immediately. If the flag isn't set, the printout has to be done manually via the menu **System • Services • Output Control** or via Transaction SP01. You should have check printing executed manually to ensure that the printer is working properly and the proper check forms are used.

Output Control Section

The **Output control** section specifies further output details in the check form (see Figure 8.6).

```
Output control
   Alternative check form        [                    ]
   Filler for digits in words    [ * ]
   Number of sample printouts    [   ]
   No. of items in payment summary [      ]
   ☐ Payment Document Validation
   ☐ Texts in recipient's lang.
   ☐ Currency in ISO code
   ☑ No Form Summary Section
   ☑ Do not Void any Checks
```

Figure 8.6   Output Control Section

Alternative Check Form
The **Alternative check form** allows the output on a different check form than the check form specified in the configuration (see Section 5.1.2 in Chapter 5).

Filler for Digits in Words
The payment amount can be output in words in the check. Blanks are replaced by this padding character that can be selected via this parameter. If the standard forms F110_PRENUM_CHCK or F110_RU_PLATJOSH are used, the padding character must be left blank.

Number of Sample Printouts
The **Number of sample printout** fields specifies how many sample checks are printed before the real checks. Sample checks are voided with void reason code 1. It's recommended not to print any sample checks.

No. of Items in Payment Summary
This field specifies the number of items in the payment summary. If you require a payment summary, set the field to 9999 to ensure that all items are printed.

Payment Document Validation

The **Payment Document Validation** field should only be set if the checks aren't printed immediately after the payment run. It validates that the payments are still valid and were not reversed in the meantime. Otherwise, a check could be issued for a payment that was reversed.

Texts in Recipient's Language

This field ensures that the text elements in the form are printed in the language of the recipient. Prerequisite is that the form is maintained in the required languages.

Currency in ISO Code

If this flag is set, all currency keys are converted into the corresponding international ISO codes. The ISO code must have been defined for each currency key via configuration.

No Form Summary Section

If this flag is set as recommended, no form summary is printed at the end of the check printing run. The form summary check is voided with void reason code 3.

Do Not Void Any Checks

The setting for this flag depends on which type of check form, blank or pre-numbered, is used and whether overflow checks are printed (see Section 5.1.2 in Chapter 5).

You should *not* set this flag if your organization uses prenumbered check forms and overflow checks are printed. In this case, the system would issue a new check number for each overflow check and void this check with void reason code 2. This ensures that the check numbers printed on the check forms and the check register are aligned. In all other cases, the flag should be set.

Reprint Checks Section

The **Reprint checks** section shown in Figure 8.7 is only used if you require reprinting check numbers from a specific check run in a mass run. In this case, set the **Void and reprint...** flag, enter the incorrect **Check numbers**, and specify a **Void reason code**.

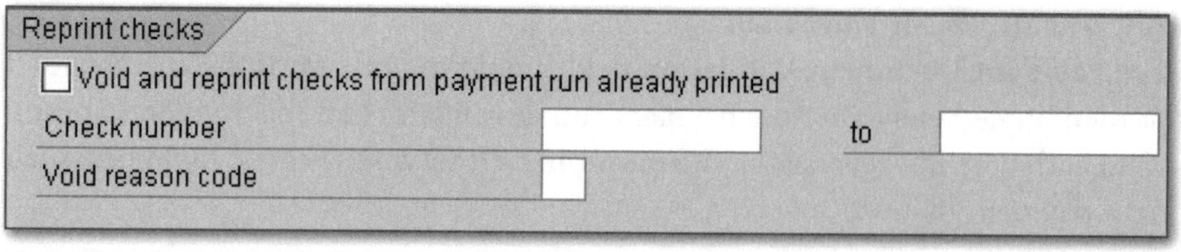

Figure 8.7 Reprint Checks Section

8.2.2 Variants

After all parameters in the check printing program are entered, the parameters have to be saved as a variant. This can be accomplished by choosing Save as Variant or via the header menu by selecting **Goto • Variants • Save as Variant.** Enter a **Variant Name** as well as a description in the **Meaning** field as shown in Figure 8.8.

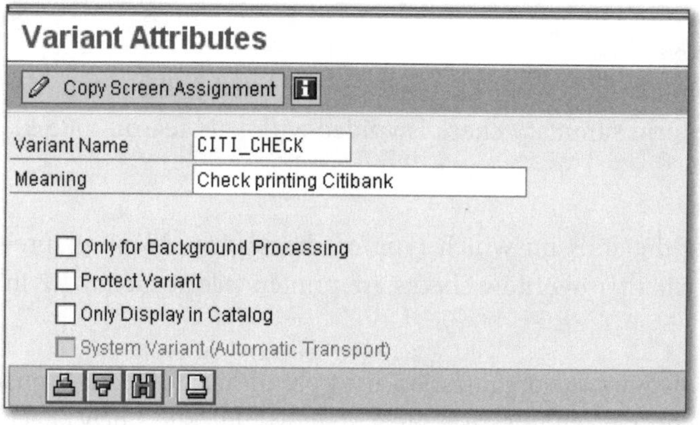

Figure 8.8 Variant Screen

After the variant is saved, it can be selected in the payment program in the Printout/data medium tab. The automatic payment program was covered in Chapter 7.

8.2.3 MICR Printer

If the check number, bank routing number, and account number have to be printed in MICR font (Magnetic Ink Character Recognition), a specific MICR-enabled printer must be used. OSS Note 94233 lists all supported printers for the MICR font.

8.3   Check Form

The SAP software delivers sample check forms in two formats, SAPscript or PDF (Adobe) format. Table 8.2 shows a list of these sample forms.

Form	Description	Format
F110_PRENUM_CHCK	Check with check number	SAPscript
F110_D_SCHECK_A4	Check in German A4 format	SAPscript
FI_PAYM_DE_CHECK	Check with check number	PDF

Table 8.2   List of SAP Sample Forms

All sample SAPscripts can be found in Transaction SE71 and Transaction SFP for Adobe forms.

8.3.1   Check Layout

During check printing, specific *windows* in the check form are available. Every window contains different content that is printed on the check. Table 8.3 gives an overview of the different windows in the check form.

Window	Content
HEADER	Company specifications, such as company name or logo
PAGE	Page number
INFO, INFO 2	Date document number, vendor account, or account clerk
ADDRESS	Vendor specifications for window envelopes and receiver address
MAIN	Line item information of the paid items and total payment amount
CARRYFWD	Carry forward for check overflow
CHECK	Check information, such as check number
CHECKADD	Check address
CHECKSPL	Amount in words

Table 8.3   Check Form Windows and Content

Figure 8.9 shows a sample check in SAPscript format with the preceding windows.

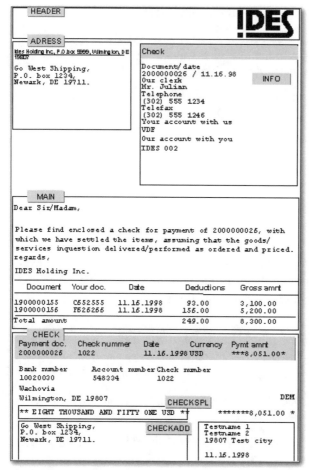

Figure 8.9 Sample Check Form in Sapscript

8.3.2 Check Form Enhancements

If information has to be printed on the check, which isn't available in the check print form or a special logic needs to be applied, the SAPscripts forms can be enhanced with a user-exit.

Changing the SAP Check Printing Program

It's not recommended to change the SAP check printing program or create a new check printing program because new developments or corrections from SAP aren't applied automatically to your own developed programs.

If an enhancement in the SAPscript form is required, a user-exit can be called directly from the form. Listing 8.1 shows a sample code of a user-exit call in a SAPScript form. The fields REGUP-BELNR, REGUP-GJAHR, and REGUP-BUZEI are passed to the user-exit GET_TEXT within program ZRFFOUSC. In return, the field W_SGTXT is passed back to the form and can be used within the form.

```
/:    PERFORM GET_TEXT IN PROGRAM ZRFFOUSC

/:    USING &REGUP-BELNR&

/:    USING &REGUP-GJAHR&

/:    USING &REGUP-BUZEI&

/:    CHANGING &W_SGTXT&

/:    ENDPERFORM
```

Listing 8.1 User-Exit Call in SAPscript Form

The user-exits are within the program ZRFFOUSC. Listing 8.2 shows the sample code for the user-exit GET_TEXT.

```
form get_text tables in_tab  structure itcsy
                     out_tab structure itcsy.
  data: w_belnr type belnr_d,
        w_gjahr type gjahr,
        w_buzei type buzei,
        w_sgtxt type sgtxt.

  clear: w_belnr, w_gjahr, w_buzei, w_sgtxt.
  read table in_tab with key name = 'REGUP-BELNR'.
  if sy-subrc = 0.
    move in_tab-value to w_belnr.
  endif.
  read table in_tab with key name = 'REGUP-GJAHR'.
  if sy-subrc = 0.
    move in_tab-value to w_gjahr.
  endif.
```

```
read table in_tab with key name = 'REGUP-BUZEI'.
if sy-subrc = 0.
  move in_tab-value to w_buzei.
endif.
select single sgtxt into w_sgtxt
       from bseg
       where belnr = w_belnr
       and   gjahr = w_gjahr
       and   buzei = w_buzei.
read table out_tab with key 'W_SGTXT'.
if sy-subrc = 0.
  move w_sgtxt to out_tab-value.
  modify out_tab index sy-tabix.
endif.
endform.                    "GET_TEXT
```

Listing 8.2 User-Exit Sample Code

Program ZRFFOUSC

The user-exit ZRFFOUSC needs to be created with the following attributes:

▶ Type: Subroutine Pool

▶ Check box: Fixed-point arithmetic

8.4 Check Management Transactions

All check management transactions can be found using the navigation path **SAP Menu • Accounting • Financial Accounting • Accounts Payable • Environment • Check Information**. Table 8.4 lists the available check management transactions.

Transaction	Description
FCH1	Check Display
FCH2	Check Display for Payment Document
FCHN	Check Register
FCH4	Renumber Checks
FCH7	Reprint Check

Table 8.4 Check Management Transactions

Transaction	Description
FCH6	Additional Info/Cash Encashment
FCHR	Online Cashed Checks
FCHT	Change Assignment to Payment
FCH5	Create Manual Checks
FCH3	Void Unused Checks
FCH9	Void Issued Checks
FCH8	Cancel Payment
FCHD	Delete Checks for Payment Run
FCHF	Delete Manual Checks
FCHE	Delete Voided Checks
FCHG	Reset Data

Table 8.4 Check Management Transactions (Cont.)

Not all check management transactions are commonly used. Therefore, only the most commonly used transactions are described in more detail in the following section.

8.5 Display Check Information

Multiple checks can be displayed by using the check register or single checks with the **Display Check** Transaction.

8.5.1 Display Checks

A single check can be displayed via Transaction FCH1 or by using the navigation path **SAP Menu • Accounting • Financial Accounting • Accounts Payable • Environment • Check Information • Display • For Check**. In the entry screen shown in Figure 8.10, the **House Bank**, **Account ID**, and **Check number** fields need to be entered.

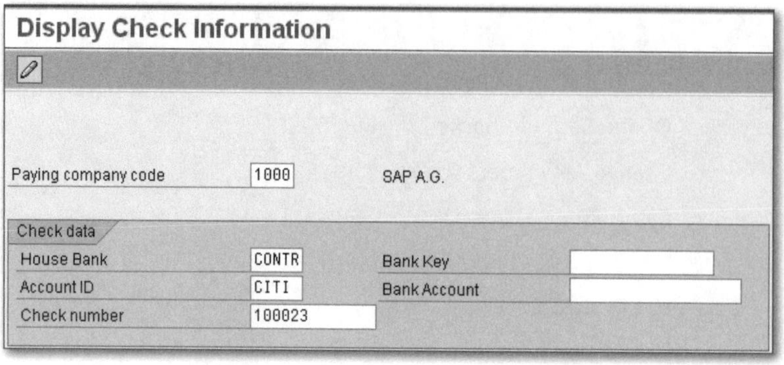

Figure 8.10 Display Check Screen

8.5.2 Check Register

An entire check register can be displayed via Transaction FCHN or by using the navigation path **SAP Menu • Accounting • Financial Accounting • Accounts Payable • Environment • Check Information • Display • Check Register**.

The check register has two tabs. In the General Selection tab, bank information as well as check numbers can be selected. The Further Selection tab allows selection by additional criteria, such as issuance date, check creation date, payment method, or payment run.

8.6 Change Check Information

Check information usually doesn't have to be changed. However on an exceptional basis, checks need to be reprinted or the encashment date needs to be changed manually.

8.6.1 Reprint Checks

A check can be reprinted via Transaction FCH7 or by using the navigation path **SAP Menu • Accounting • Financial Accounting • Accounts Payable • Environment • Check Information • Change • Reprint**. This function might be necessary if a check is lost or printed incorrectly. The result of this transaction is that the original check number is voided, and the payment is assigned to the new check number. The entry screen is shown in Figure 8.11.

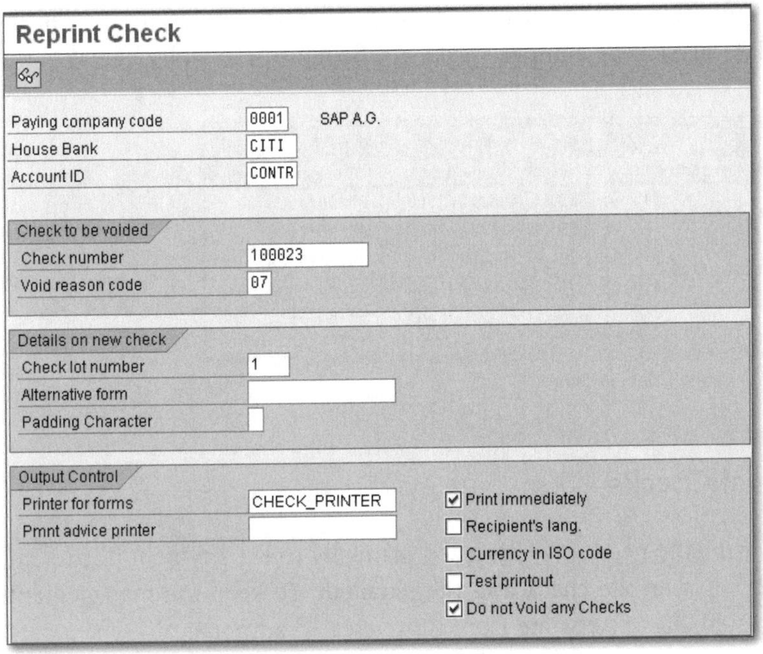

Reprint Check

Paying company code	0001	SAP A.G.
House Bank	CITI	
Account ID	CONTR	

Check to be voided

| Check number | 100023 |
| Void reason code | 07 |

Details on new check

Check lot number	1
Alternative form	
Padding Character	

Output Control

Printer for forms	CHECK_PRINTER	☑ Print immediately
Pmnt advice printer		☐ Recipient's lang.
		☐ Currency in ISO code
		☐ Test printout
		☑ Do not Void any Checks

Figure 8.11 Reprint Check Screen

To reprint the check, select **Check • Reprint** on the header menu.

8.6.2   Change Additional Information/Check Encashment

Transaction FCH6 allows you to enter manually the check encashment date for a single check. This might be necessary if an error occurs during uploading of the cashed check file or Electronic Bank Statement (EBS) and the check encashment date can't be filled automatically.

8.6.3   Online Cashed Checks

Compared to Transaction FCH6, Transaction FCH7 allows you to enter the check encashment date for multiple checks at one time. This transaction can be executed using the navigation path **SAP Menu • Accounting • Financial Accounting • Accounts Payable • Environment • Check Information • Change • Online Cashed Checks**.

As shown in Figure 8.12, for every cashed check, the **Value date** and the **Check encashment date** need to be entered.

Cashed checks				
Check number	Amount paid	Currncy	Value date	Check encashment
100010	345.75	USD	05/06/2008	05/06/2008
100016	75.45	USD	05/06/2008	05/06/2008
100017	115.34	USD	05/08/2008	05/08/2008
100019	419.25	USD	05/08/2008	05/08/2008
100023	105.84	USD	05/08/2008	05/08/2008

Figure 8.12 Online Cashed Checks Screen

8.7   Manual Checks

Checks issued manually need to be assigned manually to the payment document to create a link between the check and the payment. To keep the management of manually created checks separate from those created automatically, a separate number range should be reserved for them. Manual checks can be assigned with Transaction FCH5 or via navigation path **SAP Menu • Accounting • Financial Accounting • Accounts Payable • Environment • Check Information • Create • Manual Checks.**

8.8   Void Checks

The SAP software has two different transactions for voiding checks. Transaction FCH8 voids the check and reverses the payment at the same time. Transaction FCH9 however only voids the check.

8.8.1   Void Issued Checks

Transaction FCH9 allows you to void a single check. It is important that the check is just voided; the payment document is *not* reversed, and *no* replacement check is issued. This transaction can be executed using the navigation path **SAP Menu • Accounting • Financial Accounting • Accounts Payable • Environment • Check Information • Void • Issued Checks.**

8.8.2 Cancel Payments

In comparison to Transaction FCH9, Transaction FCH8 voids a single check and reverses the payment, which means that the invoice will be paid again in the next payment run. This transaction can be executed using the navigation path **SAP Menu • Accounting • Financial Accounting • Accounts Payable • Environment • Check Information • Void • Cancel Payment.** It is recommended to use Transaction FCH8 instead of Transaction FCH9 for check voiding, because in a usual business process the payment needs to be reversed in the case a check is voided.

8.9   Reset Check Data

Transaction FCHG allows you to reset check information, such as encashment data, extract data, or voiding data. This might be necessary if a check is incorrectly encashed or extracted. The extract data are filled automatically during the external data transfer with Transaction FCHX.

8.10   External Data Transfer/Positive Pay

The *external data transfer* functionality is also known as *positive pay*. That means that you inform your bank of all checks that were issued, canceled, or voided on a certain date to avoid check fraud. This functionality can be executed with Transaction FCHX or via the navigation path **SAP Menu • Accounting • Financial Accounting • Accounts Payable • Environment • Check Information • External Data Transfer.**

This program creates a file of all check information belonging to a paying company code, and providing this information fulfills the specified selection criteria. The data in the file is sorted according to account number and check number, and its format corresponds to the internal format of the DTACHKH and DTACHKP structures. Because currently no banking standard exists for the positive pay file format, it's recommended that you create a new program that reads the file created via Transition FCHX and then reformat this file format into the bank required format.

The selection screen of the external data transfer transaction is shown in Figure 8.13.

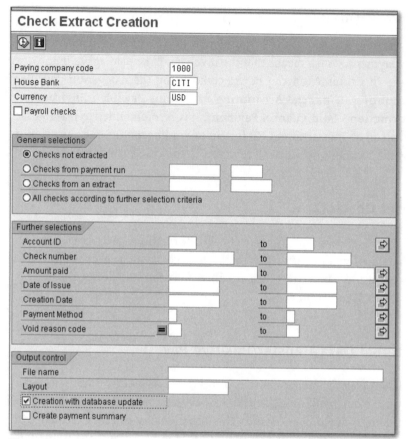

Figure 8.13 Check Extract Creation Screen

Besides the common selection criteria such as Account ID or date selection, the following parameters have special functions:

- **Checks not extracted**
- **Creation with database update**

Checks Not Extracted

If the **Checks not extracted** field is selected, all checks that were not extracted in prior extract runs are selected. This is especially important if you extract the checks on a regular basis and want to ensure that all issued checks are selected.

Creation with Database Update

The **Creation with database update** flag specifies that during the check extract, the check is updated with the extract date and time.

8.11 Create Reference for Check

Program RFCHKU00 copies the check numbers into a selected field of the corresponding payment documents. For example, the check number can be copied into the Reference or the Assignment field of the payment document, thus enabling the check to be assigned to the payment document.

This check number reference is indicated in the payment medium table so that the program ignores those check numbers already copied into the corresponding payment documents.

This program is especially helpful if you want to have the check number displayed in the assignment field of the outgoing cash line item of the payment document. Figure 8.14 shows the selection screen of report RFCHKU00.

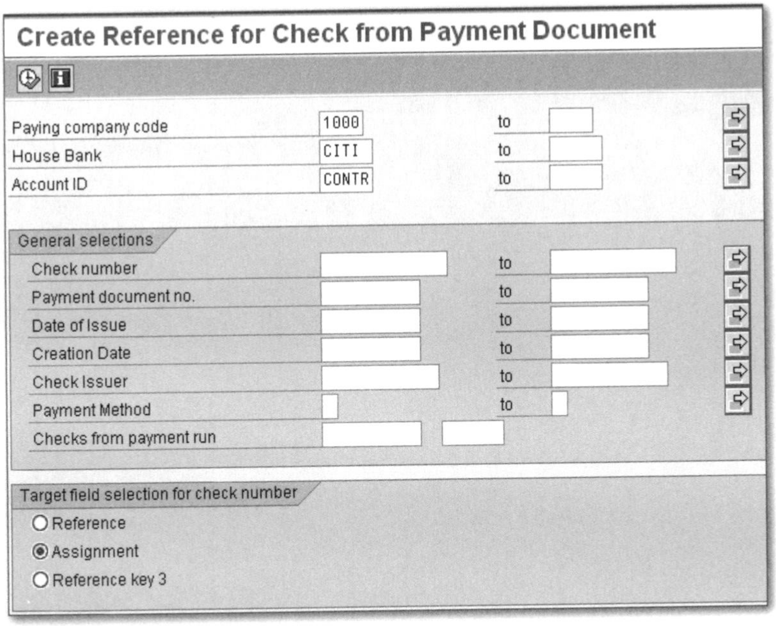

Figure 8.14 Report RFCHKU00 Selection Screen

8.12 Summary

In the Chapter, the payment issuance using checks was described. The SAP software delivers special check printing programs and has a variety of Transactions for check processing.

In the next Chapter AP payments through bank transfers is described.

Within Accounts Payable (AP), payments can be issued in different payment media formats. Bank transfer allows the submission of payments in an electronic format.

9   Bank Transfer

Even though check printing is a common form of issuing AP payments, more and more companies submit payments in an electronic format using bank transfers because bank transfers have the following advantages over check printing:

▶ Bank transfers costs significantly less than check printing because no stamps, special printer, toner, or check forms are needed.

▶ Bank transfers are more secure, due to fewer fraudulent transactions.

The bank transfer formats are usually different by country. In addition, within a country, different bank transfer types may apply. Prior to Release 4.6, SAP delivered payment programs specific to the payment format, that is, RFFOUS_T – U.S. Domestic Bank transfer or RFFOM100 – International Bank transfers. These programs had to be executed after the payment run to create the payment details in the correct payment formats. OSS Note 101440 lists all available bank transfer formats for the classic payment medium programs.

As of Release 4.6, the Payment Medium Workbench (PMW) was introduced. PMW is a generic payment medium program for all payment medium formats for which different variants are defined in configuration. The available payment formats for PMW are listed in OSS Note 395679.

Even thought the formats are different by country, fundamentally the configuration and execution steps for the bank transfers within SAP are very similar. This chapter therefore only describes in detail the ACH bank transfer format, which is commonly used in the United States for domestic payments.

9.1   ACH Payments

Within the United States, domestic payments are transferred usually using the ACH format, which stands for Automatic Clearing House. Bank transfers are executed via a private network between banks. Rules and standards are defined by the National Automated Clearing House Association (NACHA). More information can be found at *www.nacha.org*. ACH payments are used for the following:

▶ Direct payments of customer bills, such as utility bills or mortgage payments, called ACH debit payments

▶ Direct deposit of payroll or tax refunds

▶ Business-to-business payments

▶ E-commerce payments

9.1.1   ACH Payment Types

Within the ACH payment format, different ACH types are available. Table 9.1 lists the most common ACH types and their uses.

ACH Type	Description	Use
CCD	Cash Concentration or Disbursement	Payments from companies to other companies or private individuals, that is, simple vendor payments
PPD	Prearranged Payment and Deposit Entry	Payments between private individuals or from companies to private individuals, that is payroll direct deposits
CTX	Corporate Trade Exchange Note	Payments between companies, that is, vendor payments with complex note to payee records

Table 9.1 ACH Format Types and Uses

Within SAP all of these ACH types can be handled with the classic bank transfer payment Program RFFOUS_T. Within the past couple of years, banks introduced variations of the CCD and PPD format called CCD+ and PPD+, respectively. The SAP Program RFFOUS_TC_FG_PLUS handles these variations.

In addition, SAP delivers the PMW format ACH as well, which is a predefined format for all types of ACH payments.

During the implementation, you need to decide either to use the classic payment medium programs or PMW. Because SAP continues developing PMW, you should use the PMW formats instead of the classic payment medium programs.

9.2 Bank Transfer Using the Classic Payment Medium Program

As previously described, Program RFFOUS_T can be used to create a bank transfer file in the ACH format.

9.2.1 RFFOUS_T Program Sections

The bank transfer program RFFOUS_T is divided into four sections:

▶ **Company code selection**
▶ **Further selections**
▶ **Print control**
▶ **Output control**

Company Code Selection Section

In the **Company code selection** section shown in Figure 9.1, the payment proposal and company code selections are defined.

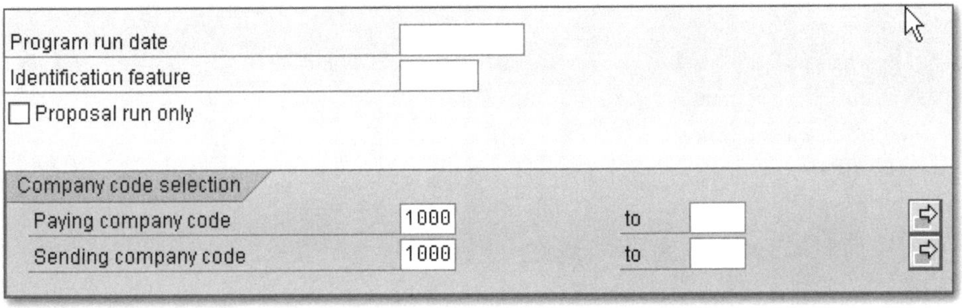

Program run date			
Identification feature			
☐ Proposal run only			
Company code selection			
Paying company code	1000	to	⇨
Sending company code	1000	to	⇨

Figure 9.1 Company Code Selection Section

Payment Proposal Selection

The payment proposal selection consists of the **Program run date** and the **Identification feature** fields. These fields only have to be filled in if ACH transfers have to be created manually by directly executing the ACH bank transfer program. Usually these fields are filled automatically during the program execution during the payment run, so they are left empty here.

Paying Company Code

In the **Paying company code** field, the company codes from where the payments are made have to be specified. This field is mandatory.

Sending Company Code

The **Sending company code** field specifies the origin company codes of the items to be paid. Multiple company codes can be entered.

Further Selections Section

The **Further selections** section shown in Figure 9.2 specifies the payment method and bank selections for the bank transfer. As a minimum, the following fields should be specified:

▶ **Standard entry class code**

▶ **House bank**

▶ **Account**

It's also recommended to specify the **Payment methods**, if your organization uses multiple payment methods.

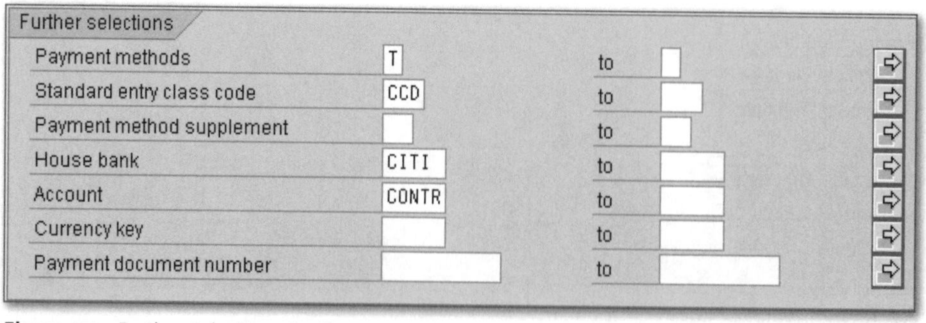

Figure 9.2 Further Selections Section

Payment Methods

The **Payment methods** field specifies the payment methods for which the bank transfer file needs to be created. You should specify the payment methods.

Standard Entry Class Code

The **Standard entry class code** field specifies the ACH payment type for the bank transfer file, such as CCD, CTX, or PPD.

Payment Method Supplement

The **Payment method supplement** field allows the selection of specific payment method supplements. Payment method supplements were covered in Section 5.2 of Chapter 5.

House Bank

The **House bank** field specifies the house bank from which the payments are made.

Account

The **Account** field specifies the bank account ID of the house bank from which the payments are made.

Currency Key

The **Currency key** field specifies the payment selection for certain currencies only.

Payment Document Number

In the **Payment document number** field, only specific document numbers can be selected for bank transfer.

Print Control Section

In the **Print control** section shown in Figure 9.3, specifications of the output and printers are made during bank transfer creation.

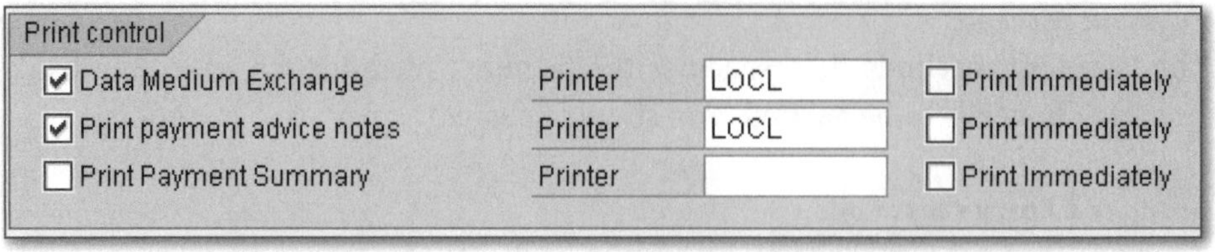

Figure 9.3 Print Control Section

Data Medium Exchange

The **Data Medium Exchange** flag needs to be set if a bank file needs to be created. At the same time, a summary form for the bank transfer file is created, which can be submitted to the bank. This form is also called an *accompanying form*. This flag should always be set.

Print Payment Advice Notes

The **Print payment advice notes** flag needs to be set if payment advices need to be printed. Payment advices are needed if the note to payee information is printed on a payment advice (see Section 5.1.2 in Chapter 5).

Print Payment Summary

The **Print Payment Summary** flag needs to be set if a payment summary needs to be printed after the bank transfer creation. The payment summary lists all payments and totals by bank account.

Printer

Specify a **Printer** for each of the selected outputs. Usually all outputs can be printed on the same printer.

Print Immediately

The **Print immediately** flag needs to be set if the printout should be executed immediately. If the flag isn't set, the printout has to be done manually via the menu **System • Services • Output Control** or via Transaction SP01.

Output Control Section

The **Output control** section shown in Figure 9.4 specifies further output details during the file creation.

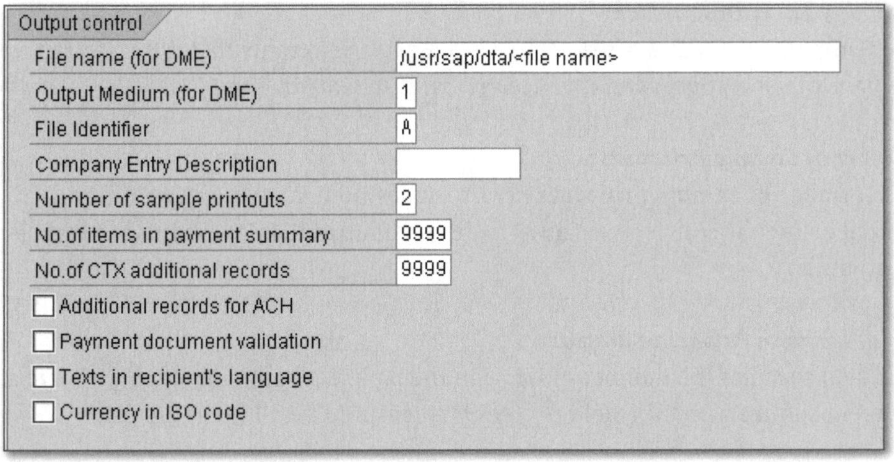

Figure 9.4 Output Control Section

The output file can be created either directly in the file system or stored within the SAP system in a temporary file called TemSe output. If the TemSe output option is chosen, the file needs to be created in a second step within the data medium administration using Program SAPMFDTA. This allows for segregation of duties if the payment program execution and bank transfer file creation needs to be handled by different departments such as the AP department and the Treasury department.

File Name (for DME)

The **File name (for DME)** needs to be specified if the file needs to be created directly in the file system. The file can be created in the application server or presentation server, depending of the file name chosen, that is, */usr/sap/dta/<file name>* or *C:\DTA\<file name>*.

Output Medium (for DME)

The **Output Medium (for DME)** field specifies if the file will be created in the TemSe area or directly in the file system. Enter "0" for a TemSe file or "1" for a direct file.

File Identifier

The **File Identifier** is used to differentiate between several files that were generated on the same day. Values 0 to 9 or A to Z are allowed.

Company Entry Description

The **Company Entry Description** is a 10-character field value that is transferred to the bank file and appears on the receiver bank statement.

Number of Sample Printouts

The **Number of sample printouts** field specifies how many sample printouts are printed before the real payment advices. It's recommended not to print any sample printouts.

No. of Items in Payment Summary

This field specifies the number of items in the payment summary. If you require a payment summary, set the field to "9999" to ensure that all items are printed.

No. of CTX Additional Records

This field is only relevant for the ACH format CTX and specifies the maximum number of information fields in which information concerning invoice items can be passed on to the payee. Using this parameter, the maximum number can be reduced if you don't want all information to be printed on the account statement, or if you always want a payment advice note to be printed. If the number of information fields isn't sufficient for all of the invoice information, a payment advice reference is created.

Additional Records for ACH

If the **Additional records for ACH** field is set, additional information, such as invoice information, is created in the bank transfer file.

Payment Document Validation

The **Payment document validation** field should only be set if the bank transfer file isn't created immediately after the payment run. It validates that the payments are still valid and were not reversed in the meantime. Otherwise, a bank transfer could be issued for a payment that was reversed.

Text in Recipient's Language

This field ensures that the text elements in the form are printed in the language of the recipient. Prerequisite is that the form is maintained in the required languages.

Currency in ISO Code

If this flag is set, all currency keys are converted into the corresponding international ISO codes. The requirement for this is that the ISO code has been defined for each currency key via configuration.

9.2.2 Variants

After all parameters in the bank transfer program are entered, the parameters have to be saved as a *variant* by choosing **Save as Variant** or via the header menu by selecting **Goto • Variants • Save as Variant**. Enter a **Variant Name** as well as a description in the **Meaning** field as shown in Figure 9.5.

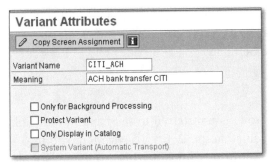

Figure 9.5 Variant Creation Screen

After the variant is saved, it can be selected in the payment program in the **Printout/data medium tab**. The automatic payment program was covered in Chapter 7.

9.2.3 Configuration Steps

Besides the configuration setting for the payment method, which was covered in Chapter 5, the following additional settings are required:

▶ Define accompanying form

▶ Define tax-ID for company code

▶ Maintain company number in house bank

Define Accompanying Form

For bank transfers, an accompanying form needs to be assigned to the payment method in the **Form Data** section. This form can be assigned in the IMG via navigation path **IMG • Financial Accounting • Accounts Receivable and Accounts Payables • Business Transactions • Outgoing Payments • Automatic Outgoing Payments • Payment Method/Bank Selection for Payment Program • Set up Payment Methods per Country for Payment Transactions.**

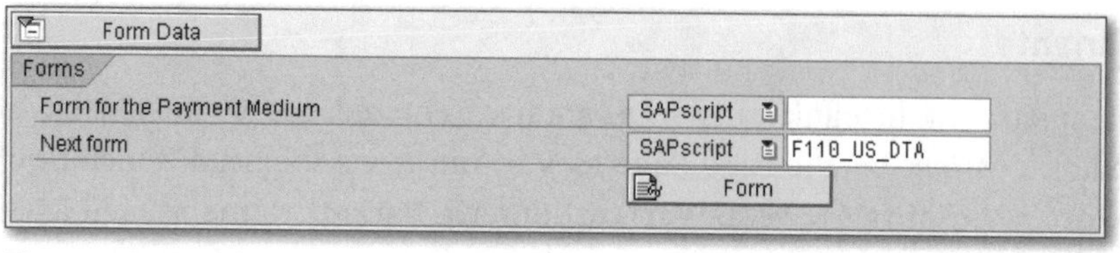

Figure 9.6 Sample Accompanying Form

As shown in Figure 9.6, the form needs to be assigned in the **Next form** field. SAP delivers sample forms in the format F110_XX_DATA. *XX* identifies the specific country, such as US for USA or D for Germany

Tax ID-Number for Company Code

The tax ID-number of the company code is transferred to the bank in the bank transfer file. This tax-ID can be maintained in the IMG via navigation path **IMG • Financial Accounting • Financial Accounting Global Settings • Company Code • Enter Global Parameters.** Select **Additional Data,** and enter the tax-ID number in the **Tax number USA (TIN)** field as shown in Figure 9.7.

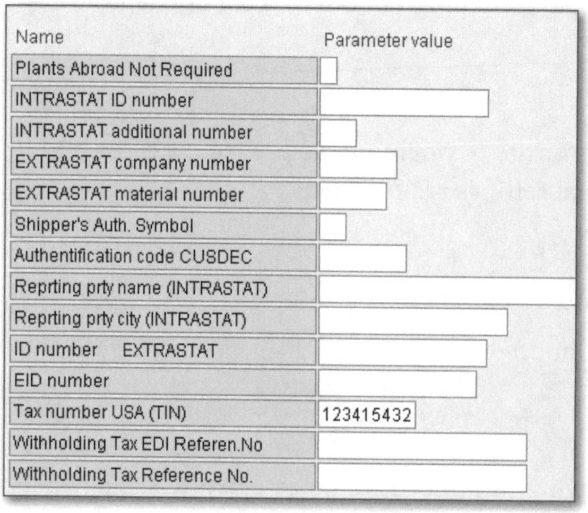

Figure 9.7 Tax ID Maintenance in Company Code

Maintain Company Number in House Bank

The **Company number** field value shown in Figure 9.8 is submitted in the ACH file to the bank and identifies a unique number assigned from the bank to your company for ACH bank files. This field can be maintained within the IMG via navigation path **IMG • Financial Accounting • Bank Accounting • Bank Accounts • Define House Banks** or via Transaction FI12.

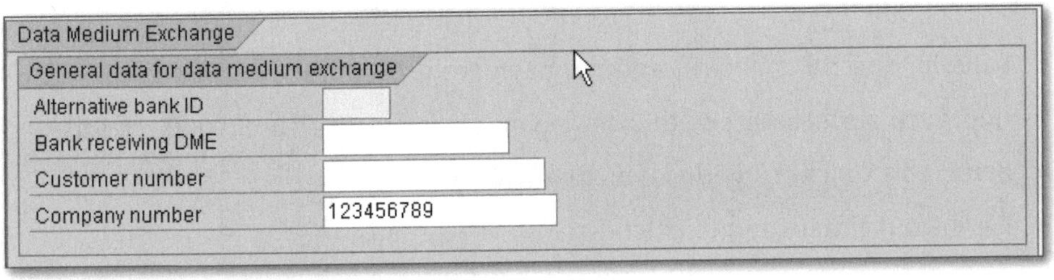

Figure 9.8 Company Number Field

The **Company number** field can be found in the **Data Medium Exchange** section of the house bank master data.

9.2.4 Enhancements

For the bank transfer Program RFFOUS_T, a variety of user-exits are available. These user-exits allow the different records to be changed during file creation. Table 9.2 lists the different user-exits available.

User-Exit	Description
RFFOX100	Change of file header record
RFFOX101	Change of batch header record
RFFOX102	Change of CCD record
RFFOX103	Change of CTX record
RFFOX104	Additional addendum records
RFFOX105	Change of batch control record

Table 9.2 User-Exits for RFFOUS_T

In general, all available user-exits for bank transfers are stored in Program RFFO-EXIT by county. All user-exits start with RFFOxxxx.

9.3 Payment Medium Workbench (PMW)

Starting with SAP Release 4.6, SAP introduced the Payment Medium Workbench (PMW). PMW is a generic tool used to configure and create payment media sent by organizations to their house banks. This generic tool will gradually phase out the classic payment medium programs (RFFO*) due to the range of advantages that it provides. Following is a list of advantages compared to the classic payment medium programs:

▶ Superior control and verification of payment procedure

▶ Improved performance with mass payments for more than 50,000 records

▶ Better sort functions with payment advice notes

▶ Easier to maintain and to extend

In this section, the ACH bank file creation using PMW is covered. The following list contains the necessary configuration steps:

1. Create the payment medium format.

2. Create/assign the payment selection variants.

3. Adjust the note to payee.

4. Assign the payment medium format.

These configuration steps are specific to PMW. In addition, the configuration steps for the classic payment medium programs, such as accompanying form, tax-ID number, and company code number in house bank, have to be done as well.

9.3.1 Create Payment Medium Format

For payments via ACH bank files, SAP software provides a fully functional PMW format with the format name ACH. This format can usually be used without additional configurations. The ACH format can be displayed in the IMG via navigation path **IMG • Financial Accounting • Accounts Receivable and Accounts Payables • Business Transactions • Outgoing Payments • Automatic Outgoing Payments • Payment Media • Make Settings for Payment Medium Formats from Payment Medium Workbench • Create Payment Medium Formats.** Figure 9.9 shows the configuration screen of PMW.

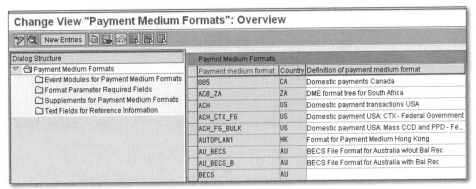

Figure 9.9 PMW Configuration Screen

For AP payment transaction via ACH, use the predefined **ACH** payment medium format for country **US**.

The detailed configuration steps of a new payment medium format aren't discussed in this section; however, in general, a payment medium format has the following characteristics, which must be configured in individual steps.

Format Output

Using PMW, non-document-based payment media are usually generated as a file. If a particular name of the format appears as a selection option on the selection screen of the generic payment medium program, the name must be entered here. It must also be selected if in addition to the payment medium, an accompanying sheet or a list is generated. You can also create documentation for the payment medium format using the text module FPM_DOCU_SAMPLE as a reference.

Level of Detail

The payments in one payment run are grouped in payment media. The criteria used to group the payments are specified by the level of detail.

Format Supplement

The format supplements translate the internal SAP term for the payment method into the language of the format, for example, entries are made in a field in the file according to the direction of payment (bank transfer/debit memo). Two payment methods are created for this in the SAP system, and the relevant format supplements for bank transfer or debit memo are assigned to these payment methods.

Length and Number of Reference Fields

The file generally contains fields that inform the recipient of the purpose of the payment on the account statement. The length and number of these reference fields need to be specified.

Implementing the Formats

If function modules are used to implement the format, entries must be made on the following interfaces:

- Event 00 - Enter sort field
- Event 05 - Enter additional reference fields
- Event 10 - Check format parameters
- Event 20 - Start/file header
- Event 25 - Open/close file
- Event 30 - Order/transaction record
- Event 40 - End/file trailer

The ACH format uses function modules, with the following function modules per event:

- Event 00 - `FI_PAYMEDIUM_ACH_00`
- Event 05 - `FI_PAYMEDIUM_ACH_05`
- Event 20 - `FI_PAYMEDIUM_ACH_20`
- Event 40 - `FI_PAYMEDIUM_ACH_40`
- Event 30 - `FI_PAYMEDIUM_ACH_30`

Format-Specific Parameters

If the format requires fields that aren't available in the SAP system, such as the company entry description for ACH payments, a structure in the Data Dictionary that contains the fields has to be created. The fields in this structure can be defined as required entry fields and provided with default values. A button is then provided on the selection screen of the generic payment medium program, which can be used to make entries in these format-specific parameters.

9.3.2 Create/Assign Payment Selection Variants

In the second configuration step, a variant in the generic payment medium creation Program SAPFPAYM needs to be defined. The variant can either be defined directly via Transaction SE38 in Program SAPFPAYM or in the IMG via navigation path **IMG • Financial Accounting • Accounts Receivable and Accounts Payables • Business Transactions • Outgoing Payments • Automatic Outgoing Payments • Payment Media • Make Settings for Payment Medium Formats from Payment Medium Workbench • Create/Assign Selection Variants.**

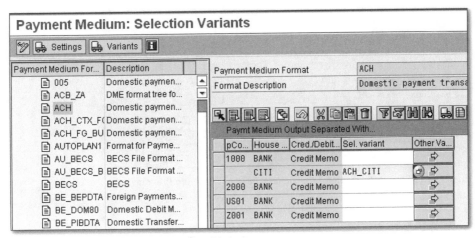

Figure 9.10 Creation of Payment Medium Variant

To create the variant from PMW as shown in Figure 9.10, select the **Payment Medium Format**, enter a variant name, and select the editing function via the menu **Variant • Edit Variant**.

The selection screen of the generic payment medium program shown in Figure 9.11 is divided into the following sections:

▶ **Format**

▶ **Print Control**

▶ **Output Control**

In the first step, enter the payment medium format "ACH". Based on the configuration of this format, the selection options on the screen are adjusted.

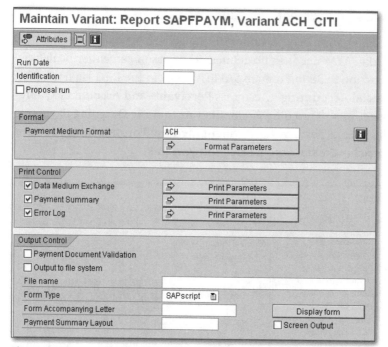

Figure 9.11 Selection Screen for the Generic Payment Medium Program

Format

The **Format** section contains the payment medium format and any additional parameters. By selecting the **Format Parameters** button, an additional screen with additional parameters appears. For payments via ACH, two additional parameters can be entered as shown in Figure 9.12.

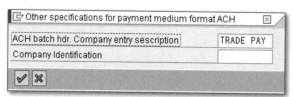

Figure 9.12 Additional Parameters for ACH Payment Medium Format

ACH Batch Hdr. Company Entry Description

The **ACH batch hdr. Company entry description** field is mandatory and transferred into the batch header of the ACH file into field BH7. The following is an excerpt from NACHA official documentation, which further explains the meaning of this field:

The Originator establishes the value of this field to provide a description of the purpose of the entry to be displayed back to the Receiver. For example, GAS BILL, REG. SALARY, INS. PREM, SOC. SEC., DTC, TRADE PAY, PURCHASE, etc.

Company Identification

The **Company Identification** field is used for creating the ACH file and contains a particular identification between the bank and your organization, such as tax number or other free number. The **Company Identification** is transferred in fields BH5 of the batch header and BC7 of the batch control record. If the field isn't filled, the system uses the value for the USA Tax Identification Number (TIN) that is maintained in the additional data for the company code as described in Section 9.2.3.

Print Control

The **Print Control** section controls whether the data file and reports will be created. As a minimum, the **Data Medium Exchange** flag needs to be set; otherwise, the ACH file won't be created. You should set all **Print Control** flags.

Output Control

The **Output Control** section specifies further output details during the file creation. The output file can be created either directly in the file system or stored within the SAP system in a temporary file called TemSe output. If the TemSe output option is chosen, the file needs to be created in a second step within the data medium administration using Program SAPMFDTA. This allows for segregation of duties if the payment program execution and bank transfer file creation need to be handled by different departments such as the AP department and Treasury department.

Payment Document Validation

The **Payment Document Validation** field should only be set if the bank transfer file isn't created immediately after the payment run. It validates that the payments are still valid and were not reversed in the meantime. Otherwise, a bank transfer could be issued for a payment that was reversed.

Output to File System

If the **Output to file system** flag is set, the file is saved directly in the file system of the application server.

File Name

The **File name** needs to be specified if the file needs to be created directly in the file system. Enter the file name, for example, "/usr/sap/dta/<file name>".

Form Type

The **Form Type** field specifies the form type of the accompanying letter form. Valid formats are SAPscript or PDF.

Form Accompanying Letter

In this field, an alternative form to the accompanying form configuration in the payment method can be entered.

Payment Summary Layout

An ALV layout can be specified in the **Payment Summary Layout** field. This layout is then used to display the payment summary.

Screen Output

To configure the payment summary layout, the list must be output on the screen by setting the **Screen Output** flag. If the layout of the payment summary is configured, the screen output can be suppressed, and the list can be sent directly to the spool.

9.3.3   Adjust Note to Payee

During the ACH file creation, you can submit additional addendum records called **Note to payee** to the receivers (see Figure 9.13). Usually one additional record is submitted with the CCD format. The predefined Note to Payee record SAP_ACH_CCD can be adjusted in the IMG via navigation path **IMG • Financial Accounting • Accounts Receivable and Accounts Payables • Business Transactions • Outgoing Payments • Automatic Outgoing Payments • Payment Media • Make Settings for Payment Medium Formats from Payment Medium Workbench • Adjust Note to Payee.**

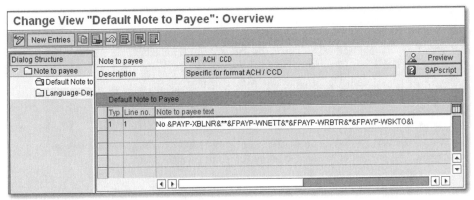

Figure 9.13 SAP Predefined Note to Payee Record

During the file creation, the variables in the note to payee are replaced with actual values. Table 9.3 shows a list of variables and their descriptions.

Variable	Description
PAYP-XBLNR	Invoice reference number
FPAYP-WNETT	Net payment amount
FPAYP-WRBTR	Gross payment amount
FPAYP-WSKTO	Discount amount

Table 9.3 Note to Payee Variables

Additional variables can be included from the structures PAYP or FPAYP.

9.3.4 Assign Payment Medium Format

In the last configuration step, the payment medium format needs to be assigned to the payment method in the IMG via navigation path **IMG • Financial Accounting • Accounts Receivable and Accounts Payables • Business Transactions • Outgoing Payments • Automatic Outgoing Payments • Payment Media • Make Settings for Payment Medium Formats from Payment Medium Workbench • Assign Payment Medium Format and Note to Payee to Payment Method.** Select the county and payment method, and assign the payment medium format and format supplement in the **Payment medium** section shown in Figure 9.14.

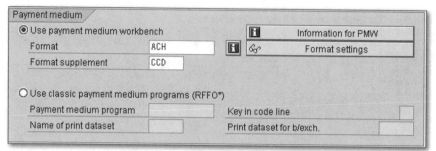

Figure 9.14 Assignment of Payment Medium Format to Payment Method

In addition, the note to payee record has to be assigned in the same configuration step. To do that, select the **Note to Payee by Origin node,** and enter the **Note to payee** record as shown in Figure 9.15.

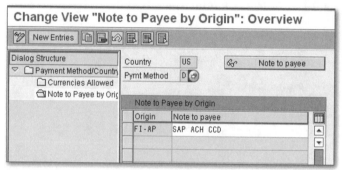

Figure 9.15 Note to Payee Configuration

9.3.5 Enhancements

If the SAP predefined payment medium formats need to be adjusted, user-defined function modules can be developed that are executed in addition to the SAP-delivered function modules. These function modules can be configured in the IMG via navigation path **IMG • Financial Accounting • Accounts Receivable and Accounts Payables • Business Transactions • Outgoing Payments • Automatic Outgoing Payments • Payment Media • Make Settings for Payment Medium Formats from Payment Medium Workbench • Adjust Payment Medium Format.**

If function modules are used to implement the format, the file can be enhanced with the following events:

- ▶ Event 00 - Fill sort field
- ▶ Event 06 - Fill additional reference fields
- ▶ Event 11 - Check format parameters
- ▶ Event 21 - Start/file header
- ▶ Event 25 - File close/open
- ▶ Event 31 - Order/transaction record
- ▶ Event 41 - End/file trailer format-specific parameters

Sample User-Exit

For example, the bank requires a bank-specific start record or header record. This record has the following value:

`$$ADD ID=ABCDEFGH BID='NWFACH11111111'`

A new function module as shown in Listing 9.1 with the name ZFI_PAYMEDIUM_ ACH_21 is created.

```
FUNCTION ZFI_PAYMEDIUM_ACH_21.
*"----------------------------------------------------------------
*"*"Local interface:
*"  IMPORTING
*"     VALUE(I_FPAYH) LIKE  FPAYH STRUCTURE  FPAYH
*"     VALUE(I_FPAYHX) LIKE  FPAYHX STRUCTURE  FPAYHX
*"     VALUE(I_FORMAT_PARAMS) TYPE  FPM_SELPAR-PARAM
*"     VALUE(I_FORMAT_PARAMS_C) TYPE  FPM_SELPAR-PARAM
*"     VALUE(I_FILENAME) LIKE  REGUT-FSNAM
*"     VALUE(I_XFILESYSTEM) TYPE  DFILESYST
*"  TABLES
*"      T_FILE_OUTPUT STRUCTURE  FPM_FILE
*"  CHANGING
*"     REFERENCE(C_FILENAME) LIKE  REGUT-FSNAM
*"----------------------------------------------------------------
DATA: BEGIN OF T_FILE OCCURS 0.
       INCLUDE STRUCTURE FPM_FILE.
DATA: END OF T_FILE.

  REFRESH T_FILE.
  IF I_FPAYH-HBKID = 'CITI ' AND
     I_FPAYH-HKTID = 'CONTR'.
   CLEAR T_FILE.
```

```
      T_FILE-LINE = TEXT-I01.
      T_FILE-LENGTH = 94.
      T_FILE-X_CR   = 'X'.
      T_FILE-X_LF   = 'X'.
      APPEND T_FILE.
      LOOP AT T_FILE_OUTPUT.
        CLEAR T_FILE.
        T_FILE = T_FILE_OUTPUT.
        APPEND T_FILE.
      ENDLOOP.
      T_FILE_OUTPUT[] = T_FILE[].
    ENDIF.
ENDFUNCTION.
```

Listing 9.1 Sample Function Module for ACH Start Record

The preceding function module moves the text defined in text element **I01** into the file header. The value of text element **I01** is shown in Figure 9.16.

Program	SAPLZFI_ACH	Active		
Text symbols	Selection texts	List Headings		
Sy	Text		dLen	mL
I01	$$ADD ID=ABCDEFGH BID='NWFACH11111111'		38	38

Figure 9.16 Text Element I01

After the function module is created, it has to be assigned to the correct event. As shown in Figure 9.17, event **21** for the file header needs to be executed because the record has to be the first record in the file.

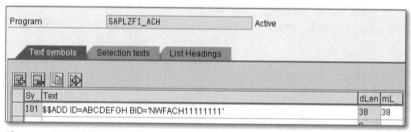

Change View "Event Modules": Overview				
New Entries				
Dialog Structure	Format	ACH		
▽ ☐ Payment Medium Forma				
☐ Event Modules	Event Modules			
☐ Format Parameter R	Event	Function module name	Imple	Relations	Standard Module
	21	ZFI_PAYMEDIUM_ACH_21		⊕ Added	FI_PAYMEDIUM_ACH_20

Figure 9.17 Event Configuration Screen

9.4 Execution of the Payment Program for Payment Medium Formats

Fundamentally, the payment program execution works the same for classic payment medium programs as for payment medium formats; however, the following minor differences apply:

9.4.1 Payment Advice

For payment medium formats, Program RFFOAVIS_FPAYM is used to print the payment advices. Similar to the classic payment format programs, a variant has to be created and assigned in the payment program in the **Printout/data medium** tab. The automatic payment program was covered in Chapter 7.

9.4.2 Schedule Payment Run

During the payment run schedule within the payment program, you should set the **Create payment medium** flag as shown in Figure 9.18. By doing that, the payment medium file is created automatically during the payment creation.

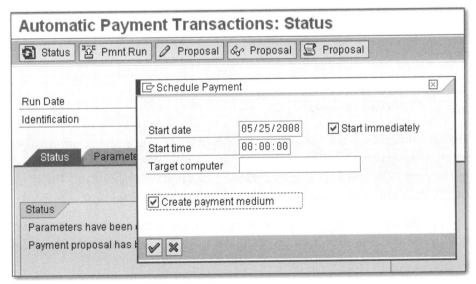

Figure 9.18 Schedule Payment Run Screen

9.4.3 Data Medium Exchange Administration

After the file is created, it can be displayed, downloaded, or payment details printed via the Data Medium Exchange (DME) Administration (see Figure 9.19). The DME administration can be accessed via Transaction FDTA or in Transaction F110 via the menu **Environment • Payment Medium • DME Administration.**

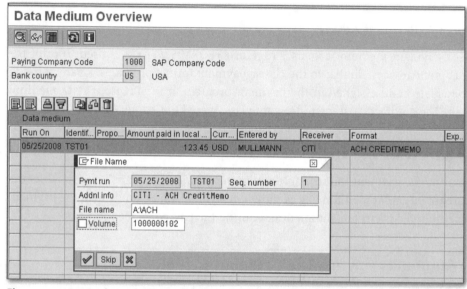

Figure 9.19 DME Administration Screen

9.5 Prenotifications

The prenotification process is an optional step used to validate bank information before real payments are submitted to the bank. A prenotification file is transferred to the bank that contains customer, vendor, or employee bank data. The bank checks this data and returns a list or file in which incorrect bank data is marked.

The prenotification programs can be accessed in Transaction F110 via the menu **Environment • Prenotification.** In detail, the following procedures are available:

- ▶ Select bank details.
- ▶ Create prenotification file.
- ▶ Import feedback.

▶ Display file.

▶ Change memo records.

9.5.1 Select Bank Details

Program RFPNSL00 can be used to select vendors or customers with newly created or changed bank information. This step is a prerequisite for the creation of the prenotification file.

9.5.2 Create Prenotification file

After the bank data are selected, the prenotification file can be created with Program RFPNFC00. Figure 9.20 shows the selection screen of the program.

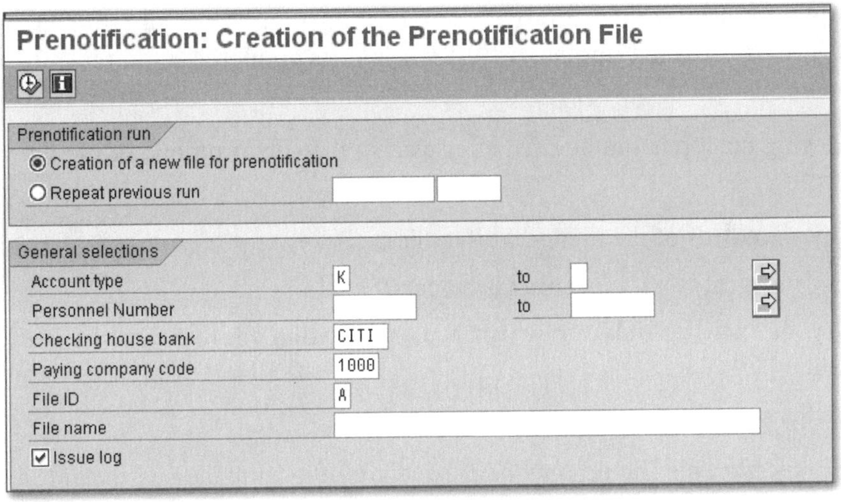

Prenotification: Creation of the Prenotification File

Prenotification run
- ⦿ Creation of a new file for prenotification
- ◯ Repeat previous run

General selections
Account type	K	to
Personnel Number		to
Checking house bank	CITI	
Paying company code	1000	
File ID	A	
File name		
☑ Issue log		

Figure 9.20 Prenotification File Creation Screen

This program generates a prenotification file in ACH format for transferring to the house bank. The data is also stored in the system, which allows for later correction of bank data. There are two alternatives on the selection screen:

▶ Selection of new records for creating a new prenotification file.

▶ Restarting a previous program by specifying the run date and the run ID. The date and ID can be determined by using the **Display File** function.

▶ A log of the selected records and bank details can be issued as well.

9.5.3 Import Feedback

If your bank returns a validation file, Program RFPNFR00 reads a file with detailed prenotification data in SAP format and transfers error messages into the SAP system for the bank data coming from the house bank. These error messages can be displayed with the **Display file** function or changed using the **Change memo record** function to correct the bank data.

The file to be imported must be in SAP format of structure PNRT. A custom conversion program that transfers the bank's file into SAP format must be created.

9.5.4 Display File

Program RFPNLS00 lists the created prenotification files. Lines from prenotification files that contain bank data marked as incorrect are highlighted in a different color. The bank data can be corrected using this function. When all errors have been flagged as corrected, the program displays the **Completed** indicator in the first column.

The following functions can be used after placing the cursor on one of the lines in the list:

▶ Display all records of the prenotification file.

▶ Display the records with incorrect bank data.

▶ Display the new records for which a prenotification file has not yet been created.

▶ Delete the prenotification file.

The prenotification file should only be deleted after the bank data has been confirmed by the house bank as being correct or the incorrect bank data has been corrected.

9.5.5 Change Memo Records

Program RFPNLS10 lists new or changed bank data and allows incorrect data to be corrected. Two different functions can be called:

▶ By choosing **Display file** and selecting a prenotification file, the records from a particular file can be edited.

- By choosing **Change memo record** and entering selection criteria, information on the prenotification file can be displayed.
- For correcting incorrect bank data, the procedure varies depending on whether the house bank's feedback is by list or file.

List Feedback

If the bank returns a list of incorrect bank information, use the following steps:

- Select **Display file,** and then display all records from a file, or select **Change memo record,** and display all of the records on the selection screen.
- Select the data recognized by the bank as being incorrect by switching to the change mode and making entries in the fields for errors.
- Save the corrected entries.

File Feedback

If the bank returns a file that was transferred into the system using the *Import Feedback* function, use the following procedure

- Place the cursor on a line with errors, and click the **Master record** button.
- Correct the bank data in the master record, and go back after saving the prenotification.
- Select the error in the first column by clicking on it as being completed.
- Save these comments. The lines affected are no longer displayed in a different color.

9.6   Summary

In this Chapter AP payments via electronic bank transfers were described. This transition method has various advantages over check payments and the SAP software delivers bank transfer formats for different countries and types. It needs to be decided during an implementation whether the classic payment medium program of the PMW will be used.

In the next Chapter the different aspects of Withholding tax reporting are described.

Withholding tax reporting within Accounts Payable (AP) includes 1099 Miscellaneous, 1099 Interest, and 1042 Tax Reporting for Non-Residents Aliens (NRA). SAP software delivers the classic and the extended withholding tax reporting tools.

10 Withholding Tax Reporting

According to the U.S. Internal Revenue Service (IRS), businesses are required to withhold money on certain payments and remit to the IRS. In this chapter, the following types of tax reporting are covered:

- 1099 Miscellaneous (MISC)
- 1099 Interest (INT)
- 1099 Government (G)
- 1042 Non-Resident Alien (NRA) Withholding Reporting

For more information about the different requirements, go to the IRS Web site at *www.irs.gov*.

1099 Miscellaneous

The most common form of withholding tax in the United States is *1099-MISC* or *1099 Miscellaneous*. Businesses must use Form 1099-MISC to report certain payments made to a person or business that isn't an employee. For example, the form is required for payments of $10 or more in gross royalties or $600 or more in rents or services. It also applies to prizes and awards, other income payments, and medical and health care payments. Businesses must file Form 1099-MISC for each person from whom they have withheld any federal income tax under the backup withholding rules regardless of the amount of the payment. In addition, businesses have to follow certain filing deadlines. 1099-MISC forms have to be sent to the recipients by the end of January for the prior tax year. By the end of March, a file has to be submitted to the IRS with all 1099 information.

1099 Interest

The rules for *1099-INT* reporting are similar to 1099-MISC. Businesses must use Form 1099-INT to report certain payments made to a person's account of $10 or more in interest or other credits. The same filling deadlines for 1099-MISC apply to 1099-INT.

1099 Government

The rules for *1099-G* reporting are similar to 1099-MISC. Government entities such as federal, state, or local governments must use Form 1099-G to report certain payments made, such as unemployment compensation, state or local tax refunds, or alternative trade adjustment assistance (ATAA) to a person's account. The same filling deadlines for 1099-MISC apply to 1099-G.

Non-Resident Alien

Payments are subject to NRA withholding if the payments are from sources within the United States, and are either:

▶ Fixed or determinable, annual or periodical (FDAP) income

▶ Certain gains from the disposition of timber, coal, and iron ore, or from the sale or exchange of patents, copyrights, and similar intangible property

In this case, the payments have to be reported on form 1042-S.

10.1 Classic Withholding Versus Extended Withholding Tax Reporting

Withholding tax reporting is one of those processes that never gets the attention it really deserves during implementations or upgrades. The reason is that withholding tax reporting isn't a main business process but rather a task that needs to be done once a year. Therefore, a lot of implementation teams decide to use simple or classic withholding tax reporting rather than extended withholding tax reporting.

The word "simple" probably implies that this function is easier to implement and use. However, experience shows that by using classic withholding tax reporting, a lot of SAP software functionality is lost, and actually the effort to implement it is the same as for extended withholding tax. For example, extended withholding tax reporting has two correction programs to identify discrepancies in the withholding tax code between your vendor master data and financial documents. Simple withholding tax doesn't provide any.

In fact, SAP recommends switching from classic withholding tax to extended withholding tax because with extended withholding tax posting you can do the following:

▶ Post tax postings on both the credit and the debit side of an entry.

▶ Make an extended withholding tax posting at the payment and invoice posting.

▶ Post several extended withholding tax categories per line item in parallel.

▶ Withhold taxes for partial payments.

▶ Consider minimum amounts, maximum amounts, and exemption limits.

▶ Split amount with withholding tax in Logistics Invoice Verification (LIV) (Transaction MIRO).

SAP has not yet announced a discontinuation of the development of classic withholding tax. However, new SAP functions, for example in contract accounting or country-specific developments, require extended withholding tax.

10.2 Migrating to Extended Withholding Tax Reporting

If your organization uses classic withholding tax reporting and wants to switch to the extended withholding tax functionality, SAP delivers a migration tool that includes all conversion steps. This migration tool can be accessed via Transaction WTMG or in the IMG via navigation path **IMG • Financial Accounting • Financial Accounting Global Settings • Withholding Tax • Withholding Tax Changeover • Withholding Tax Changeover.** Figure 10.1 shows the conversion screen with all conversion steps.

This migration tool is simple to use and well documented by SAP by clicking the **i** (info) button next to each step. Note that during the migration, no posting can be executed or data inconsistencies could occur. It's also recommend that you make a system backup before executing the migration steps because a large number of documents in your system will be changed.

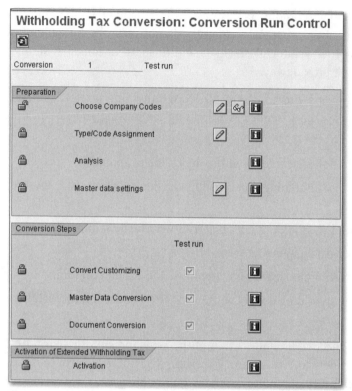

Figure 10.1 Withholding Tax Conversion Tool WTMG

10.2.1 Migration Steps

Before the migration from classic to extended withholding can be started, extended withholding tax has to be configured. The configuration steps are described later in this chapter in more detail. The migration is done in three main steps with additional activities within each step:

1. Preparation steps
   - ▸ Choose company code
   - ▸ Type/code assignment
   - ▸ Analysis
   - ▸ Master data settings
2. Conversion steps
   - ▸ Convert customizing

▶ Master data conversion

▶ Document conversion

3. Activation of extended withholding tax

Preparation Steps

The first activity within the preparation steps is the selection of the company code and country to be converted. In the second activity, the classic withholding tax types and codes have to be mapped to the extended withholding tax types and codes as shown in Figure 10.2.

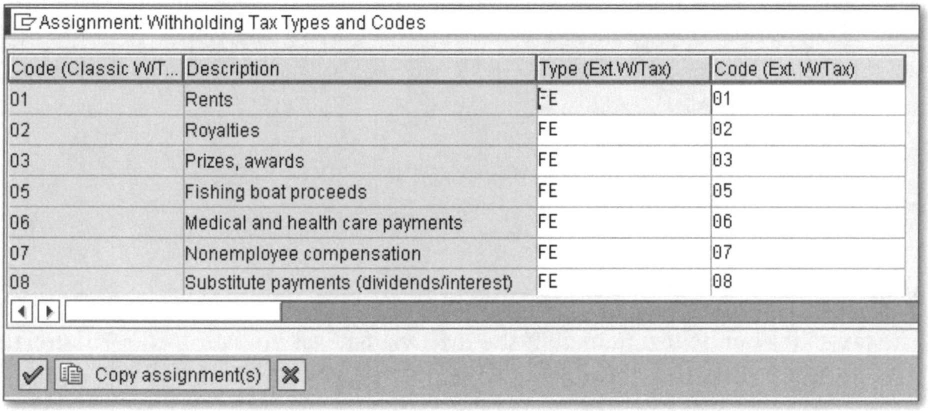

Code (Classic W/T...	Description	Type (Ext.W/Tax)	Code (Ext. W/Tax)
01	Rents	FE	01
02	Royalties	FE	02
03	Prizes, awards	FE	03
05	Fishing boat proceeds	FE	05
06	Medical and health care payments	FE	06
07	Nonemployee compensation	FE	07
08	Substitute payments (dividends/interest)	FE	08

☞ Assignment: Withholding Tax Types and Codes

✓ 📋 Copy assignment(s) ✖

Figure 10.2 Tax Code Mapping Screen

The *analysis* activity determines the number of vendor and documents to be converted. The documents include open, cleared, and parked documents. The last activity determines whether one or multiple tax types are allowed per vendor. If you're not sure, choose the multiple tax type option.

Conversion Steps

The first activity within the conversion steps converts additional configuration settings, such as account determination, from the classic withholding tax to extended withholding tax. In the second activity, all vendor master data are converted. The system determines the new tax types and codes based on the tax type and code assignment mapping.

In the document conversion activity, all documents are converted from simple to extended withholding tax. This activity usually has the longest run time.

Activation of Extended Withholding Tax

The last step activates extended withholding tax for the converted company code and completes the migration process.

10.3 1099-MISC Configuration Using Classic Withholding Tax

The configuration steps for 1099-MISC reporting using the classic withholding tax reporting tool are described in OSS Note 363650. The following configuration steps are required:

▶ Maintain tax codes.

▶ Maintain document change rules.

10.3.1 Maintain Tax Codes

The tax codes can be maintained in the IMG via navigation path **IMG • Financial Accounting • Financial Accounting Global Settings • Withholding Tax • Withholding Tax • Calculation • Maintain Tax Codes.**

Table 10.1 lists the tax codes that need to be created for 1099-MISC reporting.

Tax Code	Description
01	Rents
02	Royalties
03	Other income
05	Fishing boat proceeds
06	Medical and health care payments
07	Nonemployee compensation
08	Substitute payments in lieu of dividends or interest
09	Direct sales to a buyer for resale

Table 10.1 Tax Codes for 1099-MISC Reporting

Tax Code	Description
10	Crop insurance proceeds
13 or 3B	Excess golden parachute
14 or 3C	Gross proceeds paid to an attorney
7B	Section 409A income
15	Section 409A deferrals

Table 10.1 Tax Codes for 1099-MISC Reporting (Cont.)

For example, Figure 10.3 shows the configuration settings for tax code **07 – Non-employee compensation**.

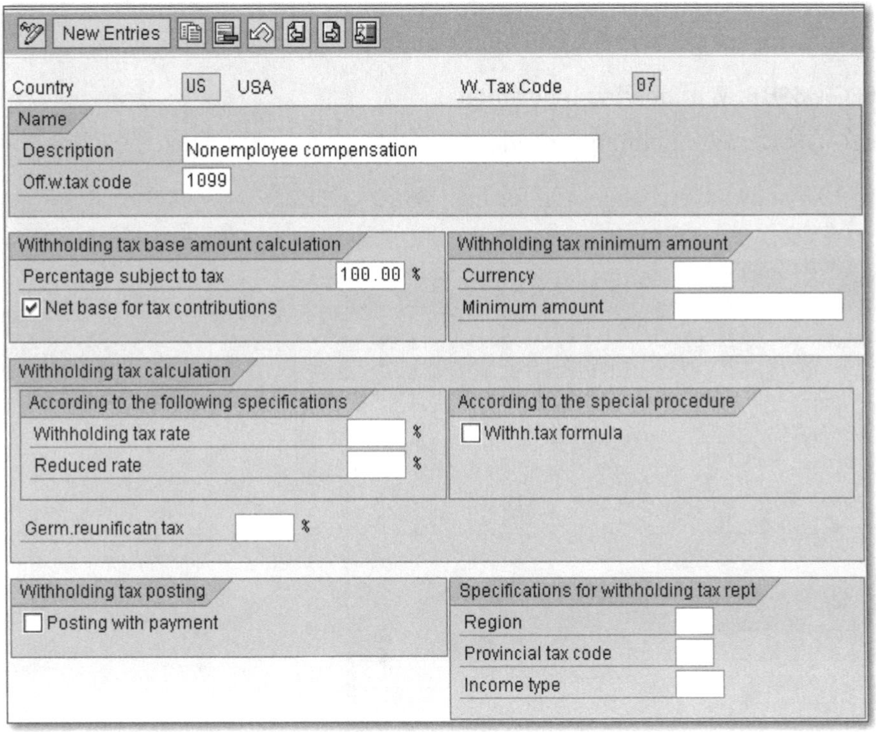

Figure 10.3 1099-MISC Tax Code Example

If a percentage of the payment amount needs to be withheld, additional tax codes need to be set up. The exact codes are listed in OSS Note 363650. From experience, however, you shouldn't withhold any amounts because this could cause issues if the vendor requests to be paid the withheld amounts after submitting documentation of tax status on a W-9 form. From a process flow, it's recommended to establish a business process where no vendor is paid before submitting a W-9 form. This ensures that invoices are recorded with the proper withholding tax code.

10.3.2 Maintain Document Change Rules

The document change rules allow the tax codes to be changed in the invoices and payments after the documents are posted. This might be necessary if the tax codes were incorrect in the vendor master data. The document change rules can be maintained in the IMG via navigation path **IMG • Financial Accounting • Financial Accounting Global Settings • Document • Line Item • Document Change Rules/Line items.**

The document change rules have to be maintained for the following fields:

▸ **BSEG-QSSHB:** Withholding base amount.

▸ **BSEG-QSSKZ:** Withholding tax code.

Figure 10.4 shows the change rule for field **BSEG-QSSKZ**.

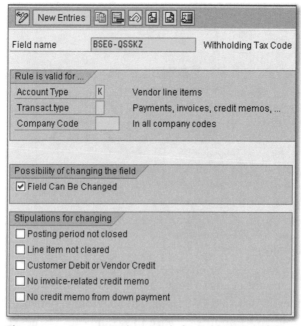

Figure 10.4 Document Change Rule for Field BSEG-QSSKZ

The flag **Field Can Be Changed** should be set, and the flag for **Line item not cleared** should not be set. This ensures that the tax code can be changed in invoices as well as in payment documents.

10.4 1099-MISC Configuration Using Extended Withholding Tax

Besides the configuration steps of the classic withholding tax tool, OSS Note 363650 also describes the configuration steps for 1099-MISC reporting using the extended withholding tax reporting tool. The following configuration steps are required:

▶ Define the withholding tax type for payment posting.

▶ Define withholding tax codes.

▶ Assign withholding tax types to the company code.

▶ Assign accounts for withholding tax to be paid over.

▶ Maintain document change rules.

10.4.1 Define the Withholding Tax Type for Payment Posting

One tax type needs to be defined for federal tax reporting (it's recommended to create the tax type as FE like Federal). The tax type can be maintained in the IMG via navigation path **IMG • Financial Accounting • Financial Accounting Global Settings • Withholding Tax • Extended Withholding Tax • Calculation • Withholding Tax Type • Define Withholding Tax type for Payment Posting.**

▶ Figure 10.5 shows the configuration setting for the federal withholding tax type. If state withholding tax needs to be withheld in addition, a second tax type for state withholding called ST needs to be created as well.

355

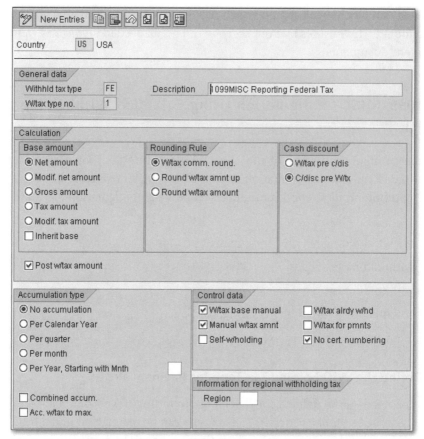

Figure 10.5 Configuration Screen for Federal Withholding Tax Type

10.4.2 Define Withholding Tax Codes

In the second step, the withholding tax codes need to be maintained in the IMG via navigation path **IMG • Financial Accounting • Financial Accounting Global Settings • Withholding Tax • Extended Withholding Tax • Calculation • Withholding Tax Codes • Define Withholding Tax Codes.** The same tax codes as listed earlier in Table 10.1 need to be created. For example, Figure 10.6 shows the configuration setting for tax code **07 – Nonemployee compensation.**

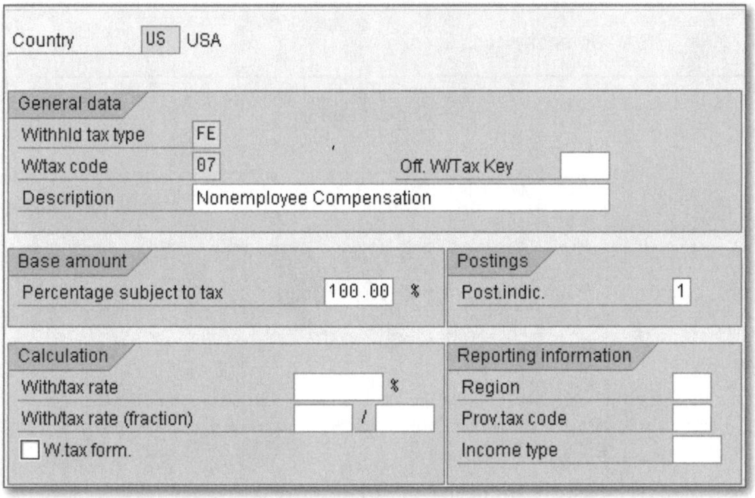

Figure 10.6 Sample Tax Code Configuration Screen

If a percentage of the payment amount needs to be withheld, additional tax codes need to be set up. The exact codes are listed in OSS Note 363650.

From experience, however, you shouldn't withhold any amounts because this could cause issues if the vendor requests to be paid the withheld amounts after submitting documentation of tax status on a W-9 form. From a process flow, it's recommended to establish a business process where no vendor is paid before submitting a W-9 form. This ensures that invoices are recorded with the proper withholding tax code.

10.4.3 Assign Withholding Tax Types to the Company Code

In the third step, the withholding tax types need to be assigned to the company codes to ensure that the tax types can be used. This assignment can be maintained in the IMG via navigation path **IMG • Financial Accounting • Financial Accounting Global Settings • Withholding Tax • Extended Withholding Tax • Company Code • Assign Withholding Tax Type to Company code**.

The configuration step needs to be done for every tax type that is allowed in the company code. Figure 10.7 shows the configuration setting tax type **FE**.

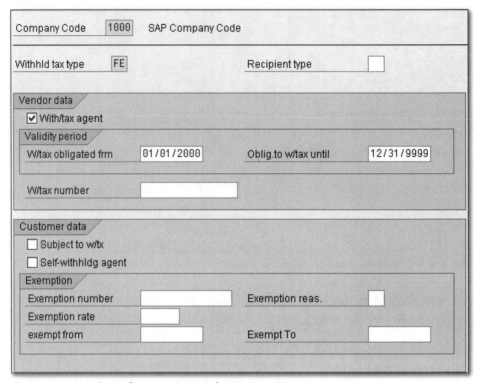

Figure 10.7 Sample Configuration Settings for Tax Type FE

10.4.4 Assign Accounts for Withholding Tax to Be Paid Over

In the next step, GL account needs to be assigned in case withholding tax is withheld. The account assignment can be maintained in the IMG via navigation path **IMG • Financial Accounting • Financial Accounting Global Settings • Withholding Tax • Extended Withholding Tax • Postings • Accounts for Withholding Tax • Define Accounts for Withholding Tax to Be Paid Over.**

10.4.5 Document Change Rules

This configuration step is the same as described in the classic withholding tax configuration section. The document change fields can be maintained in the IMG via navigation path **IMG • Financial Accounting • Financial Accounting Global Settings • Document • Line Item • Document Change Rules/Line items.**

The document change rules have to be maintained for the following fields:

▸ **WITH_ITEM-WT_QSSHB:** Withholding base amount

▸ **WITH_ITEM-WT_WITHCD:** Withholding tax code

10.5   1099 Interest Configuration

The section describes the configuration steps for 1099-INT using extended withholding tax reporting. The steps are very similar to the 1099-MISC configuration, and the following steps are required:

▸ Define the withholding tax type for payment posting.

▸ Define withholding tax codes.

▸ Assign withholding tax types to the company code.

▸ Maintain document change rules.

All these steps were explained in detail in the prior section for 1099-MISC tax reporting. For 1099-INT reporting, only a different tax type and tax code are necessary. Table10.2 lists the necessary tax code and tax type for 1099-INT reporting.

Tax type	Tax code	Description
FI	01	Interest income

Table 10.2   Tax Type and Code for 1099-INT

10.6   1099-G Configuration

The section describes the configuration steps for 1099-G using extended withholding tax reporting. The steps are very similar to the 1099-MISC configuration, and the following steps are required:

▸ Define the withholding tax type for payment posting.

▸ Define withholding tax codes.

▸ Assign withholding tax types to the company code.

▸ Maintain document change rules.

All these steps were explained in detail in the prior section. For 1099-G reporting, only different tax types and tax codes are necessary. Table 10.3 lists the necessary tax codes and tax types for 1099-G reporting.

Tax Type	Tax Code	Description
G1	1G	Unemployment compensation
G1	2G	State and local tax refund
G1	5G	Other taxable grants of greater then $600.00
G1	5B	ATAA payments
G1	5G	Taxable grants
G1	7G	Agricultural subsidy payments

Table 10.3   Tax Type and Tax Codes for 1099-G Reporting

10.7   1042-S Configuration

This section describes the configuration steps for 1042-S using extended withholding tax reporting. The steps are very similar to the 1099-MISC configuration, and the following steps are required:

- Define the withholding tax type for payment posting.
- Define withholding tax codes.
- Assign withholding tax types to the company code.
- Maintain document change rules.

All these steps were explained in detail in the prior section. For 1042-S reporting, only a different tax type and tax code are necessary. Table 10.4 lists the necessary tax code and tax type for 1042-S reporting.

Tax Type	Tax Code	Description
03	42	1042-S reporting income code 20

Table 10.4   Tax Type and Code for 1042-S Reporting

10.8   Vendor Master Data

If a vendor is subject to withholding tax, certain fields in the vendor master data need to be filled. These values are then copied into the invoice or credit memo upon data entry. Depending on whether classic or extended withholding tax reporting is used, different fields need to be filled.

In both cases, however, the social security number (SSN) or Employer Identification Number (EIN) have to be filled in the **Tax information field in the Control** tab of the vendor master data as shown in Figure 10.8. The field **Tax number 1** is used for the SSN, and **Tax number 2** is used for the EIN.

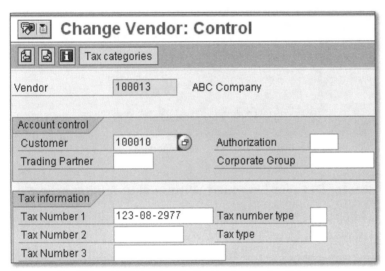

Figure 10.8   SSN and EIN Numbers in the Vendor Master Data

10.8.1   Vendor Master Data for Classic Withholding Tax Reporting

If classic withholding tax reporting is used, the tax code needs to be filled in the withholding tax code field (**W. Tax Code**) in the **Account Information** tab of the vendor master data as shown in Figure 10.9.

As described before in the differences between classic and extended withholding tax reporting, only one tax code is possible per vendor. If a vendor is subject to multiple tax codes, multiple vendors need to be created.

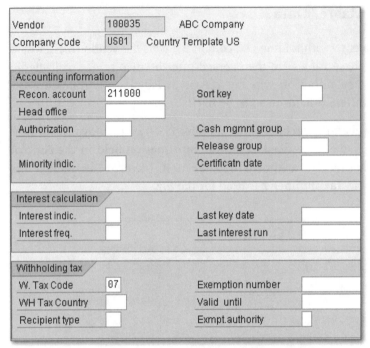

Figure 10.9 Vendor Master Data for Classic Withholding Tax Reporting

10.8.2 Vendor Master Data for Extended Withholding Tax Reporting

If extended withholding tax reporting is used, a separate tab is available in the vendor master data as shown in Figure 10.10 for the withholding tax information.

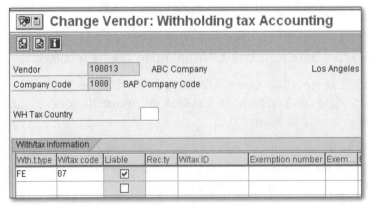

Figure 10.10 Vendor Master Tab for Extended Withholding

The fields withholding tax type (**With.t.type**) and withholding tax code (**W/tax code**) need to be filled. Multiple types and codes are possible for a single vendor. Note that the vendor is subject to withholding tax only after the field **Liable** is set.

10.9 Correction Programs

SAP delivers a variety of correction programs for withholding tax reporting. These programs are listed in OSS Note 649417. The two most commonly used correction programs are described in this section and enable you to correct invoice and payment documents if the tax type or tax code in the vendor master data are changed. These programs are only relevant for extended withholding tax reporting:

▶ **RFWT0010**
Report for generation of consistent withholding tax data in open items after the change in the vendor master data.

▶ **RFWT0020**
Creation of withholding tax data in invoices and payments.

10.9.1 RFWT0010: Adjustment of Withholding Tax Code for Open Items

This program changes open items and adjusts the withholding tax information in open items (invoices/credit memos) after withholding tax information changes in the vendor master data.

> **Consider the Following Situation:**
>
> You have forgotten to update the withholding tax code in the vendor master data. You notice your error, and update the tax information within your vendor master data via Transaction FK02. After you save the update, you see the following warning message: "Postprocess open items after changing relevant withholding tax types," which means that after you've changed the withholding tax information in your vendor master data, you need to adjust all open items. The open items need to have the same withholding tax codes as in the vendor master record. Otherwise, you won't be able process your open items through the regular payment program using Transaction F110.

Figure 10.11 shows the selection screen of Program RFWT0010.

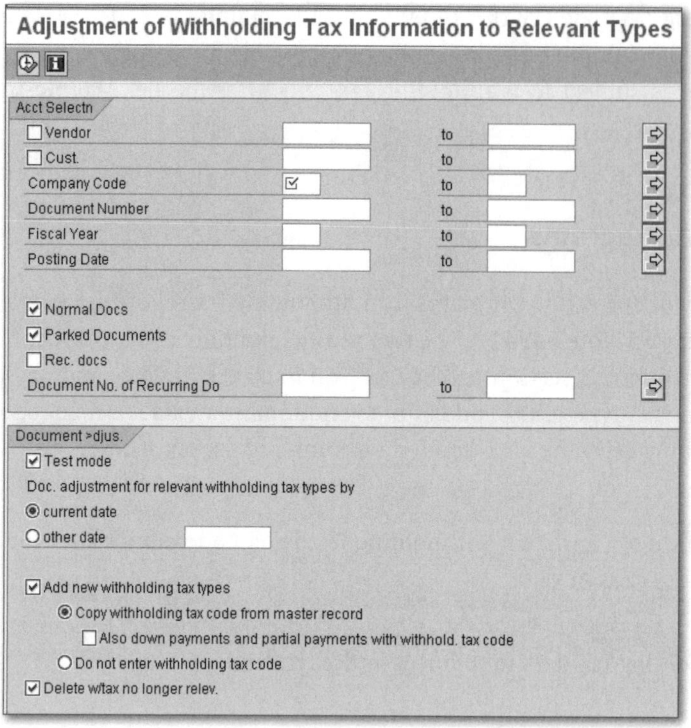

Figure 10.11 Selection Screen of Program RFWT0010

Account Selection

In the **Acct Selectn** section, the documents to be adjusted can be selected by vendor/customer, company code, and other document details such as document number, fiscal year, or posting date.

Document Adjustment

In the **Document Adjus.** section, the adjustment details need to be set. If the **Add new withholding tax types** flag is selected, the system creates new withholding tax information for open and parked documents based on the withholding tax information you entered in the vendor master data.

If the **Delete w/tax no longer relev.** flag is selected, the system deletes any withholding tax information from open and parked documents if the tax information is deleted in the vendor master data.

After all relevant selection criteria are entered, execute the program. The program lists all open and parked documents for which withholding tax information can be added, changed, or deleted. The program also lists locked entries that the program is unable to change because they are in use by other transactions. This could happen if someone is clearing open vendor items via Transaction F-44, or vendor items are still locked in a payment proposal run.

10.9.2 RFWT0020: Adjust Withholding Tax Information in Cleared Documents

The second SAP utility is Program RFWT0020. This program is able to change withholding tax information in invoices, credit memos, and payments. This functionality is needed if invoices and payments were processed with incorrect or no withholding tax information during the year, and this information needs to be changed.

Note that this program only processes tax information with a tax rate of 0%. Tax rates with 0% are tax types that do not require withholding of a fixed percentage at the time of payment. Figure 10.12 shows the selection screen of Program RFWT0020.

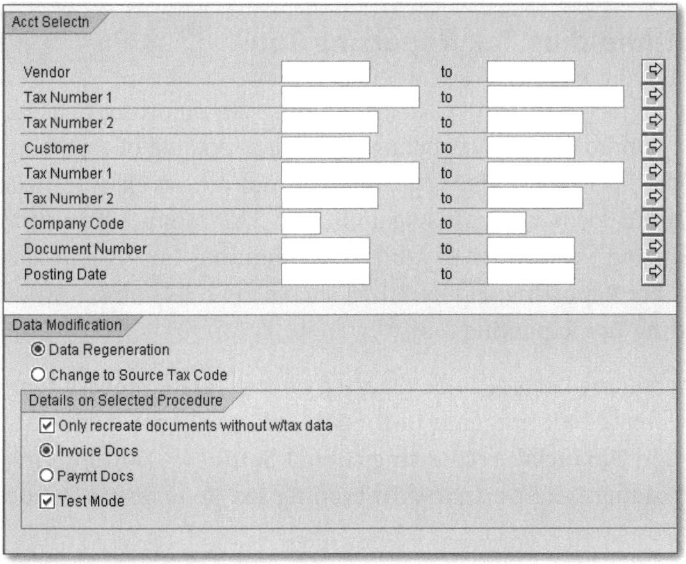

Figure 10.12 Selection Screen of Program RFWT0020

The execution and selection steps are similar to those in Program RFWT0010. Vendor and customer documents can be selected by master data information, such as vendor/customer number, tax ID, or SSN, or by document data, such as company code, document number, and fiscal year.

The withholding tax information in the payment documents is adjusted based on the withholding tax information in the invoices. That makes it necessary to adjust the invoices first. On the other side, the withholding information in the invoices can either be missing or can be wrong. To adjust all invoice and payment documents, this program should be executed four times in sequence with the selection criteria shown in Table 10.5.

Sequence	Only Recreate Documents Without Withholding Tax Date	Documents
1	Switched on	Invoice documents
2	Switched off	Invoice documents
3	Switched on	Payment documents
4	Switched off	Payment documents

Table 10.5 Execution Sequence of Program RFWT0020

10.10 Generic Withholding Tax Reporting Tool

Independent of whether classic or extended withholding tax reporting is used, SAP delivers a generic withholding tax reporting tool that is capable of reporting all described withholding tax types. This reporting tax tool can be executed via Transaction S_P00_07000134 or via the navigation path **SAP Menu • Accounting • Financial Accounting • Accounts Payable • Withholding Tax • General • Generic Withholding Tax Reporting**. Figure 10.13 shows the selection screen of the **Generic Withholding Tax Reporting** tool.

Depending on the withholding tax type to be reported on, a separate **Process Type** and **Output Group** needs to be configured in the IMG via navigation path **IMG • Financial Accounting • Financial Accounting Global Settings • Withholding Tax • Extended Withholding Tax • Generic Withholding Tax Reporting • Define Output Groups**.

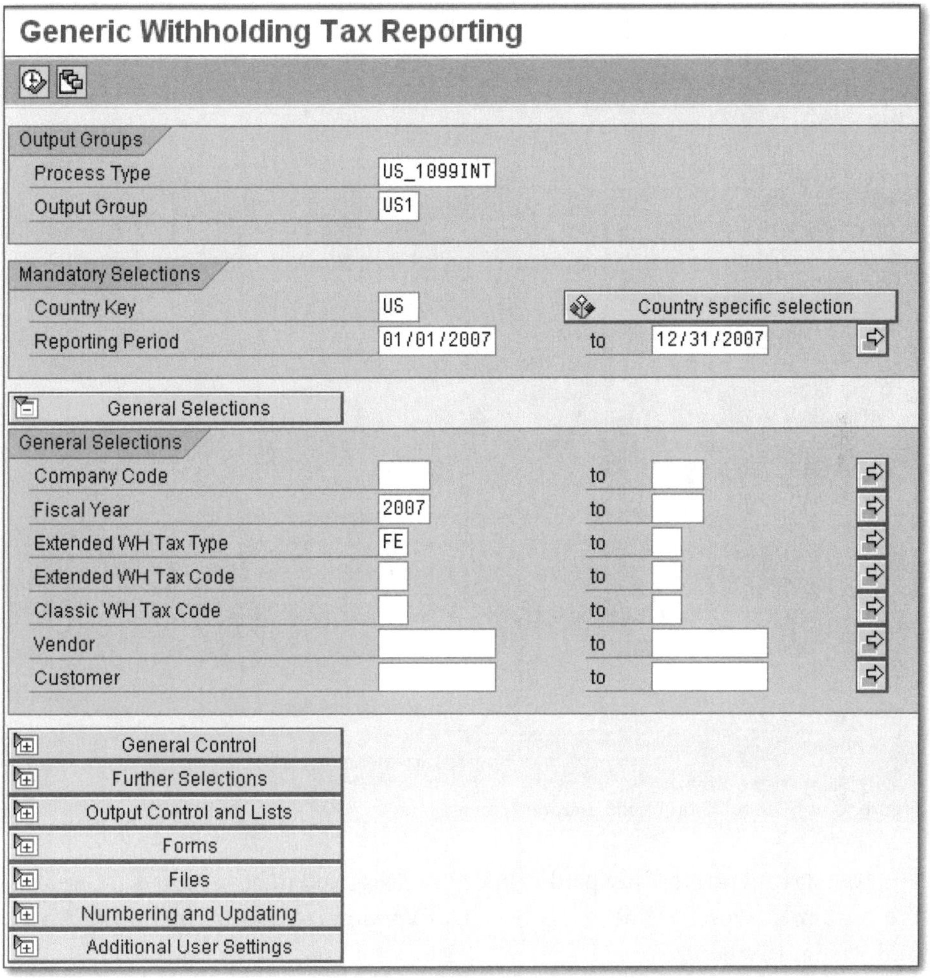

Figure 10.13 Generic Withholding Tax Reporting Tool

For each output group, it's specified what lists, printouts, and files are created
as well as which accounting documents the generic withholding tax reporting
program has to read the withholding tax information from. SAP already has pre-
delivered the output groups for 1099-MISC, 1099-INT, 1099-G, and 1042-S reporting. For example, the configuration for 1099-MISC for the **Output Group US1** is
shown in Figure 10.14.

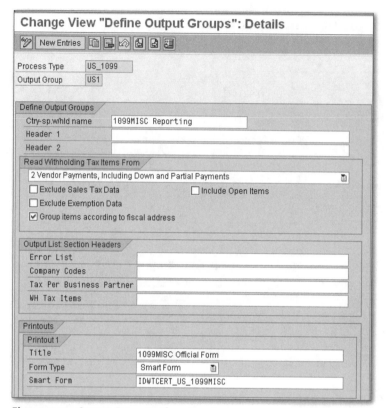

Figure 10.14 Output Group Configuration Screen

For 1099 tax reporting, only paid vendor invoices need to be reported. Therefore, the document type field needs to be set to **Vendor Payments, Including Down and Partial Payments**.

Group Items According to Fiscal Address

The field **Group items according to fiscal address** means that all payments to multiple vendors need to be combined under a single vendor and be reported under a single vendor. In the vendor master data in the **Control** tab, the **Fiscal Address** field needs to be filled with the vendor number under which the information should be combined.

Smart Forms

In the **Smart Form** field, the output form is specified. Table 10.6 lists all the smart forms for 1099 reporting.

Smart Form	Documents
IDWTCERT_US_1099MISC	1099-MISC reporting – two vendors on one form
IDWTCERT_US_1099MISC1	1099-MISC reporting – one vendor on one form
IDWTCERT_US_1099G	1099-G reporting form
IDWTCERT_US_1099INT	1099-INT reporting form
IDWTCERT_US_1042S	1042-S reporting form

Table 10.6 SAP Delivered Smart Forms

Every year in the December time frame, SAP releases required updates to the tax forms, such as background year or other regulatory changes, via OSS notes. These changes have to be imported in the system.

10.11 Summary

In this Chapter, the most common forms of Withholding Tax reporting in the U.S., such as 1099-MISC, 1099-INT, 1009-G, and 1042 reporting were described. The SAP software delivers the classic withholding and the extended withholding tax reporting tool, which has additional corrections programs and functions available. The reporting to the tax authorities is executed using the Generic Withholding Tax reporting tool.

In the next Chapter, Use tax and VAT tax reporting is covered.

Tax requirements vary greatly by country. Even within the same country, different tax rates may apply by region or jurisdiction. This chapter describes the main configuration steps for use tax in the United States and VAT tax in Europe.

11 Use Taxes and VAT Taxes

Every organization is required to collect taxes or pay taxes on purchases and sales regardless of the country, size, or type of organizations. However, great differences exist in the way the taxes are calculated, reported, and paid. Multinational companies have to comply with these tax rules, if they are doing business in different countries.

The intention of this chapter isn't to give a detailed view of the tax configuration details by country but rather to give a comprehensive overview of two common tax concepts:

▶ Use tax in the United States

▶ VAT tax in Europe

11.1 Use Tax within the United States

The use tax calculation for jurisdictions is usually based on three components:

▶ The jurisdiction in which the buyer takes possession

▶ The use of the service or material

▶ The tax status of the legal entity that purchased the service or material

Within SAP software, *use tax* is calculated using a special tax calculation procedure. Within this procedure, different rates are defined by jurisdiction code and tax code.

The *tax jurisdiction code* defines the location of the sender and receiver of the goods purchased. This is important because the sender and receiver information is needed to properly calculate use tax. The tax jurisdiction codes are usually assigned to master data such as vendor or cost center.

The tax code defines whether goods are taxable or not. Within the tax calculation procedure, the tax code is assigned to a rate by jurisdiction using the condition technique.

11.1.1 Tax Procedures

The SAP software delivers three tax procedures for the United States:

▶ **TAXUS:** Sales/use tax in United States.

▶ **TAXUSJ:** Sales/use tax with jurisdiction.

▶ **TAXUSX:** Sales/use tax with jurisdiction in an external system.

In this chapter, we'll cover the TAXUSJ procedure, which is the most commonly used procedure if no external tax calculation software is used. This procedure relies on all information stored within the SAP software to calculate the correct tax rate. This is practical for organizations that operate regionally and have simple tax calculation rules. For this procedure, the rate and conditions have to be maintained on a regular basis within the SAP software.

For large organizations that operate in multiple states with multiple product lines and procurement channels, the TAXUSX procedure is a better fit. This procedure is also jurisdiction based but communicates with an external tax calculation system. The rates and calculations are handled externally.

The third TAXUS procedure doesn't allow the calculation by jurisdiction, which isn't common. This procedure is only feasible for organizations that operate within one jurisdiction.

Figure 11.1 shows the tax calculation procedure TAXUSJ.

Each single calculation area, such as AP use tax, can have up to four different condition types that can represent different rates for state, county, or city.

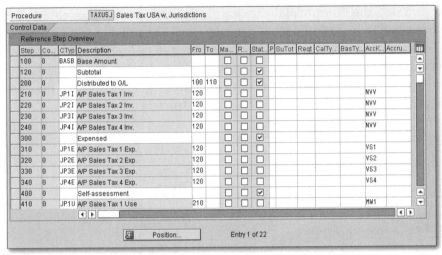

Figure 11.1   Tax Calculation Procedure TAXUSJ

11.1.2   Use Tax Configuration

The tax procedure is assigned to the country as shown in Figure 11.2 via Transaction OBBG or in the IMG via navigation path **IMG • Financial Accounting • Financial Accounting Global Settings • Tax on Sales/Purchases • Basic Settings • Assign Country to Calculation Procedure.**

Figure 11.2   Tax Procedure Assignment to Country

In the next step, the structure of the tax jurisdiction code needs to be defined. The tax jurisdiction code is usually nine characters long. The structure can be defined via Transaction OBCO or in the IMG via navigation path **IMG • Financial Accounting • Financial Accounting Global Settings • Tax on Sales/Purchases • Basic Settings • Specify Structure for Tax Jurisdiction Code.** Figure 11.3 shows the IMG configuration screen of the tax jurisdiction code structure.

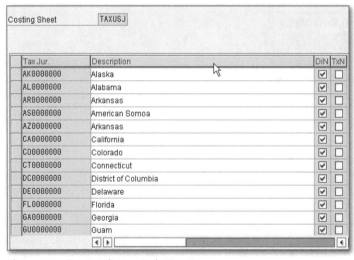

Figure 11.3 Tax Jurisdiction Code Structure

If you're using the TAXUSJ procedure, all relevant tax jurisdiction codes need to be defined for the sender as well as for the receiver jurisdictions. This task is done as shown in Figure 11.4 in the IMG via navigation path **IMG • Financial Accounting • Financial Accounting Global Settings • Tax on Sales/Purchases • Basic Settings • Define Tax Jurisdictions.**

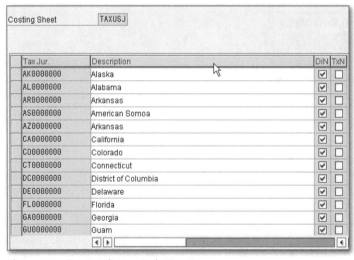

Figure 11.4 Tax Jurisdiction Code Creation

In the next step, the tax rates by tax code and jurisdiction need to be defined. The SAP software delivers a set of predefined tax codes for the tax calculation procedure TAXUSJ as shown in Figure 11.5. The tax rates can be maintain in the IMG under navigation path **IMG • Financial Accounting • Financial Accounting Global Settings • Tax on Sales/Purchases • Calculation • Define Tax Codes for Sales and Purchases.**

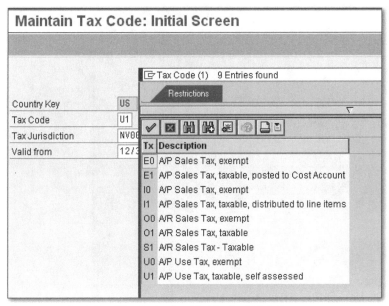

Figure 11.5 Predefined Tax Codes Provided in the SAP Software

You can adjust the description by clicking on the **Properties** button as shown in Figure 11.6.

Depending on the jurisdiction code entered, such as state, county, or city jurisdiction code, different fields are available to maintain the tax rate. This is controlled within the configuration of the condition type within the tax procedure.

Within this configuration step, the GL accounts need to be defined by transaction key. This transaction key or account key is assigned in the definition of the tax calculation procedure as shown earlier in Figure 11.1. To assign a GL account, click on the **Tax accounts** button.

The maintenance of the tax rate and GL account concludes the configuration for U.S. use tax.

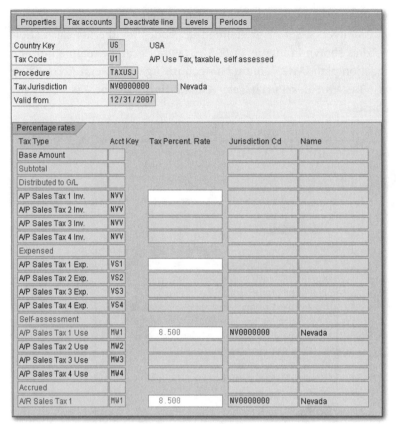

| Properties | Tax accounts | Deactivate line | Levels | Periods |

Country Key	US	USA
Tax Code	U1	A/P Use Tax, taxable, self assessed
Procedure	TAXUSJ	
Tax Jurisdiction	NV0000000	Nevada
Valid from	12/31/2007	

Percentage rates

Tax Type	Acct Key	Tax Percent. Rate	Jurisdiction Cd	Name
Base Amount				
Subtotal				
Distributed to G/L				
A/P Sales Tax 1 Inv.	NVV			
A/P Sales Tax 2 Inv.	NVV			
A/P Sales Tax 3 Inv.	NVV			
A/P Sales Tax 4 Inv.	NVV			
Expensed				
A/P Sales Tax 1 Exp.	VS1			
A/P Sales Tax 2 Exp.	VS2			
A/P Sales Tax 3 Exp.	VS3			
A/P Sales Tax 4 Exp.	VS4			
Self-assessment				
A/P Sales Tax 1 Use	MW1	8.500	NV0000000	Nevada
A/P Sales Tax 2 Use	MW2			
A/P Sales Tax 3 Use	MW3			
A/P Sales Tax 4 Use	MW4			
Accrued				
A/R Sales Tax 1	MW1	8.500	NV0000000	Nevada

Figure 11.6 Tax Rate Maintenance in Procedure TAXUSJ

11.1.3 Jurisdiction Code Maintenance in Master Data

To avoid manual input of the jurisdiction code in procurement or during invoice entry, it's recommended to enter the jurisdiction code in master data. That also means that master data need to be set up based on jurisdiction rather then area of responsibility.

For example, if the jurisdiction code is maintained in the cost center master data, it's defaulted automatically during invoice entry with Transaction FB60. In detail, the jurisdiction code can be maintained in the following master data:

▶ Company code

▶ Plant

- Storage location
- Cost center
- Internal order
- WBS-element

All of these master data items represent the receiver or ship-to jurisdiction codes. In addition, the jurisdiction also has to be maintained in the vendor master data as well to calculate the appropriate use tax rate based on the shipping address of the vendor.

11.1.4   Tax Code Maintenance in Master Data

To determine which purchases are relevant for tax, the tax codes need to be maintained in the following master data:

- GL account
- Material master

11.1.5   Tax Reporting for Use and Sales Tax

SAP software provides a standard report RFATAX00 for use and sales tax reporting. This report can be executed via Transaction S_ALR_87012394. All documents are displayed per customer or vendor account and are totaled by tax code and jurisdiction with reference to the tax base and amount.

11.2   VAT Taxes in Europe

Value added tax (*VAT*) is an indirect tax levied on the added value that results from each exchange of goods and materials. It differs from a sales tax because a sales tax is levied on the total value of the exchange.

For this reason, VAT is neutral with respect to the number of passages between the producer and the final consumer. Personal end-consumers of products and services can't recover VAT on purchases, but businesses are able to recover VAT on the materials and services that they buy to make further supplies or services directly or indirectly sold to end users. In this way, the total tax levied at each stage in the economic supply chain is a constant fraction of the value added by a business to its products, and businesses bear most of the cost of collecting the tax. VAT is the common form of taxation in most European countries.

11.2.1 Tax Procedures

SAP software delivers VAT procedures for every European country. For example, the following tax procedures are predefined:

▶ **TAXD:** Germany

▶ **TAXF:** France

▶ **TAXES:** Spain

▶ **TAXIT:** Italy

We'll only cover the tax procedure for France TAXF here because all other European tax procedures work in a similar way. Usually, the tax rates are the same within a country and don't vary by region. However, some countries such as Italy and Spain require regional codes for reporting purposes. Figure 11.7 shows the tax calculation procedure TAXF for France.

The tax calculation procedure is simpler than the U.S. tax calculation procedure TAXUSJ because no tax rates need to be defined by region.

Procedure			TAXF	Sales Tax - France												
Control Data																
Reference Step Overview																
Step	Co...	CTyp	Description	Fro	To	Ma...	R...	Stat..	P	SuTot	Reqt	CalTy..	BasTy..	AccK..	Accru..
100	0	BASB	Base Amount			☐	☐	☐							
110	0	MWAS	Output Tax	100		☐	☐	☐						MWS	
120	0	MWVS	Input tax	100		☐	☐	☐						VST	
140	0	MWVN	Non-deduct.Input Tax	100		☐	☐	☐						NVV	
150	0	NLXA	Acquisition Tax Cred	100		☐	☐	☐						ESA	
160	0	NLXV	Acquisition Tax Deb.	150		☐	☐	☐						ESE	

Figure 11.7 Tax Calculation Procedure TAXF

11.2.2 VAT Configuration

In the first step, the tax procedure is assigned to the country as shown earlier in the TAXUSJ configuration in Figure 11.1 via Transaction OBBG or in the IMG via navigation path **IMG • Financial Accounting • Financial Accounting Global Set-**

tings • **Tax on Sales/Purchases** • **Basic Settings** • **Assign Country to Calculation Procedure.**

Tax Rates

In the next step, the tax rates by tax code need to be defined. SAP software delivers a set of predefined tax codes for the tax calculation procedure TAXF as shown in Figure 11.8. The tax rates can be maintained in the IMG under navigation path **IMG** • **Financial Accounting** • **Financial Accounting Global Settings** • **Tax on Sales/Purchases** • **Calculation** • **Define Tax Codes for Sales and Purchases.**

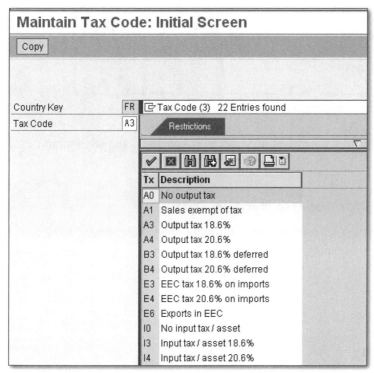

Figure 11.8 Predefined Tax Codes by SAP Software

The description can be changed by clicking on the **Properties** button as shown in Figure 11.9. Within this configuration step, the GL accounts also need to be defined by transaction key. This transaction key or account key is assigned in the definition of the tax calculation procedure as shown previously in Figure 11.7. To assign a GL account, click on the **Tax accounts** button.

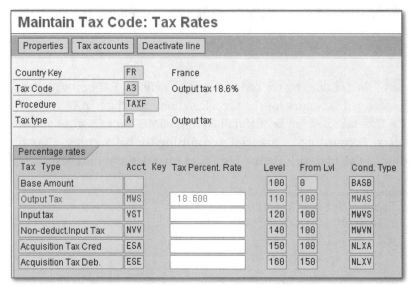

Figure 11.9 Tax Rate Maintenance

The maintenance of the tax rate and GL account concludes the configuration for VAT reporting.

11.2.3 Tax Code Maintenance in Master Data

To determine which purchases are relevant for tax, the tax codes need to be maintained in the following master data:

▸ GL account

▸ Material master

11.3 Summary

In this Chapter the most common forms of taxation in AP were described, Use tax in the Unites States and VAT tax in Europe. The SAP software delivers tax procedures by tax types and country.

In the next Chapter, AP transactions with the Special GL Indicator are described.

Special GL transactions in Accounts Payable (AP) have to be recorded separately in the General Ledger (GL) in alternative reconciliations accounts, such as down payments, retentions, or guarantees.

12 Special GL Transactions in Accounts Payable

In special situations, it's required that certain transactions be recorded in the GL in alternative reconciliation accounts. An alternative reconciliation account is a different reconciliation account than assigned in the vendor master data. Within SAP software, *special GL transactions* allow the recording and reporting of Transactions such as the following:

- Down payments
- Retention

These transactions are recorded within GL. In addition, SAP software also allows recording of special transactions, which are not visible in GL, using *noted items*. Noted items are posted to the vendor and are only visible in AP. Guarantees, for example, can be recorded on a vendor account without affecting GL.

12.1 Down Payments

In certain industries, it's common that the vendor receives a down payment for the services or goods to be delivered. After the services are delivered, and the invoice is received, the down payment is cleared against the received invoice.

Within SAP software, the down payments can be recorded in two different ways. The first option is to post the down payment directly against the vendor account and a bank account using Transaction F-48. In this case, the document has to be in balance. No payment to vendor using the payment program is executed.

The second and most common option is the *Down Payment Request* option. A down payment request allows you to enter a request for payment, which is later paid to the vendor via the automatic payment program.

The following example explains the entire down payment process using a down payment request, paying through the payment program, and clearing the down payment. The example uses the predefined Special G/L indicator "A" for down payments and "F" for down payment request.

Down Payment Example

For example, a new car over 35,000 USD is purchased from vendor 10013. Vendor 10013 requires a down payment of 10% of the purchasing amount before the delivery of the car. Upon delivery of the car, an invoice over 35,000 USD is entered, which is then cleared against the down payment. The purchase order number is 4500000065.

12.1.1 Entering a Down Payment Request

A **Down Payment Request** is entered using Transaction F-47 or the navigation path **SAP Menu • Accounting • Financial Accounting • Accounts Payable • Document Entry • Down Payment • Request.** Figure 12.1 shows the **Header Data** screen of the down payment request.

Down Payment Request: Header Data

New item

Document Date	05/21/2008	Type	KA	Company Code	1000
Posting Date	05/21/2008	Period	12	Currency/Rate	USD
Document Number				Translatn Date	
Reference	Car Down Payment			
Doc.Header Text				
Trading part.BA				

Vendor
Account 100013
Trg.sp.G/L ind. A

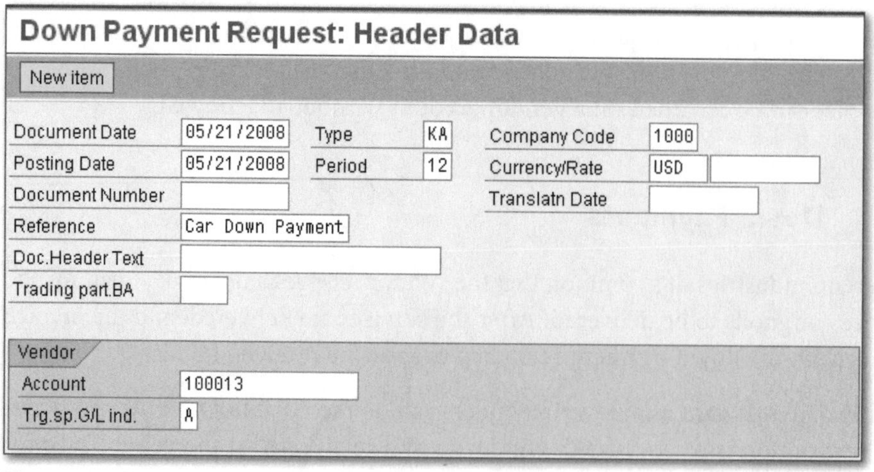

Figure 12.1 Down Payment Request: Header Data Screen

The header information contains the common document header information of an invoice such as **Posting Date**, **Document Date**, Document **Type**, and Invoice **Reference**.

Account

The **Account** field specifies the vendor to whom the down payment is made.

Target Special G/L Indicator

In the target special G/L indicator (**Trg.sp.G/L ind.**) field, the special G/L indicator for down payments is entered. Note, that the special G/L indicator of a down payment request isn't entered but instead the target special G/L indicator.

Press the **Enter** key to get to the vendor item screen after all header information is entered.

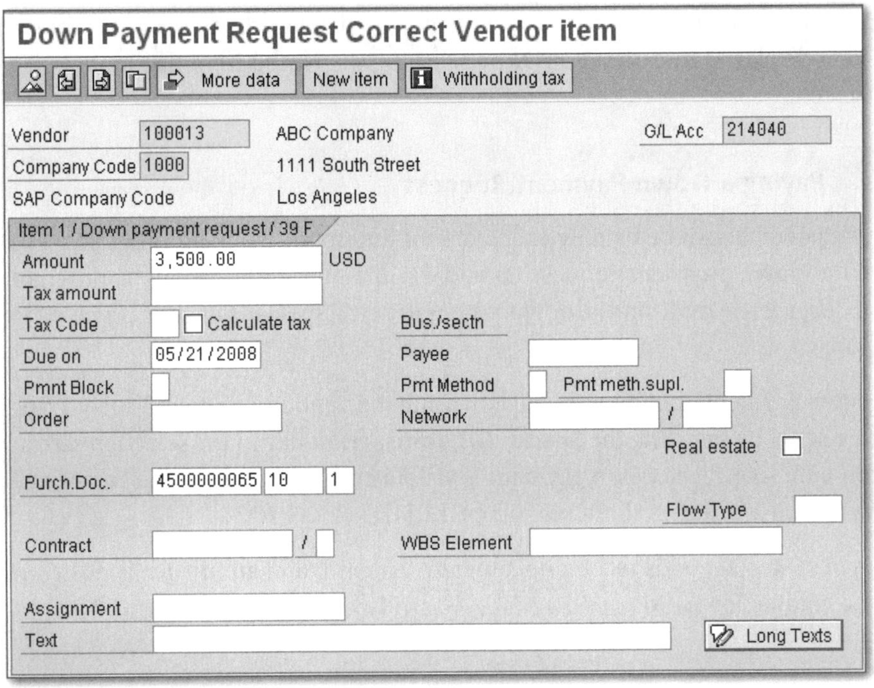

Figure 12.2 Down Payment Request Vendor Item Screen

The vendor item screen as shown in Figure 12.2 contains the down payment amount as well as payment information, such as **due date**, **payment method**, **payment supplement**, or **payment block**.

Purchasing Document

If the down payment is made against a purchase order, enter the purchase order and item number in the purchasing document (**Purch.Doc.**) field. By doing that, the down payment is visible in the purchase order, and an information message is issued during Logistic Invoice Verification (LIV), if an invoice is entered against a purchase order with a down payment.

Click the **Post** button to post the down payment request.

A down payment request is posted as a *noted item* and only visible within AP. Internally, the special G/L indicator is changed to the special G/L indicator for down payment request "F."

The down payment requests of a vendor can be displayed by using the vendor line item display Transaction FBL1N by selecting the **Noted item** flag in the selection screen.

12.1.2   Paying a Down Payment Request

A down payment can be paid by executing the automatic payment program F110. After the down payment request is paid via the automatic payment program, the request is cleared, and a down payment with special G/L indicator "A" is generated.

The down payments can be displayed by using the vendor line item display Transaction FBL1N by selecting the **Special G/L transaction** flag in the selection screen. Within purchasing, the down payment is visible in the Purchase Order History tab of the purchase order as shown in Figure 12.3.

In the next step, a goods receipt document is entered, and an invoice is posted in LIV via Transaction MIRO.

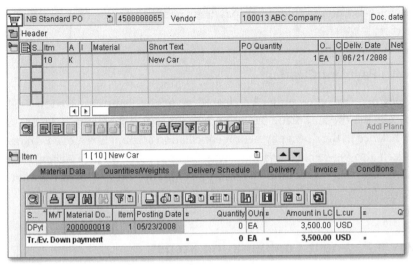

Figure 12.3 Purchase Order History Tab

12.1.3 Invoice Entry

During the invoice entry with Transaction MIRO, an information message is displayed that informs the user that a down payment is posted against the purchase order (as shown in Figure 12.4).

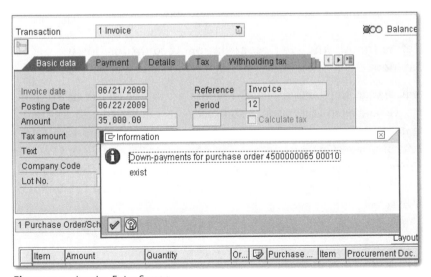

Figure 12.4 Invoice Entry Screen

After the invoice is entered, the down payment needs to be cleared against the entered invoice.

12.1.4 Down Payment Clearing

The down payment can now either be cleared manually using Transaction F-54 or automatically via the automatic payment program. After the down payment is cleared, the balance in the down payment reconciliation account is removed. Transaction F-54 can also be executed via the navigation path **SAP Menu • Accounting • Financial Accounting • Accounts Payable • Document Entry • Down Payment • Clearing.**

12.2 Down Payment Configuration Steps

SAP software already delivers the special G/L indicators for down payment request "F" and down payment "A". New special G/L indicators for down payments can be added or the existing changed, however, the special G/L indicator for down payment requests must be "F" and can't be changed.

The configuration is done in two steps:

1. Define the alternative reconciliation account for down payments.

2. Allow automatic payments for special G/L indicators.

12.2.1 Define the Alternative Reconciliation Account for Down Payment

In this configuration step, new special G/L indicators can be added, descriptions can be changed, and alternative reconciliation accounts can be assigned. The maintenance is done via Transaction OBYR or in the IMG via navigation path **IMG • Financial Accounting • Financial Accounting • Accounts Receivable and Payable • Business Transactions • Down Payment Made • Define Alternative Reconciliation Account for Down Payment.** Figure 12.5 shows the special G/L indicator maintenance screen.

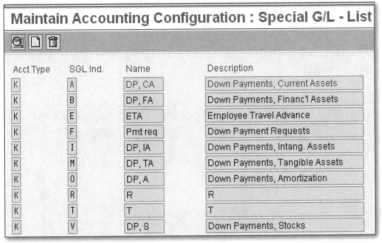

Figure 12.5 Special G/L Indicator Maintenance Screen

To create a new special G/L transaction, click on the Create button, and a new window appears that allows you to enter the new indicator, name, and description. To change the description, choose **Edit • Change Name** in the Header menu.

If you double-click on a special G/L indicator, the account assignment screen shown in Figure 12.6 appears.

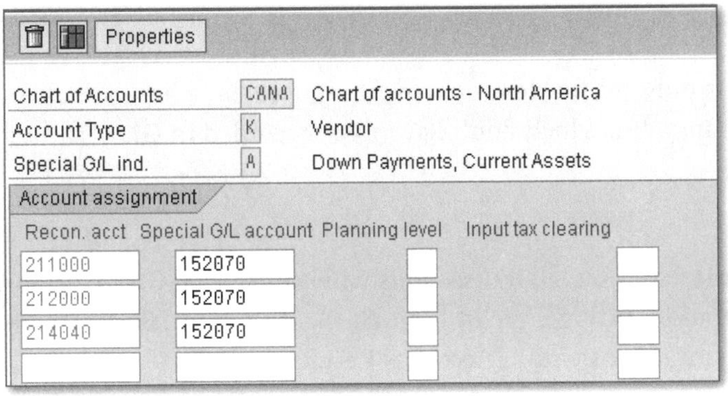

Figure 12.6 Account Assignment Screen

The **Recon. acct** column specifies the different vendor reconciliation accounts used. The **Special G/L account** column identifies the alternative reconciliation account used for down payments depending on the reconciliation account. In the preceding example, down payments are posted to the same alternative reconciliation account 152070 for three different reconciliation accounts.

By choosing the **Properties** button, the properties of the **Special G/L ind.** shown in Figure 12.7 can be changed.

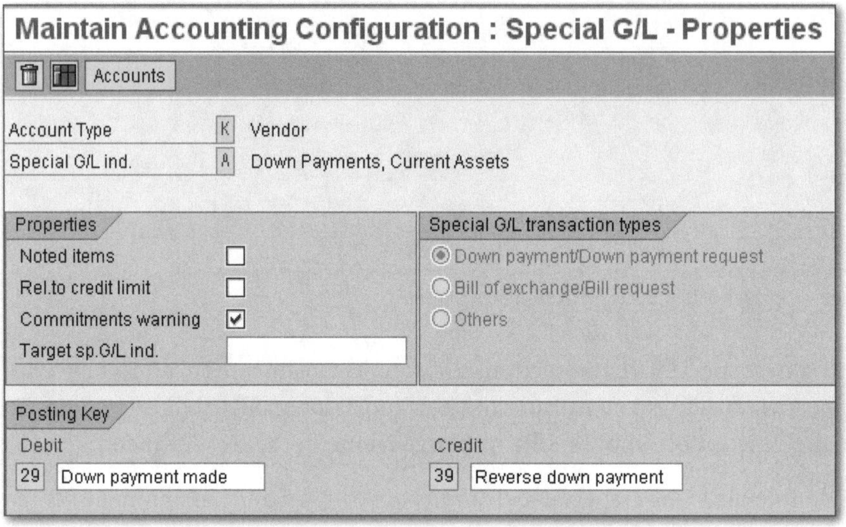

Figure 12.7 Properties of Special G/L Indicators

Noted Items

The **Noted items** flag is only set for down payment requests or other special GL transactions such as guarantees, which don't have to be recorded in GL.

Rel. to Credit Limit

If the **Rel. to credit limit** flag is set, all transactions with this special G/L indicator are taken into consideration during a credit limit check. This is usually only relevant for special G/L transactions within Accounts Receivable (AR).

Commitments Warning

The **Commitments warning** flag causes an information message to appear that informs the user of a balance in the vendor account for this special G/L indicator.

12.2.2 Allow Automatic Payments for Special GL Indicators

To pay transactions with special G/L indicators automatically, these special G/L indicators have to be specified in the configuration of the automatic payment program in the IMG via navigation path **IMG • Financial Accounting • Financial Accounting • Accounts Receivable and Payable • Business Transactions • Outgoing Payments • Automatic Outgoing Payments • Payment Method/Bank Selection for Payment Program Out • Set Up All Company Codes for Payment Transactions.** These special G/L indicators are specified in the **Sp. G/L transactions to be paid** field of the **Vendors** section shown in Figure 12.8.

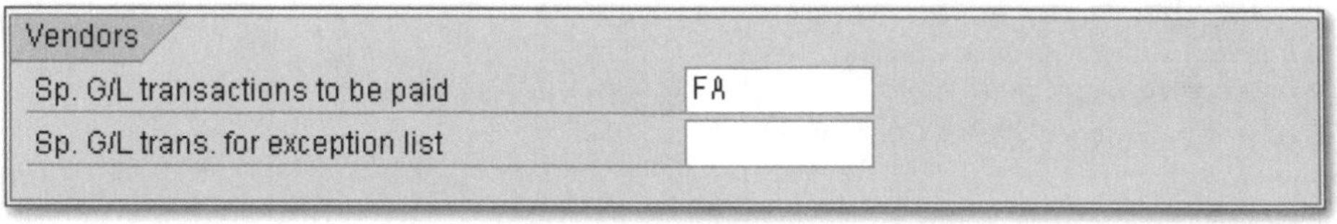

Figure 12.8   Special G/L Indicators in Payment Program Configuration

12.3   Other Special GL Transactions

If other special G/L transactions besides those for down payments are needed, these special G/L indicators can be defined via Transaction OBXT or in the IMG via navigation path **IMG • Financial Accounting • Financial Accounting • Accounts Receivable and Payable • Business Transactions • Postings with Alternative Reconciliation Account • Define Alternative Reconciliation Account for Vendors.** The configuration screens are the same as described for down payments so they are not described here further.

12.3.1   Entering Special GL Transactions

Transactions with a special G/L indicator can be entered the same way as invoices or credit memos. For example, Figure 12.9 shows Transaction FB60. In this transaction, the special G/L indicator can be entered in the **SGL Ind** field.

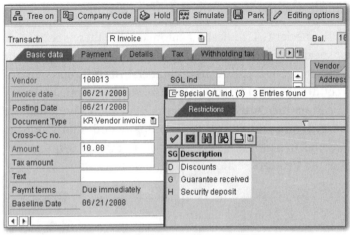

Figure 12.9 Entering Special G/L Transactions via FB60

12.3.2 Entering Noted Items

Noted items can only be entered via Transaction F-57 or via the SAP menu using the navigation path **SAP Menu • Accounting • Financial Accounting • Accounts Payable • Document Entry • Other • Noted Items.** Figure 12.10 shows the entry screen of a noted item.

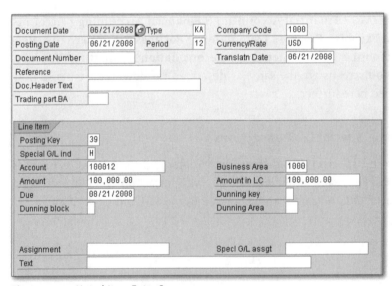

Figure 12.10 Noted Item Entry Screen

12.4 Summary

Within AP, it's required to record special transactions such as down payments, retentions, or guarantees. SAP software delivers the special G/L transaction functionality for this purpose. In this chapter, the special G/L transactions for down payments and other special G/L transactions were described include configuration and posting examples.

In the next Chapter the different transactions for reversing documents in AP are described.

The reversal functionality in SAP allows incorrect entered documents, such as invoices or payments, to be reversed. Different reversal options are available depending on the type of document to be reversed.

13   Document Reversals

As shown in the prior chapters, invoice and credit memo documents are entered through different transactions, such as FB60 for Accounts Payable (AP) invoices or MIRO for purchase order-related invoices. If incorrect documents have to be reversed, SAP has different transactions available for reversing documents. This chapter describes the different options for reversing documents. The following transactions are covered in detail:

▶ **FB08:** Individual Document Reversal

▶ **F.80:** Mass Document Reversal

▶ **FBRA:** Reset Cleared Items

▶ **MR8M:** Cancel Invoice Document in LIV

All of the preceding transactions, except Transaction MR8M, can be found within the AP application. Within AP, application documents, such as invoices or credit memos, can be reversed individually or multiple documents simultaneously through a mass reversal run. Payment documents others than check payments can be revered using the Reset Cleared Items functionality. This chapter doesn't describe the reversal of check payments, which was already covered in Chapter 8.

If invoices or credit memos that originated in LIV have to be reversed, Transaction MR8M must be chosen.

13.1   Negative Postings

Before the different reversal transactions are described in detail, you need to know about a little known but important feature in SAP software called *negative post-*

ings. Negative postings allow you to have the debit and credit balances on a vendor account adjusted as if the transaction never happed. This may be important if your organization does reporting by vendor balances or uses vendor balances in the cash flow statements. In this case, reversal documents have to be deducted. The negative postings feature is a way to have the system adjust these numbers automatically.

For clarification on how negative postings works, an invoice to vendor A is posted over $10,000, reversed, and then posted again. In the first example, the reversal is posted without negative postings. Table 13.1 shows the effect on the debit and credit balances if the negative postings feature is not used. The vendor balance can be displayed with Transaction FK10N: Vendor Balances.

Business Transactions	Debit Vendor Balance	Credit Vendor Balance
Invoice posting over $10,000		10,000-
Reversal of Invoice Document Without Negative Posting	10,000	
Invoice Posting over $10,000		10,000-
Total balance	**10,000**	**20,000-**

Table 13.1 Examples Without Negative Postings

As shown in Table 13.1, the total credit balance for this vendor is 20,000-. However, an invoice over $10,000 was entered, reversed, and entered again. In reality, the credit balance was only $10,000- because the reversed invoice needs to be deducted from the credit balance.

The second example uses the same posting sequence as in the first example, however, the negative posting function is used. Table 13.2 shows the results.

Business Transactions	Debit Vendor Balance	Credit Vendor Balance
Invoice Posting over $10,000		10,000-
Reversal of Invoice Document with Negative Posting		10,000
Invoice Posting over $10,000		10,000-
Total balance		**10,000-**

Table 13.2 Example with Negative Postings

As shown in Table 13.2, the credit balance is adjusted during the reversal posting. The result is a correct credit balance of $10,000-. However, from an accounting point of view, the posting looks incorrect because a debit posting is shown in the credit column with a positive sign. Therefore, most accounting departments choose not to activate negative postings and rather deduct reversal documents from the credit balance.

13.1.1 Configuration Steps for Negative Postings

If your organization decides to activate negative postings, the activation is done in two steps. In the first step, negative postings needs to be activated globally for the entire company code in the IMG via navigation path **IMG • Financial Accounting • Accounts Receivable and Payable • Business Transactions • Adjust Postings/ Reversal • Permit Negative Postings** as shown in Figure 13.1.

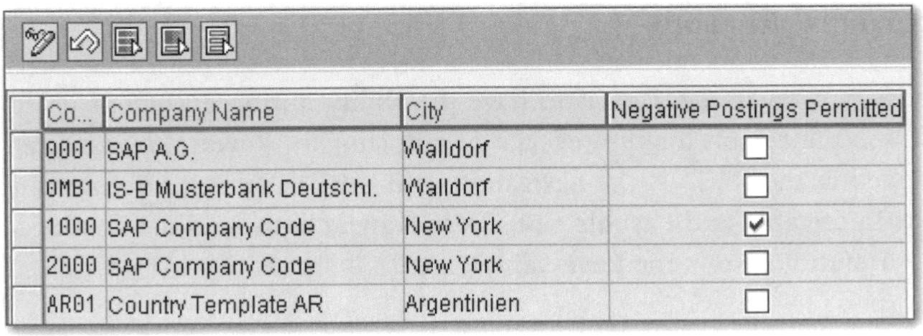

Co...	Company Name	City	Negative Postings Permitted
0001	SAP A.G.	Walldorf	☐
0MB1	IS-B Musterbank Deutschl.	Walldorf	☐
1000	SAP Company Code	New York	☑
2000	SAP Company Code	New York	☐
AR01	Country Template AR	Argentinien	☐

Figure 13.1 Activation of Negative Posting in the Company Code

In the second step, the document types to be reversed, such as invoice or credit memo document types, need to be permitted for negative postings. The document types can be maintained under the navigation path **IMG • Financial Accounting • Accounts Receivable and Payable • Business Transactions • Incoming Invoices/ Credit Memos • Carry Out and Check Document Settings • Define Document Types.** Figure 13.2 shows the **Control data** section within the document type maintenance.

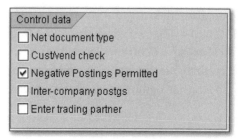

Figure 13.2 Document Type Maintenance Screen

These two configuration steps activate negative postings in the company code and for various document types. In addition, during the reversal of a document, a reversal reason has to be chosen, which allows negative postings. Reversal reasons are explained in the next section.

13.2 Reversal Reasons

The purpose of a reversal reason is to have the ability during document reversals to choose the reason for the reversal of a document. Reversal reasons can be maintained in the IMG via the navigation path **IMG • Financial Accounting • Accounts Receivable and Payable • Business Transactions • Adjust Postings/ Reversal • Define Reasons for Reversal.** Figure 13.3 shows the SAP -delivered reversal reasons.

Reason	Text	Neg.postng	Alt.pos.dt
01	Reversal in current period	☐	☐
02	Reversal in closed period	☐	☑
03	Actual reversal in current period	☑	☐
04	Actual reversal in closed period	☑	☑
05	Accrual/deferral posting	☑	☑

Figure 13.3 Reversal Reasons Configuration

The **Reason** is a two-character key, which is entered during the reversal of a document. In the **Text** field, an explanation of the reversal reason is entered.

Negative Posting

If the **Neg. postng** flag is set, the system generates a negative posting if this reversal reason is chosen during the reversal transaction, and negative postings is activated for the company code and document type to be reversed.

Alternative Posting Date Allowed

Set the alternative posting date allowed (**Alt.pos.dt**) flag if the user is allowed to choose a different posting date of the reversal document than the posting date of the original document. Usually this flag should be set because often documents have to be reversed for a closed period, and a posting date in the current period has to be entered.

13.2.1 Best Practice Reversal Reasons

The predefined reversal reasons provided by the SAP software often cause confusion for users because the descriptions are not intuitive and do not describe the reason for a reversal. It's therefore recommended to create new reversal reasons that are more explanatory. Also, if your organization doesn't activate negative postings, the predefined reversal reasons that generate negative postings can be deleted because they don't have any effect. Table 13.3 shows examples of new reversal reasons that follow these principles.

Reason	Text	Neg. Posting	Alt.pos Date
01	G/L: Incorrect Posting		X
02	G/L: Accrual Posting		X
10	AP: Incorrect Vendor		X
11	AP: Incorrect Amount		X

Table 13.3 Examples of New Reversal Reasons

As shown in Table 13.3, all reversal reasons have the Alt.pos Date flag set. This allows you to select every reversal reason for documents even if the posting period is already closed.

The configuration of the reversal reason concludes the configuration steps. In the following sections, the different reversal transactions are described.

13.3 FB08: Individual Document Reversal

Transaction FB08 is used to reverse single documents posted in GL, AR, or AP. The AP documents include invoices or credit memos. Transaction FB08 can be executed via the SAP menu path **SAP Menu • Accounting • Financial Accounting • Accounts Payable • Document • Reverse • Individual Reverse.**

Figure 13.4 shows the individual document reversal screen. To reverse a document, at a minimum, the document number, fiscal year, company code, and reversal reason have to be specified.

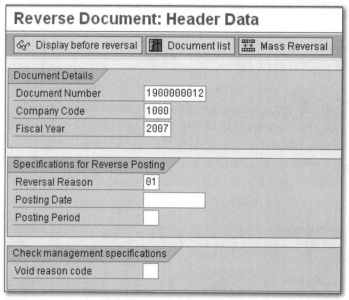

Figure 13.4 Document Reversal via FB08

Posting Date

In the *Posting Date* field the posting date of the reversal document can be specified. If the posting date field is left blank, the posting date of the document to be reversed is used. It's therefore recommended to only choose a posting date, if the period of the document to be reversed is closed.

Posting Period

The **Posting Period** only needs to be entered if the reversal document has to be posted in one of the special periods 13 to 16. A company code can have up to four special periods.

Void Reason Code

Checks are usually reversed with transactions within the check management, such as FCH8 or FCH9, which were covered in Chapter 8. If a check payment document, which doesn't contain any cleared items, needs to be reversed, the check void reason needs to be entered in this field.

After all required information is entered, click the **Post** button, and the entered document will be reversed.

If multiple documents have to be reversed simultaneously, the mass reverse Transaction F.80 can be used.

13.4   F.80: Mass Document Reversal

Transaction F.80 is used to reverse multiple documents simultaneously posted in GL, AR, or AP. Transaction F.80 can be executed via the SAP menu path **SAP Menu • Accounting • Financial Accounting • Accounts Payable • Document • Reverse • Mass Reverse**.

Figure 13.5 shows the selection screen of the mass reversal program.

> **Mass Reversal Authorization**
>
> Theoretically, Transaction F.80 allows reversing all financial documents within a client. It's recommended to give authorization to the Mass Reversal Transaction F.80 only to a selected group of users.

If the documents to be reversed are known, they can be entered in the **Document Number** field together with the **Company code** and **Fiscal Year** of the documents.

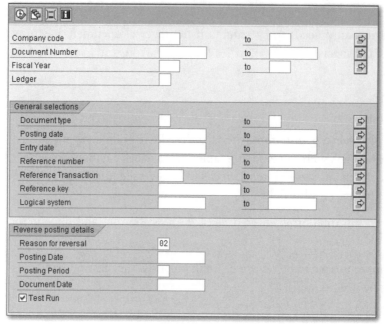

Figure 13.5 Mass Reversal Transaction

General Selection

If the documents to be reversed aren't known, the documents can be selected by other criteria, such as document type, posting date, or reference number. Additional selection criteria are available by choosing the **Dynamic Selections** button.

Reverse Posting Details

In the **Reverse posting details** sections, the **Reason for reversal**, **Posting date**, and **Document Date** of the reversal document can be specified. At a minimum, the **Reason for Reversal** needs to be selected. The mass reversal program can be executed in a **Test** run first, which is recommended.

13.5 FBRA: Reset Cleared Items

Transaction FBRA is used to reset cleared items. This might be necessary, if for example, an invoice is incorrectly cleared against a credit memo. Another example is an ACH payment document that needs to be reversed. Transaction FBRA can be executed via the SAP menu path **SAP Menu • Accounting • Financial Accounting • Accounts Payable • Document • Reset Cleared items.** Figure 13.6 shows the **Reset Cleared Items** screen.

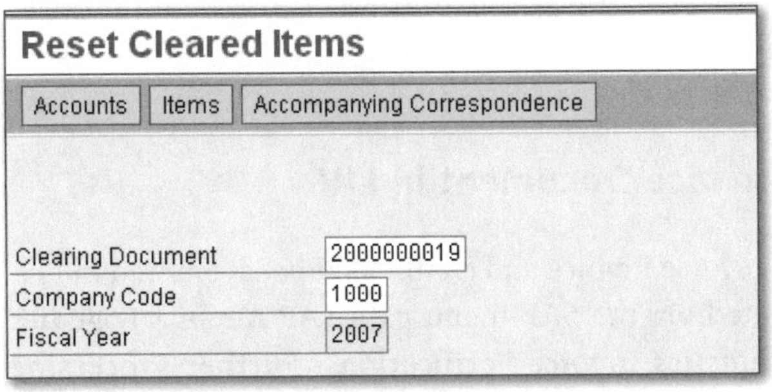

Figure 13.6 Reset Cleared Items Screen

To reset an item, the **Clearing Document** number, **Company Code**, and **Fiscal Year** need to be entered. The **Clearing Document** number can be the payment document for payments or the clearing document number for manually clearing an invoice with a credit memo. After all information is entered, click the **Reset cleared items** button, and the window shown in Figure 13.7 appears.

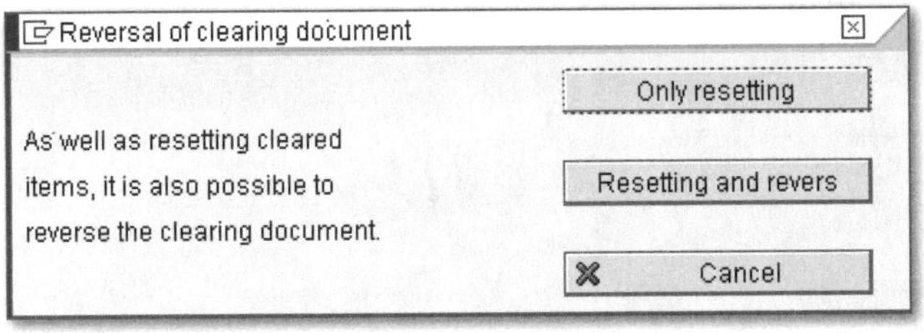

Figure 13.7 Reversal of Clearing Document window

When this window appears, there are two options available, **Only resetting** or **Resetting and revers** as described here:

▶ **Only resetting**

The cleared items are only reset; no document is reversed. For example, the incorrect invoice as cleared against a credit memo. The cleared items should only be reset. In a subsequent step, the correct invoice is cleared against the credit memo.

- ▶ **Resetting and revers**

  The cleared items are reset, and the clearing document reversed. For example, an ACH payment should be reversed. By choosing the **Resetting and revers** option, the cleared invoice is reset, and the ACH payment is reversed.

After you choose the appropriate option, the system resets or resets and reverses the entered clearing document.

13.6 MR8M: Cancel Invoice Document in LIV

Transaction MR8M is used to reverse invoice and credit documents entered in LIV. This transaction can be executed via the SAP menu path **SAP Menu • Logistics • Material Management • Logistics Invoice Verification • Further Processing • Cancel Invoice Document**. Figure 13.8 shows the **Cancel Invoice Document** screen.

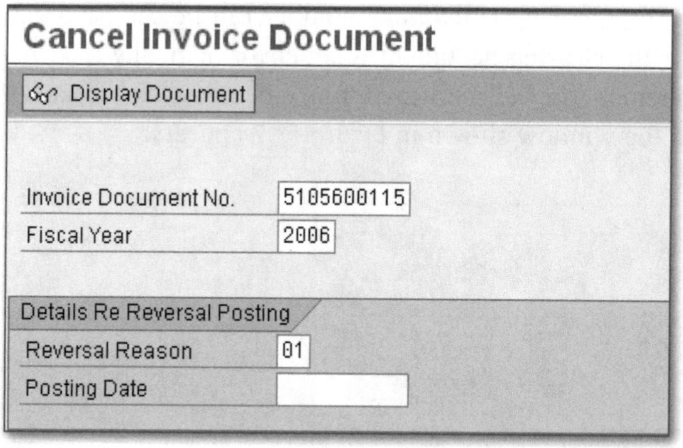

Figure 13.8 Cancel Invoice Document

Because LIV is part of materials management, no company code needs to be entered to cancel an invoice or credit memo, just the **Invoice Document No.** and the **Fiscal Year**. In addition, the **Reversal Reason** and a reversal **Posting Date** need to be entered.

After a document is reversed, you receive the following message: "Document reversed with no. XXXXXXXXXX: Please manually clear FI documents."

This message means the cancelled document is not cleared automatically with the cancellation document in the Financial Accounting component (FI), and the original invoice document has to be cleared manually with the cancellation document using Transaction F-44. Otherwise, the invoice document and the cancellation document remain open items.

> **Tip**
>
> To avoid constant manual clearing efforts, set up an automatic clearing rule for vendors with the reference number field XBLNR as the clearing criterion. Schedule the automatic clearing program SAPF124 on a regular basis (see Chapter 14).

13.7 Summary

In this chapter, we covered the different transactions to reverse documents in Accounts Payable and Invoice Verification.

In the next chapter, we'll cover the different clearing functions SAP software provides.

Vendor clearing is usually done automatically through the payment program or through document reversal. On an exceptional basis, manual clearing of vendor items is necessary through vendor clearing or internal transfer postings.

14   Open Item Management

Open item management is a process within SAP software that allows managing the reconciliation process of balance sheet accounts or sub-ledger accounts. The clearing process for balance sheet accounts can be found in the General Ledger (GL) application. Sub-ledgers in SAP software refer to applications such as Accounts Payable (AP) and Accounts Receivable (AR), where the total sub-ledger balance is posted to reconciliation accounts, but the details are stored in the AP or AR sub-ledger vendor or customer accounts.

For balance sheet accounts, the Open item management flag has to be set explicitly in the GL account master if open item management is desired. This isn't necessary for AP reconciliation accounts because they are always open item managed.

Open item management means that items within an account need to be cleared with other items in the same account. For example, within AP, an invoice is cleared with payments through the payment program or with a reversal document during document reversal.

In the previous chapters, we talked about processes such as automatic payment programs and reversals. During all these processes, vendor open items are cleared automatically. This chapter describes the manual clearing process as well as transfer with clearing transactions.

In addition, SAP software delivers a periodic process for automatic clearing. This automatic clearing program can be scheduled on a regular basis and clears open items based on configured rules per account. The main use within AP for this process is the automatic clearing of the GR/IR account, which is described in this chapter.

14.1   Manual Vendor Clearing

Manual clearing isn't a frequent used process within AP. Manual clearing might be necessary in the following situations:

▶ A credit memo is posted against a vendor, and you want to clear a specific invoice against this credit memo.

▶ An LIV document is reversed via Transaction MR8M. The system doesn't clear the documents automatically in this case, and manual clearing is necessary. In the "Automatic Clearing" section of this chapter, a process is described that allows you to clear these documents automatically.

During the clearing, the system generates a *clearing document* with a clearing date that is stored in the cleared items in the clearing document number field.

14.1.1   Manual Clearing Transition F-44

To execute manual clearing, use Transaction F-44, or execute the transaction via the SAP menu path **SAP Menu • Accounting • Financial Accounting • Accounts Payable • Account • Clear**. Figure 14.1 shows the **Clear Vendor: Header Data** screen of the manual clearing transaction.

Account

The vendor account number to be cleared needs to be entered in the **Account** field.

Clearing Date

The **Clearing date** specifies the date of the clearing. If documents are cleared that have a posting date greater then the clearing date specified, then the clearing date in the clearing document is set automatically to the greatest posting date of the cleared documents.

> **Clearing Date Determination Example**
>
> A clearing date of 6/1/2007 is specified. The documents to be cleared have the posting dates of 5/15/2008 and 6/10/2008, respectively. As a result, the clearing date in the document is automatically set to 6/10/2008.

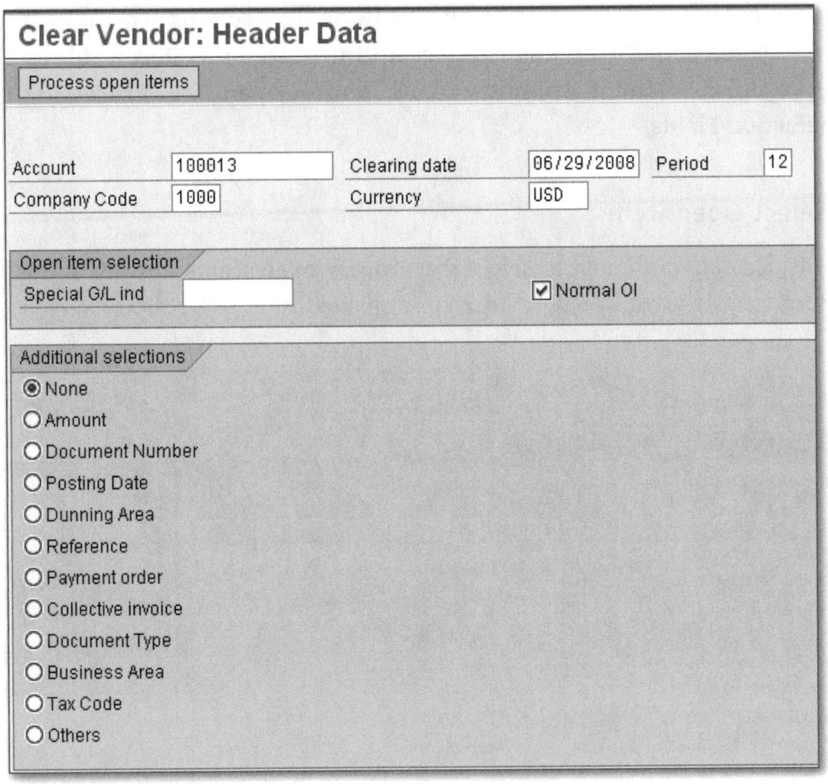

```
Clear Vendor: Header Data

 Process open items

 Account         100013      Clearing date   06/29/2008   Period   12
 Company Code    1000        Currency        USD

 Open item selection
 Special G/L ind  [        ]                    ☑ Normal OI

 Additional selections
 ⦿ None
 ○ Amount
 ○ Document Number
 ○ Posting Date
 ○ Dunning Area
 ○ Reference
 ○ Payment order
 ○ Collective invoice
 ○ Document Type
 ○ Business Area
 ○ Tax Code
 ○ Others
```

Figure 14.1 Header Screen of the Manual Vendor Clearing Transaction

Special G/L Indicator

The **Special G/L ind** allows the selection of open items that are posted with a special G/L indicator, such as down payments or retention. In this case, you have to enter the special G/L indicator key.

Normal OI

If the **Normal OI** checkbox is selected, all regular vendor open items that are posted without a Special G/L indicator are selected.

Additional Selections

The **Additional selections** section allows you to search the vendor open items by other selection criteria, such as **Posting Date** or **Document Number**. You can configure the criteria, which appear in the **Additional selections** screen, in the IMG via navigation path **IMG · Financial Accounting · Accounts Receivable and Accounts Payables · Vendor Accounts · Line Items · Open Item Processing · Choose Selection Fields.**

14.1.2 Select Open Items

After all header data are entered, select the **Process open items** button, and all open vendor items shown in Figure 14.2 are displayed.

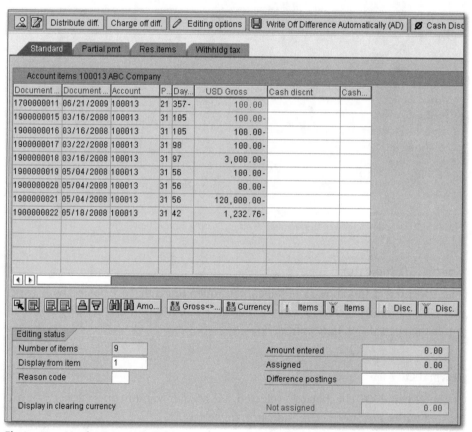

Figure 14.2 Vendor Open Item Selection

In this screen, the items to be cleared need to be selected by double-clicking on a specific line item. The **Assigned** field shows the total amount of the items selected. Any amount difference can be entered into the **Difference postings** field and will be posted to the vendor account either as a debit or credit line, depending on the sign of the difference.

The **Not assigned** field always shows any amount differences and has to be zero before the clearing document can be posted.

Partial Payments/Residual Items

By selecting the **Partial pmt** or **Res. items** tabs, items can be partially cleared. As shown in Figure 14.3, the first line item is cleared partially.

Standard | Partial pmt | Res.items | Withhldg tax

Account items 100013 ABC Company

Document ...	Document ...	Account	P...	Day...	Net amount	Payment amount	RCd
1700000011	06/21/2009	100013	21	357-	100.00	80.00	DF
1900000015	03/16/2008	100013	31	105	100.00-		
1900000016	03/16/2008	100013	31	105	100.00-		
1900000017	03/22/2008	100013	31	98	100.00-		
1900000018	03/16/2008	100013	31	97	3,000.00-		
1900000019	05/04/2008	100013	31	56	100.00-		
1900000020	05/04/2008	100013	31	56	80.00-	80.00-	
1900000021	05/04/2008	100013	31	56	120,000.00-		

Figure 14.3 Partially Clearing Screen

A reason code for partial payments can be entered in the **RCd** field. Different reason codes can be configured in the IMG via navigation path **IMG • Financial Accounting • Accounts Receivable and Accounts Payables • Business Transactions • Outgoing Payments • Manual Outgoing Payments • Overpayment/Underpayment • Define Reason Codes (Manual Outgoing Payments).**

If payment differences need to be charged off to a different account, you can define an account determination for a specific reason code. The account determination can be configured in the IMG via navigation path **IMG • Financial Accounting • Accounts Receivable and Accounts Payables • Business Transactions • Outgoing Payments • Manual Outgoing Payments • Overpayment/Underpayment • Define Accounts for Payment Differences (Manual Outgoing Payments).**

After all items to be cleared are selected, click **Post**, and the system generates a clearing document.

14.1.3 Clearing Line Layout Configuration

The line layout for the open items selected can be configured with Transaction O7Z4K or in the IMG via navigation path **IMG • Financial Accounting • Accounts Receivable and Accounts Payables • Vendor Accounts • Line Items • Open Item Processing • Define Line Layout.** Within Transaction F-44, the line layout can be selected via the menu header **Settings • Line Layout.**

14.1.4 Editing Options

Within the vendor **Open item** selection screen shown in Figure 14.2 previously, an **Editing options** button is available. This option allows you to make additional editing options available for the open items. Figure 14.4 show the available additional editing options.

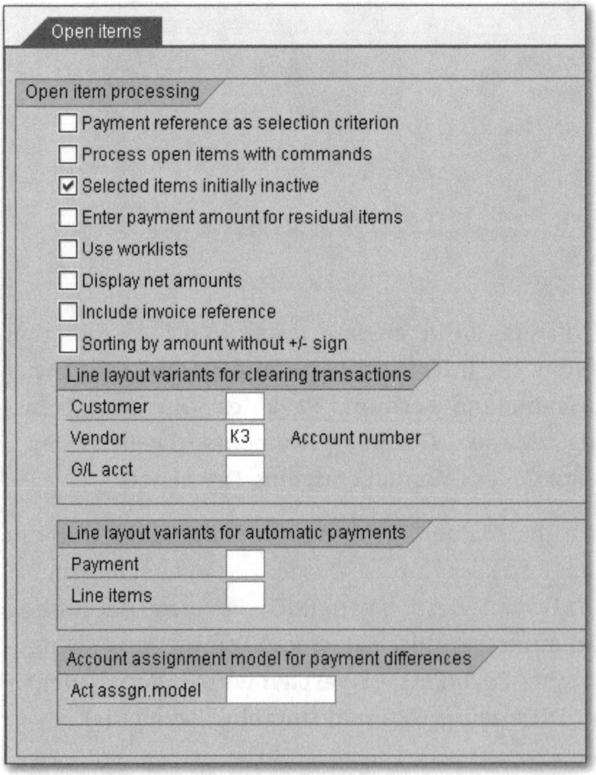

Figure 14.4 Editing Options

Selected Items Initially Inactive

When you set this checkbox, which is recommended, all open items are initially not selected, and you need to select the items to be cleared by double-clicking on the item. If this flag isn't set, all items are selected, and you have to unselect the items that should not be cleared.

Use Worklists

In the initial screen of the vendor clearing transaction, only a single vendor can be entered. However, if you require clearing between different vendors on a frequent basis, you can define a *worklist* for these vendors. The worklist can be defined in configuration under the IMG navigation path **IMG • Financial Accounting • Accounts Receivable and Accounts Payables • Vendor Accounts • Line Items • Open Item Processing • Maintain Worklists.**

After you've defined a worklist for vendors, this worklist has to be entered in the **Account** field instead of the vendor account number in the header screen of the manual clearing transaction (refer to Figure 14.1). All open items for the vendors in the worklist are then selected.

14.2   Transfer with Clearing

Another clearing transaction available within AP is the Post with Clearing transaction. Within AP, this function can be used to transfer open vendor items to another vendor account. For example, some public-sector organizations are required to transfer stale dated checks to the state as unclaimed property. In this case, a check will be issued to the state of the check payment amount.

This process can be handled by canceling the check payment first with Transaction FCH8, and then in a second step, transferring the open vendor item to a state vendor using the Post with Clearing transaction.

14.2.1   Post with Clearing Transaction F-51

To execute Post with Clearing, use Transaction F-51, or execute the transaction via the SAP menu path **SAP Menu • Accounting • Financial Accounting • Accounts Payable • Document Entry • Other • With Clearing**. Figure 14.5 shows the **Post with Clearing: Header Data** screen.

The following example shows a transfer of a vendor invoice from vendor 100013 to another vendor 100000.

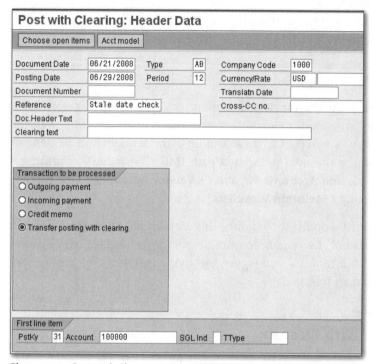

Figure 14.5 Post with Clearing Header Data Screen

First, all document header information, such as document date, posting date, document type, and reference number need to be specified.

Transaction to Be Processed

By selecting the **Transfer posting with clearing** transaction, you specify which type of manual post with clearing transaction is performed. Based on this selection, the system determines the correct posting keys. These posting keys are defined in the IMG via navigation path **IMG • Financial Accounting • Accounts Receivable and Accounts Payables • Business Transactions • Open Item Clearing • Define Posting Key for Clearing Open Items.** Define the posting keys for the clearing Transaction **UMBUCHUNG**, which stands for "transfer posting with clearing."

Posting Key Field

In the **PstKy** field, the posting key of the receiver item needs to be entered. Because an invoice is transferred from one vendor to another vendor, posting key "31" needs to be entered. Posting key "31" is a credit posting to a vendor account. For a list of posting keys, see Table 3.2 in Chapter 3.

Account

Because "31"is entered in the **PstKy** field, a vendor needs to be entered in the **Account** field.

After all header information is entered, press the **Enter** key to access the **Post with Clearing: Add Vendor item** detail screen.

14.2.2 Post with Clearing: Vendor Item

The **Vendor item** screen shown in Figure 14.6 includes all vendor line item details, such as amount, payment term, payment method, assignment, and text information.

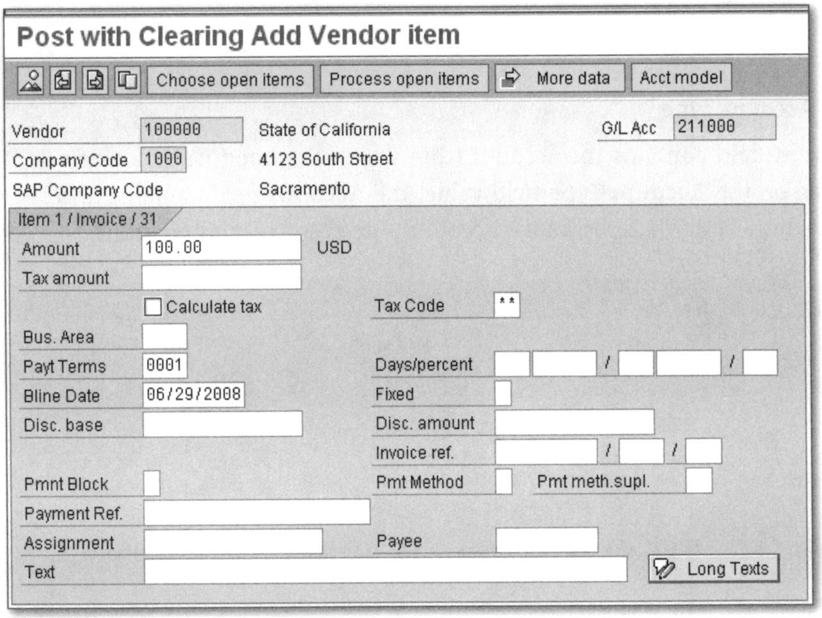

Figure 14.6 Vendor Item Detail Screen

After you enter all vendor detail information, click the **Choose open items** button to select the vendor account of the items to be cleared.

14.2.3 Post with Clearing: Select Open Items

In this screen, the **Account** number of the vendor to be cleared has to be entered. Figure 14.7 shows the selection screen.

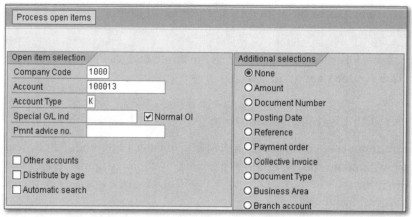

Figure 14.7 Select Vendor Open Items Screen

Account/Account Type

The **Account** field contains the account from which the open items are selected. Depending on the **Account Type** field value, the **Account** field contains different account values. Table 14.1 shows the account type/account combinations.

Account Type	Account
K	Vendor
D	Customer
S	GL account

Table 14.1 Account Type/Account Combinations

Within Transaction F-51, the account type K for vendor accounts is defaulted.

Special G/L Indicator

The **Special G/L ind** *field* allows the selection of open items, which are posted with a special G/L indicator, such as guarantees or retention. In this case, you have to enter the special G/L indicator key.

Normal OI

If the **Normal OI** checkbox is selected, all regular vendor open items that are not posted with a Special G/L indicator are selected.

Other Accounts

If the **Other accounts** checkbox is selected, a pop-up screen appears that allows you to enter additional vendor accounts. This function may be helpful if you have several vendor accounts for the same vendor and need to search for open items in all of these vendor accounts.

Distribute by Age

If the open items should be selected by age or days in arrears, the **Distribute by age** flag needs to be selected. The items to be cleared are selected automatically, and the items with the most days in arrears are selected first. If there are open items with the same number of days in arrears, then credit postings have priority over debit postings. If the amount cannot be distributed completely, then a posting on account of the remaining amount is created.

Automatic Search Indicator

If this flag is set, the system tries to find a combination of open items whose total amount corresponds with the amount entered in the bank data amount field. If the amount is found, then the items are selected. If only a near amount is found, then a window appears in which you can accept or reject the proposal.

Additional Selections

The **Additional selections** section allows you to search the vendor open items by other selection criteria, such as **Posting Date** or **Document Number**. You can configure the criteria, which appear in the **Additional selections** screen, in the

IMG via navigation path **IMG · Financial Accounting · Accounts Receivable and Accounts Payables · Vendor Accounts · Line Items · Open Item Processing · Choose Selection Fields.**

14.2.4 Post with Clearing: Process Open Items

After all information is entered, click the **Process open items** button to select the vendor open items to be transferred as shown in Figure 14.8.

Post with Clearing Process open items

| | | Distribute diff. | Charge off diff. | Editing options | Write Off Difference Automatically (AD) |

| Standard | Partial pmt | Res.items | Withhldg tax |

Account items 100013 ABC Company

Document ...	Document ...	Account	P...	Day...	USD Gross	Cash discnt	Cash...
1900000016	03/16/2008	100013	31	97	100.00-		
1900000017	03/22/2008	100013	31	90	100.00-		
1900000018	03/16/2008	100013	31	89	3,000.00-		
1900000019	05/04/2008	100013	31	48	100.00-		
1900000020	05/04/2008	100013	31	48	80.00-		
1900000021	05/04/2008	100013	31	48	120,000.00-		
1900000022	05/18/2008	100013	31	34	1,232.76-		

Figure 14.8   Process Open Items Screen

The functions and options are the same as previously described in the "Manual Clearing" section. Select the items to be transferred, and click **Post**. The result is that the open item from vendor account 100013 is transferred to vendor 10000.

14.3   Automatic Clearing

In the prior sections, manual clearing functions were described. This section describes automatic clearing through the automatic clearing program. Within AP, automatic clearing is usually used for two specific functions:

▸ Automatic clearing of LIV documents with reversal documents

▸ Automatic clearing of the GR/IR account.

Automatic clearing requires the configuration of clearing characteristics. Technically, the system clears all documents, where the balance of all clearing characteristics within an account is zero. All fields from the database Tables BKPF (document header) and BSEG (Document line item) can be used as characteristics. Up to five different characteristics can be chosen.

In addition to the characteristics, the account type and account numbers have to be specified. The account type specifies whether the accounts are GL accounts, vendors, or customers. The accounts define the account range for which the clearing characteristics are valid.

The clearing characteristics are configured in the IMG via navigation path **IMG • Financial Accounting • Accounts Receivable and Accounts Payables • Business Transactions • Open Item Clearing • Prepare Automatic Clearing.**

14.3.1 LIV Document Clearing with Reversal Documents

During the reversal of LIV documents, such as invoices or credit memos through Transaction MR8M, the system issues the following message: "Document reversed with no. XXXXXXXXX: Please manually clear FI documents." This message means that the cancelled document isn't cleared automatically with the cancellation document in the Financial Accounting component (FI), and the original invoice document has to be cleared manually with the cancellation document using Transaction F-44. Otherwise, the invoice document and the cancellation document remain open items.

To set up automatic clearing, a common clearing characteristic for the LIV document and the reversal document must be specified. Every invoice or credit memo is posted with an invoice number, which is entered into the reference field (BKPF-XBLNR). During the reversal of a document using Transaction MR8M, the invoice number from the original document is copied into the reversal document, which means that both the LIV document and the reversal document have the same invoice number. This common characteristic can therefore be used as clearing characteristic.

Figure 14.9 shows the configuration of the reference number as clearing characteristic for vendor accounts.

ChtA...	AccTy	From acct	To account	Criterion 1	Criterion 2	Crite
	K	1	9999999999	XBLNR		

Figure 14.9 Configuration of XBLNR as Vendor Clearing Characteristic

To complete the configuration, the *account type* (**AccTy**) must be specified. In this case, "K" for vendors needs to be entered. Additionally, the vendor accounts need to be defined. To make this rule available for all vendors, enter "1" in the **From acct** field and "999999999" in the **To account** field.

The execution of the automatic clearing program is described in Section 14.3.3.

14.3.2 GR/IR Account Clearing

The GR/IR account is used as an open item managed clearing account for goods receipts and invoices. The balance of this account usually contains the goods receipt balance that hasn't been invoiced. During a goods receipt entry, the GR/IR account is credited and debited during invoice entry. The clearing of the GR/IR account isn't done automatically during the invoice entry and has to be performed in a subsequent process. Due to the large data volume in this account, manual clearing isn't advisable and clearing should be performed using the automatic clearing program.

The clearing characteristic for the GR/IR account is the purchase order number (EBELN) and purchase order line item (EBELP) because the goods receipt document and the invoice document contain these common characteristics.

During the automatic clearing run, the system sums up all documents with the same purchase order and line item number. If the balance is zero, the documents will be cleared.

Figure 14.10 shows the clearing characteristic configuration for the GR/IR account. In this example, account **211010** is the GR/IR account. Because the GR/IR account is a balance sheet account, account type **S** needs to be specified.

New Entries							
ChtA...	AccTy	From acct	To account	Criterion 1	Criterion 2	Crite
	S	211010		EBELN	EBELP	

Figure 14.10 Configuration Screen for the GR/IR Clearing Account

The execution of the automatic clearing program is described next.

14.3.3 Automatic Account Clearing Execution

Automatic clearing can be executed with Transaction F.13 or via the SAP menu path **SAP Menu • Accounting • Financial Accounting • Accounts Payable • Periodic Processing • Automatic Clearing • Automatic Clearing.** The selection screen of the automatic clearing program is divided into three sections:

▸ **General selections**

▸ **Posting parameters**

▸ **Output control**

General Selections

The **General Selections** section shown in Figure 14.11 enables you to specify which customer, vendor, or GL accounts will be selected for automatic clearing.

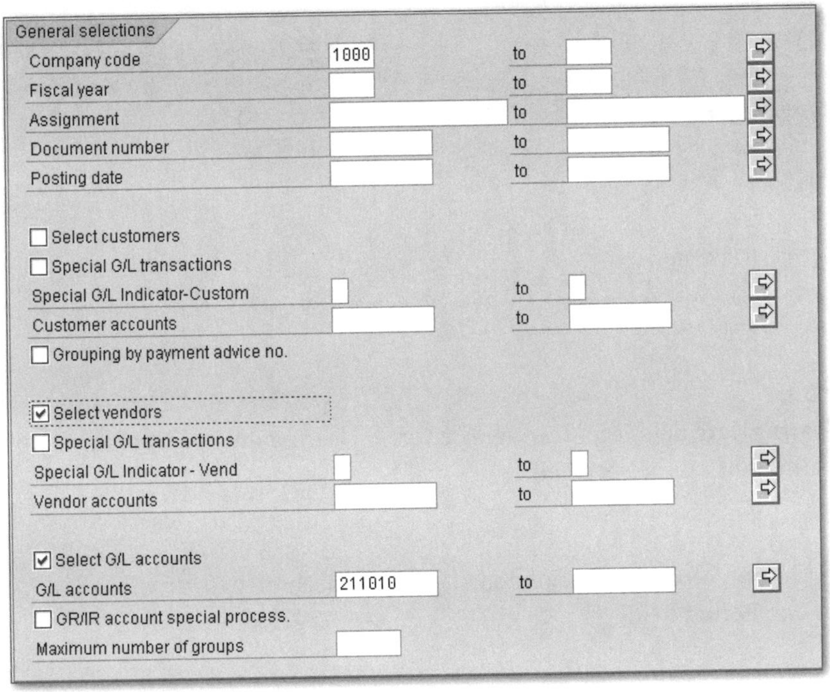

Figure 14.11 General Selections Section

To select an account group, such as vendors or GL accounts, the **Select vendors** and **Select G/L accounts** checkboxes need to be selected. In addition, the single accounts can be specified. In the preceding example, all vendors and G/L account **211010** are selected.

GR/IR Account Special Process

This flag has a special function for the GR/IR account clearing. It only needs to be selected if goods receipt based Invoice Verification is used within your organization. In this case, the clearing reference field XREF3 is used as a special clearing characteristic in addition to the purchase order number and purchase order line item.

Posting Parameters Section

The **Posting parameters** section shown in Figure 14.12 contains the specification for the clearing document postings.

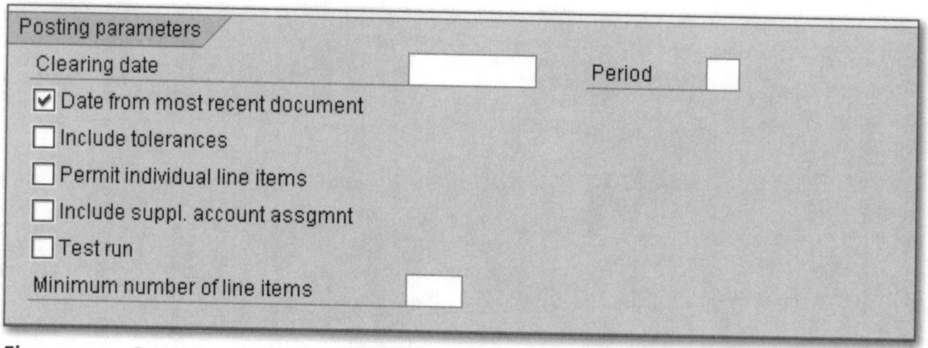

Figure 14.12 Posting Parameters Section

Clearing Date

In the **Clearing date** field, the clearing date for all clearing document of this automatic clearing run can be specified.

Period

If clearing in one of the special periods (13-16) is necessary, this period can be defined in the **Period** field.

Date from Most Recent Document

Instead of specifying a clearing date, the **Date from most recent document** flag can be selected. In this case, the posting date of the most recent document is used as the clearing date. You should choose this option over the clearing date specification.

Include Tolerances

By setting the **Include tolerances** flag, tolerances defined in the system will be taken into account during clearing.

Permit Individual Line Items

This flag allows a single line for clearing, if clearing with tolerances is used.

Include Suppl. Account Assigmnt

Within the GL account master data, the flag Supplement account assignment can be set. This flag has the effect that automatically created line items during manual clearing need to be supplemented manually with additional information, such as text information. This isn't possible during the automatic clearing program. To allow automatic clearing for accounts with the Supplement account assignment flag in the GL account master data, don't set the **Include suppl. account assigmnt** flag here.

Test Run

The automatic clearing program is executed in test mode if the **Test run** flag is set.

Output Control Section

In the **Output control** section shown in Figure 14.13, the output options of the clearing results are specified.

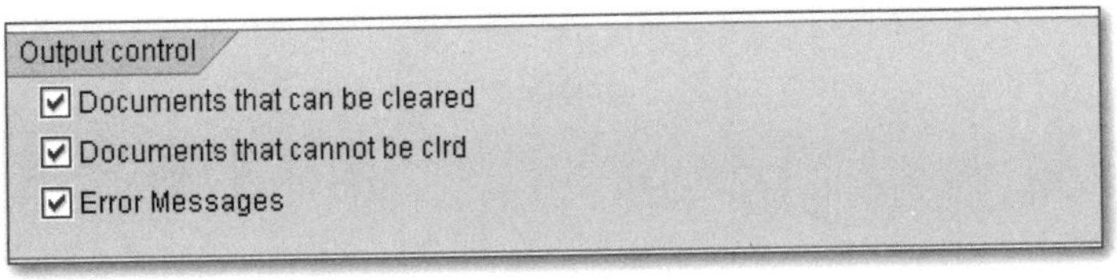

Figure 14.13 Output Control Section

After all information is entered, click the **Execute** button to execute the automatic clearing.

Automatic Clearing
Due to the usual high data volume in the GR/IR account, it's recommended to schedule a job for the clearing of the GR/IR account on a daily basis.

14.4 Summary

In this chapter, we covered the different vendor clearing transactions within AP. Manual clearing is often used to assign invoice and credit memos. The Transfer with Clearing transaction allows to transfer open vendor items to other vendors or GL accounts. The most commonly used clearing function is the automatic clearing of the GR/IR account.

In the next Chapter periodic processes within AP are described.

On a periodic basis, a number of processes have to be executed depending on your organization's business requirements. These processes include monthly processes such as interest calculation and foreign currency evaluation, or yearly processes such as balance carry forward.

15   Periodic Processing

In every organization, periodic processes have to be executed due to business requirements, accounting standard regulations, or technical reasons in SAP software. These processes need to be executed on a monthly or yearly basis. In this chapter, the following periodic processes are covered:

▶ Interest calculation

▶ Foreign currency revaluation

▶ Balance carry forward

Other periodic processes, such as automatic clearing or recurring entries, were already covered in previous chapters of this book.

15.1   Interest Calculation

Within Accounts Payable (AP), two different interest calculation processes are possible:

▶ The balance calculation method

▶ The interest on arrears method

The *balance calculation method* can be found under the SAP menu path **SAP Menu • Accounting • Financial Accounting • Accounts Payable • Periodic Processing • Interest Calculation • Balance** or via Transaction F.44. The system calculates the interest based on the account balance of a vendor rather than taking the single transactions into account.

The most commonly used interest calculation method within AP is the calculation of interest on arrears. Using this method, the interest can be calculated by vendor on open items or cleared items. Therefore, only the calculation of interest arrears is described in detail in this chapter.

15.1.1 Calculation of Interest on Arrears

Program RFKUZI00 is used to calculate interest on arrears for vendors. This program can be found in the SAP menu path **SAP Menu • Accounting • Financial Accounting • Accounts Payable • Periodic Processing • Interest Calculation • Calculate Interest on Arrears.** Different transactions codes are available based on the way the calculation program is executed. Table 15.1 lists the different transaction codes and their differences. All transaction codes, however, use program RFKUZI00 but with different predefined interest calculation types.

Transaction Code	Interest Calculation Type
F.4A	1: Calculation of interest on cleared items with interest posting. The interest is calculated based on the due date for net payment.
F.4B	2: Calculation and posting of interest on open and cleared items based on the last interest run date, which is stored in the vendor master data.
F.4C	3: Calculation of interest on open and/or cleared items without interest posting. The interest is calculated based on the due date for net payment.
F.47	Free selection.

Table 15.1 Transaction Codes for Interest on Arrears Calculation

15.1.2 Interest Calculation Process

The interest calculation follows this process:

1. The program identifies the items on which interest is to be calculated based on the rules defined in the interest indicator or any additional specifications entered when executing the program. The entered rules determine the items and transaction for which interest is calculated, such as the following:

   ▶ Cleared or open items only

   ▶ All clearing transactions or only cleared transaction with a payment

2. The program determines the days for which interest is to be calculated, taking into account the calendar type, which is specified within the interest indicator.

   ▸ There are basically two factors involved in interest calculation: the lower limit and upper limit of the calculation period specified for the interest calculation run, and the time period between the net due date and the date of the payment document. The program selects those items in which the period between the net due date and clearing date falls within the lower limit and upper limit of the calculation period. If the lower limit of the calculation period is suppressed, the program uses the value from the **Last key date** field in the vendor master data as the lower limit.

   ▸ It can be specified whether interest should be calculated as of the date of the last interest calculation. Open items, which are still open as of the date of the last interest run, are included. Cleared items are only included if the clearing date is later than the date of the last interest calculation.

   ▸ Tolerance days can be specified for the interest indicator. These days are added to the due date for net payment but are only relevant for selecting the items to be included in the interest calculation run. Interest is always calculated as of the due date for net payment without taking any tolerance days into account.

   ▸ Transfer days for cleared items can also be defined. This is a way of making allowance for when payments take longer than usual to transfer or when the relevant accounts are not cleared promptly. Transfer days are subtracted from the date of the payment document or from the clearing date.

3. After determining the items on which interest is to be calculated, the program calculates the interest amount in local currency. Interest rate changes within the calculation period are taken into account as well as minimum amounts specified for the interest indicator. The system compares the calculated interest amount with the minimum amount.

4. Correspondence forms are created if the calculated interest exceeds the minimum amount. Within the interest indicator, information for the correspondence is specified.

15.1.3 Interest Calculation Configuration

Interest calculation is configured in multiple steps. The configuration can be quite elaborate depending on your organization's requirement, therefore, only the main configuration steps are listed in this section. All of the configuration steps can be found in **IMG • Financial Accounting • Accounts Receivable and Payable • Business Transactions • Interest Calculation.**

The **Interest indicator** contains all interest configuration specifications. The following steps are the required configurations for the Interest indicator:

▶ **Define interest calculation types/indicators**
In the first step, the interest calculation indicator is defined, which specifies the calculation method: interest on arrears or balance calculation.

▶ **Prepare interest on arrears calculation**
In this step, general specifications for the interest indicator are defined, such as item selection, interest determination, amount limits, and output control.

▶ **Interest calculation**
The interest calculation configuration contains the definition of the reference interest rate, assignment of the rate to the interest indicator, and maintenance of the interest rates.

▶ **Interest posting**
In the interest posting configuration, the document type as well as GL accounts for interest postings are specified.

▶ **Print**
If a correspondence form needs to be printed, a form can be assigned to the interest indicator in this step.

15.1.4 Vendor Master Data Fields for Interest Calculation

As described in the previous section, the interest indicator contains the entire configuration relevant for the interest calculation with regards to selection, calculation, posting, and printing. This **Interest indic.** is then assigned to a vendor master in the **Account Information** tab as shown in Figure 15.1.

The interest calculation of all items for this vendor is based on the configuration of the interest indicator.

Last Key Date

The **Last key date** field specifies when the interest calculation program was executed the last time for this vendor. This field is only updated, if the **Maintain master records** flag is set during the execution of the interest calculation program.

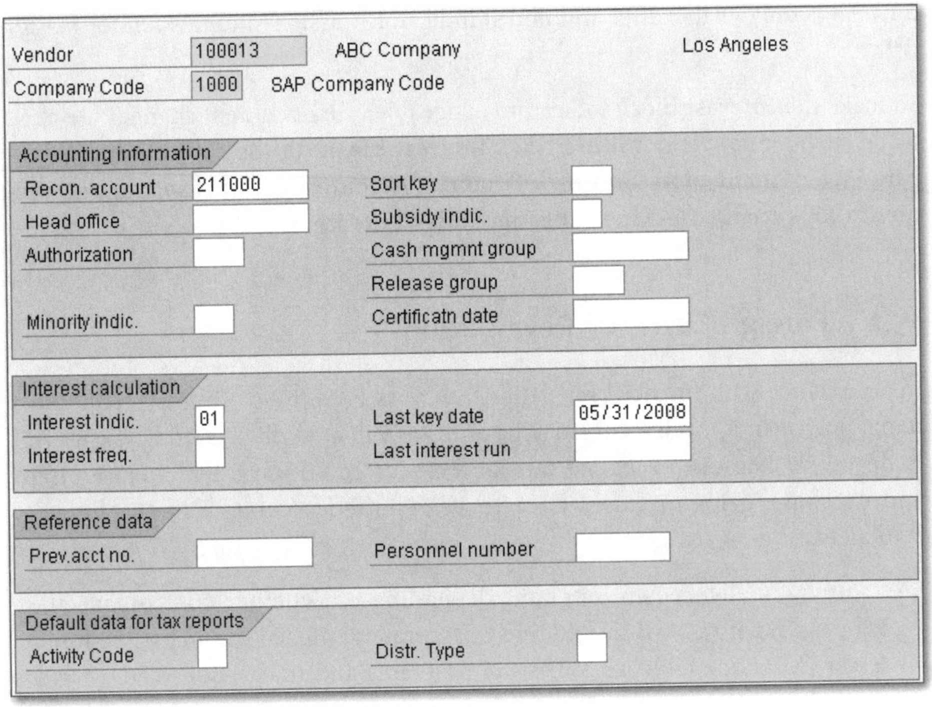

| Vendor | 100013 | ABC Company | Los Angeles |

Vendor 100013 ABC Company Los Angeles
Company Code 1000 SAP Company Code

Accounting information

Recon. account	211000	Sort key	
Head office		Subsidy indic.	
Authorization		Cash mgmnt group	
		Release group	
Minority indic.		Certificatn date	

Interest calculation

| Interest indic. | 01 | Last key date | 05/31/2008 |
| Interest freq. | | Last interest run | |

Reference data

| Prev. acct no. | | Personnel number | |

Default data for tax reports

| Activity Code | | Distr. Type | |

Figure 15.1 Interest Indicator in Vendor Master Screen

Interest Frequency

The **Interest freq.** field is only relevant for balance interest calculation and specifies the frequency of the interest calculation by months.

Last Interest Run

The **Last interest run** date field contains the date of the last balance interest calculation date. This field isn't relevant for calculating interest on arrears.

15.1.5 Exclude Line Items from the Interest Calculation

Open or cleared items can be excluded from the interest calculation using the **Interest block** indicator in the line item of a document. This indicator can be found under **Additional data** in the vendor line item. The **Interest block** indicator field is only visible after an interest indicator is assigned to the vendor master data.

To make the **Interest block** indicator changeable, the document change rule need to be changed for field **BSEG-ZINKZ (Interest block)** in the IMG via navigation path **IMG • Financial Accounting • Financial Accounting Global Settings • Document • Line Item • Document Change Rules/Line items.**

15.2   Foreign Currency Revaluation

In accordance with financial regulations, such as FASB 52 or German HGB, open items posted in a foreign currency have to be valuated on a periodic basis. This is necessary because exchange rate differences could have a monetary effect, and exchange gains or losses have to be reported accurately in the financial statements.

SAP software delivers two programs depending on whether your organization uses the classic or new GL accounting to accurately calculate and post the foreign currency valuation. Table 15.2 lists the programs and transactions codes for the classic and new GL:

General Ledger Accounting	Transaction Code	Program Name
Classic GL	F04N	SAPF100
New GL	FAGL_FC_VAL	FAGL_FC_VALUATION

Table 15.2   Foreign Currency Valuation Programs

Independent of which program your organization uses, the foreign currency revaluation includes the following activities:

▶ **Item selection**
Depending on the selection criteria specified, the program reads the items for the customers, vendors, and GL accounts that are open on the key date and adds the items together to create totals by account or group and currency.

▶ **Groupings**
The documents or balances are grouped together according to currency and account. The exchange rate type for the valuation is taken from the balance obtained for each grouping.

▶ **Valuation**

The items to be translated on the key date are summarized for each invoice reference or account/group and translated on the key date. During balance valuation, the balance is translated for each currency and account/group, and the key date exchange rate is applied.

▶ **Posting**

The program posts the valuation differences in summarized form. During valuation of the open items, the valuation posting and the reversal posting from the prior period are performed automatically.

▶ **Account determination**

The postings for accounts managed on an open item basis are made to an adjustment account and to a P&L account in the sub-ledger and GL. Accounts are determination using the valuation area.

▶ **Output**

The program generates three lists:

  ▶ List of valuated line items or GL account balances

  ▶ List of postings or posting proposals

  ▶ List of messages

These processing activities are independent of whether your organization uses the classic or new GL accounting. However, the configuration steps are different as described in the next section.

15.2.1 Configuration Steps from the Classic GL

For Classic GL accounting, the configuration activities for foreign currency revaluation can be found in the IMG via navigation path **IMG • Financial Accounting • General Ledger Accounting • Business Transactions • Closing • Valuate • Foreign Currency Valuation.**

The configuration is done with two IMG activities:

▶ Define valuation method

▶ Prepare automatic postings for foreign currency valuation

Define Valuation Method

In this activity, the *valuation method* for open items is defined. The valuation method specifies the valuation procedure, postings, and exchange rate determination. Figure 15.2 shows the valuation method configuration screen.

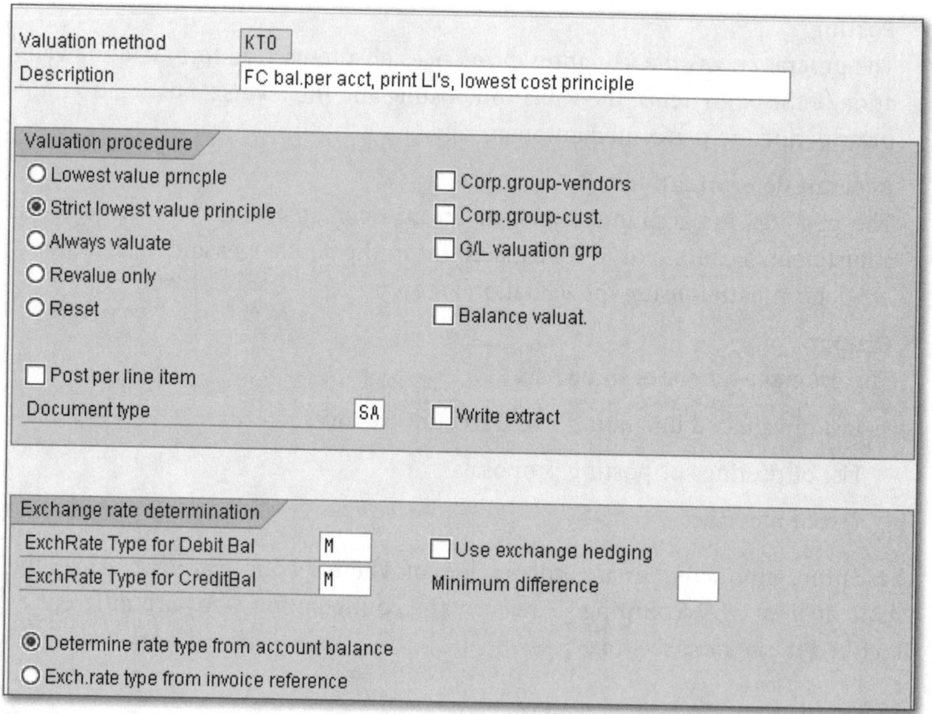

Valuation method	KTO
Description	FC bal.per acct, print LI's, lowest cost principle

Valuation procedure

- ○ Lowest value prncple
- ● Strict lowest value principle
- ○ Always valuate
- ○ Revalue only
- ○ Reset

- ☐ Corp.group-vendors
- ☐ Corp.group-cust.
- ☐ G/L valuation grp

- ☐ Balance valuat.

- ☐ Post per line item
- Document type — SA
- ☐ Write extract

Exchange rate determination

- ExchRate Type for Debit Bal — M
- ExchRate Type for CreditBal — M
- ☐ Use exchange hedging
- Minimum difference

- ● Determine rate type from account balance
- ○ Exch.rate type from invoice reference

Figure 15.2 Valuation Method Configuration

After the configuration of the valuation method, the account assignment needs to be configured.

Prepare Automatic Postings for Foreign Currency Valuation

In this activity, the account determination for automatic posting of account differences needs to be defined.

When *valuating open items*, the system posts to a balance sheet adjustment account and to an account for exchange rate differences that occur during the valuation. Exchange rate differences can be either a gain or a loss.

The *valuation of foreign currency balances* requires a special key that is assigned to the gain and loss accounts for posting any exchange rate differences that occur during valuation. This key is freely definable and is entered in the master records of the accounts to be valuated. To post the differences that are determined from a group of GL accounts to the same gain or loss accounts, enter the same key for all of these GL accounts.

15.2.2 Configuration Steps from the New GL

For New GL accounting, the configuration activities for foreign currency revaluation can be found in the IMG via navigation path **IMG • Financial Accounting (New) • General Ledger Accounting (New) • Periodic Processing • Valuate • Foreign Currency Valuation.** The configuration is done via the following IMG activities:

▶ Define valuation method

▶ Define valuation areas

▶ Prepare automatic postings for foreign currency valuation

The configuration steps are very similar to the configuration steps in Classic GL accounting and are therefore not described any further in detail.

15.3 Balance Carry Forward

Balance carry forward for vendor open items is a purely technical periodic process that must be executed once a year on the *first day* of the new fiscal year. This process calculates the ending balance of every single vendor and moves the ending balance amount into period 0 of the next fiscal year. Period 0 represents the carry-forward balance within SAP software. Without the carry forward, open items from the previous year can't be paid in the new fiscal year. In addition, if the balance carry-forward program is run before the first day of the new fiscal year, postings into the prior fiscal year are not carry forwarded automatically.

Balance carry forward can be found under **SAP Menu • Accounting • Financial Accounting • Accounts Payable • Periodic Processing • Closing • Carry Forward** or via Transaction F.07. Figure15.3 shows the selection screen of the balance carry-forward program. This program can be executed as often as desired.

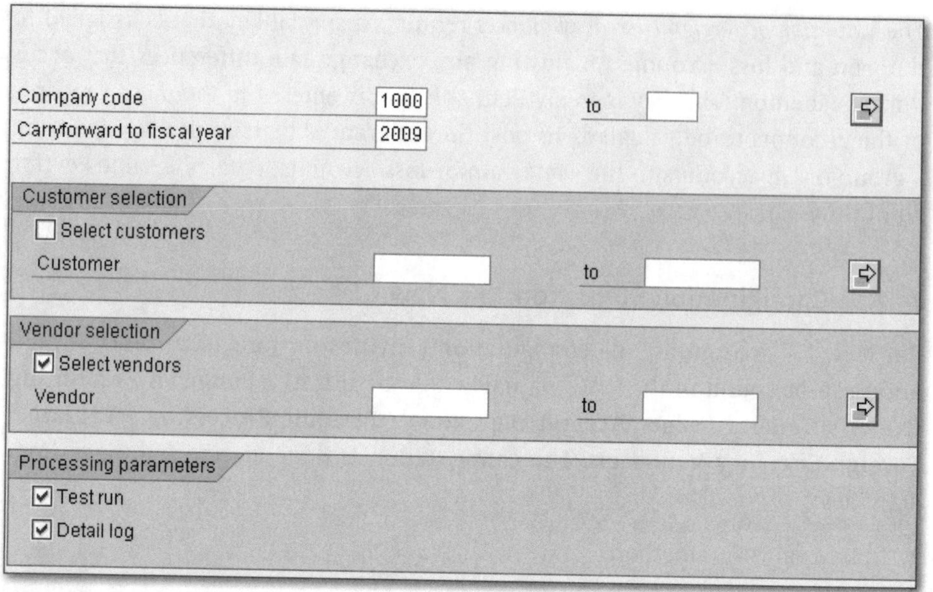

Figure 15.3 Vendor Balance Carry-Forward Program

To carry forward the vendor balances, just select the **Company code**, **Carryforward to fiscal year**, and the **Vendors** to be selected. The carry forward can be executed in a test mode by selecting the **Test run** flag.

This program can be executed multiple times.

15.4 Summary

In this chapter, we covered different transactions for period processing such as interest calculation, foreign currency evaluation, and balance carry forward.

In the next chapter, the SAP authorization concept for Accounts Payable is discussed in detail.

Authorizations define who is allowed to do what within SAP applications. There are user groups that are allowed to maintain the vendor master but are not allowed to enter invoices. Other users have only display authorizations. This chapter describes the authorization concept for Accounts Payable (AP) within SAP software applications.

16 Authorization Concept

The authorization design within every implementation is a hot topic because it takes several factors into account:

- Users need to have access to all necessary functions to perform their daily duties.
- The authorization concept has to take segregation of duty aspects into account.
- Unauthorized users should not have access to sensitive information.

16.1 SAP Authorization Concept

The SAP authorization concept protects transactions, programs, and services in SAP systems from unauthorized access. On the basis of the authorization concept, the administrator assigns authorizations to the users that determine which actions a user can execute in the SAP system after the user has logged on to the system.

To access business objects or execute SAP software transactions, a user requires corresponding authorizations because business objects or transactions are protected by *authorization objects*. The authorizations represent instances of generic authorization objects and are defined depending on the activities and responsibilities of the employee. The authorizations are combined in an authorization profile that is associated with a *user role*. The user administrators then assign the corresponding roles using the user master record so that the user can use the appropriate transactions for his tasks.

16.1.1   User Roles

Within the SAP authorization concept, roles are assigned to single users. The following different roles are available:

- Single roles
- Derived roles
- Composite roles

Single Roles

In SAP software, two different types of single roles can be used:

- **Single roles cover generic functionality**
  These roles are independent from any organizational or application-specific restriction, for example, roles for general information access and service use. These are the most common used roles in SAP, such as SAP_AP_VENDOR_MASTER_DATA.

- **Single roles used to create derived roles (Master Role)**
  These roles serve primarily as a template for the derivation rather than for production use. They include the transactions, reports, and the menu structure. But in contrast to the derived roles, there are no organizational or application-specific restrictions.

Derived Roles

Derived roles are created from single roles. A derived role inherits the selected application functions, such as transactions, reports, or websites, and the menu structure from the master role. But in contrast to the master roles, the derived roles are implemented with restrictions regarding organizational levels such as company code, cost center, plant, or application-specific control features.

Composite Roles

Composite roles are the technical equivalence of combining multiple single roles into one composite role, that is, creating one General Display role, which consists of the display roles of the different modules.

16.1.2   Authorization Objects

An *authorization object* is the lowest level in the authorization concept in SAP software. Multiple authorization objects are combined into single roles. An authorization object allows complex tests of an authorization for multiple conditions. For an authorization check to be successful, all field values of the authorization object must be appropriately maintained in the user master. The allowed authorization values for an authorization object can be displayed within an authorization object:

Authorization Object example

For example, authorization object F_LFA1_BUK (Vendor Maintenance Authorization for Company code) is shown next. This authorization object has two authorization fields,

► Activity

► Company code

The Authorization fields *Activity* controls, which functions a user is allowed to perform. The allowed activities are:

► Activity

  ► **01:** Create

  ► **02:** Change

  ► **03:** Display

  ► **05:** Lock

  ► **06:** Delete

  ► **08:** Display change documents

  ► **C8:** Conform changes

The Authorization field *Company code* controls for which company code the user is allowed to perform the activities.

If a user needs authorization to create a vendor in Company code 1000, authorization object F_LFA1_BUK needs to be maintained with the authorization fields, Activity – value "01", and Company code – value "1000". This authorization object is then assigned to a role, which is then assigned to the user.

16.2 SAP Predefined User Roles

SAP software delivers single roles for every application, which can be used as a starting point to build user-defined roles for every organization. Table 16.1 lists the delivered roles for AP and Logistic Invoice Verification (LIV).

User Role	Description
SAP_FI_AP_VENDOR_MASTER_DATA	Ability to create, change, display, and delete of vendor master data
SAP_FI_AP_DISPLAY_MASTER_DATA	Ability to display vendor and bank master data
SAP_FI_AP_INVOICE_PROCESSING	Ability to post invoices in AP
SAP_FI_AP_DISPLAY_BALANCES	Ability to display vendor balances and line items
SAP_FI_AP_DISPLAY_DOCUMENTS	Ability to display vendor documents
SAP_FI_AP_CHANGE_LINE_ITEMS	Ability to change vendor line items
SAP_FI_AP_CHANGE-REVERSE_INV	Ability to change and reverse vendor documents
SAP_FI_AP_PARK_DOCUMENT	Ability to park vendor documents
SAP_FI_AP_POST_PARKED_DOCUM	Ability to post and reject parked documents
SAP_FI_AP_CHANGE_PARKED_DOCUM	Ability to change parked documents
SAP_FI_AP_DISPLAY_PARKED_DOCUM	Ability to display parked documents
SAP_FI_AP_RECURRING_DOCUMENTS	Ability to create, change, display, and execute recurring documents
SAP_FI_AP_SAMPLE_DOCUMENTS	Ability to create, change, and display sample documents
SAP_FI_AP_CLEAR_OPEN_ITEMS	Ability to clear open items
SAP_FI_AP_PAYMENT_PROPOSAL	Ability to create and edit the payment proposal
SAP_FI_AP_PAYMENT_PARAMETERS	Ability to display the payment parameters of a payment run
SAP_FI_AP_PAYMENT_RUN	Ability to execute the payment run without payment medium

Table 16.1 Standard Delivered Sample Roles

User Role	Description
SAP_FI_AP_MANUAL_PAYMENT	Ability to execute manual payments
SAP_FI_AP_PAYMENT_CHECKS	Ability to complete the payment run for check transactions
SAP_FI_AP_PAYMENT_BILL_OF_EXCH	Ability to complete the payment run for bills of exchange transactions
SAP_FI_AP_CHECK_MAINTENANCE	Ability to edit check transactions
SAP_FI_AP_DISPLAY_CHECKS	Ability to display check information
SAP_FI_AP_INTEREST_CALCULATION	Ability to calculate interest on vendor balances and line items
SAP_FI_AP_PERIOD_END_ACTIVITY	Ability to perform closing processes within AP
SAP_FI_AP_VALUATION	Ability to perform the foreign currency valuation process
SAP_FI_AP_BALANCE_CARRYFORWARD	Ability to perform the vendor carry-forward process
SAP_FI_AP_CORRESPONDENCE	Ability to perform vendor correspondences
SAP_FI_AP_KEY_REPORTS	Ability to run AP key reports
SAP_FI_AP_INTERNET_FUNCTIONS	Ability to perform AP Internet functions
SAP_FI_AP_WITHHOLDING_TAX	Ability to run vendor withholding tax reports
SAP_MM_IV_CLERK_AUTO	Ability to run automatic settlement in LIV
SAP_MM_IV_CLERK_BATCH1	Ability to enter invoices for verification in the background
SAP_MM_IV_CLERK_BATCH2	Ability to manually process invoices verified in the background
SAP_MM_IV_CLERK_GRIR_MAINTAIN	Ability to maintain the GR/IR account
SAP_MM_IV_CLERK_ONLINE	Ability to enter invoices online
SAP_MM_IV_CLERK_PARK	Ability to park invoices
SAP_MM_IV_CLERK_RELEASE	Ability to release parked invoices

Table 16.1 Standard Delivered Sample Roles (Cont.)

16.3   Authorization Objects in Accounts Payable

SAP software delivers a large variety of authorization objects within AP that control access to vendor master data, financial documents, payments, and postings in LIV. This section lists the available authorization objects and their purposes.

16.3.1   Vendor Master Maintenance

Table 16.2 lists the authorization objects for vendor master data.

Authorization Object	Description	Purpose
F_LFA1_GRP	Vendor: Account group authorization	Ability to create, change, display, and delete of vendor master data by vendor account group
F_LFA1_GEN	Vendor: Central data	Ability to create, change, display, and delete of central vendor master data, such as address
F_LFA1_BUK	Vendor: Authorization for company codes	Ability to create, change, display, and delete of company code dependent vendor master data
F_LFA1_BEK	Vendor: Account authorization	Ability to create, change, display, and delete vendor master data based on authorization groups, which are maintained in the vendor master data
F_LFA1_APP	Vendor: Application authorization	Ability to create, change, display, and delete vendor master data based on the application, such as finance or procurement
F_LFA1_AEN	Vendor: Change authorization of certain fields	Ability to change certain vendor master data fields, based on field groups (see next section)
M_LFM1_EKO	Purchasing organization in vendor master record	Ability to create, change, display, and delete vendor master data by purchasing organization

Table 16.2 Authorization Objects for Vendor Master Data

Vendor: Change Authorization of Certain Fields

If your organization requires that certain vendor master data fields can only be changed by selected users, these fields can be grouped into field groups, and these field groups are assigned to the users using authorization object F_LFA1_AEN.

The field groups are configured in the IMG via navigation path **IMG • Financial Accounting • Accounts Receivable and Payable • Vendor Accounts • Master Data • Preparations for Changing Vendor Master Data • Define Field Groups for Vendor Master Records.**

For example, your organization requires only a selected group of users to be able to change the **Tax number 1** and **Tax number 2** fields. In the first step, a **Field group** "1" for Tax number is created as shown in Figure 16.1.

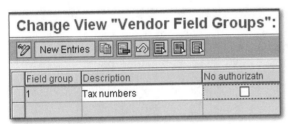

Figure 16.1 Field Group Creation

In the second step, the fields, which require change authorization check, are assigned to the field group in the IMG via navigation path **IMG • Financial Accounting • Accounts Receivable and Payable • Vendor Accounts • Master Data • Preparations for Changing Vendor Master Data • Group Fields for Vendor Master Records.**

Figure 16.2 shows fields **Tax number 1** and **Tax number 2** assigned to **Field group** "1".

Change View "Fields Of The Vendor Field Groups":

Field grp	Fld name	Field Label
1	LFA1-STCD1	Tax Number 1
1	LFA1-STCD2	Tax Number 2

Figure 16.2 Field Group Assignment Screen

The last step is the assignment of authorization object F_LFA1_AEN with the **Field group** value "1" to a user role and users.

16.3.2 Accounting Documents

Table 16.3 lists the authorization objects for accounting documents, such as invoices, credit memos, or payment documents. More authorization objects are needed to post accounting documents, such as authorizations for company code or GL accounts. These authorization objects are generic for all accounting documents and are not covered in this section.

Authorization Object	Description	Purpose
F_BKPF_BEK	Accounting document: account authorizations for vendors	Ability to create, change, or display accounting documents for vendors by authorization group
F_BKPF_KOA	Accounting document: account types	Ability to create, change, or display accounting documents by account type, such as K for vendors
F_KMT_MGMT	Maintenance and use of account assignment models	Ability to change, display, delete, or use account assignment models

Table 16.3 Authorization Objects for Financial Documents

Accounting Document: Account Authorizations for Vendors

If your organization contains sensitive vendor information, which requires that the vendor master data information and all accounting documents, such as invoices or payments, need to be protected, authorization object F_BKPF_BEK can be used for authorization control. Typical examples are invoices and payments from a payroll system, such as garnishments or health care payments.

Within the vendor master data, vendors can be assigned to **Authorization groups** in the **Central** tab as well as in the **Accounting Information** tab, depending on whether the authorization check should be performed on a vendor level or vendor/company code level. After the authorization groups are maintained in the vendor master data, the system checks the authorization object F_BKPF_BEK, anytime documents are created, changed, or displayed for this vendor. If the authorization group value in the vendor master data does not correspond to the authorization group value assigned to a user via authorization object F_BKPF_BEK, access is denied. This allows the protection of sensitive vendor master data information.

16.3.3 Logistic Invoice Verification

Table 16.4 lists the authorization objects for vendor master data.

Authorization object	Description	Purpose
M_RECH_WRK	Invoices: Plant	Ability to create, change, display, and park invoices by plant
M_RECH_AKZ	Invoices: Accept Invoice Verification differences	Ability to accept invoice differences during Invoice Verification
M_RECH_EKG	Invoice release: Purchasing group	Ability to release blocked invoices by purchasing group
M_RECH_SPG	Invoices: Blocking reason	Ability to list and release blocked invoices by blocking reason
M_RECH_BUK	Invoices: Company code	Ability to release blocked invoices by company code

Table 16.4 Authorization Objects in LIV

16.3.4 Payments

Table 16.5 lists the authorization objects for vendor master data.

Authorization Object	Description	Purpose
F_REGU_BUK	Automatic payment: Activity authorization by company code	Ability to perform specific activities in the automatic payment run by company code
F_REGU_KOA	Automatic payment: Activity authorization by account type	Ability to perform specific activities in the automatic payment run by account type

Table 16.5 Authorization Objects for Payments

Activities in the Automatic Payment Run F110

The different activities in the automatic payment creation Transaction F110 are protected via authorization objects F_REGU_BUK and F_REGU_KOA. The activity values are the same for both authorization objects. Figure 16.3 shows the available activity values.

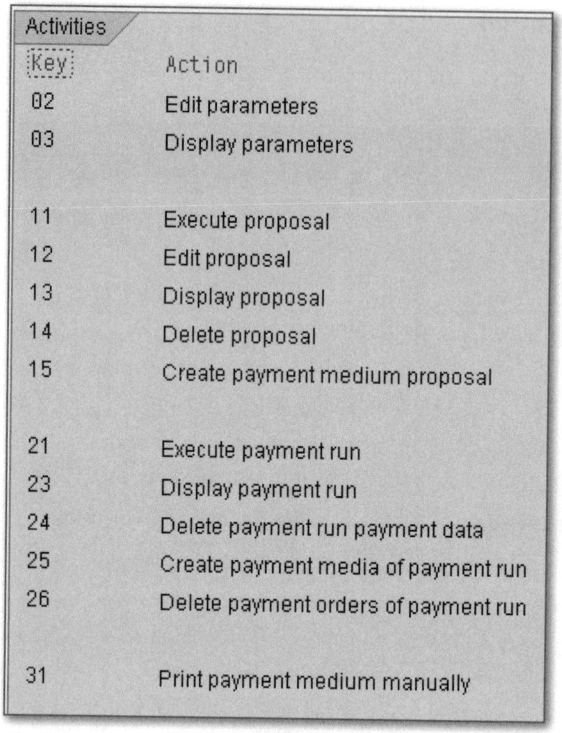

Activities

Key	Action
02	Edit parameters
03	Display parameters
11	Execute proposal
12	Edit proposal
13	Display proposal
14	Delete proposal
15	Create payment medium proposal
21	Execute payment run
23	Display payment run
24	Delete payment run payment data
25	Create payment media of payment run
26	Delete payment orders of payment run
31	Print payment medium manually

Figure 16.3 Activities in Transaction F110

16.3.5 Check Management

Table 16.6 lists the authorization objects for check management.

Authorization Object	Description	Purpose
F_PAYR_BUK	Check management: Activity by company code	Ability to change, display, or reverse checks by company code

Table 16.6 Authorization Objects for Check Management

16.4 Line Layout Protection

The authorization object S_ALV_LAYO and F_IT_ALV control the authorization for the maintenance of layouts in SAP software. Two different line item layout types are available:

▶ **Global layouts**

Global layouts start with "/" and are visible for every user. These layouts are set up as default layouts and must not be changed by an end user.

▶ **User-defined layouts**

User-defined layouts start with an alphanumeric character and are only visible to the user who created this layout. Every user should be able to maintain (create, change, delete) user-defined layouts

For example, Figure 16.4 shows layout "/AP_STND" created in Transaction FBL1N as a global layout.

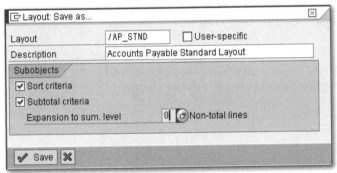

Figure 16.4 Layout Change Screen Without Global Layout Protection

From an authorization perspective, users should not be allowed to change global layouts. To restrict end users from maintaining global layouts and at the same time allow them to create, change, display, and delete only user-defined layouts, the following authorization concepts needs to be applied:

▶ **Remove authorization object** S_ALV_LAYO **from user roles**

Authorization S_ALV_LAYO and activity 23 restricts the maintenance of global layouts. If this authorization object is removed from user authorizations, the **User-specific** flag in the layout save screen is set and grayed out. Only super users should have the capability to change global layouts and have authorization object S_ALV_LAYO assigned.

▶ **Assign authorization object** F_IT_ALV **to all users with all values**

The authorization object F_IT_ALV has a field, the activity ACTVT, which can contain four permitted values: 01, 02, 03, and 70. Each of the activities 01, 02, and 70 controls the availability of particular functions of the ALV line item list:

▶ **01: Settings** • **Display Variant** • **Save...**

▶ **02: Settings** • **Display Variant** • **Current...** and **Settings** • **Display variant** • **Current Header Rows**

▶ **70: Settings** • **Display Variant** • **Administration...**

Activity 03 corresponds to the minimum authorization, which is the most restricted one: The user can only select layouts that have been configured already. In particular, all of the other functions named previously are inactive with activity 03.

After the preceding authorization concept is applied for the authorization objects S_ALV_LAYO and F_IT_ALV, the global layout will be protected. Figure 16.5 shows the change screen for global layout "/AP_STND" after this authorization concept was applied.

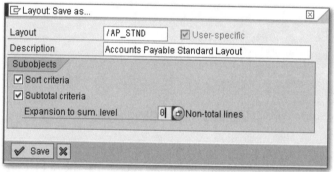

Figure 16.5 Layout Change Screen with Global Layout Protection

As shown, the **User-specific** flag is set and grayed out, which means that the user will only be able to save user-specific layouts, not global layouts.

16.5 Summary

In this chapter the AP authorization concept was described including available authorization objects and predefined roles. Explanations were provided for how to restrict change authorization for single vendor data fields, how to protect sensitive vendor data, and how to protect global ALV layouts.

In the next chapter, the AP information system is described.

SAP software delivers a variety of standard reports for Accounts Payable (AP) transactions, such as master data reports, transaction reports, and balance reports. This chapter covers the information system and enhancements that are available.

17   Accounts Payable Reporting

A large variety of standard reports within AP are delivered within the SAP system. In addition, country-specific reports are available for countries such as Germany, France, and Russia. All available reports are grouped into the following categories:

- Vendor balances
- Vendor items
- Master data
- Payment transactions

Besides the reports available in the information system, the most commonly used transaction is the *vendor line item report* via Transaction FBL1N. The line item report can be tailored with additional fields by using *special fields* or *user-defined fields*.

17.1   Information System

The information system reports can be accessed via the SAP menu path **SAP Menu • Information System • Accounting • Financial Accounting • Reports for Accounts Payable Accounting.** Figure 17.1 shows the available report transactions.

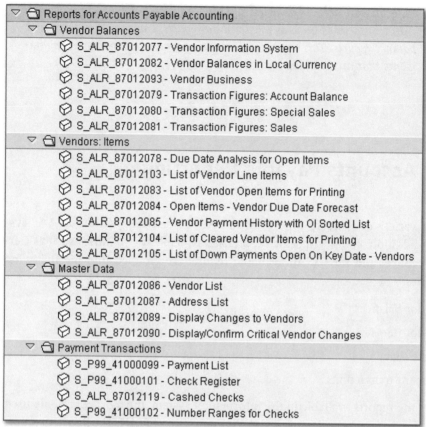

Figure 17.1 Accounts Payable Information System

17.2 Vendor Line Items (FBL1N)

The vendor line item report can be accessed via Transaction FBL1N or via the SAP menu path SAP Menu • Accounting • Financial Accounting • Accounts Payable • Account • Display/Change Line items. Figure 17.2 shows the selection screen of Transaction FBL1N.

This report allows the display of open, cleared, or all vendor line items. Based on the **Type** specified, normal documents (invoice, credit memo, or payment documents), special G/L transactions, noted items, parked documents, or customer line items are displayed.

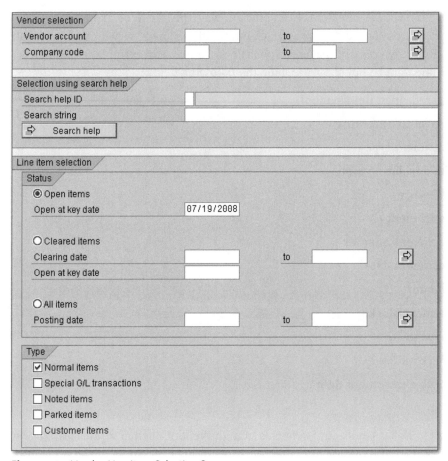

Figure 17.2 Vendor Line Item Selection Screen

AP clerks have to deal with a large volume of data and information requests on a daily basis. Typical inquiries include questions from internal as well as external parties concerning the status of invoices and payments. The AP clerk must be able to answer these questions in a time-efficient way. Typical questions include the following:

▸ Is the invoice with invoice number 11111 entered?

▸ When is the invoice going to be paid?

▸ What is the check number of the payment?

▸ Did the vendor cash the check?

To research vendor line items in an efficient way, the line item layout is especially important. You should display as much information as necessary in the line layout, and group invoices and payments visually together. For example, a good structured line item layout should include the following fields:

- **Cleared/open item symbol**
- **Special GL indicator**
- **Document type**
- **Net due date symbol**
- **Reference**
- **Assignment**
- **Document number**
- **Document date**
- **Amount**
- **Payment block**
- **Payee/er**
- **Check number**
- **Check encashment date**
- **Text**

From a technical perspective, all fields from the vendor open item and cleared item Tables BSIS and BSAS are available for display. However, some of the previously listed fields, such as **Payee** or **Check number**, aren't available in these tables. SAP software, therefore, has a function called *special fields*, which allows displaying additional fields from certain tables.

17.2.1 Special Fields

Special fields for AP line item reporting can be configured in the IMG via navigation path **IMG • Financial Accounting • Accounts Receivable and Payable • Vendor Accounts • Display Line Items • Define Additional Fields for Line Item Display.** Not all fields within the SAP database are available for display, only fields of specific database tables. Table 17.1 lists the tables from which additional fields can be selected.

Table	Description
BKPF	Accounting document header
BSEG	Account document line item
BSEC	One-time vendor information
BSED	Bill of exchange fields
PAYR	Payment medium information
BSEGC	Document data for payment cards

Table 17.1   Tables for Special Fields

As a recommendation, Figure 17.3 shows fields relevant for AP, which should be configured as special fields.

Change View "Line Layout Variant Special Fields":

New Entries

Table	Field name	Field Label
BKPF	BKTXT	Document Header Text
BSEC	NAME1	Name
BSEC	NAME2	Name 2
BSEC	ORT01	City
BSEC	PSTLZ	Postal Code
BSEC	REGIO	Region
BSEC	STRAS	Street
BSEG	EMPFB	Payee
PAYR	BANCD	Check encashment
PAYR	CHECF	Check number from

Figure 17.3   Special Fields for Accounts Payable

After the special fields are saved, they can be selected in the line item layout within Transaction FBL1N.

Report BALVBUFDEL

If no values are displayed in the ALV line layout for special fields, the ALV buffer needs to be reset via Program BALVBUFDEL. The reset of the buffer should only be necessary once per client.

449

17.2.2 User-Defined Fields via Process & Subscribe BTE 00001650

If additional fields need to be displayed that are neither available in the standard field list nor as special fields, Process & Subscribe BTE 00001650 can be used to add additional fields to the line item layout. The implementation of a BTE is described in Appendix B.

BTE 00001650 is implemented in two steps:

▶ Append structures RFPOS/RFPOSX with the additional fields.

▶ Fill the field values with BTE 00001650.

For example, the additional field *PAYR-XMANU* (Manual checks) should be displayed in the line item layout.

Append Structure RFPOS/RFPOSX

The structure RFPOS can be changed via Transaction SE11. Within the transaction, choose the **Append Structure** button to create a new append structure. Figure 17.4 shows the created append structure "ZFBL1N_RFPOS."

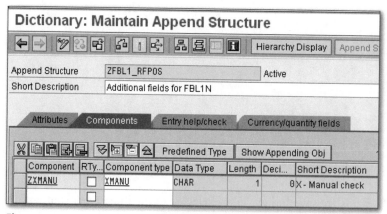

Figure 17.4 Append Structure ZFBL1N_RFPOS

It's recommended to make all additional fields begin with "Z." This is necessary in case SAP adds new fields with the same name in a later release. If that happened, the line item report would abort with a short-dump because multiple fields with the same name would exist.

In the next step, the structure RFPOSX needs to be extended with Transaction SE11 as well with the same fields as in structure RFPOS. In this example, append ZFBL1N_RFPOSX was created.

Fill Field Values with BTE 00001650

To implement the BTE, copy the SAP standard function module SAMPLE_INTERF-CAE_00001650 to a new functional module, that is, Z_INTERFACE_00001650. Listing 17.1 shows the sample code for adding the values for field *PAYR-XMANU*.

```
FUNCTION Z_INTERFACE_00001650.
*"----------------------------------------------------------------
*"*"Local Interface:
*"  IMPORTING
*"     VALUE(I_POSTAB) LIKE  RFPOS STRUCTURE  RFPOS
*"  EXPORTING
*"     VALUE(E_POSTAB) LIKE  RFPOS STRUCTURE  RFPOS
*"----------------------------------------------------------------
DATA: T_PAYR LIKE PAYR.
*------ Initialize Output by using the following line ----------
 E_POSTAB = I_POSTAB.
*----------------------------------------------------------------
* Fill field ZXMANU from table PABLE-XMANU
*----------------------------------------------------------------
 IF E_POSTAB-KOART = 'K'.
   SELECT * from PAYR into T_PAYR WHERE
                         ZBUKR = E_POSTAB-BUKRS and
                         VBLNR = E_POSTAB-BELNR and
                         GJAHR = E_POSTAB-GJAHR.
     E_POSTAB-ZXMANU = T_PAYR-XMANU.
   ENDSELECT.
 ENDIF.
ENDFUNCTION.
```

Listing 17.1 BTE 00001650 Sample Code

After the implementation of the BTE, the user-defined fields are available in Transaction FBL1N.

> **Reports RFXPRA33 and RFPOSXEXTEND**
>
> If the user-defined fields aren't visible in the field list of the line item, execute Programs RFXPRA33 and RFPOSXEXTEND, which will regenerate the line item field structure.

17.2.3   Line Item Subtotals/Sorting

The sorting and creation of subtotals for the vendor line layout is important because this allows the AP clerk to find vendor invoices and payments easily. In the following example, these sorting requirements were taken into consideration:

- ▶ Vendor open items are listed before cleared items.
- ▶ Open invoices are sorted by document date (invoice date).
- ▶ Cleared items are visually grouped by clearing document, which can be a payment or a reversal document.
- ▶ Cleared items are sorted by clearing date with the latest clearing date first.

Figure 17.5 shows the sorting and subtotaling setting for a vendor line item layout, which takes the preceding requirements into consideration.

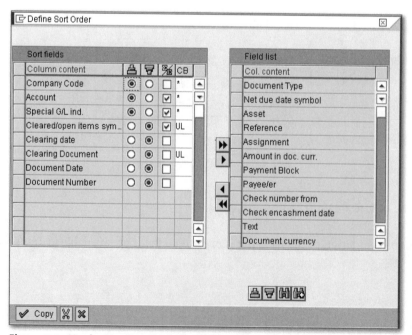

Figure 17.5   Vendor Line Item Sorting and Subtotals

17.2.4 Vendor Line Item Layout Summary

Figure 17.6 shows a vendor line layout example, which takes the recommended fields, special fields, and the sort and subtotal options into account. As a result, you have a visually appealing layout that lists items in a structured way.

	St	S	Typ	DD	Reference	DocumentNo	Doc. Date	Amount in doc. curr.	PBk	Check n	Payee/er	Date	Text
Vendor 100027 ABC COMPANY					122 SOUTH STREET NEW YORK	Tel: Fax: NY 10011						Page: 1 Date: 07/20/2008 User: MULLMAN	
□	△		KR	▣	TEST	1900000178	08/28/2006	20.00-					*test post
*	△							20.00-					
□	▢		ZP			2000000055	04/10/2008	350.99		700014			
□	▢		RE		TEST CNS INV	5105600141	04/10/2008	225.00-		700014			
□	▢		KS		TEST	1900000313	03/02/2008	80.00-		700014			
□	▢		KS		TEST	1900000313	03/02/2008	20.00-		700014			
□	▢		ZP			2000000014	08/29/2006	33.99		700000			
□	▢		ZP			2000000020	08/29/2006	33.99-		700000			
□	▢		KR		ASDFAS	1900000183	08/29/2006	56.00-		700008			
□	▢		ZP			2000000017	08/29/2006	56.00		700008			
□	▢		KR		TEST PRINT	1900000182	08/29/2006	66.00-		700002		10/29/2006	
□	▢		ZP			2000000016	08/29/2006	66.00		700002		10/29/2006	

Figure 17.6 Vendor Line Item Layout Example

17.3 Summary

In this chapter, the information system and vendor line item report were described, including special fields and user-defined fields. The next chapter covers the SAP table structure within Accounts Payable.

Even though SAP software delivers a large variety of standard reports, you may have to write your own custom programs for reporting, conversion, or interface purposes. This chapter lists the most important tables in Accounts Payable (AP) as well as useful function modules and BAPIs (Business Application Programming Interfaces).

18 Tables, Function Modules, and BAPIs

Every organization has different requirements for reporting, converting, and interfacing transactional data. This chapter lists the most important tables within AP as well as useful function modules and BAPIs.

18.1 Tables

All information within SAP software is stored in a large number of tables so that it's sometimes difficult to find the correct tables for the information needed. This section lists AP-relevant tables for vendor master data, transactional data, and payment information.

18.1.1 Vendor Master Data Table Structure

Table 18.1 lists the most commonly used vendor master data tables. These tables can be useful for either programmers or users who want to create their own queries to display vendor master data.

Table Name	Description
LFA1	Vendor master (general section)
LFB1	Vendor master (company code)
LFBK	Vendor master (bank details)
LFM1	Vendor master (purchasing organization)
LFM2	Vendor master (purchasing data)
LFZA	Vender master (permitted payee)

Table 18.1 Vendor Master Data Tables

18.1.2 Transactional Data Tables

Table 18.2 lists the most commonly used tables for transactional data such as invoices, credit memos, or payments.

Table name	Description
BSIK	Vendor open items
BSAK	Vendor cleared items
BPKF	FI document header
BSEG	FI document line items
BSEC	One-time vendor information
WITH_ITEM	Withholding tax information
PAYR	Check information data

Table 18.2 Transactional Data Tables

Tables BSIK and BSAK

All vendor line items are stored in Tables BSIK and BSAK. Table BSIK stores all open vendor line items, and Table BSAK stores cleared vendor line items. If an invoice is paid, the items are moved from Table BSIK to Table BSAK.

From a performance perspective, a report, which lists open vendor line items, should always search the line items in Table BSIK first. If additional information is needed from the document, the document header Tables BKPF and BSEG can then be selected directly.

18.1.3 Logistic Invoice Verification Tables

Table 18.3 lists the most commonly used tables for information in Logistics Invoice Verification (LIV).

Table Name	Description
RBKP	Document header
RBCO	Document line item (account assignment)
RBMA	Document line item (materials)
RSEG	Document line item (incoming invoice)
RCTX	Incoming invoices (taxes)

Table 18.3 Transactional Data Tables

18.2 Function Modules

Function modules are used to execute the same functions based on import parameters and export parameters. SAP software function modules can be displayed via Transaction SE37. Table 18.4 lists useful function modules in AP.

Function Module	Description
FIBL_CHECK_PAYR_GET_FI	Gets check information for a payment document
MR_INVOICE_DOCUMENT_READ	Reads invoice line items of LIV documents

Table 18.4 Useful AP Function Modules

18.3 BAPIs

BAPIs (Business Application Programming Interfaces) are similar to function modules. BAPIs allow a variety of functions from displaying information, changing vendor master data, to creating invoices. You can search for BAPIs using the BAPI Explorer with Transaction BAPI. Table 18.5 lists useful BAPIs in AP.

Function Module	Description
BAPI_ACC_DOCUMENT_POST	Posts an invoice document, including one-time information
BAPI_VENDOR_GETDETAIL	Returns vendor detailed information
BAPI_AP_ACC_GETOPENITEMS	Displays all vendor open items
BAPI_AP_ACC_GETBALANCEDITEMS	Displays vendor cleared items

Table 18.5 BAPIs for Accounts Payable

18.4 Summary

In this chapter useful tables, function modules and BAPIs for AP were described.

Appendices

A   Implementing a User-Exit

This appendix describes how to implement a user-exit within SAP software. A user-exit can be created using Transaction CMOD or via the navigation path **SAP Menu • Tools • ABAP Workbench • Utilities • Enhancements • Project Management.**

Often you hear the terms *enhancements* or *user-exits* used within the same context. However, there are small differences between both of them. To be exact, an *enhancement* includes one or multiple function exits, also called user-exits.

The following steps are necessary to implement a user-exit:

1. Find the appropriate enhancement.

2. Create a project.

3. Assign the enhancement to the project.

4. Enter the ABAP code in the Z program within the function module.

5. Activate the project.

Find an Enhancement

Within Transaction CMOD, all available user-exits can be displayed under the header menu by selecting **Utilities • SAP Enhancements**. In this example, a user-exit is created for vendor validation using enhancement SAPMF02K.

Project Creation

After you've found the appropriate enhancement, a project needs to be created. Within Transaction CMOD, enter a **Project** name, and click on the **Create** button as shown in Figure A.1.

In the attributes screen, enter a short text for the project, and click on the **Enhancement assignments** button.

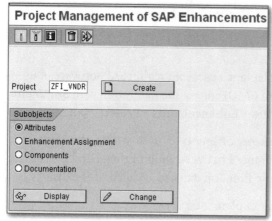

Figure A.1 Project Creation

Enhancement Assignment

In the enhancement assignment screen shown in Figure A.2, enter the name of the enhancement in the **Enhancement** field.

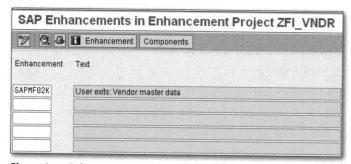

Figure A.2 Enhancement Assignment Screen

Multiple enhancements can be assigned to a single project. This might be useful if you want to group enhancements for the same business process in the same project.

After the enhancement is entered, click on the **Components** button. All available **Function exits** assigned to the enhancement are displayed (see Figure A.3). An enhancement can have multiple function exits.

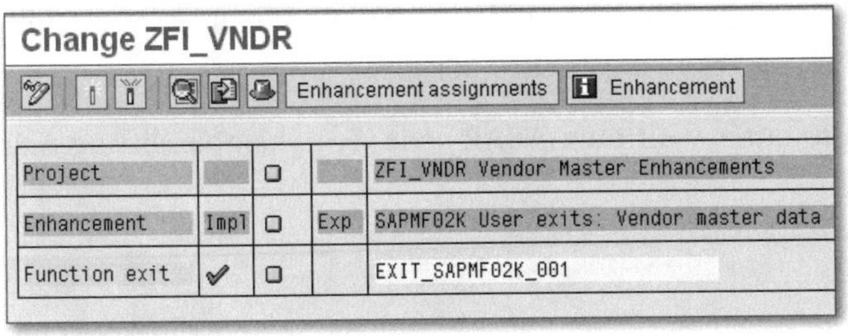

Figure A.3 Function Exit Assignment

Enter the ABAP Code

To enter the ABAP (Advanced Business Application Programming) code, double-click on the **Function exit**. The result is that the source code of the function module is displayed. Within every function module, an INCLUDE statement as shown in Figure A.4 can be found. This INCLUDE contains the ABAP code of the user-exit.

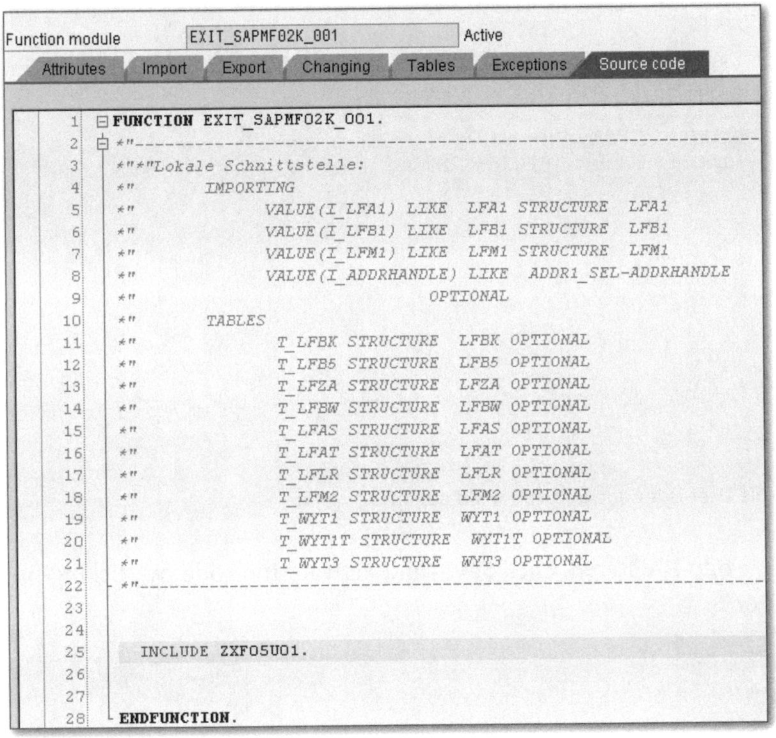

Figure A.4 Function Module Source Code

To enter your own ABAP code, double-click on the **INCLUDE**. If you get prompted to create the INCLUDE, click on **Yes** to create the INCLUDE.

At that point, you need to enter your own ABAP code. For example, listing A.1 shows a vendor validation.

```
*&-------------------------------------------------------------*
*&  Include        ZXF05U01
*&-------------------------------------------------------------*
*--------------------------------------------------------------*
* Rule 1: Validate the format of values if the Tax Number
*         field1. The values have to be in format NNN-NN-NNN
*         and only numeric values are allowed.
*         Message 010 is created in message class ZFI with
*         Transaction SE91
*--------------------------------------------------------------*
  IF NOT i_lfa1-stcd1 is INITIAL.
    IF i_lfa1-stcd1(3) cn '0123456789'.
      MESSAGE e010(ZFI).
    ENDIF.
    IF i_lfa1-stcd1+3(1) <> '-'.
      MESSAGE e010(ZFI).
    ENDIF.
    IF i_lfa1-stcd1+4(2) cn '0123456789'.
      MESSAGE e010(ZFI).
    ENDIF.
    IF i_lfa1-stcd1+6(1) <> '-'.
      MESSAGE e010(ZFI).
    ENDIF.
    IF i_lfa1-stcd1+7(3) cn '0123456789'.
      MESSAGE e010(ZFI).
    ENDIF.
  ENDIF.
```

Listing A.1 Example User-Exit Code for Vendor Validation

After the ABAP code is entered, click **Save**, and activate the code by clicking on the **Active** button.

Activate Project

The last step is the activation of the project. The assigned enhancements are processed only after the project is activated. To activate a project, go back to the initial project creation screen and click the **Activate** button, which is the first button to the left in Figure A.5.

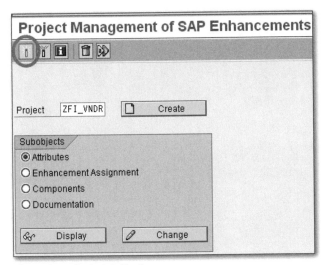

Figure A.5 Project Activation

The project and the user-exit are client independent, so they are immediately available in every client within the same system.

B   Implementing a BTE

This appendix describes how to implement a Business Transaction Event (BTE) within SAP software. A BTE can be created using Transaction FIBF or via the IMG navigation path **IMG • Financial Accounting • Financial Accounting Global Settings • Business Transaction Events.** The two types of BTEs are listed here:

▶ Publish & Subscribe Interfaces

▶ Process Interfaces

There is no real difference between these two types of interfaces, and the implementation steps are the same. In the following example, the BTE Publish & Subscribe Interface 00001440: Vendor Master Data: Final Checks will be implemented. The following steps are necessary to implement a BTE:

1. Find the appropriate BTE.

2. Create a new Z function module with the ABAP code.

3. Assign a function module to the event.

Find a BTE

Within Transaction FIBF, all available BTEs can be displayed under the header menu by selecting **Environment • Infosystem (P/S)** to display the Public & Describe Interfaces or by selecting **Environment • Infosystem (Processes)** to display the Process Interfaces. On the selection screen, click the **Execute** button without changing any default values.

Create a New Z Function Module

After you've found the appropriate BTE, select it, and click on the **Sample function module** button as shown in Figure B.1.

Business Transaction Events: Publish & Subscribe I

| ☒ | ⋘ Act. comp. | ⓘ Sample function module | ⓘ Interface | ☒ Documentation |

Selected BTEs

Event	Text
00001410	VENDOR MASTER DATA: Call GUI
00001420	VENDOR MASTER DATA: Save
00001421	VENDOR MASTER DATA: Save with data transfer
00001430	VENDOR MASTER DATA: Key texts
00001440	VENDOR MASTER DATA: Final checks
00001450	VENDOR MASTER DATA: Individual duplication check
00001460	VENDOR MASTER DATA: Auth. check: Account group

Figure B.1   Publish & Subscribe Interfaces

The system jumps to Transaction SM37 to create a new Z function module. To do that, click on the **Copy** button, and create a Z function module as a copy from the sample function module as shown in Figure B.2.

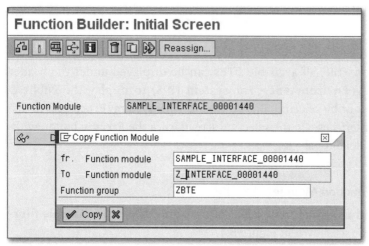

Figure B.2   Create Z Function Module

Within this new function module, the ABAP source code has to be created. For example, Listing B.1 shows the source code for a vendor validation rule.

```
TABLES: BSIK, BSAK.
*-------------------------------------------------------------*
* Rule 1: The values in Tax field 1 can only be
*         removed if no transaction data exist.
*         Message 012 is created in message class ZFI with
*         Transaction SE91
*-------------------------------------------------------------*
  IF i_lfa1-stcd1 is INITIAL and
     not i_lfa1_old-stcd1 is INITIAL.
    SELECT * FROM bsik where lifnr = i_lfa1-lifnr.
      MESSAGE e012(ZFI).
      exit.
    ENDSELECT.
    SELECT * FROM bsak where lifnr = i_lfa1-lifnr.
      MESSAGE e012(ZFI).
      exit.
    ENDSELECT.
  ENDIF.
```

Listing B.1 Sample BTE Source Code

After the ABAP code is complete, save the code, and activate the function module.

Assign Function Module to Event

The last step is the assignment of the function module to the event. There are different activation options, depending on the type of interface, such as the following:

- ▶ SAP application
- ▶ Partner
- ▶ Customer

The SAP application option and Partner option are usually reserved for SAP or SAP partner development. The following activation therefore describes the Customer activation steps. All activation steps are done within Transaction FIBF.

The first step is the creation of a customer product. The purpose of a customer product is to assign function modules to this customer product to be able to distinguish between customer and SAP function modules. The product creation is a one-time step because all BTE function modules can be assigned to the same product. A product can be created within Transaction FIBF by selecting **Settings • Product • ... of a customer**

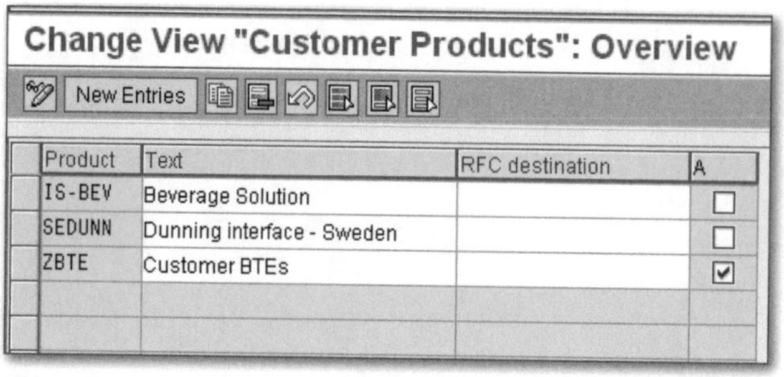
Change View "Customer Products": Overview

New Entries

Product	Text	RFC destination	A
IS-BEV	Beverage Solution		☐
SEDUNN	Dunning interface - Sweden		☐
ZBTE	Customer BTEs		☑

Figure B.3 Customer Product Creation

As shown in Figure B.3, **Product ZBTE** is created. All function modules will be assigned to this product. Ensure that the product is active by setting the flag in the **A (Active)** field.

The second step is the assignment of the function module. Depending on whether the interface is from type Publish & Subscribe or Process, choose either **Settings • P/S modules • ... of a customer** or **Settings • Process modules • ... of a customer.**

Create a new entry, and assign the function module to an event and a product. Figure B.4 shows the assignment of function module **Z_INTERFACE_00001440** to event **00001440** and Product **ZBTE**.

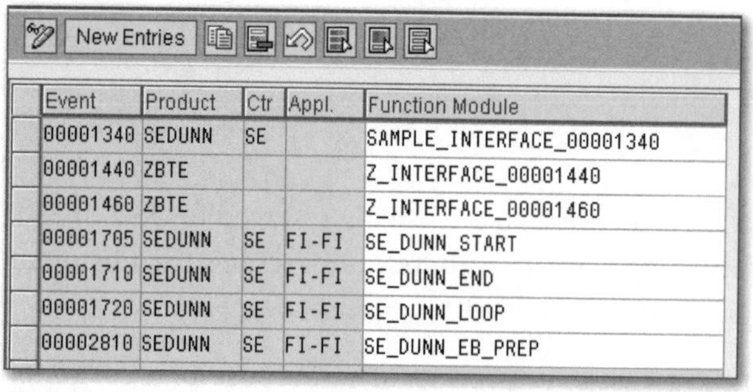
New Entries

Event	Product	Ctr	Appl.	Function Module
00001340	SEDUNN	SE		SAMPLE_INTERFACE_00001340
00001440	ZBTE			Z_INTERFACE_00001440
00001460	ZBTE			Z_INTERFACE_00001460
00001705	SEDUNN	SE	FI-FI	SE_DUNN_START
00001710	SEDUNN	SE	FI-FI	SE_DUNN_END
00001720	SEDUNN	SE	FI-FI	SE_DUNN_LOOP
00002810	SEDUNN	SE	FI-FI	SE_DUNN_EB_PREP

Figure B.4 Function MODULE assignment

The assignment configuration is client dependent and therefore has to be transported to every client within the system.

C   Implementing a BAdI

This appendix describes the implementation of a Business Add-In (BAdI) within SAP software. A BAdI can be created using Transaction SE19 or via the SAP menu via navigation path **SAP menu • Tools • ABAP Workbench • Utilities • Business Add-Ins • Implementation.** The following steps are necessary to implement a BTE:

- ► Find the appropriate BAdI.
- ► Create a BAdI implementation.
- ► Activate the BAdI.

Find a BAdI

BAdIs can be found in Transaction SE18 BAdI Definition. Within this transaction, the BadIs are grouped by SAP component, which allows a simplified search of BAdIs (see Figure C.1).

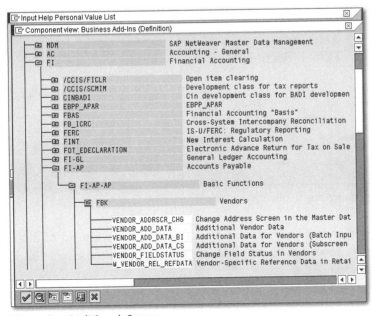

Figure C.1   BAdI Search Screen

Create a BAdI Implementation

A BAdI implementation is created with Transaction SE19. In the first step, a **BAdI Name** needs to be selected as shown in Figure C.2.

Figure C.2 Implementation Creation

After the **BAdI Name** is selected, click on the **Create Impl.** button. A new field box appears where an implementation name has to be created. This implementation name as shown in Figure C.3 contains your ABAP codes for the BAdI.

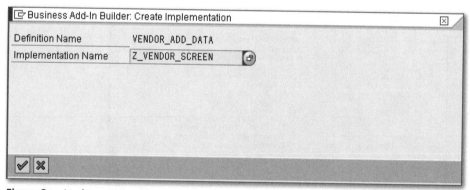

Figure C.3 Implementation Name Creation

From a technical perspective, a BAdI uses classes and methods instead of function modules, which allows you to have multiple methods within the same BAdI implementation (see Figure C.4).

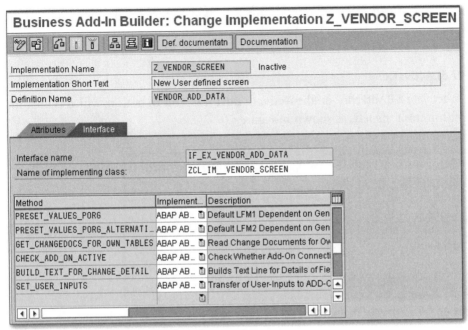

Figure C.4 Methods Within a BAdI Implementation

To create your ABAP code, just double-click on the method, and the code can be created within the method as shown in Figure C.5.

Class Builder: Class ZCL_IM__LICENDE_ADD_DATA Change

| | Pattern | Pretty Printer |

Method   IF_EX_VENDOR_ADD_DATA~CHECK_ADD_ON_ACTIVE

```
 1  method IF_EX_VENDOR_ADD_DATA~CHECK_ADD_ON_ACTIVE.
 2  *------------------------------------------------
 3  * The License Data screen (Screen Group Z1) is only
 4  * active with Transaction code XK01, XK02, XK03
 5  *------------------------------------------------
 6    IF I_SCREEN_GROUP = 'Z1'.
 7      IF SY-TCODE = 'XK01' OR
 8         SY-TCODE = 'XK02' OR
 9         SY-TCODE = 'XK03'.
10      E_ADD_ON_ACTIVE = 'X'.
11      ENDIF.
12    ENDIF.
13  endmethod.
```

Figure C.5 ABAP Code Within a BAdI

After the ABAP code is entered and activated, return to the implementation screen.

BAdI Activation

To activate a BAdI, click on the **Activate Business Add-In** button, which is the fifth button from the left, as shown in Figure C.6.

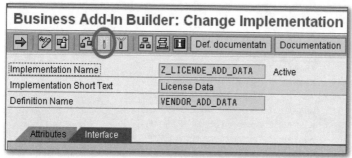

Figure C.6 Business Add-In Activation

A BAdI implementation is client independent and therefore active in all clients within a system.

D Implementing a Validation/Substitution in the Financial Accounting Component (FI) with User-Exits

This appendix describes the implementation of a user-exit for the Financial Accounting component (FI) validations and substitution. SAP software delivers within FI substitutions and validations. A *substitution* allows defaulting of values for certain fields, whereas a *validation* checks the data entry and issues messages if the validation is not fulfilled. Validations and substitutions are widely used within the different SAP financial applications. The same implementation steps as described in this appendix can be used for user-exits in the Controlling component (CO), Project Systems component (PS), or Asset Management component. In this appendix, the implementation of a FI validation as described in Section 3.14.3 of Chapter 3 is explained.

The following steps are necessary to implement a user-exit in FI for validations or substitutions:

- ▶ User-exit creation
- ▶ Maintenance of Table T80D
- ▶ Creation of substitution/validation

User-Exit Creation

Two SAP programs provide sample user-exits for validations and substitutions:

- ▶ **RGGBR000:** Validations
- ▶ **RGGBS000:** Substitutions

The first time a user-exit is implemented, the SAP sample program needs to be copied to a Z program, such as ZRGGBR00 using Transaction SE38. All subsequent changes are made in the new program.

First, the new user-exit needs to be declared within the form `get_exit_titles` as shown in Listing D.1.

```
FORM get_exit_titles TABLES etab.
```

```
DATA: BEGIN OF exits OCCURS 50,
        name(5)    TYPE c,
        param      LIKE c_exit_param_none,
        title(60) TYPE c,
      END OF exits.

exits-name  = 'UF01'.
exits-param = c_exit_param_field.
exits-title = text-001.      " Line item text required
APPEND exits.

REFRESH etab.
LOOP AT exits.
  etab = exits.
  APPEND etab.
ENDLOOP.
```
Listing D.1 User-Exit Declaration

When you declare the user-exit, keep the following items in mind:

▸ Make sure the exit-name is four characters, such as UF01.

▸ Make sure that the correct parameter is used.

  Depending on the parameter, the user-exit FORM statement is different.

  The following is a list of the parameters and the correct FORM statement of the user-exit.

  ▸ Parameter: C_EXIT_PARAM_NONE

    FORM uf01.

  ▸ Parameter: C_EXIT_PARAM_FIELD

    FORM uf01 USING business_area.

▸ Change the user-exit title by double-clicking on the text symbol, that is, text-001.

After the user-exit is declared, create the ABAP code for the user-exit. Listing D.2 shows the coding for user-exit UF01.

```
*---------------------------------------------------------------
*       FORM UF01
*---------------------------------------------------------------*
*       Line item text is required for vendor postings with
*       vendor account group 'KRED'
```

476

```
*------------------------------------------------------------------
*  ß BRESULT   T = True  F = False                          *
*-----------------------------------------------------------------*
FORM uf01 USING b_result.
  TABLES LFA1.

  B_RESULT  = B_TRUE.
  CHECK BESG-KOART = 'K'.                    "Vendor Line item
  SELECT SINGLE * FROM LFA1 WHERE LIFNR = BSEG-LIFNR.
  IF SY-SUBRC = 0.
    CHECK LFA1-KTOKK = 'KRED'.
    IF BSEG-SGTEXT IS INITIAL.
      B_RESULT  = B_FALSE.
    ENDIF.
  ENDIF.
ENDFORM.
```

Listing D.2 Example User-Exit

Maintenance of Table T80D

Table **T80D** specifies which program contains the user-exits for validations and substitutions. Originally, the entries in Table T80D point to the SAP sample programs RGGBR000 and RBBGS000. These entries need to be changed to the Z programs. To maintain Table T80D, use Transaction SM30 with **View V_T80D** as shown in Figure D.1.

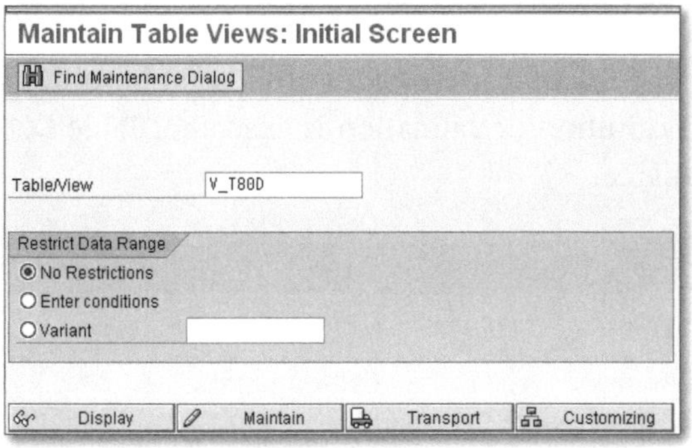

Figure D.1 Maintenance of Table T80D

Click **Maintain** to change the programs for the application areas in Table T80D. The *application area* defines which SAP software function is used. For FI valida-

477

tions, application area *GBLR* is used. For substitutions, application area *GBLS* is used. Figure D.2 shows application **GBLR** with program **ZRGGBR00**.

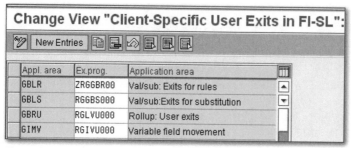

Figure D.2 Application Area Maintenance Screen

After the program is changed and saved, the SAP software regenerates automatically the underlying ABAP code.

> **Note: Generation Errors**
>
> If you encounter errors during the generation, these errors can be ignored because the SAP software delivers many validations and substitutions that are not relevant for your organization.

Substitution/Validation Creation

The last step is the creation of the validation or substitution.

The substitutions and validations are executed anytime a financial transaction is created at different call-up points. The *call-up point* defines at what point during data entry of the transaction the substitution or validation is executed. Table D.1 lists the different call-up points available.

Description	FI Substitution	FI Validation
Document header	Call-up point 1	Call-up point 1
Line item	Call-up point 2	Call-up point 2
Complete document	N/A	Call-up point 3

Table D.1 Validation and Substitution Call-Up Points

The document header substitution and validation is executed after all required document header information is filled, such as document date, posting date, or document type. At that point, the substitution and validation is called.

The line item substitution and validation are called after the line item information is entered, such as amount and account.

At call-up point 3, a complete document can be validated. The validation is executed at the time a document is saved. A FI substitution is not possible for a complete document but can be achieved with Process BTE 00001120 – Document Posting: Field Substitution Header/Line Item.

Two different transaction codes are available for the creation of validations and substitutions:

▸ **OB28:** FI Validations

▸ **OBBH:** FI Substitutions

The transactions can be found in the IMG via navigation path **IMG • Financial Accounting • Financial Accounting Global Settings • Tools • Validation / Substitution.** Figure D.3 shows validation **FI-002** at call-up point **2** for company code **1000**.

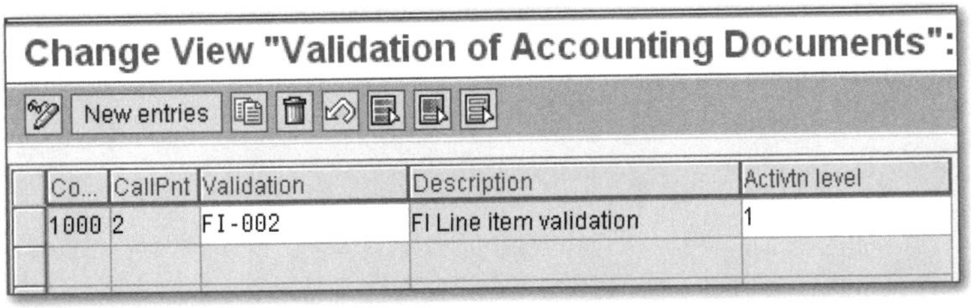

Figure D.3 Validation FI-002 Configuration Screen

Activation Level

The *activation level* specifies whether the substitution/validation is active, inactive, or only active in online transactions (not active in batch input).

To go to the detailed validation definition, choose **Environment • Validation.** Figure D.4 shows the validation definition screen.

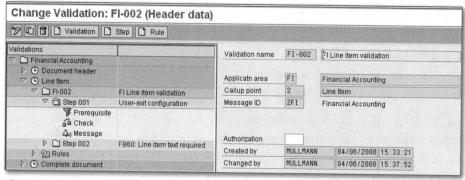

Figure D.4 Validation Definition Screen

Every validation or substitution contains different steps. A step specifies the single validation/substitution roles. To create a step, choose the **Create Step** button.

A validation is divided into three sections:

▶ Prerequisite

▶ Check

▶ Message

Figure D.5 shows the sections of a validation step.

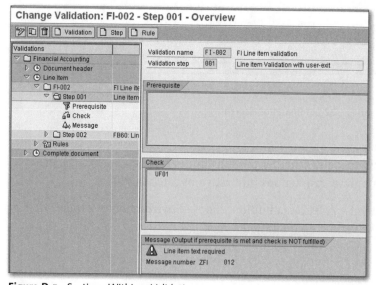

Figure D.5 Sections Within a Validation

In contrast, a substitution has only two sections, Prerequisite and Substitutions.

In the **Prerequisite** section, the rules have to be specified under which conditions the validation/substitution is executed. In the **Check** section, the validation rules need to be specified. To specify a user-exit, choose the **Exits** tab and double-click on the exit as shown in Figure D.6.

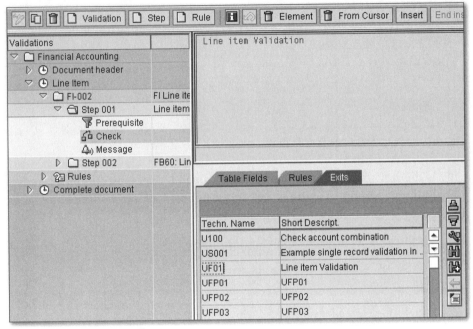

Figure D.6   User-Exit Specification

In the **Message** section, the output message needs to be specified as shown in Figure D.7. The message is displayed if the validation rule fails.

You can create user-defined messages. In addition, the message variable function allows you to display values within the message. In this case, a placeholder (&) needs to be defined within the message, and the **Message variables** field needs to be specified.

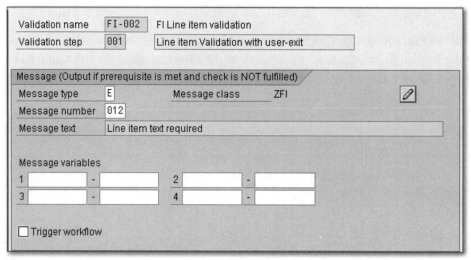

Figure D.7 Output Message Specification

This is the last step in the configuration of a validation/substitution. For additional information on validations and substitutions, look up the following notes in OSS:

▶ 48121: User Exits in Validations/Substitutions

▶ 42615: Substitution in FI

Program: RGUGBR00
If you have problems with substitutions or validations after client copies or transports, you can regenerate the substitutions or validations with program RGUGBR00.

E   The Author

Martin Ullmann has been working with SAP systems since 1994, beginning with R/3 first in Germany, then Asia, and now in the U.S. His primary focus has been on the SAP ERP Financials application and related components and sub-components.

In 2007, Martin founded DAP Consulting, a consulting company focused on public sector SAP implementations. Martin is a regular speaker on SAP ERP Financials implementation topics at conferences and a regular contributor to the FinancialsExpert publication.

He can be reached at Martin.Ullmann@DAP-Consulting.com.

Index

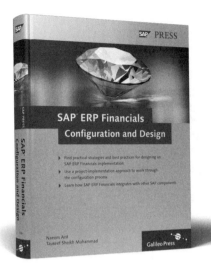

Find practical strategies and best practices for designing an SAP ERP Financials implementation

Use a project-implementation approach to work through the configuration process

Learn how SAP ERP Financials integrates with other SAP modules

Naeem Arif, Sheikh Tauseef

SAP ERP Financials:
Configuration and Design

Master the most important issues involved in designing and configuring an SAP Financial implementation using the real-world, holistic business information provided in this compre– hensive reference. You'll learn everything from the general areas of SAP Financials and how they fit in the SAP landscape, to how the General Ledger can work for you.
This invaluable guide is the one resource you need to understand the configuration and design process, the enterprise structure, reporting, data migration, Accounts Payable and Receivables, Financials integration with other modules, and all other critical areas of SAP Financials.

467 pp., 2008, 79,95 Euro / US$ 79.95
ISBN 978-1-59229-136-6

>> www.sap-press.de/1462

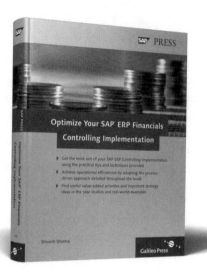

Get the most out of your SAP Controlling implementation using the practical tips and techniques provided

Learn how to make better management decisions by using the Controlling specific information in this book

Discover areas like Investment Management, Funds Management, Product Cost Controlling, and more

Shivesh Sharma

Optimize Your SAP ERP Financials Controlling Implementation

This book will answer the question, What do I do with my SAP Controlling-related requirements once the implementation is complete? Therefore, it begins where implementation guides leave off. Using tested business processes it prepares readers to make the most of their Controlling implementation.

465 pp., 2008, 79,95 Euro / US$ 79.95
ISBN 978-1-59229-219-6

>> www.sap-press.de/1807

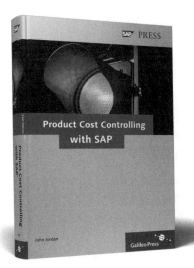

Effectively configure Controlling-Profitability Analysis with SAP using the practical instruction provided

Leverage CO-PA fundamentals to improve your company's profitability

Explore best practices for configuring costing-based and account-based CO-PA

Up to date for SAP ERP 6.0

Marco Sisfontes-Monge

Controlling-Profitability Analysis (CO-PA) with SAP

Controlling-Profitability Analysis (CO-PA) is a crucial and important part of SAP. Based on ECC 6.0, this book explores the required elements for a successful CO-PA implementation from a process-oriented perspective. This includes the fundamentals of profitability manage–ment, development of the CO-PA models and interaction with the FI component of R/3, configuration of Account-Based and Costing-Based CO-PA, extraction and retraction, and much more. This unique reference clarifies CO-PA's integration with other SAP components such as SAP NetWeaver BI, and also addresses the basic managerial questions required in any implementation.

407 pp., 2008, 79,95 Euro / US$ 79..95
ISBN 978-1-59229-137-3

>> www.sap-press.de/1463

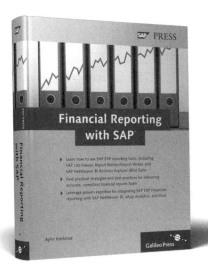

Understand and implement strategies for maximizing Financials reporting capabilities

Learn and apply best practices for simplifying, streamlining, and automating financial and management reporting

Leverage proven expertise concerning the integration of Financials reporting with BI, xApp Analytics, and Duet™

Aylin Korkmaz

Financial Reporting with SAP

This book provides finance and IT teams with best practices for delivering financial reports faster, more accurately, and in compliance with various international accounting standards. Featuring step-by-step coverage of all major FI reporting functions (including Sub-Ledger, Corporate Finance Management, and Governance, Risk & Compliance), this timely book will help you streamline and simplify financial business processes and automate financial and management reporting in SAP ERP Financials. It includes coverage of integrating FI reporting with Business Intelligence, xApp Analytics, and Duet™.

668 pp., 2008, 79,95 Euro / US$ 79.95
ISBN 978-1-59229-179-3

>> www.sap-press.de/1654

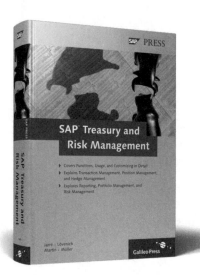

Uncover functionality, processes and complete customization details

Master transaction and position management with hedge management

Unlock the secrets of reporting, portfolio controlling and risk management

Fully up-to-date for SAP ERP 6.0

Sönke Jarré, Reinhold Lövenich, Andreas Martin, Klaus G. Müller

SAP Treasury and Risk Management

This comprehensive guide introduces you to the functionality and helps you quickly master the usage of SAP Treasury and Risk Management. Learn about the most important custo–mization settings as well as typical use cases and get straightforward solutions to many of the most common problems. With volumes of detailed screenshots, in-depth overviews and practical examples, all components of the tool are covered in detail – from transaction and position management, to risk and performance analyses, to reporting and beyond. Plus, you'll also benefit from expert guidance on interfaces and integration as well as compliance requirements. The book is up-to-date for SAP ERP 6.0.

722 pp., 2008, 99,95 Euro / US$ 99.95
ISBN 978-1-59229-149-6

>> www.sap-press.de/1520

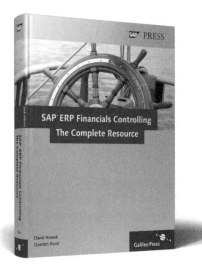

The only comprehensive, hands-on guide available for the con-figuration of SAP ERP Financials Controlling Component

Best-selling author team with long, strong track record of indus-try success and experience

Detailed, step-by-step-oriented pedagogy focused on expert, real-world knowledge transfer

David Nowak, Quentin Hurst

SAP ERP Financials Controlling: The Complete Resource

SAP ERP Financials Controlling: The Complete Resource is a comprehensive guide to the implementation and configuration of ERP Financials Controlling (CO), written by two of the leading consultants in the field. The book covers the complete configuration of the ERP Financials Controlling (CO) solution and its associated sub-components, and provides information on integrating the Financials solution with other solutions and sub-components. The book will appeal to implementation and configuration teams responsible for rolling out, upgrading, or maintaining ERP Financials Controlling as well as consultants, managers, and others. Based on ECC 6.0, it is the only comprehensive resource available for hands-on, real-world configuration scenarios for ERP Financials Controlling.
This book will be the companion title to an ERP Financial Accounting configuration book titled SAP ERP Financial Accounting: The Complete Resource, written by the same author team.

approx. 625 pp., 79,95 Euro / US$ 89.95
ISBN 978-1-59229-204-2, Jan 2009

>> www.sap-press.de/1816

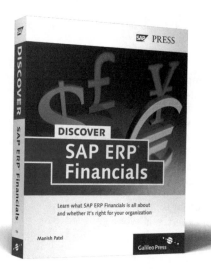

Discover what SAP Financials (FI) is all about and whether it's right for your organization

Lean how this powerful, time-tested tool can improve your financial processes and save you money

Explore the major modules, including receivable and payables, tax accounting, cost accounting, payroll accounting, travel management, and more

Manish Patel

Discover SAP ERP Financials

Business financials are an essential part of every business, large or small. Whether you just need basic accounting or you perform complex financial audits and reporting, your business needs a software tool that meets your needs. Discover SAP Financials explains how SAP can provide this solution. Using an easy-to-follow style filled with real-world examples, case studies, and practical tips and pointers, the book teaches the fundamental capabilities and uses of the core modules of SAP Financials. As part of the Discover SAP series, the book is written to help new users, decision makers considering SAP, and power users moving to the latest version learn everything they need to determine if SAP Financials is the right solution for your organization.

This is the one comprehensive resource you need to get started with SAP Financials.

544 pp., 2008, 39,95 Euro / US$ 39.95
ISBN 978-1-59229-184-7

>> www.sap-press.de/1672

Interested in reading more?

Please visit our Web site for all
new book releases from SAP PRESS.

www.sap-press.com

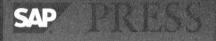